Morris Goodman, Ph. D.
1 Cypress Street
Maplewood, N. J. 07040

Curative Factors in Dynamic Psychotherapy

Curative Factors in Dynamic Psychotherapy

Edited by SAMUEL SLIPP, M.D.

Jules Bemporad   Theodore Lidz

Morris Eagle   Judd Marmor

Edrita Fried   Stanley R. Palombo

Merton M. Gill   Lloyd H. Silverman

Robert L. Hatcher   Samuel Slipp

Otto F. Kernberg   Michael H. Stone

Heinz Kohut   Saul Tuttman

Robert J. Langs   Vamık D. Volkan

Edgar A. Levenson   Ernst Wolf

Ruth W. Lidz   David L. Wolitzky

McGRAW-HILL BOOK COMPANY

New York / St. Louis / San Francisco
London / Paris / Tokyo / Toronto

Lawrence B. Apple, Suzette H. Annin, Thomas H. Quinn, and Michael Hennelly were the editors of this book. Christopher Simon was the designer. Teresa F. Leaden supervised the production. It was set in Times Roman by University Graphics, Inc.

Printed and bound by R. R. Donnelley and Sons, Inc.

Library of Congress Cataloging in Publication Data

American Academy of Psychoanalysis.
  Curative factors in dynamic psychotherapy.

  Proceedings of the annual meeting of the American
Academy of Psychoanalysis, 1978.
  Bibliography: p.
  1. Psychotherapy—Congresses. 2. Psychoanalysis—
Congresses. 3. Personality change—Congresses.
I. Slipp, Samuel. [DNLM: 1. Psychoanalytic therapy.
WM 460.6 C974]
RC475.5.A48 1981 616.89'14 80-27133

1 2 3 4 5 6 7 8 9 RRDRRD 8 0 9 8 7 6 5 4 3 2 1

ISBN 0-07-058190-8

To my wife, Sandra,
and my daughter, Elena

Contents

Contributors

Jules Bemporad, M.D., Director of Children's Services, Massachusetts Mental Health Center, Boston, Massachusetts; Associate Professor of Psychiatry, Harvard Medical School.

Morris Eagle, Ph.D., Director of Clinical Training Program, Professor of Psychology, York University, Toronto, Canada.

Edrita Fried, Ph.D., Training Analyst and Senior Supervisor, Training Department, Postgraduate Center for Mental Health, New York, New York; formerly Associate Professor of Psychiatry, Albert Einstein College of Medicine.

Merton M. Gill, M.D., Professor of Psychiatry, The Abraham Lincoln School of Medicine, University of Illinois, Chicago, Illinois; Supervisory Analyst, Chicago Psychoanalytic Institute.

Robert L. Hatcher, Ph.D., Clinical Assistant Professor, Department of Psychiatry, University of Michigan, Ann Arbor, Michigan.

Otto F. Kernberg, M.D., Medical Director, New York Hospital-Cornell Medical Center, Westchester Division, White Plains, New York; Professor of Psychiatry, Cornell University Medical College; Training and Supervising Analyst, Columbia University Center for Psychoanalytic Training and Research.

Heinz Kohut, M.D., Professorial Lecturer, Department of Psychiatry, University of Chicago School of Medicine, Chicago, Illinois; Visiting Professor of Psychoanalysis, Department of Psychiatry, University of Cincinnati; Faculty, Training, and Supervisory Analyst, Chicago Psychoanalytic Institute.

Robert J. Langs, M.D., Editor in Chief, *International Journal of Psychoanalytic Psychotherapy;* Director, Psychotherapy Training Program, Lenox Hill Hospital, New York, New York.

Edgar A. Levenson, M.D., Director of Clinical Services, William A. White Institute, New York, New York; Training and Supervisory Analyst, William A. White Institute; Clinical Professor of Psychology, Division of Graduate Studies, New York University.

Ruth W. Lidz, M.D., Clinical Professor of Psychiatry, Yale University, School of Medicine, New Haven, Connecticut.

Theodore Lidz, M.D., Sterling Professor of Psychiatry Emeritus, Yale University, School of Medicine, New Haven, Connecticut.

Judd Marmor, M.D., Franz Alexander Professor of Psychiatry Emeritus, University of Southern California, School of Medicine, Los Angeles, California.

Stanley R. Palombo, M.D., Associate Clinical Professor, George Washington University, Washington, D.C.; Faculty, Washington Psychoanalytic Institute; Faculty, Washington School of Psychiatry.

Lloyd H. Silverman, Ph.D., Research Psychologist, New York Veterans Administration, Regional Office, New York, New York; Adjunct Professor, Department of Psychology, New York University.

Samuel Slipp, M.D., Medical Director, Postgraduate Center for Mental Health, New York, New York; Clinical Professor, Department of Psychiatry, New York University, School of Medicine.

Michael H. Stone, M.D., Clinical Director, University of Connecticut Health Center, Farmington, Connecticut; Professor of Psychiatry, University of Connecticut, School of Medicine.

Saul Tuttman, M.D., Ph.D., Clinical Assistant Professor, Department of Psychiatry, New York University, School of Medicine, New York, New York; Instructor and Staff Lecturer, Training Department, Postgraduate Center for Mental Health.

Vamık D. Volkan, M.D., Medical Director, Blue Ridge Hospital, Charlottesville, Virginia; Professor of Psychiatry, University of Virginia, School of Medicine.

Ernest S. Wolf, M.D., Assistant Professor of Psychiatry, Northwestern University, School of Medicine, Chicago, Illinois; Faculty, Training, and Supervisory Analyst, Chicago Psychoanalytic Institute.

David L. Wolitzky, Ph.D., Director of Graduate Training in Clinical Psychology, Department of Psychology, New York University, New York, New York; Associate Professor of Psychology, New York University.

Acknowledgments

This book received special impetus through the leadership of the American Academy of Psychoanalysis whose Chairman of the Programs Committee, Ian Alger, appointed me Program Chairman of the National meeting of the American Academy of Psychoanalysis in Atlanta, Georgia, May, 1978. This privilege permitted me to bring together a panel of eminent clinicians who participated in a discussion of a topic of long-standing concern to me: "What Produces Change in Psychoanalytic Treatment." Their provocative and scholarly presentations served as the basis of the present volume. The rare friendship and professional support of Lloyd Silverman contributed significantly to the encouragement needed to pursue and elaborate these germinal ideas into a book.

A main source of my personal interest in this subject of curative aspects of the psychotherapeutic process came from Lewis Wolberg and his impact as a teacher during my psychoanalytic training. My interest further developed and broadened in the course of my research studies into the various aspects of psychotherapy at the Department of Psychiatry of New York University School of Medicine, under Morris Herman and subsequently Robert Cancro.

My three colleagues, Robert Langs, Saul Tuttman, and the late Benjamin Fielding, made valuable editorial suggestions for which I am extremely appreciative. I want to thank my editor, Larry Apple, for his kindness and important suggestions, Suzette Annin and Debra Weiss for the excellence of their copyediting. I wish to express my appreciation to the contributors, all of whom were most cooperative in working closely with me on their respective chapters.

The extensive library research required for this book was most ably executed by Lee Mackler, Librarian for the Postgraduate Center for Mental Health. I am especially grateful for my secretary Marie Smitelli for her efficient and enthusiastic assistance.

Most of all, I thank my wife Sandra and daughter Elena for their patience, ongoing support, and love extended continuously all through this time-consuming venture.

Curative Factors
in Dynamic
Psychotherapy

Introduction

Samuel Slipp

The most challenging issue in dynamic psychotherapy today is what actually produces change in the patient during treatment. What are these intangible yet powerful factors arising from the patient-therapist interaction that enable the patient to overcome symptoms, to give up maladaptive behavior, and to grow and develop as an individual? Recent advances in psychoanalytic knowledge have created a mounting wave of excitement and spurred the development of newer techniques that expand and enhance the usefulness of dynamic or psychoanalytic psychotherapy.[1]

Certain types of patients who formerly were considered unsuitable for psychoanalysis can now be treated by psychoanalytic psychotherapy. So often in the past, treatment with such patients was disrupted by negative therapeutic reactions, which occurred because of the defensive structure of these patients, their inability to develop a stable transference neurosis, their difficulty in establishing a therapeutic alliance, their intense rage, and their perceptual distortion of reality. The most important thrust of current psychoanalytic investigators is the work with narcissistic and borderline disorders as well as schizophrenic and depressive conditions. As we extend our analytic understanding and develop refinements in technique that enable us to engage and treat a much wider

[1]The terms dynamic and psychoanalytic will be used interchangeably.

1

group of patients, it becomes essential to evaluate the effectiveness of this treatment. The crucial question that confronts us is: what are the curative factors in dynamic psychotherapy that make it work? Are these the same as the curative factors emphasized in psychoanalysis? Yet, even in psychoanalysis, we are faced with diverse opinions about what is curative. This book will review the major factors considered to be curative and will suggest ways to evaluate them scientifically. One hopes this review will lead to better understanding of the therapeutic process and greater effectiveness in treatment, thus strengthening our common goal—to promote growth and change in our patients.

This book grew out of the Annual Meeting of the American Academy of Psychoanalysis in May, 1978. Having the opportunity to chair and organize that meeting, for three days I devoted an entire track to the important topic of what produces change in treatment. Most of the papers presented at that meeting were updated and included in this book. In order to present viewpoints representative of the entire psychoanalytic community, additional papers written by clinicians and researchers with diverse orientations were included in this volume. Most of these papers are published here for the first time. The contributors to the book were selected on the basis of the important and original work they have done in expanding our knowledge of how psychoanalysis or dynamic psychotherapy works. Each contributor was given the challenging task of writing a chapter on one aspect of the important question: what produces cure during dynamic psychotherapy?

We know that behavioral change or symptomatic improvement does indeed occur in patients as a result of suggestion, environmental manipulation, and a number of other nonspecific factors. There is a question, however, regarding the permanence of such change, which occurs without any alteration in the personality structure of the patient. Freud's original definition of cure rested on two pillars: the ability to love and the ability to work.* Cure involves not simply freedom from symptoms but also the patient's capacities to enter into intimate, loving relationships and to be productive at work. Repetitive, fixed patterns of thoughts, feelings, and behavior that may have been adaptive during childhood, but are self-defeating or limiting in the current reality, need to be relinquished to facilitate greater flexibility and better coping ability.

Freud believed that psychoanalytic cure came from insight, facilitated by the therapist's interpretations and reconstructions of associative material and dreams, and by the patient's reliving of old conflicts in the transference to the analyst. Insight served as a bridge between the past and the present. It was as if part of the patient were frozen (fixated) in the past and doomed repeatedly to act out the past through behaviors in the present. Cure was possible only

---

*It should be pointed out that this "definition" of cure may be what Freud meant by the term. No one has ever been able to find a written statement of it. Apparently Erikson, in *Childhood and Society,* 1950, p. 229, quotes Freud as having *said* something to this effect

after the patient remembered these conflicts and understood the unconscious wishes and fears underlying them. These memories contained ways of perceiving, thinking, and feeling from childhood, which, when brought to conscious awareness, could be reexamined in the light of adult functioning. The therapeutic alliance between the patient's observing ego and the therapist encourages self-observation of old conflicts as they are relived in the transference, resulting in restructuring, and expansion of the patient's ego.

Other factors that produce cure in psychoanalysis have also been suggested. These place less emphasis on insight and focus instead on the human relationship of patient and therapist, e.g., as providing a "corrective emotional experience," a "holding environment," or a second chance to relive and correct developmental arrests or deficits in the self (further to differentiate the self from the object) as well as an opportunity for the patient to identify with the analyst. These and other factors are further developed in the various chapters in the book.

Before proceeding it is important to define certain concepts that will be used and to provide a broad historical perspective for the chapters that follow. In this volume dynamic psychotherapy will be differentiated from psychoanalysis proper. Dynamic psychotherapy employs theoretical principles derived from psychoanalysis proper, but certain modifications in technique are made. Instead of the broad psychoanalytic goal of general personality change, dynamic psychotherapy as used here attempts to change specific aspects of the patient's behavior and character. The distinction between these two therapeutic approaches is not universally accepted, cannot always be clearly demarcated, and there is an area of overlap. In addition, the same patient, after sufficient ego growth in dynamic psychotherapy, may be able to benefit from psychoanalysis.

In 1954, controversy arose about whether Franz Alexander's therapeutic work could still be considered psychoanalysis, as well as about the core issue of whether the therapeutic relationship (a "corrective emotional experience") or the technical skill of the therapist was the most important factor in producing change in the patient. Taking the classical position, Rangell (1954) defined psychoanalysis in terms of technique and method of cure:

Psychoanalysis is a method of therapy whereby conditions are brought about favorable for the development of a transference neurosis, in which the past is restored in the present, in order that, through a systematic interpretive attack on the resistances which oppose it, there occurs a resolution of that neurosis (transference and infantile) to the end of bringing about structural changes in the mental apparatus of the patient to make the latter capable of optimum adaptation to life. [pp. 739–740]

Gill's (1954) definition of psychoanalysis further narrowed the classical position by emphasizing the neutrality of the analyst and the resolution of the regressive transference neurosis through the use of interpretation alone. Alexander (1954) and Fromm-Reichmann (1954) employed a broader definition of psychoanalysis, which encompassed the recognition of the importance of childhood conflict on personality development, the significance of the unconscious, and the use of transference and resistance in the treatment.

In a classic article, Bibring (1954) attempted to deal with this controversy by defining the procedures employed in all psychotherapies. He mentioned (1) suggestion, (2) abreaction, (3) manipulation, (4) clarification, and (5) interpretation. Bibring distinguishes between their use as a technique and their curative application in various treatments. He defined *suggestion* as an authority figure's inducing ideas, feelings, impluses, etc., in another person. Bibring considered that in hypnosis suggestion was curative. In psychoanalysis, suggestion is used as a technique to encourage the patient to produce dreams, memories, and fantasies, to tolerate anxiety and depression, and to face unpleasant situations. *Abreaction* concerns the therapist's acceptance or empathy with the expression of suppressed or repressed emotions. Although Freud originally considered catharsis to be curative, with the further development of psychoanalysis it became a technical tool for developing insight. In acute traumatic neurosis, however, abreaction may remain a curative factor. *Manipulation* involves giving advice and guidance, or changing the social milieu. The redirection of the patient's emotional attitudes through the therapist's words or attitudes is a subtler form of manipulation. Bibring believed that Alexander's handling of the transference to produce a "corrective emotional experience" was subsumed under this heading of manipulation. *Clarification* involves a more accurate differentiation of the self from the outside world. It increases self-awareness (feelings, thoughts, attitudes, behavior, etc.), and awareness of others and of objective reality. *Interpretation* involves the analyst's explanation of the unconscious motives and defenses that determine the patient's manifest behavior patterns.

Bibring contended that insight resulted from both clarification and interpretation, which increase self-awareness. Clarification involves little resistance, since it strengthens the patient's ego through fostering greater self-definition, more astute observation of others, and mastery over difficulties. Clarification is particularly significant in ego-psychological approaches, where the analyst's collaboration with the patient's observing ego is encouraged. Interpretation, on the other hand, arouses resistance because it brings into consciousness both repressed childhood memories that have been defended against and the release of painful affect. Bibring believed that, in psychoanalysis, all five therapeutic procedures are technically operative, but that insight through systematic interpretation is the primary curative factor. He believed that interpretations in dynamic psychotherapy tend to be less systematic and limited to partial uncovering of unconscious areas. In dynamic psychotherapy, the importance of the relationship between the patient and therapist assumes a greater significance.

Transference gratification is not always avoided, and identification with the therapist may be actively fostered through a more empathic and involved approach.

The controversy about the curative effect of relational factors versus insight was by no means resolved by Bibring. Its origins stem from an even earlier controversy between Freud and Ferenczi. Freud had carefully defined the analyst's position as one of technical *neutrality*. The transference was not to be gratified; only thus could fantasy be distinguished from reality in transference interpretations. *Interpretation* of transference and resistance was to be the main tool for change. However, Ferenczi, who worked with sicker patients, considered that maintaining this *neutral-interpretive* approach with patients who had suffered actual severe parental neglect would simply prevent engagement in treatment. Because of the patient's negative expectations, the abstinent approach would be experienced only as a repetition of parental indifference. Thus Ferenczi (1920) advocated his "active," caretaking approach, wherein the analyst was emotionally available, warm, and responsive. The patient was provided with an opportunity to regress to a symbiotic state of oneness. This provided a second chance to reexperience and grow out of the childhood neurosis, with the analyst serving as a good parental object.

This *nurturant-reconstructive* approach, as well as other aspects of Ferenczi's contributions, later found expression in the work of Alexander, Balint, Fromm-Reichmann, Guntrip, Khan, Kohut, Little, Marmor, Sechehaye, Sullivan, Thompson, and Winnicott.

Ferenczi is generally considered the father of object relations theory. He was the first to report on how patients used others to fulfill their needs by projecting their internal fantasies onto them. In addition, Ferenczi (1919) was the first to stress the importance of the analyst's being aware of both his persistent countertransferential feelings and the emotional interaction between patient and analyst. It remained for Melanie Klein, an analysand of Ferenczi's, to synthesize these insights into a systematic theory, and for the British school to develop them further into the object relations approach.

Guntrip (1968), one of the proponents of the British school, speculated on some of the differences between Ferenczi's and Freud's theory and technique. Freud placed greater emphasis on the part played by intellectual activity in analysis to produce change, an orientation that Guntrip considered masculine and phallic. The terms *in*sight and *in*terpretation themselves were indicative of active penetration. On the other hand, the analyst's stress on empathy, feelings, experiences, relationships, and interaction represented a feminine orientation. While Freud stressed the Oedipal period and sexuality, Ferenczi emphasized the pre-Oedipal period with its problems of dependency and aggression.

In this respect, Winnicott (1965) clearly believed the curative effect of therapy lay in *reexperiencing* a responsive, "good enough" mothering. The analyst provided the unconditional acceptance that served as a "facilitating" environment, comparable to the environment of infancy, which created a foundation of security and trust. In addition, the analyst created a "holding" environment which accepted and contained the patients' aggression without retaliation. Thus, patients were able to differentiate fantasy from reality through the therapeutic *relationship;* there they learned that their aggression did not destroy the object. Patients could relinquish their omnipotence and their need to control the object after they learned that the object had a separate and permanent existence. Winnicott believes that the analyst serves as a "transitional object" who enables patients to master their helplessness and distrust of the mother. Differentiation of the self and the object replaces the omnipotent fusion; thus the patient can individuate and develop a "true self" instead of a "false, compliant self."

In Freud's later work, he actively attempted to integrate the emotional and cognitive factors by concentrating his focus on the ego. Psychoanalysis changed from primarily an id psychology to an ego psychology, which encompassed drive theory but emphasized adaptation. In Freud's structural model (1923), the analysis of the ego and its defenses against the demands of the id, the superego, and the external world became paramount. In "Beyond the Pleasure Principle," Freud (1920) developed the concepts of the repetition compulsion and the ego's need to master instinctual drives as well as external forces. In Freud's new theory of anxiety (1926, 1933), a threat to the ego signaled anxiety, which in turn caused repression; previously, anxiety had been viewed simply as the result of repression of affect.

In Anna Freud's pioneering work (1936), she furthered the application of ego psychology to bring about change in psychoanalytic treatment and child analysis. Anna Freud disagreed with Melanie Klein's approach to child analysis—using early interpretations of deep unconscious fantasies revealed in the transference—since such interpretations could overwhelm the child's ego and lead to regression, uncontrolled acting out, and a negative therapeutic reaction. While Melanie Klein bypassed the ego to reach deep, instinctually generated anxieties, Anna Freud considered the ego an ally to the therapeutic process and believed that child analysis should begin on "the surface," by analyzing the ego's methods of defense. The patient was thus encouraged to participate actively in a therapeutic alliance, and the analysis of defense as well as the transference became important.

Kris (1950) elaborated this point in his concept of "regression in the service of the ego," wherein the ego participated in the analytic process of uncovering and synthesizing repressed instinctual material. Insight need not be the forced, rapid uncovering of unconscious material resulting from the analyst's dramatic interpretation, but rather, should come more slowly, with the appropriate involvement of the patient's ego. The importance of cognitive factors in adaptation to external reality was also further developed by Hartmann and his colleagues (Hartmann, 1939; Hartmann, Kris, and Loewenstein, 1951). They postulated the existence of a "conflict-free sphere" of the ego, which mediated the individual's drives and the demands of the environment for adaptive purposes. The conflict-free sphere determined what was expected and perceived, leading to a constancy of behavioral response. In addition, a model of external reality became internalized, like a cognitive map; it was termed the "inner world." Hartmann (1950) further defined the concept of the self as a separate structure within the ego, one that contained self- and object representations.

There have been further efforts to integrate the above-described theories and techniques. Kernberg (1977) considers Edith Jacobson's (1964) developmental model the most comprehensive psychoanalytic theory to date, integrating ego psychology, object relations, and drive theory. In addition, her close collaboration with Mahler (1968), whose work emphasizes the vicissitudes of early childhood development involved in separation-individuation, gave Jacobson important supportive material. Jacobson's work in turn served as a foundation for Kernberg's own important contributions to psychoanalytic theory and technique.

In his chapter in this book, Kernberg reviews theoretical issues and their applications to therapeutic work with borderline and narcissistic patients. Using the developmental schema based on Mahler's and Jacobson's work concerning stages of self- and object differentiation, Kernberg says the therapist's goal is to help these patients overcome their developmental arrest, to integrate part object relations into total object relations, to develop object constancy, and to achieve an integrated self-concept. To attain this objective, Kernberg suggests that the therapist maintain technical neutrality and interpret partial aspects of the transference. In addition, Kernberg recommends the systematic interpretation of splitting and other primitive defenses. In this way, patients can relinquish both the need to idealize and maintain omnipotent control over the analyst and the need to depreciate the analyst as an independent object to defend against the dread of empty aloneness. As patients learn that they can express their ambivalence without fear of retaliation from the analyst, their integration and differentiation improve. Kernberg's work with borderline patients (1975) has the advantage of a scientific foundation: his having been director of the Menninger Psychotherapy Research Project. This study found that borderline patients did poorly when treated by either classical psychoanalysis or supportive therapy. Those treated by expressive psychoanalytic psychotherapy did better. The degree of improvement depended on the ego strength of the patient as well as on the therapist's skill and empathy in establishing a working alliance and containing aggression.

The chapter by Kohut and Wolf elaborate another position based on extensive clinical data derived from the treatment of narcissistic disorders. Kohut (1977) has placed the self at the very center of the personality; he explains pathology and symptoms in terms of a psychology of the self. Although he acknowledges the role of drive theory and ego psychology in understanding conflict, Kohut considers their importance secondary and their explanations insufficient for a thorough comprehension of the psychopathology in the narcissistic patient. Kohut sees a weakened or defective self, a self that has not been confirmed by the parents, as the core of the patient's psychopathology. An authentic and capable self can only be built when the "mirroring" (admiring responses) and "idealizing" needs of the child are satisfied by the self-objects (parents). The unresponded-to self of the child cannot individuate and thus retains its archaic grandiosity and the wish to merge with an omnipotent self-object. Kohut prefers the term self-object transference instead of narcissistic transference to describe the type of transference narcissistic patients develop. He recognizes the need these patients have to reexperience this self-object transference ("mirror" or "idealizing") in order to make up for their developmental arrest. In their chapter, Kohut and Wolf elaborate a comprehensive psychology of the self, including a characterology of disorders of the self. Kohut is aware that others have compared his work to that of a variety of other psychoanalysts—especially Aichhorn, Hartmann, and Winnicott (and even Ferenczi, as I mentioned earlier). Kohut emphasizes, however, that his theory and technique have arisen directly out of his own clinical work and the need to transcend the limitations of classical theory. In therapy, Kohut and Wolf emphasize the importance of the therapist's empathy rather than on the interpretation of drives, since the latter may be experienced as blame. The patient needs to become aware of, to express, and to accept the unfulfilled narcissistic needs from childhood, and thus to become more accepting of himself.

The chapter by Judd Marmor develops the viewpoint that the context of the treatment situation—the patient-therapist relationship—is of greatest importance to cure. This viewpoint stems from the scientific project undertaken by Franz Alexander in 1957, which involved the objective observation and recording of psychoanalytic sessions over a period of several years. In his report, Alexander (1963) challenged the neutrality of the analyst, claiming that the analyst's values are subtly learned by the patient through verbal and nonverbal cues. Thus the therapist as a real person is also significant—especially the attributes of genuineness, warmth, and respect. These qualities help develop a therapeutic alliance that permits working through past traumatic experiences. Alexander reported that a "corrective emotional experience" occurs when the analyst's response to the patient's maladaptive behavior differs from that of past parental figures. This experience is more important than verbal interpretation in bringing about cure. It is interesting that a recent controlled scientific study by Strupp (1979), in the Vanderbilt Psychotherapy Research Project, corroborated Alexander's position; i.e., technical skill did not seem to be as significant as the human relationship, at least in short-term treatment. A group of empathic college professors were as effective as a group of highly trained psychotherapists in doing short-term treatment (25 sessions) with a homogeneous group of college students. These results were based on means or averages, however. Strupp (1980) further noted that failures by the professional therapists were caused by insufficient empathy and attention to the working alliance, an inflexible therapeutic framework, insufficient work with the negative transference, and acting out of countertransference. Thus, both empathic responsiveness *and* technical skill were important. In reviews of outcome studies before 1970 (Luborsky et al., 1971) and between 1954 and 1978 (Bachrach, 1978), these same deficiencies in the skill of therapists were understood to contribute to poor outcomes. All these studies, including Strupp's, noted that the best predictor for a positive outcome or cure is mainly the adequacy of the patient's previous personality functioning. Sicker patients did less well because of the severity of their pathology and the likelihood that they created more transference/countertransference difficulties in the treatment situation.

Robert Hatcher's chapter on insight traces the gradual evolution in psychoanalytic thinking concerning its functioning and its curative effects. Originally psychoanalytic theory held that repressed material emerged in the transference because of two reasons—its own inherent press to seek discharge as well as the repetition compulsion. In current psychoanalytic writings, the ego has assumed the more significant role, with some considering that the very motive force for psychotherapy is the mastery-seeking role of the ego. On the other hand, resistance in treatment is believed to be due to the ego's fear of dangerous thoughts, feelings, and wishes. Strachey's (1934) landmark paper stressed that only when the ego allowed certain repressed material to emerge into consciousness could it be experienced, examined, mastered, and relinquished. For interpretations to be mutative, the timing of interpretations was crucial, i.e., when the patient's impulses were emotionally alive and actively experienced in the transference. This point is further developed in Gill's chapter. Interpretations could thus lead to insight and change. The patient's superego could then identify with the more adult and realistic point of view of the analyst. Hatcher points out that the context around which insight can become effective depends on the patient's ego capacity for controlled regression, tolerance for unpleasant affect, reflective self-observation, and integrative functioning. In addition, the patient-therapist relationship provides a safe or holding environment to facilitate the process. Reorganization of the ego can occur after causal relationships, based on adult understanding, replace old meanings founded on infantile drives, fantasies, and thoughts. The gradual cumulative effect of interpretations allows the ego to expand into larger contexts for self-understanding and mastery of the environment, points that are also dealt with in the chapters by Fried, Palombo, and Stone.

In Levenson's chapter, he elaborates on the thesis advanced in his book, *The*

Fallacy of Understanding (1972). Levenson believes that cure does not result simply from the correctness of an interpretation; instead, cure is effected by the dialectical interaction—what is said and done—in the patient-therapist dyad. Levenson focuses on the very tool of psychotherapy, namely, language. The content of a communication is clothed by the nonlexical contexts, kinesics (bodily and facial gestures), as well as by the immediate social and cultural context. Bateson's (1951) use of the term "metacommunication" implies that there is a message about the message in each communication. Speech can be viewed as a form of behavior. Words are considered deeds that determine how the receiver will hear, experience, and respond to a message.

Freud himself was aware of the fact that hidden unconscious meanings are communicated through tone of voice, posture, slips of the tongue, forgetting, and other parapraxes. Astute therapists invariably pick up inconsistencies or inappropriateness in the patient's communication, especially regarding its authenticity. With borderline and narcissistic patients, who attempt to induce the therapist into feeling and behaving in certain ways, the nonverbal aspects of communication may be extremely significant as to how projective identification may operate. For example, Giovacchini (1975) and Green (1975) have commented on how narcissistic patients may try to make the analyst feel like an inanimate or nonexistent object. Others, such as Deutsch (1926), Heimann (1950), Little (1951), Racker (1953, 1957), Searles (1965), Kernberg (1975), and Langs (1976), have noted how borderline and narcissistic patients may attempt to induce countertransference responses of grandiosity, inferiority, depression, anger, or boredom in the analyst. These responses are evoked by projective identification and relate to the patient's internal objects. In turn, the therapist's own countertransference reaction (whether due to his own pathological transference or to induction by the patient) may be communicated to the patient through the context of the communication. Thus, language (paralinguistics and kinesics) may provide us with the necessary tools to study this phenomenon occurring in projective identification.

Merton Gill's chapter deals with the most critical and central issue of analytic technique: the analysis of the transference. Since the patient's neurosis finds expression in the transference to the analyst, analysis of the transference neurosis is tantamount to analysis of the neurosis. Gill's paper develops five recommendations for working with the transference in ways that enhance its curative potential. He recommends that (1) the transference be encouraged to expand, (2) interpretations of allusions to the transference help this expansion, (3) all transferences have a connection to the analytic situation, (4) resistance to awareness of the transference be interpreted, and (5) resolution of the transference be in the here and now.

Since the patient-therapist interaction is such an emotionally loaded area, transference tends to be pursued less systematically than it should be. Gill points out that the therapist as well as the patient may resist awareness of the transference. Yet this very emotionality is the stuff that cures are made of: it allows for a genuine experiencing of the transference, so that emotional insight can develop.[2] Genetic interpretations may avoid the emotionally loaded area of the therapist-patient interaction, and may lead only to an intellectual understanding that can serve as a defense against change. Although Gill emphasizes the importance of insight, as do Kleinian analysts, he is at variance with the Kleinian emphasis on the interpretation of deep genetic material. Focusing on the here and now in the patient's transference maximizes the chance that emotional insight will develop, with a resultant loosening of constrictions, correction of ego distortions, and change in personality structure.

The issue of countertransference, which has received so much attention in recent years, is reviewed and developed in Robert Langs's chapter. In recent years, the meaning of countertransference was enlarged by Winnicott (1949) to include all the reactions of the therapist to the patient. Its usefulness in treatment was further developed by Deutsch (1926), Sterba (1941), Heimann (1950), Little (1951), Racker (1953, 1957), and others. With sicker patients, the analyst does not serve simply as a screen for projections, but rather, as Bion (1970) pointed out, as a container for the patient's projective identifications. The patient projects aspects of himself into the analyst and attempts to provoke the analyst into thinking, feeling, and behaving like the patient's internalized object. The evoked behavior of the object is then reinternalized through identification. This process involves a certain fluidity of ego boundaries in the patient, and represents the patient's attempt to shape the external real world to fit his internal object world.

Langs discusses how these two forms of countertransference (pathological and inductive) operate continuously between the patient and the therapist in the "bipersonal field." When the analyst monitors his own reactions to the patient's material, the countertransference can serve as a useful therapeutic tool for understanding the patient's transference and internal objects, thereby actually contributing to the curative process. Langs further develops the concept of the "countertransference cure." Here the patient forms a "misalliance" and complies with the therapist's countertransference needs for a cure.

In my own studies of families of schizophrenics (Slipp, 1973), depressives (Slipp, 1976), and hysterics (Slipp, 1977), the treatment "misalliance" appears as a repetition of the process that originally produced the patient's pathology, e.g., the parents' need to complete themselves. The patient complies with the projective identification of the parent(s) by incorporating and acting out the

---

[2]This point is further developed in the paper by Edrita Fried.

parent's internal split objects.[3] In my opinion it is the convergence of the real world of the family with the intrapsychic world of the patient *throughout* development that contributes to the patient's continued fixation and use of primitive defenses. In therapy (as well as in other important human relations), these patients attempt to recreate this convergence of external reality with their internal objects; they use projective identification to provoke countertransference responses in the therapist. Essentially, they attempt to control the therapist's responses as they were controlled in the family. If the therapist acts out the countertransference, the pathology remains deeply fixated by external reality. Thus, Langs's contribution to the understanding and the appropriate use of countertransference is essential in helping patients to resolve their fixation in development, to differentiate fantasy from reality, to differentiate and integrate the self from the object, and to grow and change.

Vamık Volkan's chapter on identification and related psychic events explores a fascinating area of therapeutic change. Volkan reviews the literature on identification and differentiates the following terms: identification, introjection, introject, imitation, incorporation, internalization, projection, externalization, and projective identification. Ego identification with the lost object as a step toward independence that follows normal mourning was first described by Freud in "Mourning and Melancholia" (1917). Since then, considerable interest has been evoked around the curative and pathological potentials of such identification. Strachey (1934) first described the internalization of the analyst by the patient's superego emphasizing the importance of identification with the analyst during the process of change. Identification by the patient's ego with the functional representation of the therapist can also enrich the patient's personality, just as repeated introjections of the analyst as an object may lessen the harshness of the patient's superego. Volkan points out that both these processes can serve as essential components of change and cure in psychotherapy.

An interesting point developed in this chapter is that certain patients with a defect in ego organization can almost serve as a clinical laboratory in which to observe the gradual structuralization occurring during psychoanalytic treatment. These patients have failed to achieve a cohesive self-representation and lack an integrated, internalized object world. They thus relate to the therapist

---

[3]In schizophrenia, the patient acts out the parent's projected bad parental object, functioning as the family *scapegoat*. Thus the parents can displace their feared aggression onto the child and idealize their own relationship. In depression, projective-identification of the parent's good self-image occurs; the patient feels compelled to meet the parental demands for achievement and serves as the family *savior*. In hysteria, the patient acts out the parent's projected good parental object, entering into a seductive relationship with the parent of the opposite sex and serving as a *go-between* to preserve the marriage. In all these instances, the patient is bound into a symbiotic relationship that prevents individuation and results in the patient's being exploited for the parents' needs.

through introjection-projection mechanisms until cohesive self- and object representations are developed. As is usual in Volkan's other work, this chapter contains excellent presentations of clinical data.

The topic of regression, developed in the chapter by Saul Tuttman, is one that has been fraught with controversy from the beginning of psychoanalysis. Is regression necessary? If so, how much is optimal for cure? As mentioned earlier, Ferenczi (1919) believed it was necessary for patients to relive their childhood conflicts fully in the treatment situation if growth and change were to occur. Others have disagreed with the degree of regression that Ferenczi recommended; although some regression occurs in all psychoanalytic psychotherapy, it is usually more limited and more easily reversible. Such limited regression may best be subsumed under Kris's (1952) term "regression in the service of the ego." The therapeutic regression allows otherwise inaccessible material to come to conscious awareness, where it can be interpreted and worked through. Regression brings the past to life again; it is as if the past and present coalesce. This reliving adds a greater emotional impact to the transference. Stability is maintained by the working alliance, wherein the observing ego of the patient cooperates with the therapist. Thus the conditions for real emotional insight and the release from bondage to the past are created.

Tuttman deals with the problem of the therapist's distress about the patient's regression, which is accentuated in cases of intense regression. Should the therapist become more supportive and less probing? Should treatment be discontinued? My own clinical experience indicates that the serious regression that occurs as a result of the patient's life becoming more impoverished is of greater pathological significance than the regression that occurs as a result of enrichment and change in the patient's life. The latter may also be pathological (reflecting an intolerance of success), but is more often a temporary regression connected with the restructuring of the ego.[4]

Edrita Fried's chapter on working through deals with a topic whose importance is well recognized but about which little has been published. How do patients utilize insight: how is it metabolized to bring about behavioral change? This is a puzzling issue that is also dealt with in the chapters by Palombo and Stone. First of all, Fried differentiates "spectator" insight from "experiential" insight. The former is characterized as passive, distant, and intellectualized. It usually does not produce change, but may itself be used as a defense against change. On the the other hand, experiential insight is active, immediate, alive,

---

[4]In this respect, Peto (1960) stresses the temporary fragmenting effect of successful interpretations, the result of which can be regression. A transitory disintegration within the ego occurs resulting in loosening of ego boundaries or even brief depersonalization. Split-off parts of the ego then reemerge and are reintegrated into more realistic images of self and object, so that more mature identifications and sublimations can then evolve. Peto also sees this transitory disintegration-integration effect operating in dream work and play to master traumatic experiences.

and emotional. This form of insight combines both cognitive and emotional elements and is more likely to produce change. We know from laboratory experiments in the field of social psychology that changes in attitudes do not occur if people are simply given intellectual information. Change is more likely to occur if they are active, rather than passive, participants.

On a practical level, we know that simply reading about doing something that requires skill will not provide a person with the necessary ability; only doing it—experiencing the process—leads to real mastery. Insights need to be tried out repeatedly, in and out of the treatment situation, in order for the patient gradually to learn new coping methods, new ways of behaving and relating. Change occurs gradually, as new structures in the ego, which allow for a greater flow of emotions and thoughts, are built up. Fried stresses the vital importance of expressing and processing aggression during the working-through period in order to fortify the patient's ego boundaries, promoting individuation and the development of a vital and authentic self.

Lloyd Silverman's chapter on the unconscious fantasy as a therapeutic agent presents us with fascinating information from the experimental laboratory that sheds light on some of the agents of change that operate during treatment. In the 1960s, Silverman developed a dramatically new use for the tachistoscope, through which he was able to study the effects on behavior of stimulating unconscious fantasies. Subliminal stimulation appears to bypass the conscious perceptual barrier and impinge on the unconscious directly. If the stimulus corresponds to an unconscious fantasy, the fantasy is activated and produces behavioral change, which can then be measured. Certain unconscious fantasies were found to have an adaptation-enhancing effect on thought processes and affect. Silverman suggests that these very same unconscious fantasies may be activated during psychoanalytic psychotherapy, and may account for some of the changes attributed to nonspecific factors.

The most potent subliminal message was one that stimulated unconscious *symbiotic merging fantasies with mother*. This stimulus was found to be adaptation-enhancing for moderately differentiated schizophrenics, for a wide variety of other pathological conditions, as well as for a normal population. The stimulus seems to arouse memory traces of the good pre-Oedipal mother, providing a sense of security, and perhaps also inadvertently stimulating fantasies of Oedipal gratification. Thus the experimental data appear to support the importance of maternal factors in bringing about cure, as described in Ferenczi's "active" treatment, Alexander's "corrective emotional experience," Winnicott's "holding environment," Bion's "container," Kohut's emphasis on the idealizing transference, and Volkan's discussion of the introjection-projection process leading to identification in therapy.

Perhaps the most significant aspect of Silverman's findings is that both the context and the content of treatment (including the therapist's skill and technical competence) are important. They are not mutually exclusive, although, with certain types of patients, one aspect may be more important than the other. Silverman further suggests that there is now experimental evidence that stimulating the unconscious fantasy of merging with the good mother may also facilitate insight; indeed, it may be synergistic and enhancing. Thus the implications for treatment are significant.

The experimental study of dreams in the dream laboratory is presented in the chapter by Stanley Palombo. Palombo's findings indicate that the dream is not only the royal road to uncovering the unconscious but also the royal road traversed in the process of change. He believes that the integration of information generated in the analytic session takes place not in conscious cognitive awareness but during dreaming, by the convergence of associative pathways present in the patient's permanent memory. Associative material and interpretations of dreams from the analytic hour become incorporated into the dream the following night. When matching of present and past experiences occurs, this link becomes part of the permanent memory structure, which then facilitates the normal adaptive mechanisms for evaluating and sorting new experiences. Palombo calls this kind of dream the "correction dream." The process is continuous, with the "correction dream" further evoking new sets of earlier memories, which then become accessible to be worked on. These new memories, in turn, therapeutically open up new associative pathways, which create further change in treatment. Palombo found that lack of matching of present and past experiences tended to create anxiety, which awakened the dreamer. Thus the dream is introduced into waking consciousness and is generally remembered the following day. This dream, in turn, forms the day residue for the dream the following night, which attempts to resolve the mismatch in a "correction dream."

Palombo recommends that, in order to enhance the development of the "correction dream," emphasis needed to be placed on expanding the patient's associations rather than the therapist's interpretations. His work may be viewed as stressing the importance of the ego's need for mastery: its ability to evaluate and derive meaning from experiences. We have long known of the human need to reduce helplessness, as reflected in the building of myths, legends, religion, and scientific theories. Piaget's (1937) study of children's need to develop schemata to explain their experiences and to make causal connections provides another example. Palombo's discovery of how this process occurs unconsciously during dreaming may be the basis for understanding how interpretations and insight are worked through in the dream and how they are effective in bringing about change.

Michael Stone's chapter deals with the sudden and dramatic improvements, or turning points, that sometimes occur in patients during treatment. Stone considers which types of patients are more likely to demonstrate this phenomenon and then attempts to understand its occurrence. He suggests that during treatment there is an accumulation of incremental knowledge which, at one point, results in a quantum leap forward in understanding that changes the patient's life. This recalls Palombo's description of a similar phenomenon in "correction dreams." Stone also mentions that a turning point is often heralded by a dream in the patient; this he terms the "mutative dream," but he does not give it the same causal significance that Palombo does. Stone considers the dream an epiphenomenon, the end result of a complex problem-solving operation going on in the patient's mind outside of conscious awareness. Palombo, on the other hand, considers the turning-point dream to be a therapeutically active "correction dream." This dream, however, reaches the patient's conscious awareness because the unconscious solution of a major problem may in turn expose new problems that create sufficient anxiety to awaken the dreamer. Despite diverse explanations, both the astute clinician, Stone, and the careful researcher, Palombo, have highlighted this same phenomenon, the turning-point dream. Both believe this process of change occurs on an unconscious level, outside of the patient's awareness. Both view it as a continuous and gradual evolution that eventually results in the sudden resolution of a major personality problem. Both present a number of interesting clinical examples to enrich our understanding of the fascinating topic of sudden turning points in treatment.

Jules Bemporad focuses on curative factors in the treatment of depression. Depressed persons usually seek therapy after a major upheaval in their life creates a crisis in meaning around how they derive self-esteem and gratification in their existence. As a child, the depressed person was often used to complete a parent's life: the parent lived vicariously through the child's achievement. Drawing from Silvano Arieti's rich clinical experience as well as his own, Bemporad notes that the depressive's sense of worth and enrichment stems not from his or her own achievement but from parental approval. Autonomous gratification is forbidden. The depressive becomes dependent on a transferential displacement of the parent, "the dominant other," who is empowered to provide self-esteem and meaning to life. These same dynamics that Bemporad derived from retrospective case studies were found to be operative in the direct study of depressives and their families (Slipp, 1976).

Bemporad outlines three phases of treatment and lists the potential pitfalls that may hinder cure. In the initial phase, the patient will try to induce the therapist to play the role of the omniscient "dominant other," which the therapist must resist; nor should the therapist be trapped into gratifying the patient's demands. The therapist needs to encourage the patient's introspection and assumption of responsibility for his own improvement. In the second stage, resistance to change—the fear of being abandoned as punishment for becoming autonomous—has to be worked through. In the final stage, the spouse may resist change in the patient and may thus require treatment. The spouse may enter individual therapy with another therapist or both spouses may be seen in conjoint treatment to establish a new and healthier relationship.

The chapter written by Theodore and Ruth Lidz reflects the wisdom of a lifetime spent working with schizophrenics as well as studying and understanding their families (Lidz, Fleck, and Cornelison, 1965). These families were found to be incapable of fulfilling the child's needs for nurturance, personality development, basic socialization, and enculturation; nor could they provide adequate models for identification. The child is caught in the symbiotic bondage of having to complete a parent's life, and the therapist's primary task is to release the patient from this bondage. How this is accomplished is the content of the chapter. The process of treatment is developed in a clear and comprehensive fashion, including such issues as establishing a therapeutic relationship, gaining trust, avoiding the omniscient role, the therapist as participant observer, clarification of schizophrenic communication, finding a working distance, and closure of the therapeutic relationship. In therapy, the patient develops ego boundaries and becomes a separate individual able to establish proper object relations and to direct his or her own life. Many of the problems and pitfalls that the therapist must cope with are carefully elaborated, including the possibility of disruption of treatment by the family. The latter frequently occurs with young adult schizophrenics who are improving and individuating because of treatment. As Bemporad mentioned in the previous chapter, other members of the patient's family may resist change in the patient. Thus the family may need to be involved in consultation, collaborative therapy with a social worker, or conjoint family treatment in order to consolidate the gains made in individual therapy.

In the chapter, "Toward the Resolution of Controversial Issues in Psychoanalytic Treatment," Lloyd Silverman and David Wolitzky, both outstanding researchers, present some of the major controversial issues regarding what is curative in psychoanalytic psychotherapy. These issues are presented in earlier parts of the book and include (1) the problems of the self versus unconscious conflicts about sexual and aggressive drives, (2) Oedipal versus pre-Oedipal conflicts, (3) the importance of transference versus nontransference issues, and (4) the therapeutic context versus insight. Suggestions are made for the resolution of these controversies, including five research paradigms that range from naturalistic (approximating the treatment situation) to experimental (including controls and holding independent variables constant).

The final chapter by David Wolitzky and Morris Eagle reviews the important hypotheses presented by the clinicians and researchers contributing to this book regarding what is curative in psychoanalysis and dynamic psychotherapy. The current state of the field is thus presented to the reader. Each hypothesis is discussed in detail as well as in the light of the other chapters and outside literature. They address such issues as: What are the merits and problems of each of these hypotheses about what brings about change? How can these controversies be explored and possibly be resolved through further research? Indeed, some of the controversial issues may not be oppositional, but be complementary to one another. The general themes and issues raised by the contributors to the book are brought together to obtain a clearer picture of what is most effective and with whom to facilitate change in psychotherapy.

From the inception of psychoanalysis, Freud stressed the importance of its being a discipline firmly rooted in science. His own theoretical formulations were based on direct empirical findings from his work with patients. He established a carefully controlled framework for both patient and analyst in the treatment situation. Freud considered that psychoanalytic research could only be done in the therapeutic session, that to introduce other methods of investigation would change the essential process. Thus the individual case study method became the primary one and, indeed, has proved to be the richest and most creative area for the development of clinical hypotheses and therapeutic techniques. With the expansion of psychotherapy into the treatment of a broader group of patients, it becomes increasingly important to assess our therapeutic effectiveness. Evaluative procedures for psychotherapy outcome studies have become more sophisticated. In addition, the newer applications of the tachistoscope, the dream laboratory, and other scientific methods bring Freud's hope for scientific validation of psychoanalytic theories clearly within our grasp. To this end, outstanding clinicians and researchers were brought together in this book to share their creative insights and scientific knowledge to further our understanding of the curative factors in dynamic psychotherapy.

REFERENCES

Alexander, F. (1954), Psychoanalysis and psychotherapy. *J. Amer. Psychoanal. Assn.,* 2:722–733.

——— (1963), The dynamics of psychotherapy in the light of learning theory. *Amer. J. Psychiat.,* 120:440–448.

Bachrach, H. M., & Leaff, L. A. (1978), Analyzability. In: A systematic review of the clinical and quantitative literature. *J. Amer. Psychoanal. Assn.,* 26:881–920.

Bateson, G. (1951) *Communication: The Social Matrix of Psychiatry,* New York: Norton.

Bibring, E. (1954), Psychoanalysis and the dynamic psychotherapies. *J. Amer. Psychoanal. Assn.,* 2:745–770.

Bion, W. R. (1970), *Attention and Interpretation.* London: Tavistock.

Deutsch, H. (1926), Occult processes occurring during psychoanalysis. *Imago,* 12:418–433.

Ferenczi, S. (1919), On the technique of Psycho-analysis. In: *Further Contributions to the Theory and Technique of Psycho-Analysis.* London: Hogarth Press, 1926, pp. 177–180.

——— (1920), The further development of an active therapy in psycho-analysis. In: *Further Contributions to the Theory and Technique of Psycho-Analysis.* London: Hogarth Press, 1926, pp. 198–217.

Freud, A. (1936), *The Ego and the Mechanisms of Defence.* New York: International Universities Press, 1946.

Freud, S. (1910), The future prospects for psycho-analytic therapy. *Standard Edition,* 11:139–151. London: Hogarth Press, 1957.

——— (1917), Mourning and melancholia. *Standard Edition,* 14:237–258. London: Hogarth Press, 1957.

——— (1920), Beyond the pleasure principle. *Standard Edition,* 18:3–66. London: Hogarth Press, 1955.

——— (1923), The ego and the id. *Standard Edition,* 19:3–66. London: Hogarth Press, 1961.

——— (1926), Inhibitions, symptoms and anxiety. *Standard Edition,* 20:75–174. London: Hogarth Press, 1959.

——— (1933), New introductory lectures on psycho-analysis. *Standard Edition,* 22:1–182. London: Hogarth Press, 1964.

Fromm-Reichmann, F. (1954), Psychoanalytic and general dynamic conceptions of theory and of therapy: Differences and similarities. *J. Amer. Psychoanal. Assn.,* 2:711–721.

Gill, M. (1954), Psychoanalysis and exploratory psychotherapy. *J. Amer. Psychoanal. Assn.,* 2:771–797.

Giovacchini, P. L. (1975), Self projections in the narcissistic transference. *Internat. J. Psychoanal. Psychother.,* 4:142–166.

Green, A. (1975), The analyst, symbolization and absence in the analytic setting (on changes in analytic practice and analytic experience). *Internat. J. Psycho-Anal.,* 56:1–22.

Guntrip, H. (1968), *Schizoid Phenomena, Object Relations and the Self.* New York: International Universities Press.

Hartmann, H. (1939), *Ego Psychology and the Problem of Adaptation.* New York: International Universities Press, 1958.

——— (1950), Comments on the psychoanalytic theory of the ego. In: *Essays on Ego Psychology.* New York: International Universities Press, 1964.

——— Kris, E., & Loewenstein, R. M. (1951), Some psychoanalytic comments on "culture and personality." In: *Psychoanalysis and Culture,* ed. G. B. Wilbur & M. Muensterberger. New York: International Universities Press.

Heimann, P. (1950), On countertransference. *Internat. J. Psycho-Anal.,* 31:81–84.

Jacobson, E. (1964), *The Self and the Object World,* New York: International Universities Press.

Kernberg, O. (1975), *Borderline Conditions and Pathological Narcissism.* New York: Jason Aronson.

——— (1977), An ego-psychological object relations theory: The contributions of Edith Jacobson. Presented at the New York Psychoanalytic Society and Institute. (To be published in *Object and Self: A Developmental Approach,* a book in memory of Edith Jacobson, ed. S. Tuttman. New York: International Universities Press.)

Klein, M., (1948) *Contributions to Psychoanalysis,* 1921–45. London: Hogarth Press.

Kohut, H. (1977), *The Restoration of the Self.* New York: International Universities Press.

Kris, E. (1952), On preconscious mental processes. In: *Psychoanalytic Explorations in Art.* New York: International Universities Press, pp. 303–320.

Langs, R. (1976), *The Therapeutic Interaction.* New York: Jason Aronson.

Levenson, E. (1972), *The Fallacy of Understanding.* New York: Basic Books.

Lidz, T., Fleck, S., & Cornelison, A. R. (1965), *Schizophrenia and the Family.* New York: International Universities Press.

Little, M. (1951), Countertransference and the patient's response to it. *Internat. J. Psycho-Anal.,* 32:32–40.

Luborsky, L., Auerbach, A. H., Chandler, M., Cohen, J., & Bachrach, H. M. (1971), Factors influencing the outcome of psychotherapy: A review of quantitative research. *Psycholog. Bull.*, 75:145–185.

Mahler, M. S. (1968) *On Human Symbiosis and the Vicissitudes of Individuation.* Vol 1: Infanite Psychosis, New York: International Universities Press.

Peto, A. (1960), On the transient disintegrative effect of interpretations. *Internat. J. Psycho-Anal.*, 41:413–417.

Piaget, J. (1937), *The Construction of Reality in the Child.* New York: Basic Books, 1954.

Racker, H. (1953), A contribution to the problem of countertransference. *Internat. J. Psycho-Anal.*, 34:313–324.

—— (1957), The meanings and uses of countertransference. *Psychoanal. Quart.*, 26:303–357.

Rangell, L. (1954), Similarities and differences between psychoanalysis and dynamic psychotherapy. *J. Amer. Psychoanal. Assn.*, 2:734–744.

Searles, H. F. (1965), *Collected Papers on Schizophrenia and Related Subjects.* New York: International Universities Press.

Slipp, S. (1973), The symbiotic survival pattern: A relational theory of schizophrenia. *Family Process*, 12:377–398.

—— (1976), An intrapsychic-interpersonal theory of depression. *J. Amer. Acad. Psychoanal.*, 4:389–409.

—— (1977), Interpersonal factors in hysteria: Freud's seduction theory and the case of Dora. *J. Amer. Acad. Psychoanal.*, 5:359–376.

Sterba, R. (1941), The relaxation of the analyst. *Psychiatry*, 4:339–342.

Strachey, J. (1934), The nature of the therapeutic action of psychoanalysis. *Internat. J. Psycho-Anal.*, 15:127–159.

Strupp, H. H., (1980), The Vanderbilt Psychotherapy Research Project. Grand Rounds Presentation, New York University School of Medicine, Department of Psychiatry.

—— & Hadley, S. W. (1979), Specific vs nonspecific factors in psychotherapy: A controlled study of outcome. *Arch. Gen. Psychiat.*, 36:1125–1136.

Winnicott, D. W. (1949), Hate in the countertransference. *Internat. J. Psycho-Anal.*, 30:69–74.

—— (1965), *The Maturational Process and the Facilitating Environment.* New York: International Universities Press.

CHAPTER 1

The Theory
of Psychoanalytic Psychotherapy

Otto F. Kernberg

Historical Roots of Psychoanalytic Psychotherapy

Psychoanalytic exploration of the defenses and resistances, the transferences and drive derivatives of patients with severe character pathology and borderline personality organization has shown that the intrapsychic structural organization of these patients seems very different from that of better functioning patients. This finding has imposed serious constraints on the traditional theory of psychoanalytic psychotherapy. Of particular concern is that the structural characteristics of borderline patients defy applying the model of psychoanalysis to psychoanalytic psychotherapy, unless the model is modified. Yet many studies of pathological early development and object-relations theory that aim to understand severe psychopathologies recommend—implicitly or explicitly—only standard psychoanalytic techniques. We seem to have, on the one hand, a theory of psychotherapy that is not applicable to many patients in psychotherapy and, on the other hand, theories of pathological development and severe psychopathology that might require new models of psychotherapy, but

This chapter is an expanded version of a presentation at the panel "Conceptualizing the Nature of the Therapeutic Action of Psychoanalytic Psychotherapy," at the Annual Meeting of the American Psychoanalytic Association, Atlanta, Georgia, May 7, 1978.

21

are presented in terms geared mostly to psychoanalytic technique proper. One purpose of this chapter is to try to resolve this paradox.

Gill's (1954) definition of psychoanalysis as the establishment of a therapeutic setting that permits the development of a regressive transference neurosis and the resolution of this transference neurosis by means of interpretation carried out by the analyst from a position of technical neutrality contains two important implications for the theory of psychoanalytic psychotherapy. First, if the analyst's position of technical neutrality, the use of interpretation as a major psychotherapeutic tool, and the systematic analysis of the transference define psychoanalysis, then psychoanalytic psychotherapies may be defined in terms of modifications in any or all of these three technical essentials. In fact, I think the definition of a spectrum of psychoanalytic psychotherapies, ranging from psychoanalysis to supportive psychotherapies, is possible in terms of these three basic features.

Second, it needs to be stressed that the analysis of the transference is simultaneously the analysis of instinctual urges and defenses against them, and of a particular object relation within which these instinctual urges and defenses are played out. As Glover (1955) pointed out, all transference phenomena must be analyzed in terms of the principal stage of libidinal investment activated and the principal identification involved. Both contemporary ego psychology and object-relations theory take their departure from this dual nature of the transference.

It seems to me that modern ego psychology's major contributions to the theory of technique—in contrast to theories of development and psychopathology—stem from Wilhelm Reich's *Character Analysis* (1933–1934) and Fenichel's *Problems of Psychoanalytic Technique* (1941). These works expanded the analysis of resistances—including the transference as a principal resistance and source of information in the psychoanalytic situation—into the detailed analysis of the resistance function of pathological character traits. These contributions also pointed to the intimate connection between the predominance of character defenses in cases of character pathology, on the one hand, and the activation of these defenses as part of the prevailing transference resistances in all analytic treatments, on the other.

The analysis of character may well be the most dramatic practical application of psychoanalytic technique to the treatment of the neuroses. Psychoanalytic character analysis is a fundamental challenge to the traditionally pessimistic attitude of psychology and psychiatry toward the possibility of changing personality structure. From the early focus on reaction formations and inhibitory character traits to the later focus on impulsive character traits and impulse-ridden characters in general, it was only a small step to the present psychoanalytic focus on the nature of global ego "defects"—and on the puzzling relationships between ego defects and character defenses and resistances (is an ego defect a complex character resistance, or does a character resistance reflect an ego defect?).

The ego-psychology theory of psychoanalytic psychotherapy as proposed by Gill (1951, 1954), Stone (1951, 1954), Eissler (1953), Bibring (1954), and others may be defined as a psychoanalytically based treatment that does not attempt to systematically resolve unconscious conflicts, and therefore, resistances, but rather, to partially resolve some resistances, and reinforce others, with a subsequent partial integration of previously repressed impulses into the adult ego. As a result, a partial increase of ego strength and flexibility may take place, which then permits a more effective repression of residual, dynamically unconscious impulses, and a modified impulse-defense configuration that increases the adaptive—in contrast to maladaptive—aspects of character formation. This definition differentiates psychoanalysis from psychoanalytic psychotherapy in terms of both goals and the underlying theory of change reflected in these different goals.

Wallerstein formulated this difference when he proposed (1965) that the procedural stance of psychoanalysis is characterized by its lack of a specific goal (in terms of the open-ended nature of analytic work), that it aims instead at fundamental character realignment. In contrast, psychoanalytic psychotherapy focuses on certain individual circumscribed goals in that it aims for desirable modifications of behavior and character structure, without the broader goal of resolving character pathology.

The techniques employed in psychoanalytic psychotherapy were all devised to facilitate these goals and to bring about a partial shift of the dynamic equilibrium among the tripartite structures. I would modify Bibring's (1954) description of psychotherapeutic techniques to include, first of all, partial interpretation, meaning both preliminary interpretations that would remain limited to conscious and preconscious areas (or clarification), and full interpretations of some limited intrapsychic segments (leaving other segments untouched). The effect of these techniques would still be "analytic" in a strict sense, that is, at least partially uncovering unconscious motives and conflicts.

Abreaction, another psychotherapeutic technique, would permit the expression of suppressed and repressed emotions in the therapeutic situation, thereby presumably reducing intrapsychic pressures, owing to the patient's sense of being accepted by the therapist as a tolerant and empathic parental figure and, in this connection, by means of other transference gratifications as well. Suggestion, comprising a broad spectrum of psychotherapeutic techniques, includes rational counseling, advice, and emotional suggestions (e.g., hypnosis). Its effectiveness would be due to the transference implications of direct support and command from an important parental figure, the reinforcement of adaptive characterological solutions to intrapsychic conflicts, the (at least temporary) decrease of superego pressures (by their externalization, and, in this process, modification), and the facilitation of identificatory processes with the therapist's active and supportive stances toward the patient.

Manipulation would affect the intrapsychic balance of forces by indirect means, such as fostering a more favorable social environment for the patient, eliminating or controlling regressive and conflict-inducing situations in the environment, and favoring derivative expressions of the patient's unconscious needs by providing specific social outlets or situations.

Some common mechanisms by which all of these psychotherapeutic techniques may affect the patient in psychoanalytic psychotherapy have been described in the literature; for example, the "corrective emotional experience" implied in the positive human relationship developed in the course of psychoanalytic psychotherapy; the particular transference gratifications symbolically achieved in the course of the therapist's suggestive, manipulative, abreactive, and even clarifying and interpreting interventions; and, most important, the activation of identification processes in the patient by means of all of these interventions—adaptive ego identifications with the therapist would increase ego strength directly.

Combining the techniques employed in psychoanalytic psychotherapy, the ego-psychology approach defined two major modalities of treatment. The first is exploratory, insight-oriented, and uncovering—in short, expressive psychoanalytic psychotherapy; the second is suppressive, or supportive, psychotherapy.

Expressive psychotherapy is characterized by the use of clarification and interpretation as major tools. The therapist actively and selectively interprets some aspects of the transference in the light of the particular goals of treatment, the predominant transference resistances, and the patient's external reality. For the most part, technical neutrality is maintained, but neither a systematic analysis of all transference paradigms nor a systematic resolution of the transference neurosis by interpretation alone is ever attempted.

Supportive psychotherapy does use clarification and abreaction, but suggestion and manipulation predominate. Insofar as supportive psychotherapy still implies that the psychotherapist is acutely aware of and monitors the transference, and carefully considers transference resistances as part of his technique in dealing with character problems and their connection to the patient's life difficulties, it is still a psychoanalytic psychotherapy in a broad sense. By definition, however, the transference is not interpreted in purely supportive psychotherapy, and the use of suggestion and manipulation implicitly eliminates technical neutrality. A comprehensive overview of the ego-psychology theory of psychoanalytic psychotherapy can be found in Dewald's (1969) textbook.

All the ego-psychology theoreticians I mentioned earlier have stressed the difference between the structural change achieved in psychoanalysis and the more limited changes achieved in psychotherapy. Structural change as obtained in psychoanalysis implies a radical change in the equilibrium of conflictual forces involving the tripartite structural system—that is, reduction in superego pathology and pressures on the ego, reduction in the rigidity of the ego's defensive structures, sublimatory integration of previously repressed unconscious impulses, and significant increase in the scope and flexibility of adaptation to internal and external reality derived from such changes in intersystemic equilibrium.

In contrast, the changes effected by the psychotherapies would be largely behavioral. Increased adaptive functioning of certain impulse-defense configurations would predominate in the outcome of these psychotherapies. Instead of obtaining structural intrapsychic change on the basis of an interpretive approach, the therapeutic changes would be in large part adaptive, obtained, at least partly, by environmental "structuring" (in the sense of manipulation) that would help the patient deal with a more manageable environment, or by consistent "educational" guidance toward better ways of adjusting to the environment.

As suggested earlier, the major problem with this technical theory of psychoanalytic psychotherapy has been the contradiction between the theoretical model from which it stems and the structural intrapsychic organization of many patients to whom it has been applied. Thus, the ideal indication for psychoanalytic psychotherapy would be for mild cases where the "major surgery" of psychoanalysis is not warranted, and, in its supportive modality, for those with serious psychological illness (e.g., severe character pathologies) where psychoanalysis seems contraindicated (Wallerstein and Robbins, 1956). Psychoanalytic psychotherapy with patients who have relatively mild psychological illness is indeed highly effective; even brief psychoanalytically oriented psychotherapy or "focal" psychotherapy (Balint, Ornstein, and Balint, 1972) with patients who have good ego strength and motivation can be effective. The theoretical model underlying this approach holds remarkably well, then, for patients with good ego strength.

The application of this psychoanalytic psychotherapy model to patients with severe psychopathologies, however, yielded findings I have described elsewhere (Kernberg et al., 1972): Patients with ego weakness who were treated with supportive psychotherapy—following the traditional idea that such patients need to reinforce their defenses and that, therefore, resolution of resistances by interpretation is risky—did rather poorly. In contrast, borderline patients treated with expressive psychotherapy sometimes did remarkably well. As predicted, however, borderline patients treated with unmodified, standard psychoanalysis did rather poorly. In addition, the psychoanalytic exploration of defenses and resistances—particularly the transference of borderline patients—revealed findings that were hard to reconcile with the classical tripartite structural model (Kernberg, 1975).

First, these patients presented a constellation of primitive defense mechanisms centered on dissociation of contradictory ego states—or splitting—rather than on repression. Second, the transference of these patients had peculiarities that seemed very different from the more usual transference developments in better-functioning patients. Third, and most important, primitive impulses were not unconscious, but dissociated in consciousness. In this connection, the evaluation of defense-impulse constellations often did not permit a clarification of which agency within the tripartite model was defending against which impulse within which other agency. The transferences of these patients seemed to reflect contradictory ego states that incorporated primitive internalized object relations within an overall psychic matrix that did not present a clear differentiation of ego, superego, and id. In short, the cases for which the ego-psychology approach had modified classical psychoanalytic technique and formulated a theory of change by less than strictly psychoanalytic means did not seem to fit the structural theoretical model on the basis of which the psychotherapy of these cases had been conceived.

This leads us to a new psychoanalytic approach (in addition to the classical and contemporary ego-psychology ones) which attempts to deal with the phenomena just described, namely, psychoanalytic object-relations theory. As I said before, it is paradoxical that object-relations theories offer answers to problems that originally developed within ego-psychological psychoanalytic psychotherapy while many object-relations theoreticians, particularly those of the British schools, steadfastly refuse to consider any theory of technique or technical approach for patients with severe character pathologies and ego weakness other than psychoanalysis proper. What follows is an application of psychoanalytic object-relations theory to a theory of the technique of psychoanalytic psychotherapy.

In the severe psychopathologies, early, primitive units of internalized object relations are directly manifest in the transference as conflicting drive derivatives reflected in contradictory ego states. In these cases, the predominance of a constellation of early defense mechanisms centering on primitive dissociation, or splitting, immediately activates contradictory, primitive but conscious, intrapsychic conflicts in the transference. What appear to be inappropriate, primitive, chaotic character traits and interpersonal interactions, impulsive behavior, and affect storms are actually reflections of the fantastic early object-relations-derived structures that are the building blocks of the later tripartite system. These highly fantastic, unrealistic precipitates of early object relations, which do not directly reflect the real object relations of infancy and childhood and which must be interpreted until the more realistic aspects of the developmental history emerge, determine the characteristics of primitive transference. In the treatment, structural integration through interpretation precedes genetic reconstructions (Kernberg, 1979).

The interpretation of primitive transferences—which includes the systematic interpretation of splitting mechanisms and other primitive defenses—requires special psychoanalytic methods. First of all, the dangers of severe acting out and of blurring the boundaries of the psychoanalytic situation may necessitate establishing parameters of technique and/or structuring the patient's external life in order to protect the psychoanalytic situation.

Second, since verbal communication is often disturbed at primitive levels of fixation or regression, and since severe psychopathology is typically expressed nonverbally (as is all character pathology to a certain extent), the analyst's focus may have to shift from the content of free association to the total material expressed in the patient-therapist interaction, including the patient's experience of and reaction to the psychoanalytic setting, which frequently becomes a major channel of expressing the transference.

Third, under these conditions, the immediate meaning of the interpersonal relation in the transference—in terms of the activation of primitive transference dispositions—has to be interpreted with a special consideration of the patient's predominant unit of self- and object representations reflected in such interaction. Some authors have used the notion of psychoanalytic "space" (Winnicott, 1958, 1965, 1971; Bion, 1967, 1970) to refer to this translation of nonverbal interaction into a primitive object-relations structure. They have stressed the integrating function of the analyst's cognitive and emotional absorption and tolerance of the patient's chaotic material as well as the analyst's subsequent use of the integrated material in interpretive comments.[1]

Fourth, countertransference dispositions are particularly pronounced in these cases and require particular methods so that the analyst's emotional reactions can be controlled and therapeutically used.

In contrast to the facilitation of integrated ego functioning by means of the ego's overall defensive structure in patients with good ego strength, primitive defensive operations in patients with severe psychopathology have a serious ego-weakening effect. Therefore, interpretation of primitive defensive constellations such as splitting, projection, projective identification, denial, omnipotence, idealization, and devaluation improves ego strength and permits the gradual development of an observing and integrated ego function (Kernberg, 1976). Thus, within an object-relations framework, both the interpretation of defenses as clinical resistances and the interpretation of transferences as internalized object relations may—and actually should—be applied throughout the entire spectrum of psychopathology. Jacobson (1971), for example, has applied her findings regarding the psychopathology of depression and depressed borderline patients to the psychoanalytic treatment of these conditions.

---

[1]In Winnicott's terms, the analyst's affective "holding" function; in Bion's terms, the analyst's cognitive "containing" function.

While Jacobson, Mahler, and other theoreticians oriented to ego-psychology object-relations viewpoints have generally been careful in their selection of cases for psychoanalysis and have questioned the indiscriminate application of the same psychoanalytic technique to all patients, the British object-relations group, particularly the Kleinians, have applied the same unmodified technique to all patients. In the light of much accumulated clinical experience, I consider the latter approach a mistake and think that it can lead to disastrous results.

In contrast, Little, Guntrip, and, to some extent, British "middle group" clinicians in general, have tended to blur the distinctions between psychoanalysis and psychoanalytic psychotherapy, a position which can lead to considerable confusion. The approach of the British school represents precisely the other side of the paradox mentioned earlier, namely, that the theoretical and technical contributions of most interest for the psychoanalytic psychotherapy of patients with severe psychopathologies have been developed without regard for the theoretical and technical differences between psychoanalysis and psychotherapy.

I think it is possible to formulate a theory of psychoanalytic psychotherapy that uses the concepts derived from both ego psychology and object-relations theory.

A Theory of Psychoanalytic Psychotherapy

At all levels of psychopathology where psychoanalysis or psychoanalytic psychotherapy is clinically indicated, symptoms and pathological character traits reflect intrapsychic conflicts. These conflicts are always dynamically structured, that is, they reflect a relatively permanent intrapsychic organization of contradictory or conflicting internalized object relations. At severe levels of psychopathology, such dynamic structures are dissociated, thus permitting the contradictory aspects of the conflicts to remain in consciousness. Here, the interpretation of defenses and primitive transferences fosters ego integration, the consolidation of the tripartite structure, and the simultaneous transformation of primitive transferences into advanced or typically neurotic ones. Under these conditions, interpretation of the transference may bring about an alteration of the equilibrium of the forces in conflict, as well as structural intrapsychic change in the sense of integrating part object relations into total ones, consolidating ego identity, and reinforcing the boundaries of ego, id, and superego. The analysis of the transference is carried out by a direct analysis of the total analytic situation, with particular emphasis on the psychoanalytic setting and its relation to reality.

At less severe levels of psychopathology such as one finds in the standard psychoanalytic patient, the dynamically structured intrapsychic conflicts are unconscious, and are manifest largely in intersystemic conflicts between ego, superego, and id and their typical defense mechanisms. Here, the interpretation of defense mechanisms induces a partial redissolution—or rather, a loosening and shifting of the boundaries—of the tripartite structure, which facilitates both the establishment of a regressive transference neurosis and the gradual unfolding—by means of the systematic analysis of ego and superego defenses—of a regressive transference, that is more integrated than those initially formed in patients with severe psychopathologies. The analysis of the transference in patients with well-integrated tripartite structure is facilitated by the patient's observing ego and the related therapeutic alliance. The analyst must focus chiefly on free association and its distortions by the manifestation of various defense mechanisms; the focus on the analytic setting itself recedes into the background. The integration of complex repressed impulses reflecting entire constellations of repressed object relations (especially the Oedipal constellation) permits an enrichment of ego functions and experiences, as well as a reduction in the rigidity and constraint of ego defenses and superego pressures.

Although individual considerations always have priority in determining the type of treatment, generally speaking, psychoanalysis is the preferred treatment for patients with milder forms of psychopathology, except when special circumstances warrant brief psychotherapy or psychoanalytic psychotherapy. For patients with good ego strength, I would recommend psychoanalytic psychotherapy as originally defined by the ego-psychology writers I referred to earlier, as well as the combined use of various expressive and supportive techniques.[2] The following three paradigms—(1) the principal technical tools (clarification and interpretation versus suggestion and manipulation), (2) the extent to which the transference is interpreted, and (3) the degree to which technical neutrality is maintained—jointly define the nature of psychotherapy within the expressive-supportive range of treatment.

In cases of severe psychopathology—with a few exceptions where, for well-documented individual reasons, psychoanalysis is indicated and feasible—the preferred treatment is expressive psychoanalytic psychotherapy. Expressive psychoanalytic psychotherapy with such patients differs, however, from that attempted with better-integrated patients. Maintaining the three basic paradigms upon which differentiation of psychoanalysis proper from psychoanalytic psychotherapy can be established, psychoanalytic psychotherapy for severe psychopathology might be described as follows.

Because primitive transferences are immediately available, predominate as resistances, and, in fact, determine the severity of intrapsychic and interper-

---

[2]Gill (1978), however, has questioned the advisability of combining expressive and supportive techniques for patients with good ego strength, and has presented strong arguments for maintaining a strictly expressive approach with these patients.

sonal disturbances, the analyst must focus on them from the start, by interpreting them in the "here and now." Genetic reconstruction should be attempted only at later stages of treatment (when primitive transferences, determined by part object-relations, have been transformed into advanced transferences or total object-relations, thus approaching the more realistic experiences of childhood that lend themselves to genetic reconstructions). The analyst must maintain a position of technical neutrality in interpreting such primitive transferences. He must establish firm, consistent, stable reality boundaries in the therapeutic situation, and avoid getting sucked into reactivated pathological primitive object relations. Insofar as both transference interpretation and a position of technical neutrality require the use of clarification and interpretation, and contraindicate the use of suggestive and manipulative techniques, clarification and interpretation remain the principal therapeutic techniques.

In contrast to psychoanalysis proper, however, the transference analysis is not systematic. Because of the need to focus on the severity of the acting out and on the disturbances in the patient's external reality (which may threaten the continuity of the treatment as well as the patient's psychosocial survival), and also because the treatment, as part of the acting out of primitive transferences, easily comes to replace life, transference interpretation now has to be codetermined by (1) the predominant conflicts in immediate reality, (2) the overall specific goals of treatment—and the consistent differentiation of life goals from treatment goals (Ticho, 1972), and (3) the material immediately prevailing in the transference.

In addition, technical neutrality is limited by the need to establish parameters of technique, which sometimes include structuring the patient's external life and using a team approach to help the patient who cannot function autonomously during long stretches of psychotherapy. Technical neutrality is therefore a theoretical baseline from which deviations occur again and again, to be reduced by interpretation. The therapist's interpretation of the patient's understanding (or misconception) of the therapist's comments is an important aspect of this effort to reduce the deviations from technical neutrality. Further exploration of the differences between expressive psychoanalytic psychotherapy with patients presenting ego weakness and that with patients having good ego strength requires a sharper focus on both the mechanisms of action and the effects of psychotherapeutic techniques—our next issue.

The Therapeutic Action of Psychoanalytic Psychotherapy

It is interesting that little concern was expressed in the 1950s about the potentially contradictory effects of combining various interpretive and supportive techniques. Although psychoanalytic psychotherapies were classified along a spectrum ranging from the purely expressive to the purely suppressive, it was assumed that a mixture of supportive and interpretive techniques and effects was perfectly harmonious.

In retrospect, a mixture of supportive and expressive techniques does seem feasible for patients with good ego strength. For example, a therapist's suggestive and manipulative interventions in the course of an exploratory psychotherapy that focuses mostly on transference developments and their relation to the patient's immediate reality may not unduly distort such transference developments, although they naturally reduce the intensity of transference regression (particularly in driving underground the severer aspects of the negative transference dispositions, or in displacing them toward other objects). Indeed, the therapist's empathic attitude in helping the patient deal with an immediate real-life problem may lead to a favorable ego identification, without activating a primitive, pathological idealization of the "good" therapist as a defense against the activation of paranoid fears of the "bad" therapist (the potential receptacle for projected early sadistic superego forerunners). In other words, ego identification with the therapist and transference gratification may take place in the context of a mixture of supportive and expressive technical approaches with patients who have sufficiently good ego strength to be able to perceive, understand, and integrate the more positive aspects of the therapeutic relationship in spite of the underlying ambivalences in the transference.

On the other hand, this combination of expressive and supportive techniques and the respective mechanisms of their action may not work for patients with severe psychopathology. In patients with predominantly primitive transference dispositions reflecting part object-relations, all these psychotherapeutic techniques (except interpretation per se) and the mechanisms by which they are supposed to bring about therapeutic change raise new questions.

First, selectively interpreting some resistances while leaving others untouched in order to protect ego integration runs counter to the clinical observation that the predominant constellation of primitive defense mechanisms in such cases has ego-weakening effects, and that the systematic interpretation of such defenses—largely manifest as transference resistances—has an ego-strengthening effect.

Second, the very fact that the conflicting impulses—the pathologically condensed sexual and aggressive drive derivatives expressed in dissociated or split-off part object-relations—are conscious makes it imperative to deal with them: ignoring such exigent needs and impulse expressions in these patients only increases their fear of their own impulses, and displaces the most significant instinctual conflicts from the transference situation onto other relationships, thereby increasing acting out.

Third, the therapist's effort to provide a stable, reliable, and empathic parental figure who facilitates the patient's emotional growth by ego identification and transference gratification is often made impossible by the development of severely negative transferences reflected in paranoid dispositions. These paranoid dispositions must be dealt with to prevent the disruption of the psychotherapeutic relationship and to permit some semblance of therapeutic alliance to be established.

Fourth, and most important, the gratification of certain transference demands (usually stemming from the patient's need to protect the good, idealized transference relationship in the face of a threatening breakthrough of conflicts around aggression) significantly distorts the patient's perception of the therapist and of the therapeutic situation.

In short, the flexible capacity to take the best from the therapist, which patients with good ego strength have, and which, I think, has much to do with the fact that these patients respond favorably to a broad range of exploratory-supportive psychotherapeutic techniques, is missing in patients with severe psychopathology. In the latter cases, patients do not identify with the benign aspects of the psychotherapist, but rather, with highly idealized, projected forerunners of the ego ideal; because patients feel incapable of living up to such idealizations, their autonomous growth is undermined. A related problem derives from the therapist's misunderstanding of the importance of empathy for patients with severe psychopathology, a subject which I have discussed elsewhere at some length (Kernberg, 1979).

For all these reasons, a supportive technique runs counter to the therapeutic needs of patients with severe psychopathology, particularly borderline cases, with whom a modified psychoanalytic procedure or psychoanalytic psychotherapy is attempted. These patients require a purely expressive approach. I shall now spell out the three technical paradigms that jointly define expressive psychoanalytic psychotherapy with the borderline personality as well as the specific effects of these techniques.

Interpretation

Interpretation is a fundamental technical tool in psychoanalytic psychotherapy with borderline patients; in fact, in order to protect technical neutrality as much as possible, suggestion and manipulation are practically contraindicated here, except when the potential for severe acting out requires structuring the patient's external life and using a team approach to set limits and make other interventions in the social field. Such socially structuring or manipulative efforts should be considered parameters of technique, to be interpreted as often and as comprehensively as possible in working toward their gradual dissolution.

The following question has been raised: How is it possible that patients with severe psychological illness and ego weakness are able to respond to interpretation? Do these patients accept interpretations because of their actual meaning or because they are manifestations of the therapist's interest (that is, because of their magical, transference meanings)? Empirical evidence indicates that patients with severe psychological illness are indeed able to understand and integrate interpretive comments, particularly if their understanding of the therapist's interpretations is examined and interpreted in turn. In other words, the patient's difficulty in integrating verbal communication is itself a product of primitive defensive operations that can be interpreted, particularly as they are activated in the patient's reactions to the therapist's interpretations.

However, the need to explore fully the patient's understanding of the therapist's interpretations and to clarify consistently the immediate reality of the therapeutic situation—the meaning of what the therapist has been saying, in contrast to the patient's interpretation of that meaning—results in clarification taking precedence over interpretation. This technical demand creates quantitative differences between this kind of psychotherapy and psychoanalysis.

Maintenance of Technical Neutrality

This is an essential technical tool, an indispensable prerequisite for interpretive work. Once more, technical neutrality does not preclude an empathic, authentic, warm attitude on the part of the therapist, but, to the contrary, may best reflect such warmth and empathy under conditions in which the emergence of the patient's regressive aggression in the transference would naturally bring about counteraggressive reactions in the therapist. The therapist's emotional capacity to maintain an empathic attitude in such circumstances (the therapist's "holding" action) and his cognitive capacity to integrate ("contain") the fragmentarily expressed transferences are important components of such technical neutrality.

However, because the patient's potential for severe acting out and for developing life- and/or treatment-threatening situations may require structuring not only the patient's life but the psychotherapy sessions as well, technical neutrality is constantly interfered with, threatened, or limited, and a good part of the therapist's efforts will have to be devoted to reestablishing it, again and again. To put it differently, in patients with severe ego weakness or ego distortions where the nondefensive or observing part of the ego (which would ordinarily contribute to the therapeutic alliance or working relationship with the therapist) is not available, the provision of such auxiliary ego functions through clarification of the immediate reality shifts the interpretations into clarifications and may bring about deviations from technical neutrality, requiring later reductions of such deviations by interpretive means. This quantitative reduction in technical neutrality implies another difference from psychoanalysis proper.

Transference Analysis

I mentioned earlier that transference interpretation is limited in these cases, that it is codetermined by a constant focus on the immediate reality of the patient's life and the ultimate treatment goals. Moreover, because the process of interpreting primitive transferences gradually integrates part object-relations into total object-relations and, correspondingly, transforms primitive transferences into advanced or neurotic ones, the transference of borderline patients is subject to relatively sudden shifts. Neurotic or advanced transferences, reflecting more realistic childhood developments, first appear infrequently, and then increasingly often throughout the treatment. As a result, the process of transforming primitive transference structures into their integrated counterparts evolves in discontinuous, qualitatively shifting phases throughout the treatment, which gives an overall timelessness to the genetic reconstruction and interferes with its historical placement (Kernberg, 1979). These developments require an atemporal, "as if" mode of transference interpretation over extended periods of time, an additional reason for regarding such transference interpretation as less than systematic, and therefore different from that occurring in the standard psychoanalytic situation.

Nevertheless, while transference analysis is less than systematic under these conditions, the interpretation of defensive constellations is quite systematic. In contrast to expressive psychotherapy with better-functioning patients—where certain defenses may be interpreted while others are not touched—the systematic interpretation of defenses in severe psychopathology is of crucial importance in improving ego functioning and in permitting the transformation and resolution of primitive transferences. Therefore, the interpretation of the constellation of primitive defensive operations centering on splitting should be as consistent as their detection in the patient's transferences and extratherapeutic relationships permits.

The most important mechanisms of change implied in this approach (i.e., those effects that the interpretation of primitive transferences specifically attempts to achieve), are: the resolution of primitive defense mechanisms in the therapeutic situation; the integration of part object-relations into total object-relations; and the related integration and development of ego functions, particularly of ego identity, with the corresponding integration of the self concept and object constancy.

Elsewhere (1976, Chapter 6) I have described the interpretive steps that gradually transform primitive transferences into advanced ones; steps that consist, first, in defining the predominant human interaction activated at any particular time in the transference; second, in defining the self- and object components and the affect disposition (reflecting libidinal or aggressive drive derivatives) linking them in this interaction; and third, in integrating the dissociated or split-off self- and object representations under the impact of, respectively, libidinal and aggressive drive derivatives.

This specific effect of interpretation, that is, transformation by integration, is supported by the relatively nonspecific one derived from the auxiliary ego functions carried out by the psychotherapist, particularly his emotionally and cognitive integrating function reflected in his capacity to tolerate what the patient originally could not tolerate in himself. This permits the patient to accept what was previously too painful to be integrated in his own subjective experience, and in the process, provides an implicit and silent assurance that, contrary to the patient's fantasies, aggression does not necessarily destroy love

TABLE 1

Psychoanalytic Psychotherapy

	MECHANISMS OF ACTION	
TECHNICAL TOOLS	*With Good Ego Strength*	*With Ego Weakness*
Interpretation	Reduction in defenses permits emergence of repressed material	Increases ego strength by resolving primitive defenses
Transference analysis	Interpretation of selected transferences permits their gradual resolution	Interpretive integration of primitive into advanced transferences permits their eventual resolution
Technical neutrality	Fosters transference regression; permits interpretation by not gratifying transferences	Protects reality in the therapeutic situation; permits interpretation of primitive transferences

and the possibility of a deep and meaningful human relationship. These nonspecific effects may be considered "supportive," but then, all interventions are potentially supportive in their effects, as distinguished from being supportive techniques. It has been rightly stated that psychoanalysis is the "most supportive" form of therapy.

In summary, psychoanalytic psychotherapy with borderline patients uses technical tools that are similar to those used in psychoanalysis; the mechanisms of action of these tools, however, differentiate this treatment from expressive psychotherapy with patients presenting ego strength. These different mechanisms of action are outlined in Table 1.

There is one more dimension to consider in effecting therapeutic change in patients with severe character pathology and borderline conditions. This dimension has to do with the patient's increased capacity to experience subjectively what was previously dissociated and expressed in distorted behavior in the interpersonal realm. In psychoanalytic psychotherapy with severely regressed patients, patients must become subjectively aware of their relation to the psychotherapeutic setting and integrate their former expression of the uncanny in the interpersonal field. This change is analogous to the incorporation into consciousness of repressed material in patients with well-integrated tripartite structure. Again, this is a particular effect of an analytic approach that quantitatively separates psychoanalytic psychotherapy with regressed patients from the standard psychoanalytic situation as well as from psychoanalytic psychotherapy with patients presenting good ego strength.

The differences between them notwithstanding, the similarity between psychoanalytic psychotherapy and psychoanalysis is much greater in cases of severe psychopathology than in cases of milder psychological illness. One might say that, with the former, the tactical psychotherapeutic approach to each session is almost indistinguishable from psychoanalysis proper, and only from a long-term, strategic standpoint do the differences emerge. However, although the technical approach to borderline patients resembles that of psychoanalysis, the therapeutic atmosphere is quite different: the predominance of nonverbal communication and of the examination of the total interaction over the patient's communication of subjective experiences and his intrapsychic life create a special therapeutic climate.

By the same token, the difference between expressive psychoanalytic psychotherapy and supportive psychotherapy is sharp and definite in patients with severe pathology, while it may be more blurred in the less severely ill. In simple terms, it is not possible by means of psychotherapy to bring about significant personality modifications in patients with severe psychopathology without exploring and resolving primitive transferences, and this requires an analytic approach (although not psychoanalysis proper). I think that in all cases it is very helpful to maintain a clear distinction between psychoanalytic psychotherapy and psychoanalysis.

There are patients with severe character pathology, narcissistic personality, or borderline personality organization for whom both psychoanalysis and expressive psychoanalytic psychotherapy are contraindicated, and in such cases I think that a strictly supportive approach is best. Such supportive psychotherapy requires, in turn, a very sophisticated approach in using suggestive and manipulative techniques and in dealing with primitive transferences noninterpretively. All our understanding regarding supportive psychotherapy may have to be reexamined and reformulated in the light of what we now know about severe psychopathology. .

Clinical Illustration

The following segment from the psychoanalytic psychotherapy of a thirty-four-year-old single woman, a mathematician who had been unable to work for over six years and whose personality structure combined intense schizoid and masochistic features, occurred toward the end of the fourth year of treatment when, after significant improvement, a severe negative therapeutic reaction developed over a period of five months. During this time, the patient responded with subtle mockery and provocations to all of my efforts to clarify the meaning of her frequent silences, her emotional withdrawal from me, and her keeping me ignorant of important occurrences in her daily life. Over a period of months, she gradually became aware that the severe blocks and long silences in the hours reflected an internal prohibition against further improvement because of intense guilt caused by her sense that change could occur only at the cost both of her "real" mother's suffering and of the destruction and loss of her internalized mother.

On the surface, the patient's attacks on me were an attempt to make me withdraw emotionally and counterattack, which would then have permitted her to externalize her cruel internalized mother on me. In fact, there were times when a partial compromise solution took the form of her attacking me as a representation of her mother—thus partially rebelling against her—while maintaining a good surface relation with her mother in reality, thereby apparently submitting to her and keeping the treatment situation stable. She attacked her mother, bitterly complaining that her mother was cold, domineering, and yet rejecting of her. Some of the patient's descriptions of her clinging to an overpowering and aggressive mother corresponded to actual aspects of her infantile past. But all opportunities in the therapeutic situation for a true dependency on me were internally forbidden and unavailable to the patient, for which she blamed me.

Within this overall context, the following episode took place. Following a stormy session, the patient sent me a letter. What follows is a summary of that letter and the two sessions we had after I received it. Because the treatment was bilingual and the letter itself was in a foreign language, the salient features of it will be paraphrased in translation.

The patient had left for approximately a week to visit her mother, who lived in a different state. She wrote the letter soon after her arrival there, and it reached me the day before our next session. The patient wrote that she was furious at me because she felt I was just "tolerating" her; she hated my sitting "patiently" through her angry outbursts and nagging demands. She was not denying her anger and demands, but all of this was made worse by what she experienced as my detached "professional" tolerance, which angered her even more. She had fantasies of making me suffer terribly, of hurting my feelings very deeply. Without any transition, she went on to tell me how much she hated me because I never gave her any credit for anything good that she did, and never made her feel good about herself in any way. She also felt that I never acted as if we were working together, and I never showed any sense of accomplishment or pride in the progress that she had made. She felt that my emotional detachment was unfair because the progress in her treatment was not only her own work. She found my attitude one of artificial concern for her, as if I were giving her lessons in "positive feelings," and then added that one thing she hated about the treatment was that I never erred, that I never forgot that I was the therapist or slipped from that role.

The letter went on to say that she was perfectly aware what "transference" meant, that she would have to be mentally retarded not to understand this after years of treatment. But this did not take away her sense of loneliness, her sadness about not being involved in a satisfying and fulfilling relationship. And further, she added, when she did talk about this in the sessions, I twisted it around so that the problem always involved me, resulting in her feeling that I did not care at all. She really wanted to feel loved and appreciated, and instead of examining what she expected of the relationship, I only suggested endlessly that she did not appreciate what I had to give to her.

In an abrupt shift, she then wrote that instead of being angry at her parents directly, she felt angry at me for not fulfilling her parental ideals. She wanted to be loved and felt nobody loved her. In conclusion, she added that she also sometimes hated me for not being compassionate with her; she felt reduced to self-pity. She really hated me, she wrote, for the pain I had caused her over the past years without thinking twice about it. Finally, she didn't think that I deserved any good feelings from her because I never gave anything back, and she didn't need lessons in expressing "positive feelings."

In spite of the intense anger the letter expressed, it also conveyed feelings of warmth and gratitude; I experienced it as a clear indication of the patient's increased tolerance of ambivalence, her awareness of the complexity of her emotional relation with me. In short, I was very touched by it.

In our next session, which occurred the day after I received the letter, the patient complained bitterly that I did not love her, that I was "professionally" objective and cool and had no real feelings for her. As these complaints were repeated insistently, I was struck first, by the patient's sadistic tone of voice and triumphant smile; and second, by my perception of a "frozen" quality inside myself, as if indeed I had no feelings for her, accompanied by a sense of guilt—as if I owed her some real feelings. This reaction was in striking contrast to the strong positive feelings I had experienced for her at the beginning of the session. Third, I was struck by the contradiction between her unusually clear, coherent, and modulated way of expressing herself, and the content of her angry accusations. In the past, great anger had had a disorganizing effect on her communications. Fourth, I noted her references to how angry she had been with me since the last session, and how this anger had decreased only temporarily during the visit to her mother, after which she felt much better. She remarked, however, that her mother had told her she now looked "dangerously healthy" (!).

After attempting to stimulate the patient to explore how all the features I was observing might fit together, I realized that she was cutting me off every time I tried to speak, almost triumphantly making me shut up, and only remaining silent when I in turn remained silent. I told her I felt she was putting many of her internal conflicts into me because she could not tolerate them, and that she wanted to shut me up in order to avoid hearing about them. I said that behind her "simple" feeling that I had no feelings for her was a condensation of many conflicts and a fear that I would undo that condensation and face her with the conflicts that were buried in the middle of her assertion that I did not care for her.

The patient said she did feel afraid; I said that she felt afraid that I would attempt to help her understand what was going on, which was indeed very frightening. At the same time, I continued, one part of her also wanted to know what was going on, so that her fear expressed the struggle between the part of her which wanted to know and the part of her which simply wanted to get rid of her internal problems and of me.

Now the patient said she wanted me to tell her how I understood what was going on (she no longer interrupted me). I said I felt there were several layers of problems expressed in her feeling that I did not care for her. First, she felt that I was like a cold and rejecting mother with whom she was enraged for not giving her any love; second, she was taking revenge against this mother by *becoming* an aggressive, sadistic, and triumphant mother who was accusing me (representing the frightened little daughter) of not having good feelings toward her mother to whom I (she) owed everything; third, in reenacting her relation with her mother with interchanged roles, she was also attempting to spoil the good aspects of her relation with me because she felt guilty about her improvement in psychotherapy—that is, in attacking me by accusing me of not loving her, she was able to protest against her mother while remaining submissive to her.

The patient's expression changed markedly at this point; she became sad and thoughtful. She said she knew her mother wanted her to stop psychotherapy and that her mother had accused her of having a much easier life than the rest of the family. What right did she have to continue spending so much money and time on herself when other members of the family had far greater problems? And she added that I must know that her mother was also friendly and loving, and at times warm and enthusiastic. I said that it was not I she was trying to reassure that her mother could have good as well as bad sides, but herself; and that it was because she was so afraid that her hatred of her mother would also destroy everything good that she had received from her, and thus leave her completely alone, that she could neither acknowledge that hatred more directly nor accept the simultaneous existence of loving and hateful feelings for me (mother).

For the first time in several months, the patient was now able to explore further aspects of her relationship with her mother, her perception of the mother's personality, and her fear of becoming independent and grown-up.

In the following session, the patient began by saying she had left the last session feeling very sad, that she had cried on the way home and had gradually begun to feel that I had accused her of being cold and unfeeling. She said she thought that she was not cold and unfeeling and that I was accusing her of problems she had resolved long ago. She complained that I only saw her difficulties, that I could not acknowledge her improvement, and that in the middle of all of this I always maintained a self-satisfied and contented attitude stemming from my "happy satisfaction" with my own family at home. She also added that she knew that she exaggerated, but this was still the way she felt.

I told her that I understood this reaction to be a reversal of the earlier session, in which she had accused me of being cold and unfeeling, and in which I had interpreted her identifying herself with her mother in a self-satisfied, aggressive, and superior way, accusing me of being cold and ungrateful in the same way her mother had accused her. I pointed out that, in accepting my interpretation, she had felt guilty for attacking me when she realized that I was really concerned and interested in her. I added that this feeling of guilt had then changed into her sense of being the impotent victim of a sadistic mother who accused her of being cold and unloving, a reversal to the childhood experience we had discussed earlier in that session (a change reflecting the reprojection of her sadistic superego). I added that while this was going on she was aware that there was something unrealistic about her reaction, that her perception of my comments as an attack reflected her own exaggerated, self-critical oversimplification of my comments, and that I felt that, in one part of her, she was still capable of maintaining a good image of me in spite of her anger and suspicion about me (implying that she was now better able to tolerate her ambivalence toward me).

The patient, much relieved, then said she felt it was much more important to discuss her sexual difficulties than to focus so much on her difficulties with her mother; there had been such emotional storms in recent hours with me that for several sessions she had not been able to discuss her relations with her boyfriend. She also said that I was unaware of how intensely sexual her feelings about me sometimes were.

I remained silent, with an attitude of expectation of further communication from her; but she also became silent, and I finally interpreted her silence, saying that her conflicts with her mother were forcing themselves all over her mind, to such an extent that she did not have the internal freedom to explore her sexual difficulties. I also said that she might be attributing this interference to me, and that, ultimately, it was her internalized sadistic mother who was attempting to prevent her from describing her sexual feelings to me and from resolving her sexual inhibitions in the process. The patient replied that she understood better how several contradictory things were occurring in her mind, and that she had difficulty keeping them together, so that it was as if different people were experiencing different problems inside of her. I sensed considerable emotional warmth at the end of that session; the patient felt reassured by my interest and dedication without having to explore this issue verbally.

This session illustrates the persistence of the subject matter of the earlier one; the faster "replay" of the earlier resistances as part of working through; and the patient's growing awareness of the relationship between dissociative or splitting mechanisms, on the one hand, and the conflict with a sadistic primitive superego represented by her internalized mother, on the other.

Both sessions illustrate some technical characteristics of the process of structural intrapsychic change in the context of the working through of primitive transference paradigms. First, the initial manifestation of part object-relations in the early part of the first session (rapid alternation between patient and therapist of the enactment of self- and object representations reflecting the conflicts with the mother in an overall confused or chaotic transference situation) changed rapidly in the second half of the first session and throughout most of the second one into the more organized transference disposition of a higher or "neurotic" level.

Second, the material illustrates how the painful experience of not being loved could be analyzed in its genetic components involving conflicts over both love and aggression. In other words, although the transference repeated an earlier experience of not being loved by mother, that earlier experience (as well as its repetition in the transference) reflected a more complicated state of affairs. The experience of not being loved was the final outcome of the combination of the patient's need for love, her envy and jealousy of mother, the frustration and aggression stemming from mother, the patient's counteraggression and its projection onto mother, and the spiraling effect of the projection of aggression onto the image of a frightfully sadistic and destructive mother. The therapist's availability as a real object permitted, as part of the total perception of the transference-countertransference situation, a diagnosis of these various components and their analytic resolution.

A contrasting approach would have been to gratify the patient's transference demands by indicating that she was, indeed, "special" to the therapist, permitting her to think that the therapist liked her and that, in shifting from his position of technical neutrality into that of an orally giving parent, he acknowledged and responded to her needs. There are therapists, for example, who at such points might offer extra time, or express their positive feelings for the patient directly, or even hold the patient's hand. I think all these approaches are ill-advised and harmful in the long run; one pays a high price for the temporary relief that the patient experiences when his or her transference demands for love are met.

Third, the sequence illustrates the shift from a predominantly dyadic, pregenital transference into the beginning of a triadic, Oedipal one as the pregenital components are elaborated in the transference. The patient's envy and jealousy of the therapist's family contained elements of oral envy (the therapist prefers his children to the patient and feeds them with all his love) and also Oedipal elements (jealousy of the relation between the therapist and his wife and/or his adolescent daughter). In the second session the patient also directly referred to sexual fantasies and desires for the therapist, as well as expressing concern about her remaining sexual difficulties with her boyfriend.

Fourth, the overall sequence illustrates that the primitive transferences cannot be explored separately from the working through of ordinary neurotic transferences, and that there are repetitive cycles in which primitive transferences dominate, are understood and worked through, and then shift into neurotic transferences with which they are genetically connected, illustrating the intimate relation between pregenital and genital conflicts in patients with severe character pathology.

Perhaps I should repeat that the sequence occurred after approximately four years of treatment and that the patient was quite obviously on the road to improvement in terms of symptoms, social functioning, and the development of the transference. In summary, the stalemate, reflecting the patient's submission to and identification with a sadistic, primitive, internalized mother, could be resolved analytically by working through the primitive transference reflecting this internalized object relationship.

REFERENCES

Balint, M., Ornstein, P. H., & Balint, E. (1972), *Focal Psychotherapy: An Example of Applied Psychoanalysis.* London: Tavistock.

Bibring, E. (1954), Psychoanalysis and the dynamic psychotherapies. *J. Amer. Psychoanal. Assn.*, 2:745–770.

Bion, W. R. (1967), *Second Thoughts: Selected Papers on Psycho-Analysis.* New York: Basic Books, 1968.

——— (1970), *Attention and Interpretation.* New York: Basic Books.

Dewald, P. (1969), *Psychotherapy: A Dynamic Approach* (2nd ed.). New York: Basic Books.

Eissler, K. R. (1953), The effects of the structure of the ego on psychoanalytic technique. *J. Amer. Psychoanal. Assn.*, 1:104–143.

Fenichel, O. (1941), *Problems of Psychoanalytic Technique*. Albany, N.Y.: Psychoanalytic Quarterly.

Gill, M. M. (1951), Ego psychology and psychotherapy. *Psychoanal. Quart.,* 20:62–71.

——— (1954), Psychoanalysis and exploratory psychotherapy. *J. Amer. Psychoanal. Assn.,* 2:771–797.

——— (1978), Psychoanalysis and psychoanalytic psychotherapy. Paper presented at the University of California-San Francisco Medical School Continuing Education Seminar, January 20, 1978 (unpublished).

Glover, E. (1955), *The Technique of Psycho-Analysis*. New York: International Universities Press.

Jacobson, E. (1971), *Depression*. New York: International Universities Press.

Kernberg, O. (1975), *Borderline Conditions and Pathological Narcissism*. New York: Jason Aronson.

——— (1976), *Object Relations Theory and Clinical Psychoanalysis*. New York: Jason Aronson.

——— (1979), Some implications of object relations theory for psychoanalytic technique. *J. Amer. Psychoanal. Assn.,* 27:207–239.

——— et al. (1972), Psychotherapy and psychoanalysis: Final report of the Menninger Foundation's psychotherapy research project. *Bull. Menninger Clin.,* 36:1–275.

Reich, W. (1933–1934), *Character Analysis*. New York: Touchstone Books, 1974.

Stone, L. (1951), Psychoanalysis and brief psychotherapy. *Psychoanal. Quart.,* 20:215–236.

——— (1954), The Widening scope of indications for psychoanalysis. *J. Amer. Psychoanal. Assn.,* 2:567–594.

Ticho, E. A. (1972), Termination of psychoanalysis: Treatment goals, life goals. *Psychoanal. Quart.,* 41:315–333.

Wallerstein, R. D. (1965), The goals of psychoanalysis: A survey of analytic viewpoints. In: *Psychotherapy and Psychoanalysis: Theory—Practice—Research*. New York: International Universities Press, 1974, pp. 99–118.

Wallerstein, R. S., & Robbins, L. L. (1956), The Psychotherapy research project of the Menninger Foundation, Part IV: Concepts. *Bull. Menninger Clin.,* 20:239–262.

Winnicott, D. W. (1958), *Collected Papers: Through Paediatrics to Psycho-Analysis*. New York: Basic Books.

——— (1965), *The Maturational Process and the Facilitating Environment*. New York: International Universities Press.

——— (1971), *Playing and Reality*. New York: Basic Books.

CHAPTER 2

The Disorders of the Self and Their Treatment

Heinz Kohut and Ernest S. Wolf

The Emergence of a Psychology of the Self

During recent years the psychoanalytic investigation of certain frequently encountered patients has led to the recognition of a definable syndrome which at first appeared to be related to the psychoneuroses and neurotic character disorders. It was clear from the outset that these patients are characterized by a specific vulnerability: their self-esteem is unusually labile and they are extremely sensitive to failures, disappointments, and slights. It was, however, not the scrutiny of the symptomatology but the process of treatment that illuminated the nature of the disturbance of these patients. The analysis of their psychic conflicts did not result in either the expected amelioration of suffering or the hoped-for cessation of undesirable behavior. However, the discovery that these patients reactivated certain specific narcissistic needs in the psychoanalytic situation, i.e., that they established "narcissistic transferences," made effective psychoanalytic treatment possible.

The psychopathological syndrome from which these patients suffer was designated *narcissistic personality disorder*. The narcissistic transferences which are pathognomonic for these syndromes were subdivided into two types: (1) the *mirror transference,* in which an insufficiently or faultily responded-to childhood need for a source of accepting-confirming "mirroring" is revived in the

44

treatment situation, and (2) the *idealizing transference,* in which a need for merger with a source of "idealized" strength and calmness is similarly revived. As the understanding of the symptomatology, core psychopathology, and treatment of the narcissistic personality disorders increased, in particular via the investigation of the narcissistic transferences, it became clear that the essence of the disturbance from which these patients suffered could not be adequately explained within the framework of classical drive-and-defense psychology. In view of the fact that a weakened or defective self lies at the center of the disorder, explanations that focused on conflicts concerning the libidinal and aggressive impulses of these patients could illuminate neither psychopathology nor treatment process. Some progress was made by expanding the classical libido theory and by revising the classical theory of aggression. Specifically, the weakness of the self was conceptualized in terms of its underlibidinization—or cathectic deficit, to speak in the terms of Freudian metapsychology—and the intense aggressions encountered in the narcissistic personality disorders were recognized as the responses of the vulnerable self to a variety of injuries.

The decisive steps forward in the understanding of these disorders, however, were made through the introduction of the concept of the selfobject and via the increased understanding of the self in depth-psychological terms. *Selfobjects* are objects which we experience as part of our self; the expected control over them is therefore closer to the concept of the control that a grownup would expect to have over his own body and mind than to the concept of the control that one would expect to have over others. There are two kinds of selfobjects: (1) those who respond to and confirm the child's innate sense of vigor, greatness, and perfection, and (2) those whom the child can admire and merge with as an image of calmness, infallibility, and omnipotence. The first type is referred to as the mirroring selfobject; the second, as the idealized parent imago.

The *self,* the core of our personality, has various constituents that we acquire in the interplay with those persons in our earliest childhood environment whom we experience as selfobjects. A firm self, resulting from the optimal interaction between the child and his selfobjects, is made up of three major constituents: (1) one pole from which emanate the basic strivings for power and success; (2) another pole that harbors the basic idealized goals; and (3) an intermediate area of basic talents and skills that are activated by the tension arc that establishes itself between ambitions and ideals.

Faulty interaction between the child and his selfobjects results in a damaged self—either a diffusely damaged self or a self that is seriously damaged in one or the other of its constituents. If patients whose self has been damaged enter psychoanalytic treatment, they reactivate the specific needs that have remained unresponded to by the specific faulty interactions between the nascent self and the selfobjects of early life—that is, a selfobject transference is established.

Depending on the quality of the interactions between the self and its selfobjects in childhood, the self will emerge either as a firm and healthy structure or as a more or less seriously damaged one. The adult self may thus exist in states of varying degrees of coherence, from cohesion to fragmentation; in states of varying degrees of vitality, from vigor to enfeeblement; and in states of varying degrees of functional harmony, from order to chaos. Significant failure to achieve cohesion, vigor, or harmony, or a significant loss of these qualities after they have been tentatively established, may be said to constitute a state of *self disorder*. The psychoanalytic situation creates conditions in which the damaged self begins to strive to achieve or to reestablish a state of cohesion, vigor, and inner harmony.

Once the self has crystallized in the interplay of inherited and environmental factors, it aims toward the realization of its own specific program of action— a program that is determined by the specific intrinsic pattern of its constituent ambitions, goals, skills, and talents, and by the tensions that arise between these constituents. The patterns of ambitions, skills, and goals; the tensions between them; the program of action that such patterns create; and the activities that strive toward the realization of this program are all experienced as continuous in space and time—they are the self, an independent center of initiative, an independent recipient of impressions.

The Secondary Disturbances of the Self

The experiential and behavioral manifestations of the *secondary disturbances of the self* are seen in the reactions of a structurally undamaged self to the vicissitudes of life. A strong self allows us to tolerate even wide swings of self-esteem in response to victory or defeat, success or failure. Various emotions—triumph, joy; despair, rage—accompany these changes in the state of the self. If our self is firmly established, we will be afraid neither of the dejection that may follow a failure nor of the expansive fantasies that may follow a success—reactions that would endanger those with a more precariously established self.

Among the secondary disturbances are the reactions of the self to physical illness or to the incapacities of a structural neurosis, e.g., the dejection or the anger experienced when incurable muscular paralysis or chronic neurotic anxiety inhibits a person from pursuing his central self-enhancing goals. And even certain reactions of relatively undamaged layers of the self to the consequences of its own primary disturbances—such as dejection over the fact that a damaged self's vulnerability has led to social isolation—should be counted among the secondary disturbances of the self.

The Primary Disturbances of the Self

The *primary disturbances of the self* can be divided into several subgroups, depending on the extent, severity, nature, and distribution of the disturbance. If serious damage to the self is either permanent or protracted, and if no defensive structures cover the defect, the experiential and behavioral manifestations are those that are traditionally referred to as *the psychoses*. The nuclear self may have remained noncohesive (schizophrenia) either because of an inherent biological tendency, or because its totality and continuity were not responded to with even minimally effective mirroring in early life, or because of some combination of biological and environmental factors.

In other instances, the self may have obtained a degree of cohesion, but because of the interaction of inherent organic factors and a serious lack of joyful responses to its existence and assertiveness, it will be massively depleted of self-esteem and vitality ("empty" depression). During the crucial periods of its formation the self may have been almost totally deprived of the repeated wholesome experience of participating in the calmness of an idealized adult (i.e., of a merger with an idealized selfobject), with the result—again decisively influenced by inherent biological factors—that an uncurbed tendency toward unrealistically heightened self-acceptance (mania) or self-rejection and self-blame ("guilt" depression) remains a serious central weak spot in its organization.

A second subgroup of primary disorders of the self is the *borderline states*. Here the breakup, enfeeblement, or functional chaos of the nuclear self is also permanent or protracted, but, in contrast to the psychoses, the experiential and behavioral manifestations of the central defect are covered by complex defenses. Although in general it is not advisable for the therapist to tamper with these protective devices, it is sometimes possible to make the patient's use of them more flexible by reconstructing the genesis of both the central vulnerability and the chronic characterological defense. For example, it may be helpful to the patient to understand the sequence of events, repeated on innumerable occasions, when as a child his need to establish an autonomous self was thwarted by the intrusions of the parental selfobject. In other words, at the very point when the nascent self of the child required the accepting mirroring of its independence, the selfobject, because of its own incompleteness and fragmentation fears, insisted on maintaining an archaic merger.

A significantly more resilient self is found in the next subgroup, the *narcissistic behavior disorders,* even though the symptoms which these persons display—e.g., perverse, delinquent, or addictive behavior—may expose them to grave physical and social dangers. But the underlying disorder—the breakup, enfeeblement, or serious distortion of the self—is only temporary in these cases, and with the support of increased insight into the genetic roots and the dynamic purpose of their symptomatic behavior, they may become able to relinquish it in favor of more mature and realistic supports for their self-esteem.

Closely related to the narcissistic behavior disorders are the *narcissistic personality disorder,* where breakup, enfeeblement, or serious distortion of the self is also only temporary but where the symptoms—e.g., hypochondria, depression, hypersensitivity to slights, lack of zest—primarily concern the person's psychological state rather than his actions and interactions.

Of the patients who suffer from disorders of the self, only those with narcissistic behavior and personality disorders are capable of tolerating the frustrations of the narcissistic needs of their vulnerable self that are reactivated in the working through process of analysis without a protracted fragmentation or depletion of the self. In other words, of all the primary disorders of the self, only narcissistic behavior and personality disorders are analyzable.

The Etiology of Self Pathology

In view of the fact that the disorders of the self are, by and large, the results of miscarriages in the normal development of the self, we will first present an outline of the normal development of the self. It is difficult to pinpoint the age at which the baby or small child may be said to have acquired a self. To begin with, it seems safe to assume that, strictly speaking, the neonate is without a self. The newborn infant arrives physiologically preadapted to a specific physical environment—i.e., the presence of oxygen, food, a certain range of temperature—outside of which it cannot survive. Similarly, the infant's psychological survival requires a specific psychological environment—i.e., the presence of responsive-empathic selfobjects. It is in the matrix of a particular selfobject environment that, via a specific process of psychological structure formation called *transmuting internalization,* the *nuclear self* of the child will crystallize. Without going into the details of this structure-building process, we can say: (1) that it cannot occur without a previous stage in which the child's mirroring and idealizing needs have been sufficiently responded to; (2) that it takes place in consequence of the minor, nontraumatic failures in the responses of the mirroring and the idealized selfobjects; and (3) that these failures lead to the gradual replacement of the selfobjects and their functions by a self and its functions. And it must be added that, while gross identifications with the selfobjects and their functions may temporarily and transitionally occur, the ultimate wholesome result—the autonomous self—is not a replica of the selfobject. The analogy of the intake of foreign protein in order to build up one's own protein is very serviceable here—even as regards the splitting up and rearrangement of the material that has been ingested.

If we keep in mind the processes by which the self is created, we realize that, however primitive the nuclear self may be in comparison with the adult self, at its very inception it is already a complex structure, the endpoint of a developmental process which may be said to have its beginnings with the formation of specific hopes, dreams, and expectations concerning the future child in the minds of the parents (especially the mother). When the baby is born, the encounter with the child's actual physiological and psychological equipment will, of course, influence the parents' preconceived imagery about its future personality. But the parental expectations will exert a considerable influence on the baby's developing self from birth onward. Thus the self arises from the interplay between the newborn's innate equipment and the selective responses of the selfobjects through which certain developmental potentialities are encouraged while others are not encouraged or are even actively discouraged. Out of this selective process there emerges, probably during the second year of life, a nuclear self which, as stated earlier, is currently conceptualized as a bipolar structure: archaic nuclear ambitions form one pole; archaic nuclear ideals form the other. The tension arc between these two poles enhances the development of the child's nuclear skills and talents—rudimentary skills and talents that will gradually develop into those that the adult employs in the service of the productivity and creativity of the mature self.

The strength of these three major constituents of the self, the choice of their specific contents, the nature of their relationship—e.g., which one of them will ultimately predominate—and their progress toward maturity and potential fulfillment through creative actions will be less influenced by those responses of the selfobjects that are shaped by their philosophy of child rearing than by those that express the state of their own nuclear self. In other words, it is not so much what the parents *do* that will influence the character of the child's self, but what the parents *are*. If the parents are at peace with their own needs to shine and to succeed insofar as these needs can be realistically gratified, if, in other words, the parents' self-confidence is secure, then the proud exhibitionism of the budding self of their child will be responded to acceptingly. However grave the real-life blows to the child's grandiosity, the proud smile of the parents will keep alive a bit of the original omnipotence, which will form the nucleus of self-confidence and inner security that sustains the healthy person throughout life. And the same holds true with regard to our ideals. Despite our disappointment when we discover the weaknesses and limitations of the idealized selfobjects of our early life, their strong, confident, secure caretaking and the merging of our anxious selves with their tranquility—via their calm voices or via our closeness with their relaxed bodies as they hold us—will be retained by us as the nucleus of the strength and calmness we experience as adults under the guidance of our inner goals.

It is only in the light of our appreciation of the crucial influence exerted on the development of the self by the personality of the selfobjects of childhood that we are able to trace the genetic roots of the disorders of the self. Psychoanalytic case histories have tended to emphasize certain dramatic incidents, certain grossly traumatic events—from the child's witnessing the "primal scene" to the loss of a parent in childhood. But we have come to believe that such traumatic events may be no more than clues that point to the truly pathogenic factors, such as the unwholesome atmosphere to which the child was exposed during the formative years of the self. In other words, individual traumatic events cause less serious disturbances than the chronic ambience created by the deep-rooted attitudes of the selfobjects. Even the still vulnerable, developing self can cope with a serious trauma if it is embedded in a healthy, supportive milieu.

The essence of the healthy matrix for the growing self of the child is a mature, cohesive parental self that is in tune with the changing needs of the child. It can mirror the child's grandiose display with a glow of shared joy one minute, yet, perhaps a minute later, if the child becomes anxious and overstimulated by its own exhibitionism, the parental self will curb the display by adopting a realistic attitude vis-à-vis the child's limitations. Such optimal frustrations of the child's need to be mirrored and to merge into an idealized selfobject, hand in hand with optimal gratifications, generate the appropriate growth-facilitating matrix for the self.

Some parents, however, are not adequately sensitive to the needs of the child but instead respond to the needs of their own insecurely established self. Here are two characteristic illustrations of pathogenic selfobject failures. They concern typical events that emerge frequently during the analysis of patients with narcissistic personality disorders during the transference repetitions of those childhood experiences that interfered with the normal development of the self. We must add here that the following events are indicative of a pathogenic childhood environment only if they represent the selfobjects' *chronic* attitude. Put differently, they would not emerge at crucial points of a selfobject transference if they had occurred as the consequence of a parent's unavoidable *occasional* failure.

First illustration: A little girl comes home from school, eager to tell her mother about some great successes. But the mother, instead of listening with pride, deflects the conversation from the child to herself and begins to talk about her own successes, which overshadow those of her little daughter.

Second illustration: A little boy is eager to idealize his father; he wants his father to tell him about his life, the battles he engaged in and won. But instead of joyfully acting in accordance with his son's need, the father is embarrassed by the request. He feels tired and bored and, leaving the house, finds a temporary source of vitality for his enfeebled self in the tavern, through drink and mutually supportive talk with friends.

Psychopathology and Symptomatology

We shall now describe some syndromes of self pathology that arise in consequence of the developmental failures described in the preceding section. It is clear that in many, if not most, patients the various forms of self disturbance which we distinguish in the following classification will not be clearly identifiable. Mixtures of the experiences characteristic of different types will often be present and, even more frequently, the same patient will experience different pathological states of the self at different times, often in close proximity to one another. The following descriptions should be clinically helpful, however, because they point out frequently occurring clusters of experience.

The *understimulated self* is a chronic or recurrent condition of the self that arises in consequence of a prolonged lack of stimulating responsiveness from the selfobjects in childhood. Such personalities are lacking in vitality. They experience themselves as boring and apathetic, and they are experienced by others in the same way. Persons whose nascent selves have been insufficiently responded to will use any available stimuli to create a pseudo excitement in order to ward off the painful feeling of deadness that tends to overtake them. Children employ the resources appropriate to their developmental phase, such as head-banging among toddlers, compulsive masturbation in later childhood, and daredevil activities in adolescence.

Adults have at their disposal an even wider armamentarium of self-stimulation—in particular, in the sexual sphere, addictive promiscuous activities and various perversions; and, in the nonsexual sphere, such activities as gambling, drug- and alcohol-induced excitement, and a lifestyle characterized by hypersociability. If the analyst is able to penetrate beneath the defensive facade presented by these activities, he will invariably find empty depression. Prototypical is the compulsive masturbation of lonely, "unmirrored" children. It is not healthy drive pressure that leads to the endlessly repeated masturbation, but the attempt to substitute pleasurable sensations in *parts* of the body (erogenous zones) when the joy provided by the exhibition of the *total* self is unavailable.

The *fragmenting self* is a chronic or recurrent condition of the self that arises in consequence of the lack of integrating responses to the nascent self in its totality from the selfobjects in childhood. Occasional fragmentation states of minor degree and short duration are ubiquitous. They occur in all of us when our self-esteem has been taxed for prolonged periods and when no replenishing sustenance has presented itself. We all may walk home after a day in which we suffered a series of self-esteem-shaking failures, feeling at sixes and sevens within ourselves. Our gait and posture will be less than graceful at such times, our movements will tend to be clumsy, and even our mental functions will show signs of uncoordination.

Patients with narcissistic personality disorders will not only be more inclined to react to even minor disappointments with such fragmentation symptoms, but their symptoms will tend to be severer. If a normally well-dressed patient arrives in our office looking disheveled—if his tie and shirt are grossly mismatched and his socks out of harmony with his shoes—we will usually not go wrong if we ask ourselves whether we were unempathic in the last session, whether we failed to recognize a narcissistic need.

Still more serious degrees of fragmentation will be encountered during the psychoanalytic treatment of the most severely disturbed patients with narcissistic personality disorders. Such a patient might respond to even minor therapeutic or real-life rebuffs with a deep loss of the sense of the self's continuity in time and cohesiveness in space—a psychic condition that produces profound anxiety. In particular, the feeling that various body parts are no longer held together by a strong, healthy awareness of the totality of the body self leads to apprehensive brooding about the fragments of the body, often expressed by patients in the form of hypochondriacal worry. Unlike the chronic hypochondriacal preoccupations encountered in some psychoses, however, even the severest, quasi-delusional analogous worries in the narcissistic personality disorders are the direct consequence of some specific, identifiable narcissistic injury, and they disappear, often with dramatic speed, as soon as a bridge of empathy with an understanding selfobject has been built. A typical sequence of events in the analysis of patients who have established a mirror transference will demonstrate this point. When the mirror transference is in balance, the patient, sensing the analyst's empathic attention, feels whole and self-accepting. Subsequent to an erroneous interpretation, however—e.g., following a session in which the analyst addressed some *detail* of the patient's psychic life when, in fact, the patient had offered his *total* self for approval—the patient's feeling of wholeness, which had been maintained via the transference, disappears. It is reestablished when the analyst restores the empathic tie to the selfobject by correctly interpreting the sequence of events that led to its disruption.

The *overstimulated self* tends toward recurrent states of overstimulation in consequence of unempathically excessive or phase-inappropriate responses from the selfobjects of childhood to the activities of the grandiose-exhibitionistic pole of the child's nascent self, the activities of the pole that harbors the guiding ideals, or both.

If the grandiose-exhibitionistic pole of a person's self was exposed to unempathic overstimulation in childhood, then that person cannot obtain a healthy glow of enjoyment from external success. Since such people are subject to flooding by unrealistic, archaic fantasies of greatness that produce painful tension and anxiety, they will try to avoid situations in which they could become the center of attention. In some such persons creativity may be unimpaired so long as no exhibition of the *body* self is involved, directly or indirectly. In most of them, however, the creative-productive potential will be diminished because their intense ambitions, which have remained tied to unmodified grandiose fantasies, will frighten them.

Furthermore, in view of the fact that the selfobjects' responses focused prematurely and unrealistically on the fantasied performance or products of the self but failed to respond appropriately to the exhibitionism of the nascent nuclear self of the child as the initiator of the performance and as the shaper of the products, throughout life the self will be experienced as separate from its own actions and weak in comparison with them. Such people will tend to shy away from creative activities because their selves are in danger of being destroyed by being siphoned into their own performance or products.

If the pole that harbors a person's ideals was overstimulated in childhood— e.g., by the unempathically intense and prolonged display of a parental selfobject in need of admiration—then it will be the persisting intense need for the merger with an external ideal that will threaten the equilibrium of the self. Since contact with the idealized selfobject is therefore experienced as a danger and must be avoided, the healthy capacity for enthusiasm will be lost—the enthusiasm for goals and ideals which people with a firm self can experience vis-à-vis the admired great ones who are their guides and examples, or with regard to the idealized goals that they pursue.

Closely related to the overstimulated self is the *overburdened self.* But whereas the overstimulated self's ambitions and ideals have been unempathically responded to in isolation, without sufficient regard for the self *in toto,* the overburdened self has not been provided with the opportunity to merge with the calmness of an omnipotent selfobject. In other words, the overburdened self has suffered the trauma of unshared emotionality. The result of this specific empathic failure of the selfobject is the absence of the self-soothing capacity that protects normal persons from being traumatized by the spreading of their emotions, especially anxiety. A world that lacks such soothing selfobjects is an inimical, dangerous world. No wonder, then, that a self that was exposed in early life to states of overburdenedness because of the lack of soothing selfobjects will in certain circumstances experience its environment as hostile.

During states of overburdenedness in adult life—e.g., after the therapist has been unempathic, particularly by failing to give the patient the right interpretation with regard to his emotional state, or by pouring too much insight into him all at once, oblivious to the fact that the patient's capacity to absorb new understanding has been exceeded—a patient might dream that he lives in a poisoned atmosphere or that he is surrounded by swarms of dangerous hornets; and, in his waking awareness, he will tend to respond to otherwise hardly noticeable stimuli as if they were attacks on his sensibilities. He will, for example, complain of noises in the therapist's office or of unpleasant odors. These reactions of patients with narcissistic personality disorders, especially when they involve an overall attitude of irritability and suspiciousness, may at times strike us as alarmingly close to those we encounter in the psychoses, particularly in paranoia. Unlike the more or less systematized, chronic suspiciousness and counterhostility of the paranoiac, however, these manifestations of the overburdened state of the self—like the analogous hypochondriacal preoccupations in states of self-fragmentation—always appear as the direct consequence of a specific narcissistic injury, i.e., the unempathic, overburdening response of a selfobject. They disappear speedily when an empathic bond with the selfobject has been reestablished, i.e., when a correct therapeutic interpretation has been made.

Characterology

The suffering associated with diseases of the self impels the sufferer to undertake psychological moves that will ameliorate his condition. The resulting behavioral manifestations, however, are not the direct expression of the still persisting, normal self-assertive needs of childhood. Because of the intensity of these needs and the patient's conviction that they will not be responded to, they arouse deep shame which, in turn, leads to their suppression. Sometimes, particularly in the narcissistic behavior disorders, suppression alternates with bursts of ragefully expressed but ineffectively pursued demands that the wrong that has been done be set right. But it is not only the fact that total suppression of narcissistic needs alternates with stridently expressed demands for their immediate fulfillment that differentiates the behavior of the adult with self pathology from the healthily assertive behavior of the normal child. The demands themselves—whether they take the form of fantasies (in the narcissistic personality disorders) or are openly expressed through words and behavior (in the narcissistic behavior disorders), and whether they involve grandiose-exhibitionistic display or acceptance by idealized figures—are not a manifestation of the normal narcissism of childhood. Having been deprived of the appropriate responses from their selfobjects in childhood, such persons either chase after fragments of the never experienced normal narcissistic fulfillment or disavow their needs by the imperious assertion of invulnerability and omnipotence.

The delineation of various character types in the narcissistic realm, especially when combined with the study of the specific failures of the selfobjects of childhood that are the decisive genetic factors in character formation, will serve as a guide for the therapist's activities vis-à-vis patients' self pathology. Some of the narcissistic character types that we will delineate overlap to some extent with some of the syndromes of self pathology presented in the preceding section. In contrast to the earlier descriptions, however, our emphasis here will be not primarily on chronic or recurring states of the self but on the behavior and experiences of those who suffer from various specific self disorders. The same qualifications that we gave concerning mixed and shifting cases of self pathology also apply to the following attempt to delimit some specific personality types in the narcissistic realm.

Mirror-hungry personalities thirst for selfobjects whose confirming and admiring responses will nourish their famished self. They are impelled to display themselves and to evoke the attention of others in order to counteract, however fleetingly, their inner sense of worthlessness and lack of self-esteem. Some of them are able to establish relationships with reliably mirroring others that will sustain them for long periods. But most of them will not be nourished for long, even by genuinely accepting responses. Thus, despite their discomfort about their need to display themselves and despite their sometimes severe stage fright, they must go on trying to find new selfobjects whose attention and recognition they seek to induce.

Ideal-hungry personalities are forever in search of others whom they can admire for their prestige, power, beauty, intelligence, or moral stature. They can experience themselves as worthwhile only so long as they can relate to idealized selfobjects. Again, in some instances, such relationships last a long time and are genuinely sustaining to both people involved. In most cases, however, the inner void cannot forever be filled by these means. Ideal-hungry persons feel the persistence of the structural defect and, as a consequence of this awareness, begin to look for—and, of course, inevitably find—some realistic defects in their god. They then continue the search for new idealizable selfobjects, always with the hope that the next great figure they attach themselves to will not disappoint them.

Alter-ego-hungry personalities need a relationship with a selfobject that confirms the existence and the reality of the self by conforming to the self's appearance, opinions, and values. At times, alter-ego-hungry personalities, too, may be able to form lasting friendships—relationships in which each of the partners experiences the feelings of the other as if they had been experienced by one's self.

> If thou sorrow, he will weep;
> If thou wake, he cannot sleep.
> Thus of every grief in heart
> He with thee doth bear a part.

Shakespeare, *The Passionate Pilgrim*

But again, in most instances, the inner void cannot be permanently filled by the twinship. The alter-ego-hungry person discovers that the other is a separate self and, as a consequence of this discovery, begins to feel estranged from the other. It is thus characteristic for most of these relationships to be short-lived.

Like the mirror- and ideal-hungry personalities, the alter-ego-hungry personality is prone to look restlessly for one replacement after another.

The above-mentioned three narcissistic character types are frequently encountered in everyday life and, in general, should be considered variants of the normal human personality, with its assets and defects, rather than forms of psychopathology. Stated in more experience-distant terms, it is not primarily the *intensity* of their need that brings about the attitude and behavior typical of these types, but rather, the *specific direction* in which they are propelled in their attempt to remedy a circumscribed weakness in the self. It is the location—not the extent—of the self defect that produces the characteristic stance of these individuals. By contrast, the following two types are characterized less by the location of the defect and more by its extent. In general, they must be considered as lying within the spectrum of pathological narcissism.

Merger-hungry personalities impress us by their need to control their selfobjects in an effort to obtain self structure. Here, in contrast to the types sketched above, the need for merger dominates the picture; the specific type of merger, however—i.e., merger with a mirroring selfobject, an idealized selfobject, or an alter ego—is less important in determining the person's behavior. Because the self of such persons is seriously defective or enfeebled, they need selfobjects in lieu of self structure. Their manifest personality features and behavior are thus dominated by the fact that the fluidity of the boundaries between them and others interferes with their ability to discriminate their own thoughts, wishes, and intentions from those of the selfobject. Because they experience the other as their own self, they feel intolerant of his or her independence: they are very sensitive to separations from the selfobject and they demand—indeed they expect without question—the selfobject's continuous presence.

Contact-shunning personalities are the reverse of the merger-hungry types. Although for obvious reasons they attract the least notice, they may well be the most common of the narcissistic character types. These persons avoid social contact and become isolated, not because they are uninterested in others, but, on the contrary, just because their need for them is so intense. The intensity of their need not only leads to great sensitivity to rejection—a sensitivity of which they are painfully aware—but also, on deeper and unconscious levels, to the apprehension that the remnants of their nuclear self will be swallowed up and destroyed by the yearned-for, all-encompassing union.

The Treatment of the Narcissistic Behavior and Personality Disorders

The essential therapeutic goal of depth psychology is the extensive amelioration or cure of the central disturbance, not the suppression of symptoms by persuasion or education, however benevolently brought to bear. Since the central pathology in the narcissistic behavior and personality disorders is the

defective or weakened condition of the self, the goal of therapy is the rehabilitation of this structure. True, to external inspection, the clusters of symptoms
and personality features that characterize the narcissistic behavior disorders,
on the one hand, and the narcissistic personality disorders, on the other hand,
are completely different: the self-assertive claims of the first group appear to
be too strong, and those of the second group not strong enough. But depth-
psychological investigation demonstrates that the psychopathological basis of
both disorders—the disease of the self—is in essence the same.

With regard to those patients with narcissistic behavior disorders who make
overloud narcissistic claims and whose behavior appears to be too self-assertive,
the therapist might be tempted to persuade them to relinquish their demands
and to accept the limitations imposed by the realities of adult life. But doing
this is like trying to persuade patients who suffer from a structural neurosis to
give up their phobia, hysterical paralysis, or compulsive ritual. The overtly
expressed, excessive narcissistic demands and self-assertiveness of these
patients are not the manifestations of an archaic narcissism that was never
tamed, but are instead a set of characterologically embedded symptoms.

Indeed, it is the essence of the disease of these patients that access to their
childhood narcissism is barred. The unfulfilled narcissistic needs of their childhood, which they must learn to get in touch with, to accept, and to express, lie
buried deep beneath their clamorous assertiveness, guarded by a wall of shame
and vulnerability. If, on the basis of a therapeutic maturity- or reality-morality,
the therapist concentrates on censuring the patient's manifest narcissism, the
patient's repressed narcissistic needs will be driven more deeply into repression—or the depth of the split in the personality that separates the sector of
the psyche that contains the unresponded-to autonomous self from the noisily
assertive one that lacks autonomy will increase—and the unfolding of the narcissistic transference will be blocked.

These considerations apply whether the patient's overt narcissistic demands
are expressed via quietly persistent pressure, attacks of scathing narcissistic
rage, or emotional means that lie between these two extremes. We all know
people who annoy us by asking us again and again to repeat our favorable
comments about some successful performance of theirs. And we all also know
others who, throughout their lives, go from one selfishly demanding rage attack
to another, seemingly oblivious to the rights and feelings of those toward whom
their demands are directed. If the analyst responds to these demands by exhor-
tations concerning realism and emotional maturity or, worse still, blamefully
interprets them as the expression of an insatiable oral drive that needs to be
tamed or of an evil primary destructiveness that needs to be neutralized and
bound by aggression-curbing psychic structures, then, as we said, the development of the narcissistic transference will be blocked.

But if the analyst can show to the patient who demands praise that, despite the availability of average external responses, he must continue to "fish for compliments" because the hopeless need of the unmirrored child in him remains unassuaged; and if the analyst can show to the raging patient the helplessness and hopelessness that lie behind his rages, can show him that his rage is indeed the direct consequence of his inability to assert his demands effectively, then the old needs will slowly begin to make their appearance more openly as the patient becomes more empathic with himself. And when the repressions are thus ultimately relinquished—or when the split maintained via disavowal is bridged—and the narcissistic demands of childhood begin to make their first shy appearance, the danger is not that they will run to extremes, but that they will again go into hiding at the first rebuff or unempathic response. In other words, experience teaches us that the therapist's major effort must be concentrated on the task of keeping the old needs mobilized. If the therapist succeeds in this, then they will gradually—and spontaneously—be transformed into normal self-assertiveness and normal devotion to ideals.

The foregoing conclusions also hold with regard to those with self pathology or narcissistic personality disturbances who are overtly shy, unassertive, and socially isolated, but whose conscious and preconscious fantasies—"the secret life of Walter Mitty"—are grandiose. If the therapist believes that the patient's timidity, shyness, and social isolation are due to the persistence of archaic illusions, specifically, to the persistence of untamed childhood grandiosity as manifested in grandiose fantasies, then he will feel justified in applying educational and moral pressure to persuade the patient to relinquish these fantasies. But neither the patient's fantasies nor his social isolation are the cause of his illness. On the contrary, together they constitute a psychological unit which, as a protective device, attempts to maintain the patient's precariously established self by preventing its dangerous exposure to rebuff and ridicule. If the therapist is educational rather than analytic, merely trying to persuade the patient to give up his fantasied grandiosity, then the distance between the patient's defective self, on the one hand, and the therapist as the hoped-for empathic responder to the patient's narcissistic needs, on the other hand, will increase, and the spontaneous movement toward the first significant breach in the wall of sensitivity and suspicion—the establishment of a narcissistic transference—will be halted.

If, however, the therapist can explain without censure the protective function of the grandiose fantasies and the social isolation, and thus demonstrate attunement with the patient's disintegration anxiety and shame concerning his precariously established self, then the spontaneously arising transference mobilization of the old narcissistic needs can proceed unhindered. Despite disintegration fears and shame, the patient will then be able—cautiously at first, later more openly—to reexperience the need for the selfobject's joyful acceptance of childhood grandiosity and for an omnipotent surrounding—

healthy needs that were not responded to in early life. Again, as in the case of the narcissistic behavior disorders, the remobilized needs will gradually and spontaneously be transformed into normal self-assertiveness and normal devotion to ideals.

In the foregoing we demonstrated that our therapeutic principles and correlated therapeutic strategy are based on the understanding of the central psychopathology of the analyzable disorders of the self and that they have as their aim the amelioration and cure of this central psychopathology. Since in both major types of analyzable disorders the psychopathology is the same, it follows that despite their divergent symptoms—noisy demands and intense social activity in the narcissistic behavior disorders, shame and social isolation in the narcissistic personality disorders—the process of treatment too is, in essence, the same. And, of course, the nature of the wholesome result that is achieved by the treatment is also the same: that is, the firming of the formerly enfeebled self, both in the pole that carries the patient's self-confidently held ambitions and in the pole that carries his idealized goals. We need only add that the patient's revitalized self-confidence and enthusiasm for his goals will ultimately make it possible for him to resume the pursuit of the action-poised program arched in the energic field that established itself between his nuclear ambitions and ideals—thus making it possible for him to lead a fulfilling, creative, and productive life.

REFERENCES

Kohut, H. (1971), *The Analysis of the Self*. New York: International Universities Press.
——— (1972), Thoughts on narcissism and narcissistic rage. *The Psychoanalytic Study of the Child*, 27:360–400. New York: Quadrangle.
——— (1977), *The Restoration of the Self*. New York: International Universities Press.
Wolf, E. S. (1976), Ambience and abstinence. *Annual Psychoanal.*, 4:101–115. New York: International Universities Press.

CHAPTER 3

Change in Psychoanalytic Treatment

Judd Marmor

What do we mean by change in psychoanalytic treatment? I believe we would all agree that basically one of the things which distinguishes the goal of psychoanalytic treatment from that of most other therapies is that it aims not simply at removal of symptoms but at basic characterological change. Whether these changes are subsumed under the concept of genitality, as in libido theory, or under such concepts as self-realization or the full development of the self, I believe it is clear that they are concerned with basically similar goals of improving the ego-adaptive capacity of individuals, of helping them to achieve greater emotional maturity, to love unselfishly, to have meaningful and satisfying sexual relationships, to work effectively, and to be socially responsible and productive human beings within the limits of their capacities. Although these are ideal goals, any movement in the direction of these goals is what we mean when we speak of change as a result of psychoanalytic treatment.

Traditionally and historically, change in psychoanalytic treatment has always been ascribed to one of two factors, or to a combination of the two: (a) increased cognitive awareness via the insight or the interpretations that the analyst made to the patient; and/or (b) the release of repressed affect, which

An earlier version of this chapter was presented at the Annual Meeting of the American Academy of Psychoanalysis, Atlanta, Georgia, May 1978, and appeared in the *Journal of the American Academy of Psychoanalysis,* 7:345–357, New York: Wiley, 1979.

Freud called abreaction. Freud linked abreaction to the recall of infantile traumata and the release of affect bound up with these traumata. Ideally, change
in analytic treatment has been considered most likely to occur with a combination of cognitive awareness and release of affect, or so-called "emotional
insight."

As time went on, however, the concept of the analytic process became more
complicated, not necessarily in terms of its essence, but with regard to how this
goal could be achieved. First and foremost, Freud himself gave up the idea that
abreaction or cognitive awareness, in and of itself, was sufficient to achieve
analytic change, and placed increasing emphasis on what he called the "working through" of resistances. He conceived of these resistances primarily as
resistances to remembering the repressed infantile memories whose recovery
he considered essential to analytic change. Gradually, however, a number of
other tenets became tied to the concept of analytic technique and change in
psychoanalytic treatment. For example, it was considered important to maintain a certain level of tension during the analytic hour by means of some frustration of the patient. The use of the couch, of course, was traditional. Sessions
were expected to be daily, if possible, but under no circumstances to be less
than four times a week for "proper" analytic therapy. Great emphasis was put
on the "correct" timing and content of interpretations in achieving analytic
change. The analyst ideally was expected to maintain the "neutral mirror"
model, which involved a certain degree of passivity, the maintenance of analytic incognito, and the maintenance of a value-free attitude of neutrality with
regard to moral judgments. Later analytic theoreticians placed great emphasis,
also, on the promotion of regression in the analytic technique, and on the
revival and reliving of the infantile neurosis as an essential element in achieving
psychoanalytic change in treatment. Finally, in more recent years, there has
been an increasing recognition of the importance of countertransference factors
in the analytic process, but their actual role in achieving change in psychoanalytic treatment has never been clearly delineated.

Over the years, as my own experience with analysis and analysts grew, I
found myself troubled by a basic question. If "correct" cognitive interpretation
and "correct" cognitive insight were key factors in analytic change, why was
it that patients seemed to respond favorably to analysts with disparate theoretical views? Certainly, it seemed to me, there had to be some common
denominator that underlay the different schools of analytic thought, all of
whom were helping their patients, as far as I could tell. Moreover, why did I
have the impression that colleagues who adhered strictly to the "neutral mirror" model seemed, on the whole, to do less well with their patients than those
who related more warmly, actively, and empathically? Third, I found myself
questioning, more and more, whether it was actually ever possible to be totally
neutral or value free in the analytic situation. Did not our very focus on what

we interpreted as healthy or neurotic, mature or immature, appropriately masculine or feminine, bespeak certain values which we were reflecting as products of our own particular cultural context? Fourth, I found myself asking whether the insights for which we strove and which we considered indispensable to the achievement of change in psychoanalysis were really so indispensable. Finally, I must take note of the important influence upon my thinking of the Alexander and French book (1946) on psychoanalytic therapy, with its emphasis on the principles of flexibility and its concept of the corrective emotional experience as a significant factor in analytic change.

My admiration for Alexander's thinking ultimately led to our friendship and to my participation with him and several other colleagues in a four-year research study, beginning in 1957, on the nature of the psychotherapeutic process as practiced by psychoanalysts. As many of you know, this was a study in which the transactions between several experienced psychoanalysts and their patients were observed through one-way screens and meticulously recorded by other analysts over a period of several years. A basic premise of this study was that no analyst or patient could adequately observe or describe what went on in their work together because their involvement in the process itself precluded their being able to do so with true objectivity—only an outside observer could be expected to accomplish this. Before that time it had been assumed generally that such observation would introduce an impurity that would seriously modify or alter the observed process, but we found—what we all know now—that, except for some initial self-consciousness on the part of both therapist and patient (more the therapist!), the psychotherapeutic and psychoanalytic processes went on as usual.

In brief, I think it is fair to say that probably the single most important awareness that emerged from this study was a recognition of the subtlety, multiplicity, and complexity of the interacting variables, *both verbal and nonverbal,* that enter into the psychoanalytic process. What we had previously thought of as something that an analyst did for or to a patient was actually a complex transactional process taking place *between* them, with the analyst's particular "techniques" being only one of many factors involved. Indeed, over the years, I have come to the conclusion that these variables enter into all psychotherapeutic processes, nonanalytic as well as analytic, but for the purpose of this discussion I will focus only on change in the analytic process.

Let me begin by stating the obvious (although it sometimes seems to be overlooked in the psychoanalytic literature). Psychoanalysts are not uniform, interchangeable units like safety-razor blades. Not only do patients differ—e.g., in the nature of their psychopathology, their ego strengths and ego defenses, their capacity to verbalize, their values, their motivation to change, their life situations and support systems—but so do psychoanalysts, e.g., in their capacities for warmth and empathy, their style, knowledge, appearance, sophistication, reputation. Add to these the disparate conscious and unconscious emotional needs, ambitions, and value systems of different analysts, and we begin to get some inkling of the numerous variables and transference-countertransference reactions that play a fateful part in the outcome of every psychoanalytic process. Taken all together, these constitute the complex network of elements that shape the patient-therapist relationship that is the fundamental matrix of the analytic process and critical to its success or failure in producing change. I wish to emphasize that these elements encompass not only unconscious factors but also the real attributes—physical, psychological, and situational—of both patient and therapist. Basic reality obstacles can defeat even the best analytic technique.

Although a good patient-therapist relationship is probably the single most important factor producing change in psychoanalytic treatment, there are other factors that play significant contributory roles.

We are all aware of the therapeutic value of catharsis, particularly in the opening phase of the analytic process. This term, coined by Freud, reflects his concept of it as a discharge of repressed libidinal tension. To appreciate its meaning within an ego-psychological framework, however, we must recall that it takes place in the context of the troubled patient's faith, hope, and expectancy of receiving help from the analyst whose social role carries the promise that such help can be forthcoming. I believe that what holds true for catharsis also holds true for the phenomenon of abreaction. We all know by now, as Freud was the first to discover, that abreaction in and of itself is not necessarily therapeutic. Yet the belief in its value continues to persist in countless forms of contemporary therapies. The reason for this, I believe, is not in its function as a discharge phenomenon, but rather that an atmosphere of heightened suggestion and expectation that improvement will occur can indeed produce feelings of well-being.

One of the primary distinguishing features of the analytic process is its effort to uncover and identify the unconscious psychodynamic factors, both past and present, that lie behind the patient's adaptive difficulties. Although many other forms of psychotherapy may occasionally employ aspects of this approach, the emphasis on it is uniquely psychoanalytic, as are the techniques of transference- and dream-interpretation as major ways of achieving it. Such understanding, which we term "insight," has generally been considered essential to achieving change in psychoanalysis. Over the years I have come to question this assumption for the simple reason that again and again I have encountered patients who have clearly benefited, both subjectively and objectively, from their analytic treatment without any clear cognitive conception of how or why this improvement has taken place.

Moreover, as I have indicated, the "insights" that patients receive from adherents of different analytic schools vary greatly, so that the specific form of the insight cannot be considered essential for change to take place. Finally, we have all seen patients who seem to have considerable cognitive awareness of the basis of their difficulties, but who fail to change behaviorally. The least we can say in such instances is that insight alone is not enough.

I would not want these brief remarks to be interpreted as meaning that I place no value on insight in the analytic process. If there were no reason other than that it represents an effort to create a rational foundation for the understanding of how and why psychopathology develops, and thus is part of scientific tradition, I would consider it indispensable. But, over and above this, I believe there is reason to believe that therapeutic results achieved with the aid of insight have a more solid underpinning and are more likely to be lasting. A number of comparative studies of behavioral versus psychodynamic therapies have demonstrated that, although results are achieved more quickly with certain behavioral approaches, they tend to last longer after insight-oriented psychotherapy.

If changes in psychoanalytic treatment do not necessarily depend on insight, what other elements are involved? I believe that there are four other important factors that contribute to change in analytic treatment: (1) operant conditioning, by means of explicit or implicit approval-disapproval cues from the analyst as well as via corrective emotional experiences in which the analyst's responses to the patient's maladaptive behavior differ from those experienced at the hands of significant figures in the patient's developmental past; (2) suggestion and persuasion, usually implicit, rarely explicit; (3) identification with the analyst; and (4) repeated reality-testing or practicing of new adaptive techniques, both in the analytic situation and in the outside world, in the context of consistent emotional support from the analyst.

The recognition that the analytic process involved a significant amount of operant conditioning was one of the important discoveries that emerged from the aforementioned research study that Alexander and his colleagues undertook in the late 1950s. One of our major observations was the striking degree to which the analyst's values and therapeutic goals were conveyed nonverbally, even when care was being taken not to express them verbally. Facial reactions, a look of approval or disapproval, a slight lift of the eyebrows, a barely perceptible nod of the head or shrug of the shoulders, became important channels of communication to the patient. Even behind the couch, the subtle nuance of an mm-hmm, the pattern of the silences, the analyst's shifting movements, or the tonal quality of comments served as cues to the patient whose antennae were highly sensitive to the slightest indication of interest or lack of interest, approval or disapproval. Other studies around the same time (Krasner, 1958; Mandler and Kaplan, 1956) were able to demonstrate experimentally that such minimal signals not only acted as a subtle operant conditioning system—reinforcing approved thought and behavior, and discouraging that which was disapproved of—but also clearly influenced the content of the patient's communication.

Although nondirective analytic treatment presumably eschews suggestion, the latter weaves willy-nilly like a continuous thread throughout the therapeutic process. The patient's expectation of being helped, the implication that such help will be forthcoming if there is compliance with the analytic program, and the analyst's every indication that certain patterns of behavior and thought are healthier or more mature than others involve implicit, if not explicit, elements of suggestion and persuasion. The greater the degree of positive transference, the greater the faith, hope, and expectancy, and the more responsive the patient is apt to be to these cues.

Another unexpected finding from our extensive observations of analytic treatment was the surprising degree to which patients unconsciously tended to adopt certain of the analyst's patterns of thought and behavior after a while. This process occurs without the analyst's consciously intending it or fostering it and is often described as a form of identification. Strachey (1934) attributes it to what he calls "dosed introjects of the analyst's superego" (p. 159). Miller and Dollard (1941) would probably consider it just another form of social learning.

Finally, the process of repetitive reality testing is one of the critical factors in achieving change in analytic treatment. Although Freud originally applied the concept of "working through" to the laborious and repetitive process of overcoming the patient's resistances to the uncovering process in analysis, more and more ego-oriented analysts have been applying the term to the equally laborious and important task of overcoming the patient's resistances to change, in terms of the achievement of new patterns of thought and behavior. Neither insights nor confrontations nor transference interpretations, in and of themselves, necessarily produce fundamental change, although occasionally we may be gratified to see change occur on that basis alone. More often than not, however, particularly in the treatment of difficult character disturbances and of severe phobic reactions, we find it necessary, sooner or later—as Freud himself (1919) was the first to note—gently and persistently to begin to encourage the patient to come to grips directly with the anxiety-provoking situation, and by a series of graduated successes eventually to achieve the desired sense of mastery. For most patients this does not come easily; there is much resistance to giving up their long-established defensive patterns. Analytic work usually takes years not because the uncovering process takes that long but because the process of enabling the patient to generalize the insights achieved in the transference situation and to apply them to the wider arenas of his life does not usually come easily and requires patient, repetitive interpretation of perceptual distortions and defensive rationalizations under an umbrella of benign and consistent emotional support.

To summarize what I have said thus far, I believe that the elements that produce change in analytic treatment can be subsumed under the following main categories:

(1) A basic matrix of a good patient-therapist relationship resting on both real and fantasied qualities that each brings to their work together—e.g., the therapist's real abilities, values, genuineness of interest, empathy, and respect for the patient; and the patient's belief system, expectancies, motivation to change, and capacity to relate. This matrix includes both conscious and unconscious elements, and encompasses such concepts as "rapport" and "therapeutic alliance," in addition to the transference-countertransference aspects of the patient-therapist relationship.

(2) Release of emotional tension. This encompasses the concepts of both catharsis and abreaction associated with being able to remember and discuss with a helping person painful memories and feelings within the context of heightened expectations and hopes that help will be forthcoming.

(3) Cognitive learning, or the acquisition of insight into the nature and sources of the presenting problem. This insight may be presented in the context of a number of different theoretical frameworks—Freudian, neo-Freudian, Jungian, etc.—and still be effective as long as the other therapeutic elements are operative also. That is, the specific content of the insight is in itself not essential to the change process as long as it presents a plausible and internally logical explanation for the patient's difficulties.

(4) Operant conditioning, by means of subtle and often nonverbal cues of approval or disapproval, as well as by corrective emotional experiences in the relationship with the analyst.

(5) Suggestion and persuasion, usually implicit, occasionally explicit.

(6) Unconscious identification with the analyst, both conceptually and behaviorally.

(7) Repeated reality testing and "working through" in the context of the analyst's sustained and consistent emotional support.

Although I first presented these ideas in 1962 and 1964, various other similar models have since appeared in the literature. To mention only a few, Hans Strupp (1976, p. 97) describes three basic "conditions" for therapeutic change: (1) a basic helping relationship "created and maintained" by the therapist, and characterized by "respect, interest, understanding, tact, maturity, and a firm belief in his or her ability to help"; (2) condition one provides what Strupp calls "a power base" from which the therapist can influence the patient through (a) suggestion and persuasion, (b) encouragement of communication and honest self-scrutiny, (c) interpretations of unconscious material, (d) providing a model of maturity, and (e) manipulation of rewards; and (3) the third condition is that the patient have both the "capacity and willingness to profit from the experience."

Jerome Frank (1976, pp. 83–85) believes all therapies, including analysis, share six therapeutic functions:

(1) Strengthening the therapeutic relationship.

(2) Inspiring the patient's hope for help.

(3) Providing opportunities for both cognitive and experiential learning.

(4) Stimulating emotional arousal as a motive power for change in attitudes and behavior.

(5) Enhancing the patient's sense of mastery and competence by providing or stimulating success experiences.

(6) Encouraging "working through" and the application of what has been learned in therapy to daily living.

Finally, Jules Masserman (1980, pp. 86–89), with his usual felicitous turn of phrase, has recently described the basic ingredients of therapeutic change in what he calls the "Seven Pil-R's of Biodynamic Therapy":

(1) Reputation of the therapist
(2) Rapport
(3) Review of the history—assets as well as liabilities
(4) Reconsideration and reorientation
(5) Reeducation and rehabilitation (recycling)
(6) Resocialization
(7) Relief of symptoms

Before bringing this discussion to a close, there are a few other issues that I would like to touch on briefly as important ingredients in producing change in analytic treatment.

The first of these is warmth. Numerous studies have experimentally confirmed the fact that therapists who convey a quality of empathic warmth to their patients consistently tend to achieve better therapeutic results. This finding has an important bearing on the therapeutic usefulness of the impersonal "neutral mirror" model in classical analytic technique. This recommendation of Freud's had great merit in the context in which it was originally made— namely, at a time when he was exploring the still totally uncharted area of the "unconscious" and therefore wanted to exclude, as much as was humanly possible, any external "impurities" from the pristine free associations of his patients. What is good for research, however, is not necessarily good for treatment, and from all that we have now come to learn about the nature of the therapeutic process, it seems safe to say that a strictly impersonal and "neutral" approach to our analytic patients is not conducive to the best therapeutic results. It goes without saying that this does not mean that an analyst should react to patients with unprofessional effusiveness or seductiveness. It does mean, however, that the ability to transmit to our patients feelings of empathic warmth and genuineness of interest within the context of professional objectivity *is* an important ingredient of the therapeutic matrix. Incidentally, it is worth noting that, from all we know about the way Freud actually practiced, he *did* convey these qualities, despite his written emphasis on the mirror model.

The second issue is the importance of the therapist's being an active rather than a passive participant in the analytic process; by this I mean being a participant observer (as Sullivan [1953] put it) rather than a passive one. Obviously, this does *not* mean acting out in the analysis, indulging in wild analytic interpretations, or being directive and telling the patient what to do. It *does* mean actively confronting defenses and resistances, responding empathically to patient distress without forsaking objectivity, and never losing sight of the fact that the goal of analysis is not the interminable exploration of primary-process material as an end in itself, but the utilization of all insights toward the focused goal of enabling patients to cope more adaptively with their problems of living. This is a point that Leon Salzman (1976) has also emphasized. The understanding received from transference and dream interpretations *must* be translated wherever possible into more generalized applications to other situations and other interpersonal relationships; otherwise, there is a danger that they will remain sterile and useless. This kind of activity on the part of the therapist serves a number of constructive therapeutic purposes: (1) it is an indication to the patient of the analyst's concern and interest both in the patient and in the therapeutic objective; (2) it maintains a high level of therapeutic tension more effectively and constructively than does the old rule of frustration; (3) it helps to maintain a therapeutic focus and does not allow the patient or the analytic process to lapse into long and sterile periods of silence, passivity, or fruitless digression. Thus it tends to promote therapeutic change more rapidly, on the whole, than does a classically passive technique.

Finally, over the years I have come to appreciate the great importance of setting a termination point to the analytic process. The first analyst to set a termination date in analytic treatment was Freud (1918) himself in his treatment of the Wolf Man in 1912. Subsequently, Ferenczi and Rank did considerable experimenting with it and, indeed, Rank made it one of the cornerstones of his therapeutic method. In the late 1940s Franz Alexander called attention to it again as an important technical device, and more recently, a number of psychoanalysts, notably Sifneos (1972), Mann (1973), and Malan (1976), have made it the central feature of their short-term psychoanalytic therapeutic techniques.

In recent years, particularly since the germinal research work of Mahler (1968) and Bowlby (1969, 1973), the central importance of the separation-individuation issue has come sharply to the fore, not only in human personality development but also in the analytic process itself. As a result we have become more aware of the dependency elements that are potentially involved in the analytic process itself, and the entire issue of analysis, terminable and interminable, takes on a new dimension. Alexander was one of the first to point out that the very process of daily visits in analysis can foster an unhealthy dependency in some patients, and Rado (1956) indicated that the fostering of regression in classical analytic technique can have a similar result.

What I am indicating circuitously is that occasionally we analysts are somewhat remiss in prolonging the treatment of our patients more than is absolutely necessary. If we are totally honest with ourselves, it may be that occasionally the conflict of interest that is inherent in the fact that we have a stake in keeping our schedules filled plays a role in this state of things. But putting this aside, I merely want to call to your attention the psychodynamic value of the analyst's setting a termination date at some suitable point in the analytic process rather than waiting, as is traditionally done, "for both patient and analyst to somehow arrive at such a conclusion mutually." When the analyst sets the termination date, it inevitably brings the issue of separation and individuation to the fore in a way that can no longer be conveniently avoided or ignored. The analytic work becomes more sharply focused on that issue and on the dissolution of the transference. The setting of the date conveys another important message. It implicitly says to the patient: "I, the analyst, now have sufficient confidence in your strength and capacity to function autonomously that I can cut you loose." Although the initial reaction of patients is one of separation anxiety and even feelings of rejection, once these feelings have been worked through, patients usually take a giant step forward in self-confidence and autonomy. Thus, letting the patient go is the final and quintessential therapeutic maneuver in the production of change in analytic treatment!

REFERENCES

Alexander, F., & French, T. M. (1946), *Psychoanalytic Therapy*. New York: Ronald.
Bowlby, J. (1969), *Attachment and Loss, Vol. I: Attachment*. New York: Basic Books.
——— (1973), *Attachment and Loss, Vol. II: Separation*. New York: Basic Books.
Frank, J. (1976), Restoration of morale and behavior change. In: *What Makes Behavior Change Possible?*, ed. A. Burton. New York: Brunner/Mazel, pp. 73–95.
Freud, S. (1918), From the history of an infantile neurosis. *Standard Edition*, 17:7–122. London: Hogarth Press, 1955.
——— (1919), Lines of advance in psycho-analytic therapy. *Standard Edition*, 17:157–168. London: Hogarth Press, 1955.
Krasner, L. (1958), Studies of the conditioning of verbal behavior. *Psychol. Bull.*, 55:148–170.

Mahler, M. (1968), *On Human Symbiosis and the Vicissitudes of Individuation.* New York: International Universities Press.

Malan, D. H. (1976), *The Frontier of Brief Psychotherapy.* New York: Plenum.

Mandler, G., & Kaplan, W. K. (1956), Subjective evaluation and reinforcement of a verbal stimulus. *Science,* 124:582–583.

Mann, J. (1973), *Time-Limited Psychotherapy.* Cambridge, Mass.: Harvard University Press.

Marmor, J. (1962), Psychoanalytic therapy as an educational process. In: *Science and Psychoanalysis,* Vol. V, ed. J. Masserman. New York: Grune & Stratton, pp. 286–299.

—— (1964), Psychoanalytic therapy and theories of learning. In: *Science and Psychoanalysis,* Vol. VII, ed. J. Masserman. New York: Grune & Stratton, pp. 265–279.

Masserman, J. (1980), *Principles and Practice of Biodynamic Psychiatry.* New York: Thieme-Stratton.

Miller, N. E., & Dollard, J. C. (1941), *Social Learning and Imitation.* New Haven: Yale University Press.

Rado, S. (1956), Recent advances in psychoanalytic therapy. In: *Psychoanalysis of Behavior.* New York: Grune & Stratton.

Salzman, L. (1976), The will to change. In: *What Makes Behavior Change Possible?,* ed. A. Burton. New York: Brunner/Mazel, pp. 13–33.

Sifneos, P. E. (1972), *Short-Term Psychotherapy and Emotional Crisis.* Cambridge, Mass.: Harvard University Press.

Strachey, J. (1934), The nature of the therapeutic action of psychoanalysis. *Int. J. Psycho-Anal.,* 15:127–159.

Strupp, H. (1976), The nature of the therapeutic influence and its basic ingredients. In: *What Makes Behavior Change Possible?,* ed. A. Burton. New York: Brunner/Mazel, pp. 96–112.

Sullivan, H. S. (1953), *Interpersonal Theory of Psychiatry.* New York: Norton.

CHAPTER 4

Insight and Self-Observation

Robert L. Hatcher

The Development of the Concept of Insight in Psychoanalysis

Insight in Freud's Early Analytic Technique

In 1893 Breuer and Freud published a remarkable new theory of hysteria. Its central thesis was that "hysterics suffer mainly from reminiscences"—split-off or suppressed memories loaded with unspent affect were denied the usual release through associational pathways in consciousness enjoyed by normal affect experiences. Consequently, they pressed for discharge, leading to the formation of hysterical symptoms, which were symbols of the suppressed memories. The cure for the symptom was relatively simple. It consisted in restoring the memory, its accompanying affect, and the details of the surrounding circumstances to consciousness, where affect was able to dissipate through the various available nervous connections and to achieve catharsis by motor discharge in speech.

During this early period, Freud's concepts of neurosis and its cure were

An earlier version of this chapter appeared in *Journal of the American Psychoanalytic Association,* 21:377–398, 1973, New York: International Universities Press.

My appreciation is due to Joseph B. Adelson and George A. Richardson for their critical readings of earlier drafts of this paper.

essentially mechanistic. The patient's role was passive: to obstruct the physician's view of the unconscious as little as possible. While the theory of cure placed great emphasis on consciousness, it did not require *active* consciousness from the patient. Rather, the hidden memories were *made* conscious by the physician, who thereby effected a cure through the establishment of links between repressed affects and their normal discharge channels. One can compare the physician's role (as Freud often did) to the surgeon who would cut through the superficial tissue to excise a neoplasm. At first, the patient's passivity was sought through light hypnosis, a kind of mental local anesthetic.

Even when the patient's active though unconscious resistance tó this cure forced Freud to replace light hypnosis with his forehead-pressure technique, and later with free association, his motives were to circumvent the patient's activity and to get the unconscious into consciousness. Any route which led to the conscious discovery of the repressed would do. The patient could remember directly, or the analyst could piece together the traumatic incident for him. But information from relatives or acquaintances would serve just as well (cf. the case of the "happily married young women," in Breuer and Freud, 1895, pp. 274–275).

Freud's contact with resistance gradually forced him to pay increased attention to the patient's role in bringing the unconscious to consciousness. With the advent of free association, Freud asked his patients to suspend their critical faculties by themselves (Freud, 1900, pp. 101–102). Physicians no longer exercised their will directly against the resistance; rather patients would try to follow the "basic rule" themselves. Patients were confronted with the fact that it was their *own* task to contact their unconscious, and their own resistance that blocked their way. At same time, Freud's theory of cure became more psychological. The earlier theory of an automatic cure following the release of pent-up energies through restoration of the memory to consciousness fell away, and increased stress was placed on the control exercised by the preconscious system *(Pcs.)* over the unconscious system *(Ucs.)* (Freud, 1900, pp. 577–578). The work of analysis changed from a quick abreaction to a gradual—Freud called it "laborious"—mastery of the *Ucs.* by the *Pcs.*

Emotional Insight and the Importance of Experiencing

From this developing vantage point, Freud recognized his technique of twenty years before as "intellectualist" (Freud, 1913). He had discovered that patients must experience their resistances directly, and be convinced of the latter's power, before they can give them up. As patients yield their resistances, they are able to experience the emerging repressed contents directly. Without going through this process, the therapy becomes an "intellectualist" process, and the phenomenon Freud described as "knowing but not knowing" occurs. An intellectual knowledge of the repressed contents sits above and separate from the actual working of the unconscious conflict. The patient does not grapple directly with the *Ucs.*, and so the *Pcs.* gains no dominance over it. Freud found that direct experience with the resistance, leading to discovery of the repressed contents, is attained primarily through the transference neurosis. Patients are exposed to a "real but conditional" experience of their neurosis in the transference (1914); here their intellectual comprehension struggles with the repressed contents directly. This patient participation represents a considerable change from the dreamy hypnotized hysteric of the *Studies on Hysteria*.

It was not until 1934, after the advent of the structural theory, that the development of these ideas appeared again in the literature. The importance of vivid contact with the *Ucs.* is a significant theme of Strachey's landmark paper of that year, "The Nature of the Therapeutic Action of Psychoanalysis," in which he presents his concept of the "mutative interpretation." Interpretations are mutative only if they deal with active, living impulses. "Every mutative interpretation must be emotionally 'immediate'; the patient must experience it as something actual" (p. 150). Hence, to be maximally effective, the interpretation must be delivered when the impulse is active in the transference. In contrast, "the purely informative, 'dictionary' type of interpretation will be non-mutative, however useful it may be as a prelude to mutative interpretations" (p. 150).

Through the years, analysts have returned to this theme again and again. The danger of "dictionary" analysis threatens the analyst whose own intellectualizing tendencies lead him to collude with his patient's wish to avoid the full range of mental experience. Beyond this problem, however, is the inherent verbal, intellectual nature of interpretation itself. As Bibring put in in 1954,

The fact that interpretations are explanatory concepts carries with it the danger of intellectualization, . . . a form of resistance in that the patient "accepts" interpretations on the basis of their plausibility, their ability to make sense (i.e., to explain certain clinical data), but without "feeling" that this is so; or when the patient adopts the analytic language and readily produces all kinds of interpretations with great ease but without any emotion, etc. [p. 758].

Richfield (1954) reviewed this problem on a more logical, philosophical level. Citing Betrand Russell, he points out that "There are two fundamentally different ways in which we can know things . . . knowledge by *acquaintance* and knowledge by *description*" (p. 400). Knowledge by acquaintance involves a direct, experiential contact with the known subject. Knowledge by description, on the other hand, is "knowledge *about* that subject, and may be independent of any acquaintance with that same subject" (p. 400). Because therapy depends on the ego's recognition and mastery of alien contents, it must meet these contents on a direct, dynamic level, which requires knowledge by acquaintance. In the idea of descriptive insight we quickly recognize Freud's early (1913) concept of "knowing but not knowing."

With many others (Strachey, 1934; Bibring, 1954; Greenson, 1967), Richfield stresses the importance of descriptive awareness (also called intellectual or "dictionary" interpretation, or clarification) in leading the patient to a more direct acquaintance with a conflict. The task of analysis is then to fill out the first descriptive awareness of these unconscious conflicts with direct, emotional experience.

There is, however, a complementary problem in analysis. Strongly *emotional* contact with a conflict may obscure the intellectual understanding of its meaning. Valenstein (1962) describes this as the defense of "affectualization," which complements "intellectualization" and is prevalent in hysterics. We can see then that *emotional insight demands a balanced integration of emotional contact and intellectual comprehension into a full-bodied experience of the meaningfulness of an unconscious conflict.*

The Therapeutic "Split"

Patients experience their feelings about the analyst as real. Freud was painfully confronted with this fact in his abortive analysis of Dora (1905). The discovery of transference—the fact that the patient's feelings for the analyst are repetitions of old object ties from the past—helped solve this problem. Feelings for the analyst are real, but not *really* real. As Freud (1914) put it, transference "is a piece of real experience, but . . . it is of a provisional nature" (p. 154). But the recognition of this fact places a special demand on the patient. "The physician cannot as a rule spare his patient this phase of treatment. He must get him to re-experience some portion of his forgotten life, but must see to it, on the other hand, that the patient retains some degree of aloofness, which will enable him, in spite of everything, to recognize that what appears to be reality is in fact only a reflection of a forgotten past" (Freud, 1920, p. 19).

This problem was discussed by Strachey and Sterba in papers published side by side in 1934. Sterba proposed the term "dissociation of the ego" for the phenomenon Freud described. Strachey dealt in detail with the shifts in the ego which accompany the first phase of a mutative interpretation, in which repression is lifted and the ego gradually allows transference to develop. The second phase begins when the transference has developed into a vivid experience of feeling for the analyst and an interpretation is offered to the patient. Strachey points out that "the successful outcome of this phase depends upon his [the patient's] ability, at the critical moment of the emergence into consciousness of the released quantity of id energy, to distinguish between his fantasy object and the real analyst" (p. 146). The patient's reality testing is bolstered by the analyst's own sense of reality, which Strachey thinks is introjected into the patient's superego. This "auxiliary superego" gives advice to the ego which is "consistently based on *real* and *contemporary* considerations" (p. 140).

Sterba describes the dissociation in the ego that is required at the moment of interpretation.

> The subject's consciousness shifts from the center of affective experience to that of intellectual contemplation. The transference situation is *interpreted,* i.e., an explanation is given which is uncolored by affect and which shows that the situation has its roots in the subject's childhood. Through this interpretation there emerges in the mind of the patient, out of the chaos of behavior impelled by instinct and behavior designed to inhibit instinct, *a new point of view of intellectual contemplation* [p. 121].

This dissociation is followed by a process of synthesis or assimilation of the hitherto unconscious contents into the working life of the ego. Much of this assimilation occurs preconsciously over an extended period of time. Like Strachey, Sterba points to the superego as the prototype of the dissociated, observing ego, tracing the analyst's contribution to this function to the patient's superego identification with the analyst's more adult and realistic point of view.

The ego's ability to shift flexibly from the unreflective immediacy of transference and free association to a reflective contemplation of these experiences is a basic requirement for psychoanalytic therapy, and its importance has been recognized by virtually every writer on the subject (e.g., Stone, 1961; Loewenstein, 1963; Greenson, 1967; Stern, 1970).

Insight as a Process

In the early days of analysis, gaining insight was a reasonably simple matter. Pressure on the forehead or associations to a dream brought up the unconscious for the analyst's interpretation. But we can see that as Freud grew to appreciate the power and value, first of resistance and then of transference, and complemented these with the notion of working through, the acquisition of insight was recognized as a much more complex process. Sterba and Strachey offered the first systematic views of this process, gained from the organizing perspective of the ego-psychological, structural viewpoint. Reviewing their presentations, we see that during the analytic hour patients more or less lose themselves in their transferences and associations. When the analyst interprets, the patient's observing ego is reactivated, which lets the patient consider the interpreted material from a dissociated, detached perspective. The ego then reintegrates, bringing the new material into the everyday life of the ego.

Insight is thus a complex process that depends on the integrated, sequential operation of several different ego functions, which have been described by Kris (1956). Kris suggests that, in addition to the capacity for detached, objective self-observation, insight requires the use of controlled ego regression. As Freud points out, patients must actively suspend many of their logical and moral considerations during free association (1900, pp. 101–102). This suspension permits direct experience of the fresh material that arises for observation. Insight also requires control over the discharge of affects. Affect must be accessible, it must contribute to a vivid reexperiencing in memory and the transference, but it must not overwhelm the patient or be channeled into acting out. Tolerance of unpleasant affect is a major requirement for insight and self-observation. Finally, Kris notes the importance of the integrative function of the ego in bringing insight into useful connection with the everyday functioning of the ego. Each of these components has its own pathologies that hamper the functioning of the insight process. Kris stresses that insights develop slowly in analysis, based as they are on repeated interpretation by the analyst. It takes a long time for the patient to make extensive use of interpretation. In the earlier stages of analysis, the synthesis is often quickly submerged by new anxieties and conflicts, and at best it proceeds preconsciously, if it proceeds at all. Insight has to be resupplied by the analyst when the interpreted conflict returns later. As patients gain increasing mastery, however, they are able to sustain their insights as the conflicts reappear in new guises.

Myerson (1960, 1963, 1965) has developed the extremely important concept of *modes of insight*. A mode of insight describes a certain *type* of insight, and it implies a certain *process* through which the insight is reached. Myerson (1965) describes two different modes of insight which appear late in analysis, and which are important in postanalytic self-analysis. He calls them "psychoanalytic insight" and "reality-oriented insight." Psychoanalytic insight is an internalized version of the analytic process itself, and leads to a dynamic and genetic understanding of an unconscious conflict. The mode has four steps; (1) an active effort to understand the conflict, followed by (2) suspension of active attention and a move toward attempted mastery through fantasy, leading to (3) self-observation and then (4) reintegration. (We can see the imprint of Sterba's 1934 concepts on Myerson's thought.) To summarize a typical example from Myerson's 1965 paper: late in his analysis a patient found himself feeling very angry at his little daughter, who was misbehaving at a family party. The patient recognized the inappropriate strength of his anger and began to wonder about it in the analytic hour. Unable to make headway by a directed conscious approach to the problem, he allowed himself to have a fantasy which expressed some hostility toward his sister's daughter and some restitution to the sister. Next, the patient recognized the immediate significance of the situation: he was extremely angry at his daughter because she had rejected him. From this, he moved to sibling and Oedipal contexts—past and present—in which he had experienced the same feeling, and which closely paralleled the fantasy about the sister's daughter.

There were thus four steps in the activation of this mode of self-awareness.

The first was the recognition that some self-aspect needed to be dealt with further, and a beginning attempt at a direct cognitive confrontation with the problem. In the second, a specifically analytic tack was taken, allowing fantasies to arise by relaxing the vigilant cognitive and defensive attitudes to the problem. As Myerson points out, it takes a good deal of courage and trust to abandon one's defenses and plunge into the analytic process when frightening content is involved. The third step came in looking at this fantasy from an analytic context that had been painstakingly constructed over several years of analysis, and the last step involved a reintegration of the new material into the ego.

The reality-oriented mode operates with much less openness to unconscious conflict. It begins with the patient's direct effort to renounce the conflicted part of himself. When that fails, a superego-ridden fantasy emerges, demonstrating regressive loss of mastery of the conflict. Because he is unable to master the conflict through fantasy, self-observation is activated, and the patient faces conflict over his impulse. But he does not allow himself to explore the conflict further through associations. Instead, he turns to the reality situation to separate his fantasy from the facts. In the first example given, the patient would have stopped when he recognized that it was his daughter's rejection that was upsetting him, and reminded himself that, rejected as he felt, there was little objective reason to be upset with her, so he might as well simply tolerate his feelings for her.

Although the patient may use the reality-oriented mode defensively, we can see that it has useful application in the clarification used to prepare for interpretation.

The Motives and Autonomy of Insight Acquisition

As Kris (1956) and Myerson (1960, 1963, 1965) have stressed, the acquisition of insight is often not an autonomous process. Freud's early expectation that patients' wish for cure would lead them to tell all was quickly dashed by the phenomenon of resistance. He came to rely on the power of the positive transference to overcome resistance (1913, 1914), although Dora (1905) made the hazards clear. But the wish to comply with the analyst has remained an important motive in the patient's struggle to follow the basic rule. The basic rule as an analytic ego ideal was first formulated by Sterba (1934) and Strachey (1934). Kris (1956) and Miller et al. (1965) have since stressed the role of compliance and identification in adopting analytic forms of insight and self-observation.

More generally, Miller et al. (1965) have reviewed the various influences the analyst may use to help patients observe themselves. The analyst may "stimulate and exhort" patients to activate their observational skills; interpret patient's difficulties with self-observation; actively instruct patients in self-observation; and serve as a model for identification through his or her own patterns of observation and insight.

Kris (1956) and Myerson (1960, 1963, 1965) provide useful discussions of defensive and pathological motives for the acquisition of insight. The entire process may gratify libidinal or aggressive aims. Kris, for example, points out that insight gained in compliance with the analyst gratifies libidinal wishes for union with him or for his love and praise. The stability of these insights is linked to the positive transference. Certain aggressive aims are gratified by the wish to become independent of the analyst. This wish leads to premature efforts at self-analysis, and, as Kris puts it, "a by-and-large competitive attitude tinged by hostility holds the field."

Myerson (1960, 1963, 1965) is also concerned with the motives for insight and self-observation. He suggests that self-observation may be motivated by the wish to escape anxiety and guilt; it may be undertaken to restore happy ties to a loved one, or to cope better with a demanding or competitive reality. Myerson tends to imply that autonomous self-observation and insight are noble ideals to strive for: in compliance with the analytic process itself (Kris, 1956), the patient should be determined to know and master the unconscious, regardless of the pain and frustration involved.

Certain specific ego functions, components in the insight process, may also be distorted for dynamic reasons—for example, the tolerance of affect may be inhibited in an effort to avoid "messy" feelings. The intereferences with insight acquisition that we have described are fundamentally motivational (i.e., dynamic in nature). These interferences are standard fare in every analysis and are generally responsive to interpretation. More serious interferences occur when profound conflict, hereditary deficit, or severe characterological distortions stunt the component ego functions involved in insight acquisition. There may be deficits in any of the five major functions: the capacity for controlled ego regression, the tolerance and control of affect discharge, the capacity for reflective self-observation, and the integrative function of the ego. While it is clear that these different functions overlap, it is possible to consider them separately.

The regression-enhancing features of the analytic situation may precipitate the well-known problem of uncontrolled regression in certain patients. These regressions often disrupt the other ego functions involved in insight acquisition and place a severe strain on the therapeutic alliance. Recent studies (Atkins, 1967; Dickes, 1967; Frosch, 1967) suggest that these apparently uncontrolled regressions may be relatively circumscribed in many patients. Even patients whose regressions are broad, deep, and long-lasting may be able to work effectively in analysis (Atkins, 1967).

The capacity for reflective self-observation may be impaired, especially in impulse-ridden characters. Stern (1970) has recently described a "therapeutic playback technique" in which patients with weak self-observational capacities may relisten to an hour on a tape recorder. This allows them to listen to themselves more reflectively, supplementing their reflective self-observational skills.

The integrative function of the ego is implicated in all of the component ego functions involved in insight acquisition. As originally described by Kris, the integrative function serves to bring insights into working interrelation with the rest of the ego. The synthetic function may generate plausible insights from diverse free-associative data, but without the activity of the integrative function, these insights remain isolated from the ongoing activity of the ego and therefore useless (Kris, 1956). Recent work on the borderline patient, however (Kernberg, 1966, 1967), suggests that certain failures of the integrative function may be effectively influenced by analysis.

Self-Observation

As an introductory definition, we may describe the function of self-observation as the observation of any and all contents, characteristics, and activities of the person, and the relationships among these features. Self-observation is an ego function. Like any other ego function, it is defined by certain basic properties: the functions it performs; its relations to other functions of the ego and to the demands of the drives, the superego, and reality. Self-observation may thus be directed toward the other functions of the ego in the service of insight; it may be responsive to defensive needs, such as the denial of unpleasant affect; it may work hand in hand with the reality-testing function in the effort to differentiate objective reality from subjective preferences; and so on.

Like reality testing, self-observation by its nature operates in conjunction with the ego function of consciousness. While the contribution of consciousness may be minimal—self-observation occurs during dreaming, for example—the notion of preconscious, automatized self-observation raises thorny questions.

In relation to the id, self-observation may be libidinized in certain pathological forms of self-consciousness (narcissistic characters, inhibited forms of exhibitionism, etc). It may be aggressivized through the superego in depressions and psychoses. It may be more or less affected by realistic comments and criticisms, and by the effects of one's own actions. Self-observation has more general stylistic characteristics as well. It may be impressionistic, subtle, psychologically-minded, outer or inner directed, shallow, penetrating, limited, honest, deep, spotty.

With this overview in mind, we may turn to a more detailed consideration of the function of self-observation.

Types of Self-Observation

Our introductory definition does little to illuminate the complexity of the self-observing function. Freud (1900) made an important early refinement with his distinction between self-observation and reflection:

> I have noticed in my psycho-analytical work that the whole frame of mind of a man who is reflecting is totally different from that of a man who is observing his own psychical processes. . . . In both cases attention must be concentrated, but the man who is reflecting is also exercising his *critical* faculty; this leads him to reject some of the ideas that occur to him after perceiving them, to cut short others without following the trains of thought which they would open up to him, and to behave in such a way towards still others that they never become conscious at all and are accordingly suppressed before being perceived. The self-observer, on the other hand, need only take the trouble to suppress his critical faculty. If he succeeds in doing that, innumerable ideas come into his consciousness of which he could otherwise never have got hold [1900, pp. 101–102].

Kris (1956) presents a modern description of a similar distinction:

> It might be preferable . . . to distinguish two cases, the one in which the ego observes the self and the other in which it observes its own functioning. In the latter case, one of the functions of the ego, that of observing, may be thought of as pitted against others [pp. 451–452].

The first form of self-observation that Kris describes is closer to experience than is the second. This "experiential" self-observation is a report of whatever is noticed about the self at a given moment, when the person simply lets his or her thoughts flow. It is the work of a passive, free-associative, observing ego. The second is the more detached (cf. Sterba), reflective form of self-observation, which occurs when the ego is taking an active, organizing view of the functioning of the mind.

It is clear that the distinction between these two types of self-observation is not hard and fast, for the two extremes are joined by every imaginable shade and degree. There is some reflective awareness of the self, and some conceptual editing in "experiential" self-observation—for example, the free-associative ideal is constrained by the need to remain comprehensible to the analyst (Kris, 1956). On the other hand, there is some affect in reflective self-observation; it is more than "detached intellectual contemplation." As we have seen, insight becomes effective only when it meets emotionally living material.

In general, then, we can imagine many other varieties of self-observation occurring outside analysis or going on unobserved within it. Chief among these is *silent* self-observation. Silent self-observation need not be communicated subsequently in the analysis, and, in fact, may make little use of words at all. Although Freud placed great emphasis on the importance of words in mastering the unconscious (see, e.g., 1900, 1923), it is not certain that the patient's capacity for therapeutically effective self-observation is limited by his verbal skills.

Self-Observation and Insight

Self-observation is not to be confused with insight, of which it is a major component, as Kris (1956) has pointed out. Insight is a *process* which makes use of the ego function of self-observation in both its experiential and reflective forms. The first provides material for understanding, and the second makes an active effort to understand.

While self-observation often serves insight, it is worthwhile to consider it separately from its involvement in insight acquisition. A good deal of the self-observation in therapy does not serve the immediate goal of attaining insight. The patient or the analyst may observe aspects of the self which appear unrelated to the immediate themes of the therapeutic hour, but which in the long run contribute to the understanding of the patient. Self-observation serves many other masters as well. In cases of depression and obsessional neuroses, it serves the critical superego in its review of guilty deeds. It serves the narcissistic character in the admiration of the self, and so on. In any case, there is much to be learned from separating out the function of self-observation for direct consideration, with an eye to its contribution to the analytic process.

The Nature of Self-Observation

Before we venture into the analytic situation, however, we need to take a closer look at the nature of self-observation. Self-observation of the type I have called "experiential" is in many respects simpler than the "reflective" variety because its function is to report what is visible to the inner eye. It does not attempt new integrations, but instead faces the immediate flux of experience— not an easy task, but a cognitively less complex one. Even so, there is a great range of individual differences in the complexity of the material observed, as well as in the breadth and vividness of the content covered. The obsessive patient typically focuses his observation on the minutiae of his mental life, to the exclusion of the broader gestalt and the emotional vividness of his experience. The hysteric tends to lose the complexity of experience in a rush of vagueness and emotionality (Valenstein, 1962; Shapiro, 1965).

In contrast to experiential self-observation, the hallmark of reflective self-observation is its organizing activity. In this respect it is the keystone of the insight process. The contents which have emerged in the "experiential" phase are recognized as elements in a larger, unifying frame of reference, or *context*.

The search for or emergence of this *context* is the core of reflective self-observation.

A context is an organized cognitive system of meaningfully related contents. The meaning that relates the contents may be a specific fantasy and its dynamic, economic, genetic, structural, and adaptive correlates; it may be a certain trait and all the circumstances in which that trait appears; or it may be a certain reality situation and the feelings, impulses, and fantasies that situation arouses. In other words, a context places an isolated thought, fantasy, or chain of associations or behaviors in a meaningful setting. Experientially, this leads to an "understanding" of the fantasy, thought, etc. The context established by reflective self-observation serves as an explanation of the behavior under consideration. For example, the day before a patient had a cystoscopy, she was unwilling to have intercourse with her husband. The evening after, she was depressed, felt inadequate and uninteresting, and had the following dream: An art museum was being plundered of its marble statues while its tough, masculine female curator struggled helplessly to prevent the loss. We may understand these disparate behaviors in the context of the patient's unconscious fantasy that she possessed a penis hidden in her vagina or urethra, which would be stolen from her by the intruding penis.

Rapaport (1957) and Kris (1950) also use the concept of context. Rapaport extends it to mean the underlying cognitive organization of a particular thought or thought process, making it possible not only to specify the exact context of a given self-observation, but also to group self-observations according to more general cognitive features that are embodied in each context.

The most relevant feature is the degree of intrapsychic focus in the self-observations. The simplest self-observations are relatively global, unsophisticated forms in which the role of intropsychic factors is little recognized—for example, "Pushy people are offensive to me." The most complex forms show an increasing appreciation of the contribution of the self to experience, so that the locus of explanation shifts from the outside to the inside of the self. "Pushy people offend me" becomes "I don't like pushy people because they remind me of my older brother, who always used to push me around because he was jealous." It is clear that the differentiation of the intrapsychic dimension allows a subtler and more complex understanding of the contribution of external as well as internal factors in experience—especially the motives and limitations of others. For research purposes (Hatcher, 1972), it is possible to establish and rank groups of self-observations according to the extent and quality of their intrapsychic focus, and so to construct a hierarchy of increasingly complex *"modes"* of self-observation.

This close look at the cognitive features of self-observation illustrates how an ego function is composed of many complex and subtle characteristics. Closer examinations of many ego functions remain to be made. For example, consciousness, reality testing, and the integrative function are relatively unexplored. Furthermore, ego functions seem to overlap and interrelate to a remarkable degree, and a systematic exploration of these interrelations would be desirable.

Self-Observation in Analysis

Experiential and reflective self-observation have different but related roles in analysis. A good deal of the early work in an analysis is directed at modifying experiential self-observation. As time goes on, as interpretive work moves to discover and create new contexts for understanding the patient's behavior, reflective self-observation becomes increasingly important.

Experiential self-observation is the process that provides the content of the analysis. When they begin analysis, patients have two obstacles to overcome in their attempts to communicate to the analyst. First, patients are usually ignorant of the analytic situation and unfamiliar with the unrestricted self-observation required of them. Second, patients' defenses interfere with their efforts to observe their inner experiences richly. They need to be taught, to a greater or lesser extent, how to observe themselves. Miller et al. (1965) have suggested that the analyst encourages patients directly, and indirectly by example, in their efforts at self-observation. The analyst must interpret the specific inhibitions in self-observation that restrict its scope or meaningfulness. He or she will design confrontations with character traits having similar inhibiting and distorting effects on self-observation.

These efforts help the patient's self-observation become more autonomous, both from internal conflict and from compliance with the analyst. Miller et al. (1965) trace a sequence of stages reflecting these changes in spoken self-observation (i.e., self-observation communicated to the analyst). The sequence begins with a compliant, externally oriented, unemotional form of communication they call "reporting" and culminates in an autonomous, inwardly oriented, emotionally rich form they call "imparting."

The analyst builds his interpretation on the patient's self-observations by proposing a new or revised context in which the associations can be understood, thus replacing old, stunted contexts. From this point of view, one may consider the neurosis to be the result of the burden of infantile, fantasy-ridden, and often unconscious contexts. These old contexts are restructured and assimilated into new contexts through interpretation. Hartmann (1939) describes this role of interpretation:

Defenses (typically) not only keep thoughts, images, and instinctual drives out of consciousness, but also prevent their assimilation by means of thinking. When defensive processes break down, the mental elements defended against and certain connections of these elements become amenable to recollection and reconstructions. Interpretations not only help to regain the buried material, but must also establish correct causal relations, that is, the causes, range of influence, and effectiveness of these experiences in relation to other elements. I stress this here because the theoretical study of interpretation is often limited to those instances which are concerned with emerging memories of corresponding reconstructions. But even more important for the *theory of interpretation* are those instances in which the causal connections of elements, and the criteria for these connections, are established. We cannot assume that the ways in which children connect their experiences, and which later become conscious in the course of psychoanalysis, could satisfy the requirements of the mature ego, not to speak of the requirements of a judgment which has been sharpened by psychoanalytic means of thinking [p. 63].

The new contexts contained in interpretations reflect more sophisticated modes of understanding and so provide a more accurate and detailed picture of the patient's behavior.

In the analytic hour, the analyst's interpretation serves as a signal, activating the patient's *reflective* self-observation. Patients listen to the interpretation and—more or less consciously—review their recent behaviors and associations in the light of the new context. At first, the patient's ability to take a fresh look at his or her associations may be shaky. The interpretation raises new anxieties and touches on deeper secrets; the review may quickly be abandoned to the preconscious level of thought (Kris, 1956). As time goes on, these new anxieties and secrets, too, are interpreted, and the original subject returns again and again. Each time, as the associations emerge from the preconscious, they are better organized by the new context offered by the interpretation (Kris, 1950). The patient is able to take longer, more searching looks at the material from the new context until it becomes a more or less readily available perspective whenever the conflict arises. This gradual assimilation of interpretations leads the patient to make ever-expanding use of more complex contexts of self-observation. Progress is made from nonautonomous experiential self-observation, distorted by inhibition and character traits, to more spontaneous, freely ranging, affectively modulated self-observation. Reflective self-observation, at first vague and rigid, becomes both more specific and more encompassing.

These improvements are by no means independent of one another—in fact, the distinction between reflective and experiential self-observation is more heuristic than real. Interpretations of the defenses that block free experiential self-observation often imply a hidden neurotic context. "You have to be silent because you are threatened by some angry feelings for me" is an example. These interpretations guide the patient's associations into an implicit context—in this case, transference fantasies about the analyst's reactions to anger. A subsequent interpretation of these fantasies might fill out the implicit context and contrast it with the reality of the analyst—for example, "My silence repeats your father's silent reaction to your anger, when you were afraid that he was holding back an explosive rage at you." The activated reflective self-observation will assimilate this interpretation, which will begin to organize the patient's feelings about his anger, so that the next time they arise, his associations will move more directly to the transference fantasies behind them. *This feedback process linking experiential and reflective self-observation may eventually result in a flexible transition between the two in the patient's continued self-analysis after termination.*

Self-Observation, Insight, and the Analytic Cure

It is striking how little has been written about the analytic cure, not to mention the role of self-observation and insight in its accomplishment. There is, in fact, a certain mystery behind analytic efficacy, despite Freud's complaint (1937) that, on this subject, "the interest of analysts . . . [is] quite wrongly directed. Instead of an enquiry into how a cure by analysis comes about (a matter which I think has been sufficiently elucidated) the question should be asked of what are the obstacles that stand in the way of such a cure" (p. 221).

Certainly it is possible to construct a theory of cure based on what we see of the results of analyses that are deemed successful: in fact, it has been done repeatedly. Freud's famous statement (1933) about insight and the therapeutic effect of analysis puts the argument succinctly: "Their object is to strengthen the ego, to make it more independent of the superego, to widen its field of vision, and so to extend its organization that it can take over new portions of the id. *Where id was, there ego shall be.* It is a work of culture—not unlike the draining of the Zuyder Zee" (p. 80).

The concept of context described above helps articulate this process of ego mastery. Every thought, every fantasy, every behavior of any kind may be seen as organized in a larger context. Psychoanalysis searches out meaningful contexts that help the patient organize—or reorganize—his disturbing fantasies, thoughts, or behaviors. Searching out and articulating the unconscious (or preconscious) context for a set of thoughts and behaviors may be valuable to the patient in and of itself. The hitherto isolated behavior and thoughts, and the context which makes them meaningful, are linked up with other systems of meaning and influence in consciousness, enhancing ego mastery. They are placed in perspective, to put it another way, and tend to lose their earlier poignancy because of it. The interconnection of contexts circumscribes the significance of any one context, making each a part of a meaningful whole.

Loewald (1960) conceptualizes the value of insight in somewhat similar terms and includes the fact that the search for contexts is a mutual effort led by the analyst.

The patient, who comes to the analyst for help through increased self-understanding, is led to this self-understanding by the understanding he finds in the analyst. The analyst operates on various levels of understanding. . . . the analyst structures and articulates, or works towards structuring and articulating, the material and the productions offered by the patient. If an interpretation of unconscious meaning is timely, the words by which this meaning is expressed are recognizable to the patient as expressions of what he experiences. They organize for him what was previously less organized and thus give him the "distance" from himself which enables him to understand, to see, to put into words and to "handle" what was previously not visible, understandable, speakable, tangible. A higher stage or organization, of both himself and his environment, is thus reached, by way of the organizing understanding which the analyst provides [p. 24].

The particular context used at any given time in interpretive work may capture the phenomena more or less adequately. What we might call a "trait" context (e.g., "It is just like me to drop things in the kitchen") may capture a good deal less of the meaning of a parapraxis than an "analytic" context (e.g., "I need to be and feel clumsy in the kitchen to ward off the triumphant, guilty fantasy of being a better cook, wife, and mother than my own mother"). It is important to keep in mind, however, a point that Klein (1958) discussed in relation to the problem of "exact" or "accurate" perception. He argued that exhaustive perception is impossible because there are an infinite number of ways in which reality may be viewed. He suggested that the only useful criterion is that perception be effective for the purpose it serves. A similar argument may be applied to self-perception. We cannot claim *a priori* that analytic self-observation is better or more adequate than trait-level awareness. Rather, we must specify the conditions under which one is more satisfactory than the other. Neurosis is the condition that is most interesting from the point of view of psychotherapy research—and the question becomes: is analytic self-observation more effective than trait-level self-observation in overcoming neurotic difficulties? If the argument about the role of contexts in psychoanalysis is correct, the answer must be yes.

Wallerstein (1965) observes that, in our thinking about insight and its relation to cure, we make a "tacit assumption that the two develop together and in appropriate correspondence to each other—that is, that the achievement of analytic insights in the process of making the unconscious conscious is the constant and the necessary and the (implicitly) sufficient concomitant of the achievement of the outcome goals, to be able to live and to work" (p. 763). Perhaps this assumption requires further investigation.

Further Developments in the Study of Insight and Self-Observation

Analysts have continued to investigate the motives leading to insight, the process itself, and the manifold interferences in the effort to acquire insight. A series of papers by authors from the San Francisco Psychoanalytic Institute (Weiss, 1967, 1971; Sampson, 1976; Bush, 1978) have stressed the mastery-seeking role of the ego in analytic work. Freud accounted for the emergence of repressed instinctual drives in the transference by the repetition compulsion and the tendency of the repressed unconscious to seek actual discharge in behavior, particularly following the analysis of resistance. These authors find that the ego plays a much larger role in bringing forbidden or dangerous thoughts, feelings, and wishes into play in the analysis. The ego wishes to master and integrate the repressed, providing thereby the forward push to the analytic work. On the other hand, the ego makes continuous unconscious assessments of the risks involved in experiencing the repressed more directly and consciously (Weiss, 1971).

These unconscious ego assessments are based on the unconscious ego's erroneous ideas of the dangers posed by the repressed impulses. These ideas are based on infantile experiences and fantasies involving fears of castration, loss of love, loss of the superego's love, and separation, which are the major motives for defense (Freud, 1926; see also Bush, 1978; Hatcher, 1980). Analysis of defense and resistance involves detecting and integrating these unconscious fears of the ego, bringing them into connection with the judgment of the mature ego. The ego then feels safe in allowing the repressed more direct expression.

We should note that this approach must come to terms with the role of the press of the repressed for discharge and the repetition compulsion as motivators in the analytic process (Friedman, 1969, 1977, 1978).

These considerations have direct bearing on our understanding of the process of insight acquisition. They are one aspect of an increasing recognition of the unconscious and preconscious mental activity involved in acquiring and utilizing insight. Kris's 1956 paper is again a landmark on this path:

Interpretation naturally need not lead to insight; much or most of analytic therapy is carried out in darkness, with here and there a flash of insight to lighten the path. A connnection has been established, but before insight has reached awareness (or, if it does, only for flickering moments), new areas of anxiety and conflict emerge, new material comes, and the process drives on: thus far-reaching changes may and must be achieved without the pathway by which they have come about becoming part of the patient's awareness [p. 452].

Kris calls the conscious understanding *insight,* and leaves the unconscious (or preconscious) connections unnamed. Some authors have chosen to call these connections *unconscious insight* (Nagera, 1978), a preliminary stage in the development of conscious insight. Kris's (1956) description of the "good hour" connects with this idea. The patient's preconscious ego organizes the themes of his material leading to conscious insight. These hours represent the culmination of much previous analytic work.

Part of the challenge posed by these ideas is that they suggest that extensive understanding can occur and significant changes result from the work of the unconscious (and preconscious) ego. Insight has been linked with consciousness since the earliest days of psychoanalysis. Nevertheless, in his recent article, Blum (1979) calls our attention to an early case report of Freud's (1893) in which he provides mutative insight to a hypnotized patient. Blum was not trying to demonstrate the point at issue here. But Freud's patient, a mother who could not breast-feed her child, did not recall the interpretation Freud made when she awoke from the hypnosis.

There is increasing opinion, then, that the contexts we have described above may be established and utilized for change outside of the patient's awareness.

The Anna Freud–Hampstead Center Symposium on Insight, held by the Michigan Psychoanalytic Society in November, 1978, resulted in many reviews and new contributions to the understanding of insight. Many of these papers were published as a supplement to the *Journal of the American Psychoanalytic Association* (Volume 27). Hansi Kennedy's (1979) contribution developed an important and little-studied aspect of the insight process, investigating the developmental factors that limit the child's use of insight. Many of the ego functions required to acquiring insight are detailed by Kris (1956), and Kennedy reviews the child's slow development of these ego capacities. Children's use of insight is limited by their inability to tolerate painful affects and their dominance by the pleasure principle; by their limited capacity for distinguishing reality and fantasy and to assess, understand, and process external reality and cause and effect; by their egocentrism, concrete thinking, and lack of capacity for abstract thinking; by their tendency to act instead of reflect; by their lack of frustration tolerance; by the lack of conflict over some impulses; and by their belief in the omnipotence of adults. In his recent paper, Nagera (1978) demonstrates how frequently these same problems persist into adult life, limiting the use our adult patients can make of the insight process.

It is still the case, however, that "insight is a *sine qua non* of the psychoanalytic process and is a condition, catalyst, and consequence of the psychoanalytic process" (Blum, 1979).

Summary

Insight has been a key tool in psychoanalytic treatment since its earliest days. Analytic thought has come to view the acquisition of insight as a complex process, in which the ego function of self-observation is a major component. After tracing the evolution of this line of thought, detailed consideration is given to self-observation; its nature, its structure, and its place in the analytic process.

REFERENCES

Atkins, N. (1967), Comments on severe and psychotic regressions in analysis. *J. Amer. Psychoanal. Assn.,* 15:584–607.

Bibring, E. (1954), Psychoanalysis and the dynamic psychotherapies. *J. Amer. Psychoanal. Assn.,* 2:745–770.

Blum, H. (1979), The curative and creative aspects of insight. *J. Amer. Psychoanal. Assn.,* 27:41–69.

Breuer, J., & Freud, S. (1893), On the psychical mechanism of hysterical phenomena: Preliminary communication. *Standard Edition,* 2:3–17. London: Hogarth Press, 1955.

—— (1895), Studies on hysteria. *Standard Edition,* 2:19–305. London: Hogarth Press, 1955.

Bush, M. (1978), Preliminary considerations for a psychoanalytic theory of insight: Historical perspective. *Internat. Rev. Psycho-Anal.,* 5:1–13.

Dickes, R. (1967), Severe regressive disruptions of the therapeutic alliance. *J. Amer. Psychoanal. Assn.,* 15:508–533.

Freud, S. (1893), A case of successful treatment by hypnotism. *Standard Edition,* 1:115–128. London: Hogarth Press, 1966.

—— (1900), The interpretation of dreams. *Standard Edition,* 4 & 5. London: Hogarth Press, 1953.

—— (1905), Fragment of an analysis of a case of hysteria. *Standard Edition,* 7:3–124. London: Hogarth Press, 1953.

—— (1913), On beginning the treatment (Further recommendations on the technique of psycho-analysis I). *Standard Edition,* 12:123–144. London: Hogarth Press, 1958.

—— (1914), Remembering, repeating and working-through (Further recommendations on the technique of psycho-analysis II). *Standard Edition,* 12:147–156. London: Hogarth Press, 1958.

—— (1920), Beyond the pleasure principle. *Standard Edition,* 18:46. London: Hogarth Press, 1955.

—— (1923), The ego and the id. *Standard Edition,* 19:3–66. London: Hogarth Press, 1961.

—— (1926), Inhibitions, symptoms and anxiety. *Standard Edition,* 20:77–175.

—— (1933), New introductory lectures on psycho-Analysis. *Standard Edition,* 22:5–182. London: Hogarth Press, 1964.

—— (1937), Analysis terminable and interminable. *Standard Edition,* 23:216–253. London: Hogarth Press, 1964.

Friedman, L. (1969), The therapeutic alliance. *Internat. J. Psycho-Anal.,* 50:139–153.

—— (1977), Conflict and synthesis in Freud's theory of the mind. *Internat. Rev. Psycho-Anal.,* 4:155–170.

—— (1978), Trends in the psychoanalytic theory of treatment. *Psychoanal. Quart.,* 47:524–567.

Frosch, J. (1967), Severe regressive states during analysis: Introduction. *J. Amer. Psychoanal. Assn.,* 15:491–507.

Greenson, R. (1967), *The Technique of Practice of Psychoanalysis,* Vol. 1. New York: International Universities Press.

Hartmann, H. (1939), *Ego Psychology and the Problem of Adaptation.* New York: International Universities Press, 1958.

Hatcher, R. (1972), Self-observation in psychoanalytic psychotherapy. Unpublished doctoral dissertation, University of Michigan.

—— (1980), The unconscious ego. Unpublished paper presented to the Michigan Psychoanalytic Society.

Kennedy, H. (1979) The role of insight in child analysis: A developmental viewpoint, Psychoanal. Assn. Supplement, 27:9–28. J. Amer.

Kernberg, O. (1966), Structural derivations of object relationships. *Internat. J. Psycho-Anal.,* 47:236–253.

——— (1967), Borderline personality organization. *J. Amer. Psychoanal. Assn.,* 15:641–685.

Klein, G. (1958), Cognitive control and motivation. In: *Perception, Motives, and Personality.* New York: Knopf, 1970, pp. 201–231.

Kris, E. (1950), On preconscious mental processes. In: *Psychoanalytic Explorations in Art.* New York: International Universities Press, 1952, pp. 303–319.

——— (1956), some vicissitudes of insight in psychoanalysis. *Internat. J. Psycho-Anal.,* 37:445–455.

Loewald, H. (1960), On the therapeutic action of psychoanalysis. *Internat. J. Psycho-Anal.,* 41:16–33.

Loewenstein, R. (1963), Some considerations on free association. *J. Amer. Psychoanal. Assn.,* 11:451–473.

Miller, A., Isaacs, K., & Haggard, (1965), On the nature of the observing function of the ego. *Brit. J. Med. Psychol.,* 38:161–169.

Myerson, P. (1960), Awareness and stress: Post-psycho-analytic utilization of insight. *Internat. J. Psycho-Anal.,* 41:147–156.

——— (1963), Assimilation of unconscious material. *Internat. J. Psycho-Anal.,* 44:317–327.

——— (1965), Modes of insight. *J. Amer. Psychoanal. Assn.,* 13:771–792.

Nagera, H. (1978), The problem of insight: A comparison between children and adults. Unpublished paper presented to the Michigan Psychoanalytic Society, 1979.

Rapaport, D. (1957), Cognitive structures. In *The Collected Papers of David Rapaport,* ed. M. Gill. New York: Basic Books, 1967, pp. 631–664.

Richfield, J. (1954), An analysis of the concept of insight. *Psychoanal. Quart.,* 23:390–408.

Sampson, H. (1976), A critique of certain traditional concepts in the psychoanalytic theory of therapy. *Bull. Memminger Clin.,* 40:255–262.

Shapiro, D. (1965), *Neurotic Styles.* New York: Basic Books.

Sterba, R. (1934), The fate of the ego in analytic therapy. *Internat. J. Psycho-Anal.,* 15:117–126.

Stern, M. (1970), Therapeutic playback, self-objectification, and the analytic process *J. Amer. Psychoanal. Assn.,* 18:562–598.

Stone, L. (1961), *The Psychoanalytic Situation.* New York: International Universities Press.

Strachey, J. (1934), The nature of the therapeutic action of psychoanalysis. *Internat. J. Psycho-Anal.,* 15:127–159.

Valenstein, A. (1962), The psychoanalytic situation (affects, emotional reliving, and insight in the psychoanalytic process). *Internat. J. Psycho-Anal.,* 43:315–324.

Wallerstein, R. (1965), The goals of psychoanalysis. *J. Amer. Psychoanal. Assn.,* 13:748–770.

Weiss, S. (1967), The integration of defenses. *Internat. J. Psycho-Anal.,* 48:520–524.

——— (1971), The emergence of new themes: A contribution to the psychoanalytic theory of therapy. *Internat. J. Psycho-Anal.,* 52:459–467.

CHAPTER 5

Language and Healing

Edgar A. Levenson

Psychoanalysis has, ever since Anna O. so felicitously named it, been known as the "talking cure." Leo Stone (1973) called speech "the veritable stuff of psychoanalysis" (p. 58), and, more recently, Paul Ricoeur (1971) has said that "there enters into the field of investigation only that part of experience which is capable of being said" (p. 838). I quote these two contemporary sources to affirm that this is by no means a vestigial concept. Yet we know that all the talk in the world doesn't change patients, that persuasive formulations of psychodynamics can fall flat, and that neophyte analysts more often talk too much than too little. This mastery of the commonplace seems a sorry virtuosity. Talk seems too ordinary an instrument for so difficult an enterprise as psychoanalysis. Yet, as I shall elaborate, from a structural linguistic perspective on psychoanalytic process, there are extremely subtle and intricate ramifications to this most ordinary and unself-conscious function.

To begin with, it seems most likely that what these authors really imply is that psychoanalysis is the *nonacting* cure: that is, what is acted out—rather than talked about—cannot be encompassed in the treatment. This would certainly be consistent with Freud's (1914) position in "Remembering, Repeating

An earlier version of this chapter was presented at the Annual Meeting of the American Academy of Psychoanalysis, Atlanta, Georgia, May 1978, and appeared in the *Journal of the American Academy of Psychoanalysis,* 7:271–282, New York: Wiley, 1979.

and Working Through": "He [the therapist] celebrates it as a triumph for the treatment if he can bring it about that something that the patient wishes to discharge in action is disposed of through the work of remembering" (p. 154).

But the distinction between speech and action is often very obscure. Some acting out seems clearly more like a vivid nonverbal language than pure evasion; and it is often precisely at this elusive interface of action and speech that the most impressive psychoanalytic insights take place. Consider the patient who announces that he could not possibly be angry at the therapist and who then kicks over the therapist's cocktail table; or the therapist who is unaware of being angry with the patient and is horrified to find that he has forgotten to appear for a session. These examples might be considered simple parapraxes, yet they are one end of a continuum of behavior that ranges through more precise symbolic reenactments of psychoanalytic content to behavior that reflects an extremely subtle resonance between the subject material, the "talk" of therapy, and the patterning of the transference.

For example, a patient dreams she is sitting in a Japanese restaurant, unable to decipher the menu. At a table next to her sits a man with graying hair who holds the menu up in the air and points out a rather simple shrimp dish. She now knows what to order. When asked what she makes of this dream (she does not volunteer an explanation), the patient replies, "At first, it didn't make any sense to me, but then I thought to myself, what would *you* say about it?" She then proceeds to present a quite sophisticated explication of the transference aspects of the dream and even some of the countertransference implications. Does she not *play out* the content of the dream between us? She must read the therapist's instructions (even if they are "simple" or "tiny"). She does it everywhere: she can only arrive at a decision by first applying the template of someone else's experience. Surely, all this between us is mediated through speech, but is it not also action, speech as behavior?

The debate begins to sound sadly familiar. Is it acting out, "acting in" (in Eidelberg's phase [Kohut, 1957]), or parapraxis? Should the term "acting out" be limited only to behavior that repeats earlier infantile experience? It seems much the same ambiguity that pervades the discussion of countertransference. What is real, what is not real, what is regression, how much "participation" on the part of the therapist is permissible? The distinctions so clear to Fenichel and Menninger become, for many of us, increasingly obscure. If transference is the "playground" Freud (1914) considered it to be, what happens in the playground? If there is regression in the transference, is it only talked about? Can it be only talked about because the therapist will not "play"? Or is the transference a variety of that old playground activity, "show and tell"? These dilemmas have been increasingly festooned with metapsychological elaborations designed to bridge the widening gap between orthodox restraint and more radical participant observation.[1] It is, to some extent, like bolstering a sinking house by adding another story. Certainly we must agree that speech mediates therapy, but why not look at the nature of the medium, in addition to what is carried?

This apparent dilemma about talk and action—about what can be said and what must be shown—is, I suspect, more apparent than real and depends on a series of misconstruings about the nature of language and its role in psychoanalysis. The confusion begins with the failure to distinguish between speech and language. De Saussure, the Swiss linguist, clearly delineates *parole* and *langue* (1970, pp. 43ff). *Parole* is, of course, "talk," the spoken aspect of language. Language is, in De Saussure's aphorism, "speechless speaking." It is the whole set of linguistic habits that allow an individual to understand and be understood. That is, it encompasses those conventions, rules, or givens that govern the syntax, grammar, and semantics of the spoken communication as it emerges from this matrix.[2]

Further, one must distinguish language from semiotics, first defined and named by the American philosopher C. S. Peirce (1955). Semiotics refers to "the transmission of signals, signs, signifiers and symbols in any communication system whatever" (Wilden, 1972, p. 111). At the bottom of the communication system hierachy is speech; then comes the intricate machinery for processing speech (language); and finally, there is a more extensive system of coded communication (semiotics), which involves speech, nonverbal cuings, and most important, the cultural and social context of communication—what Peirce called the "pragmatics" of communication.[3] Psychoanalysts have traditionally been concerned with pragmatics. Jacques Lacan, the stormy petrel of French psychoanalysis, with his emphasis on "symbolic, real, and imaginary" imagery, seems primarily interested in the semantics of semiotics. His preoccupation with the "word" (with meaning) makes him very difficult for psychoanalysts (or anyone else, for that matter) to read, since there is absolutely no pragmatic base for the applicability of his position (Lacan, 1977). It

---

[1]Particularly in object-relation theory and its application to borderline syndromes, where much emphasis is put on appropriate and useful responses.

[2]This distinction between speech and language is perhaps most vividly illustrated by ethological studies with chimpanzees, which have no speech capacity but considerably more language resources than we had heretofore suspected. Washoe, the first chimpanzee to be cultivated linguistically, had an extensive repertory of sign language symbols and could recognize hundreds more. Lucy, another chimpanzee, was able to construct compound words: "cry-hurt-food" for a hot radish, "dirty cat" for a cat she didn't like. This is certainly semantic creation. See Emily Hahn (1978) for an instructive review of animal communication.

[3]This can open a can of worms, since the French treat language as more encompassing than semiotics, and the Americans follow the hierarchy I have indicated. See Percy (1954) for extended discussion of this issue.

is all very well (and correct from the structuralist viewpoint) to claim that the unconscious is structured like a language. But how does one talk with it?

It must be understood, then, that speech is only a small part of an extensive semiotic communication that takes place between the two participants in the analytic process. I am not suggesting that one merely pay attention to how the patient sits or looks. I am suggesting something considerably more elaborate— that there are other extensively coded communications, as informational as speech, that take place in the intersubjective realm.

To begin with, language is also a form of behavior. As Wittgenstein put it, "Words are also deeds." This concept is familiar as Bateson's (1951) "metacommunication"; that is, every communication has a message about the message. There is an extensive literature on this subject, but it is generally agreed that the metamessage acts on the environment as a "command" or set of instructions (Bateson, 1951). Thus, language not only communicates, it also acts on the environment. It is a process of making. To put it simply, when we talk with someone, we also act with him. This action or behavior is, in the semiotic sense, coded like a language. *The language of speech and the language of action will be transforms of each other;* that is, they will be "harmonic variations" on the same theme. The resultant behavior of the dyad will emerge out of this semiotic discourse.

In other words, the therapist's interpretation is not exclusively an intellectual appraisal of what he has been hearing from the patient, it is also a piece of behavior which resonates to the patient. This interpretation qua behavior will be an extension of the problem under immediate examination, and the therapist's participation will be a transform of the problem. The therapist will become an extension of the patient's problem in order to become part of the solution (Levenson, 1972). The therapy proceeds, not out of the correctness of the interpretation, but out of the dialectical interaction of what is said and what is done in the patient-therapist dyad. How this interaction occurs may be the core issue of therapy.

The patient is a man in his early fifties who has just entered therapy for an incapacitating depression. He has a history of severe mood swings either caused by, or resulting in, vicissitudes in career and life status. He has had extreme ups and downs in his circumstances. He has also had a great deal of traditional therapy so that he is totally conversant with his dynamics. With great facility, he supplies explanations and interpretations, but all without visible effectiveness. He is also a person of considerable talent and verve. The therapist spends the first few sessions giving a virtuoso demonstration of what H. S. Sullivan called "expertness." He inquires, makes correlations, finds fresh perspectives. The patient's condition continues to decline.

After several sessions, the therapist begins to realize that the patient is making no effort at all. There are no dreams; the patient does not follow up or expand on any area of inquiry. He is like a drowning man who will not reach for a life belt. Proffering this interpretation would be quite useless, since the accompanying covert therapist behavior would be anger at the patient for failing to applaud his performance; i.e., "I give you my best and it is not enough for you!" Thus the therapist, instead of pointing out the patient's passivity and nonparticipation, contributes his own experience, saying that he feels obliged to dazzle the patient with his virtuosity, and moreover, he thinks that this is the way the patient has performed in his life; lots of flash but no solid work.

Two dreams follow. One has to do with work, stupendous tasks, one of which was getting two immense trees which are side by side to bend apart. This leads, as one might have expected, to the patient's first admission of his inability to arouse his wife's sexual interest.

The second dream I shall present in more detail. The patient arrives at a dock prepared to leave with his wife and children on an ocean cruise. A man intercepts him and indicates that he must first return home for some documents. He is offered a ride in a motorcycle sidecar, but is afraid of the wind and exposure. Suddenly he finds himself riding an old school bus, going very slowly. (The patient never rides public transportation, a point he makes each time he arrives by cab.) He is struck by the fact that as they proceed every small detail of the landscape is vividly etched; every crack, every building, every turn in the road.

The patient doesn't know what to make of this dream. He offers a few Freudian homilies from his kit bag; e.g., the cracks are vaginas, water means birth. These may well be correct, but behaviorally he is demonstrating his immense fatuousness. The therapist, delighted with the dream, which he perceives as a transference dream signaling the first real hope for change, rushes to interpret: arriving at the "Doc," intercepted by the therapist, told that he must first document himself before cruising off into the sunset, in some way afraid of or perhaps addicted to exhilaration and risk-taking, then the insight that the therapy consists of going slowly, reviewing his life, capturing the details; for once, not his offhand slipshod brilliance but *real* work. The patient is delighted with this effort; the therapist is equally delighted until it occurs to him that he has given another performance with a dream that should have been obvious to the patient with a little real effort. Again, the content of the interpretation is accurate, but the participation is a transform of the patient's facile virtuosity. The therapist finds that he feels manic in the sessions and delighted with his performance (which is usually a prodrome of disaster).

If the therapist had resisted the temptation to interpret the dream, surely an opportunity would have been lost. Or, would the patient have interpreted it himself? I think not. So, to interpret is to act out the content under discussion; to fail to interpret is to act out another aspect of the content under discussion, namely, the patient's impotence and sense of insufficiency in the face of life tasks. This is, I suspect, the dilemma inherent in the speech-action transform. Certainly it can be resolved. The patient emerged entirely from his depression after this session, settling comfortably into a detailed inquiry into his life.

Perhaps resolution lies in what is essentially an expansion of awareness of this bind. The patient brings in material, the therapist interprets, the interpretation has a spoken component that brackets or defines the issue under inquiry. It has also a behavioral component that reenacts the issue. Change may occur because the therapist is able, through his awareness of participation, to shift the homeostasis of the system; or, as I rather suspect, the simple repetitive restatement/reenactment of the critical issue in the patient's life may be what gradually makes for change. In this sense, the "working through" *is* the therapy; it is not a mere preliminary to interpretive insight.

Therapy is a process of entrapment and either extrication or explication, as I suggested above. The therapist cannot be therapeutic by endeavoring to be correct. The therapist cannot do therapy by maintaining the vaunted mythic neutrality or by "participating" in some wonderful way. His participation must be authentic rather than sincere (Levenson, 1974). (It is an irresistible digression to remind the reader that *sincere* derives etymologically from "to be without fault" and *authentic* from "to be one's own author"; or, alternately and oddly, "to be a murderer" [*Webster's New World Dictionary,* College edition]. To take responsibility for one's own actions, to act without the sanction of the gods, was anathema to the classical Greeks.) If interpretation is behavior, then with each interpretation the therapist risks himself authentically, discovers his meaning in transaction with the patient, and mobilizes his cure by participatory observation.

This has always been implicit in H. S. Sullivan's (1955) concept of participant observation. In its original discrete use it meant, I believe, to behave with the patient so as to maximize communication. Later it came to mean to use one's participation as a more extensive communication to and from the patient. But, ultimately, from both the operational viewpoint and the semiological, it means that every communication is a participation, which enlarges the communication, which in turn enlarges the participation. Every line of inquiry, including silence, is a choice of alternative participations. Every therapeutic situation—regardless of the therapist's restraint—involves interaction with the patient.

So, to understand the effect of an intervention, one must consider both the semantics and the pragmatics. The effect depends on the attribution of meaning, plus the behavior of the dyad around what is being said. This is akin to Strawson's (1963) division of a statement into what you are saying and what you are saying about it. In some cases this is obvious. For example, a therapist can make a quite accurate interpretation out of anger or a need to distance or seduce a patient. The patient will perceive the underlying meaning of the communication in the therapist's behavior. But, as I have suggested, there are subtler implications.

The patient, a young adult, dreams of being the princess with the pea under her mattress. The therapist suggests that she may be referring to an excessive touchiness or sensitivity to criticism. The patient feels hurt and begins to cry. This kind of resonance between content and behavior illuminates, I believe, the heart of the therapeutic dilemma. The therapist must deal with both the content of the interpretation and the simultaneous transformation of his participation into the sadistic accuser. Surely the patient's tearfulness is both confirmation and resistance, and surely any reasonably competent therapist can handle such an impasse without semiotics. But willy-nilly the therapist is practicing a semiotic skill. I must agree with Edelson's (1975) claim that psychoanalysis is a semiotic science and that:

... linguistic competence—the internalized knowledge of language that is possessed without conscious awareness of it or even the ability to explicate it—is a significant foundation of the psychoanalyst's clinical skill.... Much of the understanding the psychoanalyst attributes to empathy, intuition, or conscious or unconscious extralingual information actually derives from his own internalized linguistic (and semiological) competence, of whose nature and existence he may be altogether unaware [p. 63].

I would emphasize that this view of linguistics lies within the purview of structuralism and reflects its particular perspectives.[4] Structuralism claims that all human endeavor, not just speech, is coded like a language and that this pervasive coding may reflect the basic structuring of human thought. From this perspective there is no thought without language. What about dreams, which are largely visual? I suspect the answer would be that we do not see the dream, we have only the report of the patient. Moreover, one can easily make a case for a pictographic language, what Fromm (1951) called "the forgotten language." If one sees all human endeavor as systematically patterned, as a code, then speech, cultural manifestations such as myths or ceremonials, aspects of developmental psychology, artistic productions, psychoanalysis all become different transformations of the same holistic theme: every aspect of culture reflects and participates in every other aspect. Every piece is complete in itself and yet a part of the larger order (Levenson, 1976).

This particular world view is inherent in structuralism, and in a biological variant of structuralism, general systems theory, which has recently been popularized in Arthur Koestler's (1978) *Janus*. Although it may not be the last word, structuralism is both heuristically appealing and a prerequisite for

---

[4]Chomskian linguistics is another matter and presents a different paradigm for a linguistic psychoanalysis (see Edelson, 1975).

understanding the relevance of, say, Lévi-Strauss, Barthes, Lacan, and even Piaget. Lacan's (1977) statement that the unconscious is structured like a language and Barthes's (1970, p. 136) statement that all human discourse is one giant sentence reflect this viewpoint. We need only add that human behavior is an aspect of human discourse.

To recapitulate my four postulates: First, speech and language are not coterminous; second, language is to be subsumed under the larger rubric of semiotics; third, language is simultaneously behavior; and last, behavior is structured like a language, i.e., behavior is simultaneously language. Taken singly, these postulates are not terribly radical, but combined, several conclusions become inescapable. First, there is no real discontinuity between speech and action. They are simply harmonic variations on the same theme. Second, "acting in" the transference is not something that occurs intermittently at times of distress; it is a semiotic dimension that goes on continually. The relationship between the patient and the therapist is played out, over time, in a patterned, structured way. This *discourse of action* is isomorphic with whatever the patient and therapist are talking about. It is also isomorphic with whatever the patient has told the therapist about his outside life, past and present. All the dimensions of the therapy—the patient's history, contemporary issues in the patient's life (and the therapist's), dreams, memories, acting out, acting in, transference, countertransference—are of a piece. The ability to range across these transformational variations of the patient's theme is, as Edelson's statement affirms, the therapist's true métier.

From this perspective, countertransference cannot be considered a response only to the patient's infantile experience, or, obversely, only to the patient's real and present self. It must be an authentic response across *all* dimensions. Nor can it be only feeling about the patient; it must be also behavior toward him. We are interested in countertransference, not only because it distorts the truth of what we tell the patient, but because it determines the way we behave with him. And it is the correspondence of that behavior with other "languages" of the therapy which makes the treatment go.

Let us suppose that a patient is reporting inexplicable childhood beatings at the hands of his father. The therapist listens in silence. The patient accumulates and expands his sense of fury and finally abreacts in an explosion of heretofore suppressed rage. But it is quite likely that the patient is identified with his father and therefore subtly sadistic toward his own children or the therapist. He cannot hate the father without hating the father in himself. Thus his abreaction leads into another morass, namely, his self-loathing. Suppose that the therapist, instead of listening quietly, asks for more details, attempts to establish what the father was so angry about and what the context of the beatings was. Certainly this is a different participation. It may undercut the patient's anger, but it may also make the father more comprehensible and release the patient from his self-loathing. Let us suppose, as a third alternative, that the therapist listens to the tearful report and thinks to himself, "I can understand why someone might want to bash this guy." This may not demonstrate the proper psychoanalytic sangfroid, but it does cue the therapist to some aspect of the patient's behavior that the father was unable to deal with rationally.

All these approaches constitute initially different participations with the patient around the same material. One might argue that all but the inactivity are bad technique. Presumably the patient will progress along his own trajectory if the therapist waits it out. But silence *is* a participation. It might qualify as a universal nostrum if the patient always got around to further explication, but that does not always happen; sometimes resolution requires the therapist's participation, often at some risk to his neutrality. Sometimes our best results follow countertransferential acting out, losing our tempers, making mistakes. We may be left with a sneaking feeling that if things had proceeded properly, nothing would have resulted. Did H. S. Sullivan have this in mind when he reputedly said, "God keep me from a therapy that goes well!"? The material may never emerge if action is not taken; sometimes interaction with the patient must precede explanation. This is particularly true with patients we label borderline or schizoid. For these distrustful people, the correspondence of word and deed must be very high.

Therapeutic effectiveness, then, depends on the correspondence of "show" and "tell." In my earlier examples I focused on how the *patient* replays in the dyad the material that is being talked about. What does the *therapist* do? Interpretation is not enough, since an interpretation, though factually accurate, can be contextually wrong. A variety of working through takes place; not analysis of the patient's resistance to the interpretation, but rather a changing, or at least expanded, participation with the patient around the material. In some way the therapist must operate with the patient so as to be "heard."

Let us take that classical purveyor of therapists' despair, the masochistic patient. What is a sadist? Someone who is kind to a masochist, goes the old joke. Sadomasochistic impasses are not resolved by recourse to interpretations, which progressively become acts of desperation or rage on the part of the therapist. Something must happen between therapist and patient. The therapist who feels benign is not only remote, he is being sadistic. The therapist who feels kindly is repressing his rage and is afraid of his sadism. What is left? There is a Zen koan: "What do you do when you are hanging over a cliff, holding on with one hand?" "Open your fist!" is the answer. The therapist must recognize that there is no way to "hear" the patient without feeling angry and sadistic. There is no way to keep such feelings out of the therapy except by dissembling, and a lie in behavior is no less abusive than a lie in speech, so the therapist is, again, sadistic. Perhaps a true discourse requires that the therapist feel sadistic, but without mystification or double-binding of the patient. This would establish a harmonic integrity between the transference and the rest of the patient's life. The message might then be heard, and the discourse, in the structuralist sense, enriched. Corrective emotional experiences largely disappear in the tar pit of the patient's self-equilibrating system. I doubt that the patient grows because he is supplied with a nurturing environment. I suspect the patient must be engaged and experienced and responded to. If behavior is a language, then it must be heard. The therapist who is detached from an angry patient may hear him on the speech level but does not hear him on the action level.

I do not mean to imply that all the patient's communications are characterological fly traps. One also hears simple requests, quiet messages. To those, the therapist can answer directly. For example, the therapist informs the patient that he is going on vacation. The patient says, "Oh. Where?" Whether the therapist says nothing, asks for fantasies, or casually (perhaps even enthusiastically) answers the patient's question depends on his "third ear"—his unconscious linguistic skills. He could be wrong, but at least he listened. Doctrinaire positions about how one should handle this kind of exchange (e.g., the patient *always* feels deserted) seem to me sincere but not authentic. Perhaps one should first listen and then respond.

There is another genre of exchange often touted in the literature as proper technique. This example is from Greenson (1976, pp. 272–273). A patient points out that when he expresses political opinions that match the therapist's he get marginal cues of approval; when he doesn't, he is subjected to masked hostile analysis. He documents this position with examples. The therapist, decently and honestly, is amazed at his blind spot. He validates the patient's perception, admits his fault, and then asks, "Why do you feel obliged to satisfy my political views?"—just at the time when the patient has struck back! He plays out exactly that kind of authoritarian inquiry that the patient complained about. The discourse doubles back on itself and stops. The therapist says, in effect, "Very well, you caught me and you were right; now, let's get back to working on you." Why not wonder how they got into that subtle coercion? How does it match with other aspects of the patient's life? What was called out in the therapist? Let us suppose the patient was always very submissive to his father's opinions. That in itself does not explain why the therapist coerced him. Or, if we suppose the therapist has the tendency to coerce others, that still does not explain why he coerced this patient, or why he was so astonished at being caught out. Would it be unscientific to suggest that therapist and patient talk about their mutual experience rather than "analyze" it?

To summarize: Psychoanalysis originally postulated a serious antinomy between word and deed. It was the "talking cure," and what was acted upon could not be spoken about—that is, could not be analyzed. Classical psychoanalysis had no real lexicon for behavior, and it fell to H. S. Sullivan to introduce the operational concept of participant observation, a concept that others have broadened considerably since its introduction.[5] It now encompasses a rather wide range of behaviors and perceptions on the part of the therapist. Kohut (1971), Kernberg (1975), Muslin and Gill (1978), and Schafer (1978) have recently championed similar but more orthodox revisionisms of traditional psychoanalytic theory.

The concept of transference makes very little sense if one conceptualizes the patient as only talking or fantasying in the field of an inactive, blank-screen analyst. Such a view denies the operational reality that communication (if not speech) is always going on and that the transference arena is subtle ongoing discourse between the two participants even when the therapist is totally silent.

Linguistic concepts make it possible to view language as more than speech but much less than the total field of semiotic communication. From this viewpoint action, or behavior, *is* a language that is a precise transform of the speech. In the therapeutic context, whatever the dyad talks about will simultaneously be shown or played out between them. *The power of psychoanalysis may well depend on what is said about what is done* as a continuous, integral part of the therapy. Wittgenstein somewhere said, "What can be shown cannot be said," by which I suspect he meant that action and speech are really different modalities, parallel but not interchangeable. Therefore, I am not suggesting that the therapist match his behavior to what the patient says, for example, by being the good father. The interaction must be as authentic and perplexing an aspect of the total discourse as is speech. I don't think it is yet possible to know why therapeutic change occurs, since the neuropsychological mechanisms involved in language are still a "black box" for us; i.e., we do not know the brain mechanisms which mediate communication. There is some suggestive evidence from Pribram's work that there are a number of simultaneous languages of the brain. Insight, change, reprogramming of perception may require some synchronous fit or lining up of these different languages. Pribram (1971) postulates a holographic component to thinking which is too elaborate to discuss in detail here. But, according to his view, thought is "a search through the distributed holographic memory for resolution of uncertainty, i.e., for the acquisition of relevant information . . . the term relevant information includes appropriate *configurations* . . . when problems generate thought, contextual and configurational matchings are sought, not just specific items of information" (p. 370). I feel reasonably sure change is not as a consequence of the communication of meaning alone, although that may be a large part of it. The linguistically alert therapist, by paying attention to the concordance of spoken

---

[5]See Chrzanowski (1977) for a review of contributions to the participant-observation paradigm.

and acted language, facilitates the process even if he cannot say exactly what it is he is doing.

The psychoanalyst—he-who-talks-with-his-patients —then, is trying to understand and clarify an ordinary process, really most naturally performed without much thought about it. Cloaked in structuralist trappings, the inquiry has tones of grandeur. As Barthes (1970) put it, "Once again the exploration of language, conducted by linguistics, psychoanalysis, and literature, corresponds to the exploration of the cosmos" (p. 144). But, in a humbler simile, we are perhaps more like the centipede, trying to figure out how we manage to put one foot in front of the other without falling on our faces in the process.

REFERENCES

Bateson, G. (1951), *Communication: The Social Matrix of Psychiatry*. New York: Norton.

Barthes, R. (1970), To write: An intransitive verb? In: *The Structuralist Controversy*, ed. R. Macksey and E. Donato. Baltimore: Johns Hopkins Press.

Chrzanowski, G. (1977), *Interpersonal Approach to Psychoanalysis: Contemporary View of Harry Stack Sullivan*. New York: Gardner Press.

De Saussure, F. (1970), On the nature of language. In: *Introduction to Structuralism*, ed. M. Lane. New York: Basic Books.

Edelson, M. (1975), *Language and Interpretation in Psychoanalysis*. New Haven: Yale University Press.

Freud, S. (1914), Remembering, repeating, and working through. *Standard Edition* 12:147–156. London: Hogarth Press, 1958.

Fromm, E. (1951), *The Forgotten Language*. New York: Rinehart.

Greenson, R. (1976), *The Technique and Practice of Psychoanalysis*. New York: International Universities Press.

Hahn, E. (1978), A reporter at large (Animal communications: Part II). *The New Yorker*, April 24, pp. 42ff.

Kernberg, O. (1975), *Borderline Conditions and Pathological Narcissism*. New York: Jason Aronson.

Koestler, A. (1978), *Janus*. New York: Randon House.

Kohut, H. (Rep.) (1957), panel report: Clinical and theoretical aspects of resistance. *J. Amer. Psychoanal. Assn.*, 5:551.

—— (1971), *The Analysis of the Self: A Systematic Approach to the Psychoanalytic Treatment of Narcissistic Personality Disorders*. New York: International Universities Press.

Lacan, J. (1977), *Ecrits*. New York: Norton.

Levenson, E. (1972), *The Fallacy of Understanding*. New York: Basic Books.

—— (1974), Changing concepts of intimacy in psychoanalytic practice. *Contemp. Psychoanal.*, 10(3):359–369.

—— (1976), A holographic model of psychoanalytic change. *Contemp. Psychoanal.* 12(1):1–20.

Muslin, H., & Gill, M. (1978), Transference in the Dora case. *J. Amer. Psychoanal. Assn.*, 26(2):311–328.

Peirce, C. S. (1955), *Philosophical Writings*. New York: Dover.

Percy, W. (1954), *The Message in the Bottle*. New York: Farrar, Straus & Giroux.

Pribram, K. (1971), *Languages of the Brain*. Englewood Cliffs, N.J.: Prentice-Hall.

Ricoeur, P. (1971), The question of proof in Freud's writing. *J. Amer. Psychoanal. Assn.,* 25(4).

Schafer, R. (1978), *Language and Insight*. New Haven: Yale University Press.

Stone, L. (1973), On resistance to the psychoanalytic process. In: *Psychoanalysis and Contemporary Science,* Vol. 2, ed. B. Rubinstein. New York: Macmillan.

Strawson, P. F. (1963), On referring. In: *Philosophy and Ordinary Language,* ed. C. Caton. Urbana: University of Illinois Press.

Sullivan, H. S. (1955), *The Interpersonal Theory of Psychiatry,* ed. H. S. Perry & M. L. Gawel. New York: Norton.

Wilden, A. (1972), *System and structure: Essays in communication and exchange*. London: Tavistock.

CHAPTER 6

The Analysis of the Transference

Merton M. Gill

The analysis of the transference is generally acknowledged to be the central feature of analytic technique. Freud regarded transference and resistance as facts of observations, not as conceptual inventions. He wrote:

> . . . the theory of psychoanalysis is an attempt to account for two striking and unexpected *facts of observation* which emerge whenever an attempt is made to trace the symptoms of a neurotic back to their sources in his past life: the *facts* of transference and of resistance . . . anyone who takes up other sides of the problem while avoiding these two hypotheses will hardly escape a charge of misappropriation of property by attempted impersonation, if he persists in calling himself a psychoanalyst [1914b, p. 16]. (Italics mine)

Rapaport (1967) agrued in his posthumously published paper on the method of psychoanalysis that transference and resistance inevitably follow from the fact that the analytic situation is interpersonal.

An earlier version of this chapter appeared in the *Journal of the American Psychoanalytic Association* (supplement), 27:263–288, New York: International Universities Press, 1979. A case illustration has been added to the present revised and expanded version. It is a partial summary of a forthcoming monograph. Its preparation was supported in part by Research Scientist Award, NIMH grant #30731. Drs. Samuel D. Lipton, Irwin Hoffman, and Ilse Judas have helped me develop and clarify the ideas expressed in this paper.

Despite this general agreement on the centrality of transference and resistance in technique, it is my impression from my experience as a student and practitioner, from talking to students and colleagues, and from reading the literature that the analysis of the transference is not pursued as systematically and comprehensively as I think it could and should be. The relative privacy in which psychoanalysts work makes it impossible for me to state this view as anything more than my impression. But even if I am wrong, I believe it will be useful to review issues in the analysis of the transference and to explore why an important aspect of the analysis of the transference—namely, resistance to the awareness of the transference—is often slighted in analytic practice.

I must first distinguish clearly between two types of interpretation of the transference. The one is an interpretation of resistance to the *awareness* of transference. The other is an interpretation of resistance to the *resolution* of transference. This distinction has been best spelled out by Greenson (1967) and Stone (1967). The first kind of resistance may be called defense transference. Although that term is used mainly to refer to a phase of analysis characterized by a general resistance to the transference of wishes, it can also refer to a more isolated instance of transference of defense. The second kind of resistance is usually called transference resistance. With some oversimplification, one might say that in resistance to the awareness of transference, the transference is what is resisted, whereas in resistance to the resolution of transference, the transference does the resisting.

The distinction between resistance to the awareness of transference and resistance to the resolution of transference can be more descriptively stated in terms of implicit or indirect references to the transference versus explicit or direct references to the transference. The interpretation of resistance to awareness of the transference is intended to make the implicit transference explicit, whereas the interpretation of resistance to the resolution of transference is intended to make the patient realize that the already explicit transference does indeed include a determinant from the past.

It is also important to distinguish between the general concept of an interpretation of resistance to the resolution of transference and a particular variety of such an interpretation, namely, a genetic transference interpretation, that is, an interpretation of how an attitude in the present is an inappropriate carry-over from the past. While there is a tendency among analysts to deal with explicit references to the transference primarily by genetic transference interpretations, there are other ways of working toward a resolution of the transference. This paper will argue, first, that not enough emphasis is being given to interpretation of the transference in the here and now—that is, to the interpretation of implicit manifestations of the transference—and second, that interpretations intended to resolve the transference as manifested in explicit references to the transference should be primarily in the here and now rather than genetic interpretations.

A patient's statement that he feels the analyst is harsh, for example, is at least to begin with probably best dealt with not by interpreting that the patient is displacing his feeling that his father was harsh but by elucidating some other aspect of the patient's here-and-now attitude, such as what in the analytic situation seems to him to justify his feeling, or what anxiety made it so difficult for him to express his feelings. How the patient experiences the actual situation is an example of the role of the actual situation in a manifestation of transference, which will be one of my major topics.

Of course, both interpretations of the transference in the here and now and genetic transference interpretations are valid and together constitute a sequence. We presume that a resistance to the transference ultimately rests on the displacement toward the analyst of attitudes from the past.

Transference interpretations in the here and now and genetic transference interpretations are of course exemplified in Freud's writings and are in the repertoire of every analyst, but they are not distinguished sharply enough.

Because Freud's case histories focus much more on the yield of analysis than on the details of the process, they are readily but perhaps incorrectly construed as emphasizing work outside the transference much more than work with the transference and, even within the transference, as emphasizing genetic transference interpretations much more than work with the transference in the here and now (see Muslin and Gill, 1978). Freud's case reports may have played a role in establishing what I consider to be a common maldistribution of emphasis—not enough emphasis on the transference and, within the transference, not enough emphasis on the here and now.

Before I turn to the issues in the analysis of the transference, I will only mention a primary reason for failure to deal adequately with the transference. It is that work with the transference involves both analyst and patient in the most affect-laden and potentially disturbing interactions of analysis. Both participants in the analytic situation are motivated to avoid these interactions. Flight away from the transference and to the past can be a relief for both patient and analyst.

I divide my discussion into five parts: (1) The principle that the transference should be encouraged to expand as much as possible within the analytic situation because the analytic work is best done within the transference; (2) The interpretation of disguised allusions to the transference as a main technique for encouraging the expansion of the transference within the analytic situation; (3) The principle that all transference has a connection with something in the present actual analytic situation; (4) How the connection between transference and the actual analytic situation is used in interpreting resistance to the awareness of transference; and (5) The resolution of transference within the here and now and the role of genetic transference interpretation.

The Principle of Encouraging the Transference to Expand within the Analytic Situation

Surely all analysts will agree on the importance of transference interpretations; many will also agree that transference interpretations are more effective than interpretations outside the transference; but what of the relative roles of interpretation of the transference and interpretation outside the transference?

Freud seems to alternate between saying that the analysis of the transference is auxiliary to the analysis of the neurosis and saying that the analysis of the transference is equivalent to the analysis of the neurosis. The first position is supported by his statement that the transference resistance must be analyzed in order to get on with the work of analyzing the neurosis (1913, p. 144). It is also implied in his reiteration that the ultimate task of analysis is to remember the past, to fill in the gaps in memory. The second position is supported by his statement that victory must be won on the field of the transference (1912, p. 108) and that the mastery of the transference neurosis "coincides with getting rid of the illness which was originally brought to the treatment" (1916–1917, p. 444). In addition, he says that after the resistances are overcome, memories appear relatively easily (1914a, p. 155).

These two positions also find expression in the two very different ways in which Freud speaks of the transference. In the same paper he refers to the transference on the one hand as "*the most powerful resistance* to the treatment" (1912, p. 101) but on the other hand as doing us "the inestimable service of making the patient's . . . impulses immediate and manifest. For when all is said and done, it is impossible to destroy anyone *in absentia* or *in effigie*" (1912, p. 108).

I believe it can be demonstrated that his principal emphasis falls on the second position. He wrote once in summary: "Thus our therapeutic work falls into two phases. In the first, all the libido is forced from the symptoms into the transference and concentrated there; in the second, the struggle is waged around this new object and the libido is liberated from it" (1916–1917, p. 455).

That Freud advocated expanding the transference as much as possible within the analytic situation can be shown by clarifying that resistance is primarily expressed by repetition; that repetition takes place both within and outside the analytic situation but that the analyst seeks to deal with it primarily within the analytic situation; that repetition occurs not only in the motor sphere (acting) but also in the psychical sphere; and that the psychical sphere is not confined to remembering but includes current experiences too.

Freud's emphasis that the purpose of resistance is to prevent remembering can obscure his point that resistance shows itself primarily by repetition, whether inside or outside the analytic situation: "The greater the resistance, the more extensively will acting out (repetition) replace remembering" (1914a, p. 151). Similarly, in "The Dynamics of Transference," he said that the main reason that the transference is so well suited to serve the resistance is that the unconscious impulses "do not want to be remembered . . . but endeavor to reproduce themselves . . ." (1912, p. 108). The transference is a resistance primarily insofar as it is a repetition.

The point can be restated in terms of the relationship between transference and resistance. The resistance expresses itself in repetition, that is, in transference both inside and outside the analytic situation. To deal with the transference is therefore equivalent to dealing with the resistance. Freud emphasized transference as repetition *within* the analytic situation so strongly that it has come to be defined as such, even though conceptually speaking repetition outside the analytic situation is also transference. Freud himself once used the term that way:

We soon perceive that the transference is itself only a piece of repetition, and that the repetition is a transference of the forgotten past not only to the doctor but also as to all other aspects of the current situation. We . . . find . . . the compulsion to repeat, which now replaces the impulsion to remember, not only in [the patient's] personal attitude to his doctor but also in every other activity and relationship which may occupy his life at the time [1914a, p. 151].

It is important to realize that the expansion of the repetition inside the analytic situation (whether or not in a reciprocal relationship to repetition outside the analytic situation) is the avenue to control the repetition: "The main instrument for curbing the patient's compulsion to repeat and for turning it into a motive for remembering lies in the handling of the transference. We render the compulsion harmless, and indeed useful, by giving it the right to assert itself in a definite field" (1914a, p. 154).

Kanzer has discussed this issue well in "The Motor Sphere of the Transference" (1966). He writes of a "double-pronged stick-and-carrot" technique by which the transference is fostered within the analytic situation and discouraged outside the analytic situation. The "stick" is the principle of abstinence, as exemplified in the admonition against making important decisions during treatment, and the "carrot" is the opportunity afforded the transference to expand within the treatment "in almost complete freedom," as in a "playground" (Freud, 1914a, p. 154).

As Freud put it: "Provided only that the patient shows compliance enough to respect the necessary conditions of the analysis, we regularly succeed in giving all the symptoms of the illness a new transference meaning, and in replacing his ordinary neurosis by a 'transference neurosis' of which he can be cured by the therapeutic work" (1914a, p. 154).

The reason it is desirable for the transference to be expressed within the treatment is that there it "is at every point accessible to our intervention" (1914a, p. 154). Freud later made the same point this way: "We have followed this new edition [the transference neurosis] of the old disorder from its start, we have observed its origin and growth, and we are especially well able to find our way about in it since, as its object, we are situated at its very center" (1916-1917, p. 444). It is not that the transference is forced into the treatment; rather, it is spontaneously but implicitly present and is encouraged to expand and become explicit in the course of analysis.

Freud emphasized *acting* in the transference so strongly that one can overlook that repetition in the transference is not necessarily *enacted*. Repetition need not go as far as motor behavior. It can also be expressed in attitudes, feelings, and intentions, and indeed it often does take such forms. Such repetition is in the psychical, rather than the motor, sphere. It is important to make that point clear, because Freud can be mistakenly understood as saying that repetition in the psychical sphere can only mean remembering the past, as when he writes that the analyst "is prepared for a perpetual struggle with his patient to keep in the psychical sphere all the impulses which the patient would like to direct into the motor sphere; and he celebrates it as a triumph for the treatment if he can bring it about that something the patient wishes to discharge in action is disposed of through the work of remembering" (1914a, p. 153).

It is true that the analyst aims to convert acting in the motor sphere into awareness in the psychical sphere, but transference may be in the psychical sphere to begin with, albeit disguised. The psychical sphere includes awareness in the transference as well as remembering.

One objection of both analysts and patients to a heavy emphasis on transference interpretation of associations about the patient's real life is that such interpretation means the analyst is disregarding the importance of what goes on in the patient's real life. This criticism is not justified. To emphasize the transference meaning is not to deny or belittle other meanings of the content, but to focus on the particular meaning that is the most important for the analytic process for the reasons I have just summarized.

Interpretations of resistance to the transference can also appear to belittle the importance of the patient's outside life if they unduly emphasize the patient's outside behavior as an acting out of the transference. Some of the patient's actions in the outside world may be an expression of and resistance to the transference—that is, acting out. But the interpretation of associations about actions in the outside world as having transference implications need mean only that the patient's choice of outside action to figure in his associations is codetermined by the need to express a transference indirectly. It is because of the resistance to awareness of the transference that the transference has to be disguised. When the disguise is unmasked by interpretation it becomes clear that, despite the inevitable differences between the outside situations and the transference situation, the content is the same for the purpose of the analytic work. Therefore the analysis of the transference and the analysis of the neurosis coincide.

I stress this point particularly because some readers of earlier versions of this paper understood me to be advocating the analysis of the transference for its own sake rather than in the effort to overcome the neurosis. But as I cited above, Freud wrote that mastering the transference neurosis "coincides with getting rid of the illness which was originally brought to the treatment" (1916–1917, p. 444).[1]

How the Transference Is Encouraged to Expand within the Analytic Situation

The analytic situation itself fosters the development of attitudes with primary determinants in the past, i.e., transferences. The analyst's reserve provides the patient with few and equivocal cues. The purpose of the analytic situation is to foster the development of strong emotional responses, and the very fact that the patient has a neurosis means, as Freud said, that "it is a perfectly normal and intelligible thing that the libidinal cathexis [we would now add negative feelings] of someone who is partly unsatisfied, a cathexis which is held ready in anticipation, should be directed as well to the figure of the doctor" (1912, p. 100).

Thus the analytic setup itself fosters the expansion of the transference within the analytic situation; the interpretation of resistance to the awareness of transference will further this expansion.

There are inportant resistances to awareness of the transference in both

---

[1]In response to a suggestion by the editor of this volume, I add the following clarification: Freud's statement that the mastery of the transference neurosis is tantamount to the analysis of the patient's original neurosis implies that the neurosis can be expressed wholly in terms of the relationship between patient and analyst. This does not amount to a denial of intrapsychic organization in favor of interpersonal manifestations; rather, it is to say that the neurosis as intrapsychically organized expresses itself in the interpersonal interaction. Presumably the resolution of the transference neurosis is marked by a revision of the intrapsychic organization, i.e., the so-called structural change. Nor does Freud's view imply that a neurosis is simply the intrapsychic result of the interpersonal experiences of development. For the way in which interpersonal experience is understood and incorporated into the intrapsychic organization is codetermined by innate factors, whether these are called drives, instincts, primarily autonomous apparatuses, or by the term with the fewest restrictive connotations: schemata.

patient and analyst. The patient's resistances stem from the difficulty in recognizing erotic and hostile impulses toward the very person to whom they have to be disclosed. The analyst's resistances stem from the patient's tendency to attribute to him the very attitudes that are most likely to cause him discomfort. Patients often will not voice the attitudes they believe the analyst has toward them because of a general feeling that it is impertinent to concern themselves with the analyst's feelings and because of a more specific fear that the analyst will not like having such attitudes ascribed to him. Thus the analyst must be alert not only to the attitudes patients have toward him but also to the attitudes patients ascribe to him. The analyst will be much more attuned to this important area of transference if he is able to see himself as a participant in an interaction, as I shall discuss below.

The investigation of the attitudes ascribed to the analyst makes easier the subsequent investigation of the intrinsic factors in the patient that played a role in such ascriptions. For example, the exposure of the patient's ascription of sexual interest in him to the analyst, and genetically to the parent, makes easier the subsequent exploration of the patient's sexual wish toward the analyst, and genetically toward the parent.

The patient's resistances to awareness of these attitudes cause them to appear in various disguises in his manifest associations, and the analyst's resistances cause a reluctance to unmask the disguise. The most commonly recognized disguise is displacement, but identification is an equally important one. In displacement, the patients' attitudes are narrated as being toward a third party. In identification, the patient attributes to himself attitudes he believes the analyst has toward him.

To encourage the expansion of the transference within the analytic situation, the disguises in which the transference appears have to be interpreted. In the case of displacement, the interpretation will be of allusions to the transference in associations not manifestly about the transference. This is a kind of interpretation that every analyst often makes. In the case of identification, the analyst interprets the attitude the patient ascribes to himself as an identification with an attitude he attributes to the analyst. (See Lipton [1977b] for illuminating illustrations of such disguised allusions to the transference.)

Many analysts believe that transference manifestations are infrequent and sporadic at the beginning of an analysis and that the transference does not dominate the patient's associations until a transference neurosis has developed. Other analysts, including myself, believe that the patient's associations have transference meanings from the beginning to the end of analysis. I think those of the former school of thought fail to recognize the pervasiveness of indirect allusions to the transference, that is, the resistance to the awareness of the transference.

In his autobiography, Freud wrote: "The patient remains under the influence of the analytic situation even though he is not directing his mental activities on to a particular subject. We shall be justified in assuming that nothing will occur to him that has not some reference to that situation" (1925, pp. 40–41). Since it is obvious that associations are often not directly about the analytic situation, the interpretation of Freud's remark rests on what he meant by the "analytic situation."

What Freud meant is, I believe, clarified by reference to a statement he made in "The Interpretation of Dreams" (1900): that when the patient is told to say whatever comes to his mind, his associations become directed by the "purposive ideas inherent in the treatment," of which there are two: one relating to the illness and the other—about which Freud said the patient has "no suspicion"—relating to the analyst (1900, pp. 531–532). If the patient has "no suspicion" of the theme relating to the analyst, what are clearly implied are the patient's implicit references to the analyst. My interpretation of Freud's statement is that it not only specifies the themes inherent in the patient's associations but also means that the associations are *simultaneously* directed by these two purposive ideas, not sometimes by one and sometimes by the other.

One important reason why the early and continuing presence of the transference is not always recognized is that it is considered to be absent in the patient who is talking freely and apparently without resistance. As Muslin and I (Gill and Muslin, 1976) pointed out in a paper on the early interpretation of transference, resistance to the transference is probably present from the beginning, even if the patient appears to be talking freely. Issues that do not manifestly involve the transference may nevertheless also be allusions to the transference, but the analyst has to be alert to the pervasiveness of such allusions to discern them.

The analyst should, then, proceed on the assumption that the patient's associations have pervasive transference implications. This assumption is not to be confused with denial or neglect of the current aspects of the patient's life situation. Theoretically, it is always possible to give precedence to a transference interpretation if only one can discern it through its disguise by resistance. I am not disputing the desirability of learning as much as one can about the patient, if only to be in a position to make more correct interpretations of the transference. One therefore does not interfere with an apparently free flow of associations, especially early in analysis, unless the transference threatens the analytic situation to the point where its interpretation is mandatory rather than optional.

With the recognition that even the apparently freely associating patient may also be showing resistance to awareness of the transference, the formulation that one should not interfere as long as useful information is being gathered should replace Freud's dictum that the transference should not be interpreted until it becomes a resistance (1913, p. 139).

Connection of All Transference Manifestations with Something in the Actual Analytic Situation

As a prelude to a further discussion of the interpretive technique for expanding the transference within the analytic situation, I will argue that every transference has some connection with some aspect of the current analytic situation. Of course, all the determinants of a transference are current in the sense that the past can exert an influence only insofar as it exists in the present. What I am referring to is the current reality of the analytic situation, that is, what actually goes on between patient and analyst in the present.

All analysts would doubtless agree that there are both current and transference determinants of the analytic situation, and probably no analyst would argue that a transference idea can be expressed without contamination, as it were—that is, without connection to anything current in the patient-analyst relationship. Nevertheless, I believe the technical implications of this fact are often neglected in practice, as I will discuss later. Here I want only to argue for the connection.

As several authors (e.g., Kohut, 1959; Loewald, 1960) have pointed out, Freud's early use of the term transference in "The Interpretation of Dreams" (1900)—albeit in a connection not immediately recognizable as related to the present-day use of the term—reveals the fallacy of considering that transference can be expressed free of any connection to the present. That early use referred to the fact that an unconscious idea can only be expressed as it becomes connected to preconscious or conscious content. In the dream, the phenomenon with which Freud was then concerned, transference took place from an unconscious wish to a day residue. In "The Interpretation of Dreams," Freud in fact used the term transference both for this general rule—that an unconscious content is expressible only as it becomes transferred to a preconscious or conscious content—and for the specific application of this rule to a patient's transference to the analyst. Just as the day residue is the attachment point of the dream wish, so must there be an analytic situation residue— though Freud did not use that term—as the attachment point of the transference wish.

Analysts have always limited their behavior, both in variety and intensity, to increase the extent to which the patient's behavior is determined by his idiosyncratic interpretation of the analyst's behavior. Unfortunately analysts sometimes limit their behavior so much, as compared to Freud's practice, that they even conceptualize the entire relationship with the patient as a matter of technique without any nontechnical personal relationship, as Lipton (1977a) has pointed out.

But no matter how far analysts attempt to limit their behavior, the very existence of the analytic situation provides patients with innumerable cues that inevitably become their rationale for transference responses. In other words, the analytic situation is real and cannot be ignored. It is easy to forget this truism in one's zeal to diminish the role of the current situation in determining the patient's responses. One can try to keep past and present determinants relatively distinct from one another, but one cannot obtain either in "pure culture." As Freud wrote: "I insist on this procedure [the couch], however, for its purpose and result are to prevent the transference from mingling with the patient's associations imperceptibly, to isolate the transference and to allow it to come forward in due course sharply defined as a resistance" (1913, p. 134). Even "isolate" is too strong a word in the light of the inevitable intertwining of the transference with the current situation.

If analysts remain under the illusion that the current cues they provide to the patient can be reduced to the vanishing point, they may be led into a silent withdrawal that is not far removed from the caricature of an analyst as someone who does indeed refuse to have any personal relationship with the patient. In such cases, silence has become a technique rather than merely an indication that the analyst is listening. The patient's responses then can be mistaken for uncontaminated transference when they are in fact transference adaptations to the silence.

The recognition that all transference must take its point of departure from the actual analytic situation has a crucial implication for the technique of interpreting resistance to the awareness of transference, to which I turn now.

The Role of the Actual Situation in Interpreting Resistance to the Awareness of Transference

Once the analyst becomes persuaded of the centrality of transference and the importance of encouraging it to expand within the analytic situation, he has to identify the presenting and plausible interpretations of resistance to the awareness of transference that he should make. Here his most reliable guide is the cues offered by what is actually going on in the analytic situation: on the one hand such events as a change in time of session or a specific interpretation, and on the other hand the patient's experience of the analytic situation as reflected in explicit remarks about it, however fleeting they may be. This is the primary technical yield of the recognition that any transference must be linked to the actuality of the analytic situation. The cues point to the nature of the transference just as the day residue for a dream may point to latent dream thoughts.

Focusing attention on the current stimulus for a transference elaboration will keep the analyst from making mechanical transference interpretations— from seeing allusions to the transference in associations not manifestly about the transference without offering any plausible basis for such an interpretation.

Attending to the current stimulus also offers some protection against the analyst's inevitable tendency to project his own views onto the patient, either because of countertransference or because of a preconceived theoretical bias.

The analyst may be very much surprised at what it is in his behavior that the patient finds important, for the patient's responses will be idiosyncratically determined by the transference. The patient may respond to seemingly trivial things because, as in dream displacement to a trivial aspect of the day residue, dream displacement onto something trivial can better serve resistance in analysis.

Because the stimulus to the transference is connected to conflictful material, it may be difficult to find. It may be so quickly disavowed that the patient's awareness of it is only transitory. With the discovery of the disavowal, the patient may also gain insight into how it repeats a disavowal made earlier in life. In search for the present stimuli that the patient is responding to transferentially, the analyst must therefore remain alert to fleeting, apparently trivial manifest references to himself as well as to the events of the analytic situation.

If the analyst interprets the patient's attitudes in a spirit of seeing their plausibility in the light of the information the patient has rather than in the spirit of either affirming or denying them, the way is open for their further expression and elucidation. Thus the analyst respects the patient's effort to be plausible and realistic rather than seeing his transference attitudes as manufactured out of whole cloth.

I believe it is so important to make a transference interpretation plausible to the patient in terms of current stimuli that, if the analyst is persuaded that the manifest content has an important transference implication but cannot see a current stimulus for the attitude, he should explicitly say so if he decides to make the transference interpretation anyway. The patient himself may then be able to identify the current stimulus.

It is sometimes argued that the analyst's attention to his own behavior as a precipitant of the transference will increase the patient's resistance to recognizing the transference. I believe, on the contrary, that because of the inevitable interrelationship of the current and transference determinants, it is only through interpretation that they can be disentangled.

It is also argued that the transference cannot be advantageously interpreted until it has reached optimal intensity. It is true that too quick an interpretation of the transference can serve a defensive function for the analyst and deny him the information he needs to make a more appropriate transference interpretation. But it is also true that delaying interpretation may result in an unmanageable transference. Deliberate delay can be a manipulation in the service of abreaction rather than analysis and, like silence, can lead to a response to the actual situation which is mistaken for uncontaminated transference. Obviously, important issues of timing are involved. I believe an important clue to when a transference interpretation is appropriate lies in whether it can be made plausibly in terms of something in the current analytic situation.

A reader of an earlier version of this paper understood me to be saying that all the analyst need do is interpret the allusion to the transference; that I did not see the necessity of interpreting why the transference had to be expressed by allusion rather than directly. Of course the second kind of interpretation is necessary, as I meant to imply in saying that, when the analyst approaches the transference in the spirit of seeing how it appears plausible to the patient, he paves the way for its further elucidation and expression.

The Relative Roles of Resolution of the Transference within the Analytic Situation and by Genetic Transference Interpretation

Freud's emphasis on remembering as the goal of the analytic work implies that remembering is the principal avenue to the resolution of the transference. But his delineation of the successive steps in the development of analytic technique (1920, p. 18) makes clear that he saw this development as a change from an effort to reach memories directly to the utilization of the transference as the necessary intermediary to reaching the memories.

Freud also described resistance as being primarily overcome in the transference, with remembering following relatively easily thereafter:

From the repetitive reactions which are exhibited in the transference we are led along the familiar paths to the awakening of the memories, which appear without difficulty, as it were, after the resistance has been overcome (1914a, p. 154–155);

and:

This revision of the process of repression can be accomplished only in part in connection with the memory traces of the process which led to repression. The *decisive* part of the work is achieved by creating in the patient's relation to the doctor—in the 'transference'—new editions of the old conflicts . . . Thus the transference becomes the battlefield on which all the mutually struggling forces should meet one another [1916–1917, p. 454; emphasis added].

It was this primary insight that Strachey (1934) clarified in his seminal paper on the therapeutic action of psychoanalysis.

There are two main ways in which work with the transference in the here and now fosters resolution of the transference. The first lies in clarifying the cues in the current situation that are the patient's point of departure for a transference elaboration. The exposure of the current point of departure at once raises the question whether it is adequate to support the conclusion drawn from it. Relating the transference to a current stimulus is, after all, part of the patient's effort to make the transference attitude plausibly determined by the present. The reserve and ambiguity of the analyst's behavior increase the range of apparently plausible conclusions the patient may draw. If an examination of the basis for such conclusions makes clear that the actual situation is subject to meanings other than the one the patient discerned, he will more readily consider his preexisting bias, that is, his transference.

A reader of an earlier version of this paper suggested that, in speaking of the current analytic relationship and the relation between the patient's conclusions and the information on which they seem plausibly based, I am implying some absolute conception of what is real in the analytic situation, with the analyst as the final arbiter. That is not the case. My statement that the patient must come to see that his information is subject to other possible interpretations implies the very contrary to an absolute conception of reality. In fact, analyst and patient engage in a dialogue in the spirit of attempting to arrive at a *consensus* about reality, not at some fictitious absolute reality.

The second way in which work with the transference in the here and now fosters resolution of the transference is through the patient's experience of something new in the very interpretation of the transference. The patient is being treated in a way that differs from what he expected. Analysts seem reluctant to emphasize this new experience, as though it endangers the role of insight and argues for interpersonal influence as the significant factor in change. Strachey's (1934) emphasis on the new experience in the mutative transference interpretation has unfortunately been overshadowed by his views on introjection, which have been mistakenly seen as advocating manipulation of the transference. In fact, Strachey saw introjection of the more benign superego of the analyst as only a temporary step on the road toward insight. The new experience is not only to be distinguished from the interpersonal influence of a transference gratification; it is also to be seen as accompanying insight—into both the patient's biased expectation and the new experience itself. As Strachey points out, what is unique about the transference interpretation is that insight and the new experience take place in relation to the very person who was expected to behave differently, and it is this that gives the work in the transference its immediacy and effectiveness. While Freud did stress the affective immediacy of the transference, he did not make the new experience explicit.

It is important to recognize that transference interpretation is the joining of experience to insight. Both are needed to bring about and maintain the desired changes in the patient. It is also important to recognize that no new techniques of intervention are required to provide the new experience. It is an inevitable accompaniment of interpretation of the transference in the here and now.

It is often overlooked that although Strachey said that only transference interpretations are mutative, he also noted with approval that most interpretations are outside the transference. In a further explication of Strachey's paper and entirely consistent with Strachey's position, Rosenfeld (1972) has pointed out that clarification of material outside the transference is often necessary to determine the appropriate transference interpretation and that both genetic transference interpretations and extratransference interpretations play an important role in working through. Strachey said relatively little about working through, but surely nothing against the need for it, and he explicitly recognized a role for recovery of the past in the resolution of the transference.

My own position is to emphasize the role of the analysis of the transference in the here and now both in interpreting resistance to the awareness of transference and in working toward its resolution by relating it to the actuality of the analytic situation. I agree that extra transference and genetic transference interpretations, and of course working through, are important too. The matter is one of emphasis. I believe interpretation of resistance to awareness of the transference should figure in the majority of sessions, and that if this is done by relating the transference to the actual analytic situation, the very same interpretation is the beginning of work toward the resolution of the transference. To justify this view more persuasively would require detailed case material.

It may be considered that I am siding with the Kleinians, who many analysts believe mistakenly give the analysis of the transference too great a role, if not an exclusive one, in the analytic process. It is true that Kleinians emphasize the analysis of the transference more, in their writings at least, than do the general run of analysts. Indeed Anna Freud's (1968) complaint that the concept of transference has become overexpanded seems to be directed against the Kleinians. One of the reasons the Kleinians consider themselves the true followers of Freud in technique is precisely because of the emphasis they put on the analysis of the transference. Hanna Segal (1967), for example, writes as follows: "To say that all communications are seen as communications about the patient's phantasy as well as current external life is equivalent to saying that all communications contain something relevant to the transference situation. In Kleinian technique, the interpretation of the transference is often more central than in the classical technique" (pp. 173–174).

Despite the Kleinians' disclaimers, my reading of their case material leads me to agree with the apparently general view that Kleinian transference interpretations often deal with so-called deep and genetic material without adequate connection to the present analytic situation and thus differ sharply from the kind of transference interpretation I am advocating.

The insistence on exclusive attention to any particular aspect of the analytic process, such as the analysis of the transference in the here and now, can become a fetish. I do not say that other kinds of interpretation should not be made, but I believe the emphasis on transference interpretations within the analytic situation needs to be increased, or at least reaffirmed, and that we need more clarification and specification of just when other kinds of interpretations are in order.

Of course it is sometimes tactless to make a transference interpretation. Surely one reason for not making a particular transference interpretation, even if one seems apparent to the analyst, would be preoccupation with an important extratransference event; another would be an inadequate degree of rapport, to use Freud's term, to sustain the sense of criticism, humiliation, or other painful feeling the particular interpretation might engender, even though the analyst had no intention of evoking such a response. The issue may well be, however, not whether an interpretation of resistance to the transference should be made, but whether the therapist can find that transference interpretation that, in the light of the total situation—both transference and current—the patient is able to hear and benefit from primarily as the analyst intends it.

Transference interpretations, like extratransference interpretations or indeed any behavior on the analyst's part, can have an effect on the transference which in turn needs to be examined if the result of an analysis is to depend as little as possible on unanalyzed transference. The result of any analysis depends on the analysis of the transference, the persisting effects of unanalyzed transference, and the new experience that I have emphasized as the unique merit of transference interpretation in the here and now. It is especially important to remember this lest one's zeal to ferret out the transference itself becomes an unrecognized and objectionable actual behavior, with its own repercussions on the transference.

The emphasis I am placing on the analysis of resistance to the transference could easily be misunderstood as implying that it is always easy to recognize the transference as disguised by resistance or that analysis would proceed without a hitch if only such interpretations were made. I mean to imply neither. I believe that the analytic process will have the best chance of success if correct interpretation of resistance to the transference and work with the transference in the here and now are the core of the analytic work.

Case Illustration

I believe the most faithful rendering of the therapeutic process is by the report of a full session. No single session is likely to demonstrate all the points made in this paper, however, nor can I find any session that is not open to criticism of some kind.

I chose the following session for these reasons: Though the therapist may well be considered too intrusive, his very activity increases the number of illustrations of interpretation of the transference. Indeed, the therapist himself comments on the degree of his activity. (In a later session, it becomes clear that the patient feels competitve in seeing connections and interprets the therapist's activity as besting him in this contest.) Since the patient is being seen only once a week, most people would call this treatment "psychotherapy." I am of the opinion that the range of settings—defined as frequency of sessions, couch or chair, type of patient, and experience of therapist—in which the technique of analysis of the transference is appropriate is far broader than is usually considered to be the case, so this illustration serves to exemplify that view, too. The session is only the second of the therapy and thus illustrates what I mean by employing this technique from the beginning. My comments will be largely restricted to how the analysis of the transference is being exemplified, though of course much else could be said.

The patient understood that in return for being seen by an experienced therapist the hours would be recorded and used for teaching purposes. The context of the second hour was that the first hour was to have been followed by a gap of three weeks because the therapist would be away. His plans changed, however, and so he phoned the patient to offer an earlier appointment. There was some difficulty in finding a time that suited both therapist and patient. The second hour took place ten days after the first. To save space, the account is given in summary rather than verbatim, but it follows the transcript faithfully.

The patient began by saying he keeps a diary and had written something in it that he thought might be helpful. He asked if he should read it and the therapist said that was all right. It was an expression of great loneliness. The therapist asked if it had been written for him. The patient did not think so, but rather that after writing it he thought it might be helpful to share it. In response to a question, he said the central issue in the material he read is his loneliness. The therapist asked whether he had felt he could communicate this better by writing it down, and he said he had. The therapist asked when he had written the diary entry and established that it was before he had phoned the patient. The therapist said that he nevertheless wondered if the loneliness implied a reference to the long time the patient had anticipated waiting before the second appointment.

This is an interpretation which suggests that the material not manifestly about the relationship alludes to the relationship. It is made plausible by an event in the therapy—the anticipated long wait for the second appointment.

The patient said this might be true and that he was supposed to have had a last summing-up appointment with his previous therapist but he too had been away. This seems like an indirect confirmation of the interpretation. The therapist suggested this indicated there might be something to what he had said, and the patient said: "What you're saying sounds valid and hits a nerve." He added that perhaps he is expecting a lot from the therapist. He referred to this as "setting himself up," and the therapist suggested this meant he feared an awful letdown.

The patient agreed, but the therapist, instead of following this up as he well might have, asked what the patient's reaction had been to the phone call. He said he had been surprised and the therapist asked if that was all. He said he had been angry because he had had to rearrange his schedule. The therapist asked why he hadn't refused the offer. He said it had seemed important to the therapist. When the therapist said the patient then was accommodating him, the patient replied that he thought he was making himself look bad.

The therapist suggested that the patient apparently felt the therapist might react by feeling that it was inappropriate for the patient to talk as though he were doing the therapist a favor after the therapist had put himself out. The patient agreed.

The therapist asked whether the patient had speculated about what had motivated the offer of an appointment. The patient said the therapist had wanted to maintain continuity. The therapist responded that apparently his concern was unnecessary since the patient had been prepared to wait. But, after all, was it not true that the patient's loneliness did indicate that he was reacting to the long gap between appointments?

The therapist seems defensive here. He may indeed be reacting to the spurning of his concern. In fact, his motivation may well have included a wish to have a session for the class he was teaching. It is not impossible that this speculation had occurred to the patient (it has in similar situations) and that therapist and patient were colluding to keep this thought unspoken.

The therapist suggested that perhaps the patient's reaction was a denial of how strongly he felt about the long wait till the next appointment. The patient responded that "this will sound dumb," but sometimes he feels like abandoning everything and just devoting himself to working out his problems—but, after all, he has a job and other responsibilities.

The therapist suggested that the patient had apparently interpreted the interpretation as a rebuke that he was not sufficiently interested in the therapy. This is an example of an interpretation of an allusion to the patient's experience of the relationship made plausible by what the therapist had said. It is an example of how the transference is an amalgam of past and present, or contributions from both therapist and patient.

The patient said the interpretation didn't "ring exactly true." The therapist tried to justify his interpretation by reminding the patient that he had introduced his response by saying it would sound dumb. The patient still didn't accept it and said it was ironic that he had rushed away from a religious service to keep the appointment. But, after all, he continued, this was also a cleansing of the soul.

The therapist asked about a Hebrew expression the patient had used in his initial reading from his diary, and the patient explained he had spent a year in Israel and was good at languages. The therapist had indicated he thought the patient's knowledge of Hebrew was extensive.

After a pause the patient said he was feeling intensely emotional and was surprised at feeling this way. The therapist asked for clarification of the feeling and the patient responded that he felt the therapist was "zeroing in" on sore spots the patient would prefer not to deal with. He is surprised at the therapist's ability to touch on important issues even though he doesn't know the patient very well.

The therapist asked for an illustration and the patient responded that it was the therapist's speaking of his loneliness, but then he recognized that he had introduced that topic himself. The therapist interpreted that the patient might be feeling two ways: on the one hand he wants to be understood, but on the other hand he would prefer that the therapist not deal with sore points so directly and rapidly. The patient agreed and said he didn't feel ready to trust the therapist and was afraid of his own thoughts and feelings.

The therapist asked for a further clarification of what made the patient feel he was "zeroing in" so rapidly and the patient said he was not sure. The therapist asked if the patient was finding this therapy different from his previous one. The patient replied that he had built up a lot of trust in the previous therapist. He did not think the (current) therapist was acting differently from the people he was used to.

The therapist said he was concerned that he had been directing the conversation too much and he would wait for the patient to take the lead. After a pause, the patient said he had had a strange experience the week before. A girl had invited him to stay at her apartment because they came home very late from a date. He believed she expected him to make a sexual advance but he did not and he is concerned because he feels he should have.

The therapist might have interpreted here that this association—clearly spontaneous—was an allusion to the fact that the appointment had been initiated by the therapist's call, that is, that he had been issued the invitation. The interpretation need not have included a sexual parallel.

The patient then spontaneously referred to his concern about homosexuality (possible evidence that the phone call was felt to be a homosexual seduction but probably premature to interpret); he said that a sexual experience relieved his loneliness a little and that he felt like a "weirdo" because he had never had intercourse with a woman.

The patient had been pausing frequently and the therapist called attention to these pauses, saying that the patient apparently was not accustomed to speaking about himself in therapy without pausing for replies. He replied that his previous therapist had said that he was afraid to talk about his homosexuality and would start and stop in talking about it as if offering a kind of bait. The therapist said he was not suggesting that the patient was using it as bait but was asking whether the patient was aware of not taking the initiative; the therapist was concerned that he might be directing the conversation. The therapist explained that they would be more likely to deal with the patient's concerns if he would take more initiative in the conversation. He disavowed wanting the patient to continue with the topic of homosexuality but raised the question of how the patient saw the relation between homosexuality and loneliness. The therapist then stopped himself, saying he was again directing, but asked whether the patient feared he would stress homosexuality and ignore the loneliness. The patient thought not and said he was primarily wondering how the woman had interpreted his behavior.

After a pause, the patient said he was concerned about his job because he had given notice some time before and the job was finally being offered to someone else. The patient had introduced this topic by saying his language gave him away; the therapist had asked what he had been reluctant to reveal. The reply was that he feared being told not to worry so much about his job. Then he said he feared he was second-guessing himself and that the therapist would think him a "total idiot."

The therapist suggested that this was perhaps why he was guarding his language. The patient said he wondered why he was guarding himself. The therapist suggested that he felt the therapist could see his sore spots too clearly and was reluctant to reveal them because he didn't know the therapist well enough to trust him. The patient responded that he wanted to give himself away and to hide himself at the same time.

The patient then said he could never please his father. The therapist asked whether the patient felt he was reacting the way he might with his father and whether the therapist had in some way indicated that the patient couldn't please him. Through these questions the therapist deals with the patient's spontaneous comment about the past as a possible flight from the present. The patient's response to the latter question was negative, and he added that he himself was casting the therapist in the father role as he had his previous therapist.

The patient referred to his having thought in the previous session that the therapist had judged him, but the therapist had denied it. The therapist said it was understandable that the patient might not believe that denial since he knew so little about the therapist. This response illustrates the therapist's emphasis on the plausibility of the patient's experience of the relationship.

The patient said his eyes keep tearing; the therapist said that was an example of his difficulty in admitting his feelings. The patient said he was ashamed and the therapist responded that the patient apparently expected to be criticized; again it was understandable that he was in conflict about whether to trust the therapist so soon. The patient agreed.

When the hour was over, the patient said he felt bad that his name was on the tape. At first the therapist said he would blank it out, but then he said that if the patient were to accept taping at all, he would have to trust the therapist to some degree. The patient agreed, and the therapist said he should nevertheless feel free to talk about the taping whenever he wished.

As he left, the patient wished the therapist a good vacation, though the therapist had not given any reason why he would have been unable to see the patient for three weeks.

Summary

I distinguish between two major resistances to the transference. One is resistance to awareness of the transference and the other is resistance to resolution of the transference.

I argue that the bulk of the analytic work should take place in the transference in the here and now. I detail Freud's view that the transference should be encouraged to expand within the analytic situation. I suggest that the main technique for doing so, in addition to the analytic setup itself, is the interpretation of resistance to the awareness of transference by searching for allusions to the transference in associations not manifestly about the transference; that in making such interpretations one is guided by the connection to the actual analytic situation that every transference includes; that the major work in resolving the transference takes place in the here and now both by examining the relation between the transference and the actual analytic situation from which it takes its point of departure, and by the new experience that the analysis of the transference inevitably includes; and that while genetic transference interpretations play a role in resolving the transference, genetic material is likely to appear spontaneously and with relative ease after the resistances have been overcome in the transference in the here and now. Working through remains important and it too takes place primarily in the transference in the here and now.

I close with a statement of a conviction designed to set this paper into a broader perspective of psychoanalytic theory and research. The points I have made are not new. They are present in varying degrees of clarity and emphasis throughout our literature. But like so many other aspects of psychoanalytic theory and practice, they fade in and out of prominence and are rediscovered again and again, occasionally with some modest conceptual advance, but often with an air of discovery attributable only to ignorance of past contributions. There are doubtless many reasons for this phenomenon. But not the least, in my opinion, is the almost total absence of systematic and controlled research in the psychoanalytic situation (in contrast to the customary clinical research). I believe that only with such systematic and controlled research will analytic findings become solid and secure knowledge instead of being subject again and again to erosion by waves of fashion and by what Ernst Lewy (1941) called the "return of the repression"—the retreat of psychoanalysts from insights they had once reached.

REFERENCES

Freud, A. (1968), Acting out. *Internat. J. Psycho-Anal.*, 49:165–170.

Freud, S. (1900), The interpretation of dreams. *Standard Edition*, 4 & 5. London: Hogarth Press, 1953.

―――― (1912), The dynamics of transference. *Standard Edition*, 12:99–108, London: Hogarth Press, 1958.

―――― (1913), On beginning the treatment (further recommendations on the technique of psycho-analysis, I), *Standard Edition*, 12:123–144, London: Hogarth Press, 1958.

―――― (1914a), Remembering, repeating and working through (further recommendations on the technique of psycho-analysis, II), *Standard Edition*, 12:147–156, London: Hogarth Press, 1958.

―――― (1914b), On the history of the psychoanalytic movement, *Standard Edition*, 14:7–66, London: Hogarth Press, 1957.

―――― (1916–1917), Introductory lectures on psycho-analysis. *Standard Edition*, 15 & 16. London: Hogarth Press, 1963.

―――― (1920), Beyond the pleasure principle. *Standard Edition*, 18:7–64, London: Hogarth Press, 1955.

―――― (1925), An autobiographical study. *Standard Edition*, 20:7–74, London: Hogarth Press, 1959.

Gill, M., & Muslin, H. (1976) Early interpretation of transference. *J. Amer. Psychoanal. Assn.*, 24:779–794.

Greenson, R. (1967), *The Technique and Practice of Psychoanalysis*, Vol. 1 New York: International Universities Press.

Kanzer, M. (1966), The motor sphere of the transference. *Pychoanal. Quart.*, 35:522–539.

Kohut, H. (1959), Introspection, empathy and psychoanalysis. *J. Amer. Psychoanal. Assn.*, 7:459–483.

Lewy, E. (1941), The return of the repression. *Bull. Menninger Clin.*, 5:47–55.

Lipton, S. (1977a), The advantages of Freud's technique as shown by his analysis of the Rat Man. *Internat. J. Psycho-Anal.*, 58:255–274.

―――― (1977b), Clinical observations on resistance to the transference. *Internat. J. Psycho-Anal.*, 58:463–472.

Loewald, H. (1960), On the therapeutic action of psychoanalysis. *Internat. J. Psycho-Anal.*, 61:16–33.

Muslin, H., & Gill, M. (1978), Transference in the Dora case. *J. Amer. Psychoanal. Assn.* 26:311–328.

Rapaport, D. (1967), The scientific methodology of psychoanalysis. In: *Collected Papers*, ed. M. Gill. New York: Basic Books, pp. 165–220.

Rosenfeld, H. (1972), A critical appreciation of James Strachey's paper on "The nature of the therapeutic action of psychoanalysis." *Internat. J. Psycho-Anal.*, 53:455–462.

Segal, H. (1967), Melanie Klein's technique. In: *Psychoanalytic Techniques,* ed. B. Wolman. New York: Basic Books, pp. 168–190.

Stone, L. (1967), The psychoanalytic situation and transference. *J. Amer. Psychoanal. Assn.,* 15:3–57.

Strachey, J. (1934), The nature of the therapeutic action of psychoanalysis. *Internat. J. Psycho-Anal.,* 15:127–159; (reprinted) 50:275–292.

CHAPTER 7

Countertransference
and the Process of Cure

Robert J. Langs

It is now rather well known that countertransference (narrowly defined to mean those primarily inappropriate and pathological responses of a psychotherapist or psychoanalyst that are based on pathogenic unconscious fantasies, memories, and introjects, and related inner disturbances; see Langs, 1976c) was first viewed entirely as an obstacle to the cure of the patient in psychotherapy or psychoanalysis (see Freud, 1910, 1937). Largely as a result of Heimann's (1950) landmark paper, it subsequently was recognized that countertransference reactions, even when restricted to the narrow definition proposed here, could prove useful in understanding the patient, and could therefore contribute positively to the curative process. Eventually, writers on this subject attempted to develop a balanced view of the potentially constructive and damaging effects of countertransference.

In this presentation, I undertake a rather careful study of both the detrimental and the helpful consequences of countertransference. I will concentrate on relatively new perspectives, beginning with a broad conceptualization. I will then offer specific comments on the influence of countertransference on the therapist's selection and use of a given treatment modality, demonstrating its effects in the choice of one of three basic therapeutic procedures. I will also focus on how countertransference influences the conceptualization of, and therapeutic techniques with, resistances and will briefly indicate how countertrans-

127

ferences shared among therapists and analysts have interfered with the development of a valid conceptualization of the process of cure.

The Process of Cure

Before I take up our main themes, a brief definition of psychoanalysis and psychoanalytic psychotherapy is in order. (Hereafter I will refer to the two interchangeably.) Together, they may be viewed as treatment modalities that take place in a specified setting and under a particular set of conditions. They are geared toward alleviation of symptoms through cognitive-affective insight into unconscious processes and contents, and by means of inevitable positive introjective identifications with a therapist capable of sound management of the framework and valid interpretations. According to this definition, there are two major avenues of cure: one that is object-relational and interactional, involving unconscious identificatory processes; and the other involving the achievement of affectively meaningful, valid cognitive insights. In general, the former tends to be broadly ego-enhancing, whereas the latter entails specific forms of nonsymptomatic adaptive resolutions of specific unconscious fantasy-memory constellations (Langs, 1976a, 1976c).

In the interest of focusing solely on countertransference issues, we must bypass many other issues pertinent to the process of cure, including those contributions that stem from the analyst's essentially sound and valid functioning (his noncountertransference-based endeavors; see Langs, 1976c). It should be recognized, however, that the analyst's contributions always fall somewhere on a continuum; that is, no intervention, attitude, or response of the analyst is ever either entirely pathological or entirely free from a modicum of disturbance. Further, the therapist's inner state and the emergence of countertransferences are consistently under the influence of the patient's communications, and are always but one element of the conscious and—especially—unconscious interaction between patient and therapist: (in that sense, they are products of the bipersonal field; Langs, 1976a, 1978).

Countertransference as an Impediment to Cure

The difficulties that analysts through the years have had in understanding and mastering countertransference are foreshadowed in Freud's (1910, 1937) few terse comments on this critical topic. Freud restricted himself entirely to the detrimental and limiting aspects of countertransference, stating that no analyst could carry an analysis further than his own countertransferences would permit (1910). Much later, he wrote (1937) that analysis was an impossible profession, and briefly described some of the special stresses of analytic work and the need for occasional periods of reanalysis. Freud noted that countertransferences could interfere with the analyst's function as a model for the patient (a precursor of the writings of those who followed Freud on the influence of countertransferences on the identificatory processes in analysis) and, in addition, commented on the readiness with which some analysts become inappropriately defensive and divert the implications of the patient's material away from themselves.

These few remarks on countertransference stand in contrast to Freud's (1912a, 1912b, 1913, 1914, 1915) more extensive writings on transference. A review of Freud's case histories (1905, 1909, 1918) reveals that countertransference is almost entirely neglected (e.g., in the Dora case, where it is obviously implicit and yet not discussed; see Freud, 1905; Langs, 1976b).

With this background, let us now consider the detrimental consequences of countertransference. Much has been written about the limitations and wide range of negative therapeutic effects that can derive from the therapist's own psychopathology. Virtually any unusual subjective experience of the therapist, or any unsatisfactory or idiosyncratic intervention or behavior, signals the presence of countertransference (Cohen, 1952; Langs, 1974). Far more difficult to recognize are the countertransferences reflected in the therapist's accepted, long-standing, basic attitudes toward the patient, and in interventions that seem natural and appropriate at first glance. There is therefore a need to review and monitor every therapeutic intervention—and period of silence—for possible countertransference-based influence, and to pay special attention to the patient's responsive material as a *commentary* on each intervention (Langs, 1978). In this approach the therapist examines the indirect, derivative material from the patient for valid unconscious (nontransference) perceptions and responses to countertransference-based communications before addressing distorted, transference-based reactions. Nonvalidation of an intervention is also taken as a sign of countertransference, it being proposed that sound interventions receive Type Two derivative confirmation—i.e., indirect, disguised extensions of the analyst's interpretations in which truly unique and unanticipated realizations appear so that previously disparate material finds new unification and integration (in essence, the intervention generates the emergence of a *selected fact*—a realization that unites previously disparate observations; Bion, 1977; Langs, 1978).

A reevaluation of the clinical psychoanalytic literature reveals that therapists have several major blind spots regarding the detrimental influence of countertransferences. First, therapists fail to recognize the evident pervasiveness of countertransference expressions. Second, they fail to appreciate that countertransference expressions may significantly traumatize patients and result in treatment stalemates and distinctly poor therapeutic outcomes. Further, countertransferences may serve to "fix" the patient's psychopathology to a degree that virtually precludes insightful cure. At some point, pervasive unresolved countertransferences call for the termination of the therapy. In such cases, termination must be undertaken tactfully and entirely at the behest of the patient's derivative communications, which will consistently include the patient's unconscious realization that therapy is not feasible because of the therapist's disturbances.

Many analysts view countertransference as an essentially intrapsychic process that is sometimes evoked by the patient; in this view, countertransference is generally well-mastered by the analyst and is relatively peripheral to the therapeutic work with the patient except for occasional major interferences or blocks (Reich, 1951, 1960; see Langs, 1976c). Many believe that countertransferences (somewhat less than transferences) belong to the realm of fantasy and are an inner problem of the therapist with only secondary consequences for the patient.

A distinctly different perspective arises when countertransference is viewed as an inevitable, continuous, and essential component of the communicative interaction between patient and therapist (Langs, 1979a). In this view, the therapist's interventions are appreciated not only for their manifest contents and functions but for their full latent implications as well. Thus the pervasiveness of the unconscious component of the analyst's work comes to the fore, as does the realization of the inevitability of a modicum of disturbance—*inevitable countertransferences* (Langs, 1979a)—in every silence and intervention of the therapist, even when these are essentially sound and valid. Beyond this expected minimum are more pervasive expressions of the analyst's pathology: *preponderant countertransferences*.

In this characterization, countertransference is part of the actualities of the here and now in psychotherapy: those immediate realities filled with unconscious implications that reverberate with dynamic and genetic aspects for both participants (see Chediak, 1979). Countertransference-based expressions are therefore conveyed through the therapist's conscious and unconscious communications to the patient; the latter are actualities containing both surface and deeper meanings and functions, and their unconscious influence will override any other conscious intention or meaning of the therapist's interventions.

Thus, the detrimental aspects of countertransference are best conceived as critical conscious and—especially—unconscious disruptive communications from the therapist to the patient. These communications are unconsciously perceived and introjected by the patient, generating valid perceptions and introjects which are distinctly destructive and negative. On rare occasions, these processes take place consciously, but the analyst cannot depend on such direct identification by the patient. The psychoanalytic literature indicates that countertransference is characteristically acknowledged by the analyst only in the presence of a manifest error, or on direct confrontation from the patient. The far more subtle (though sometimes gross) continuous expressions of countertransference, as well as the patient's continuous unconscious introjective and cognitive responses, have been very much neglected.

The analyst's countertransference-based expressions have a multitude of negative effects. On some level, such attitudes and behaviors repeat earlier childhood traumas that contributed to the patient's neurosis and therefore justify and reinforce it. In Racker's (1957) terms, the analyst's actual behavior corresponds to a current pathological introject in the patient, itself derived from intrapsychic factors and earlier traumatic experiences.

Other effects of countertransference include the patient's valid unconscious belief that he and the analyst are alike in some important way (Little, 1951)—another way the patient justifies his neurotic adjustment. This belief also reflects a loss of the essential differentiating gradient that renders the therapist a more mature and integrated object than the patient (Loewald, 1960), thereby interfering with the therapist's serving inevitably as a growth-promoting introject. In addition, in the presence of significant countertransferences, the unconscious and functional therapeutic work will be directed more toward the therapist than toward the patient (Searles, 1975; Langs, 1976a). At such times, the *designated therapist* becomes the *functional patient,* and both participants in the treatment situation unconsciously engage in curative efforts directed toward the therapist's "neurotic" manifestations. And while some benefit may accrue to the patient when this type of unconscious curative endeavor proves beneficial to the therapist, he nonetheless suffers an interlude during which his own neurosis is largely set to the side. Despite such neglect of the patient's psychopathology, he may experience some degree of symptom alleviation, leading to the false conclusion that an insightful process is occurring.

The problem of establishing criteria, however broad, of junctures at which the therapist's countertransferences have so traumatized the patient and so interfered with the usual process of cure that termination—and possibly referral—is necessitated has seldom been addressed (see, however, Greenson, 1967; Langs, 1976c). The first step in dealing with therapeutic stalemate or regressive reactions in patients who are not responding to therapeutic work is to obtain supervisory consultation. The therapist should simultaneously make extended efforts at self-analysis and, if the problem is of large and fixed proportions, return to personal analysis or therapy. These endeavors are far less destructive to patients than sending them directly for consultation—a measure that modifies the confidentiality of the treatment situation and disrupts the essential one-to-one therapeutic relatedness. As I have shown elsewhere (Langs, 1975b, 1979c), on an unconscious level such disruptions exert uniformly detrimental effects on the patient and tend to reflect significant countertransference difficulties in the analyst—however shared and common they may be.

It should be recognized, however, that a critical factor in resolving countertransference-based treatment stalemates (and clinical experience indicates that many treatment stalemates *are* countertransference-based) is the therapist's effort at self-analysis as a means of gaining access to the underlying unconscious fantasies on which the countertransference-based reactions are based. At such times, unconsciously and through derivative communications, patients will usually engage in strong therapeutic efforts on the therapist's behalf. By carefully monitoring the patient's material for such efforts, the therapist can rectify countertransference influences while simultaneously analyzing the patient's responsive material.

It is essential, too, that as quickly as possible the main therapeutic thrust be centered again on the patient's illness. All too often, the primary unconscious therapeutic work deals with the analyst's rather than the patient's pathology; this is a serious and detrimental distortion of the therapeutic process. It is well to realize, however, that there are therapeutic interactions which ultimately succumb to the analyst's countertransferences. These can be recognized by persistent evidence of the presence of pathological input from the therapist and from a sensitive monitoring of the patient's material in that light. Embedded in such material are, as a rule, unconscious directives that would lead the therapist toward an appropriate and necessary termination under these conditions.

With the recent emphasis on the positive potential of countertransference, one must not forget its consistently destructive consequences. There can be no doubt that unrecognized and unresolved unconscious countertransference fantasies exert a continuing detrimental influence on the therapeutic interaction and that they have a wide range of negative consequences for the patient— e.g., pathological acting out, symptomatic crises, and untoward regressive episodes. Unrecognized countertransference is the single most frequent basis for therapeutic failure. It is countertransference, rather than transference (as stated by Freud, 1905; and Bird, 1972), that is by far the hardest part of analysis—and therapy.

The Effects of the Resolution of Countertransference

Having specified the ever-present negative consequences of countertransference, we can now consider the ways in which countertransferences may ultimately contribute to the cure of the patient. As a bridge to that topic, we may briefly reflect on those therapeutic interludes of major countertransference-based expressions, after which the therapist recognizes his or her error (via self-analysis and by monitoring the patient's derivative material), rectifies it in the therapeutic bipersonal field, and analyzes and works through the patient's reactions to the disturbance so generated. In such work, the therapist gives full credence to the patient's nontransference functioning—his valid unconscious perceptions and introjects of the therapist's psychopathology—by implicitly accepting the validity of such communications and in no way treating them as essentially distorted or inappropriate. Later, the therapist moves on from this valid core to work with the patient's subsequent distortions and the extensions of his reactions from the nontransference to the transference sphere. The latter responses constitute expressions of psychopathology evoked largely by the therapist's countertransferences; when these are both rectified and the patient's responses successfully analyzed, we have one type of therapeutic interlude in which disturbances in the therapist have indeed contributed to the process of cure.

To summarize, the type of therapeutic interlude described above has the following central characteristics:

(1) Countertransference expressed as a technical error—the analyst repeats on some level an earlier pathogenic interaction

(2) Unconscious perception and introjection by the patient (reinforcement of pathological introjects and neurotic maladaptations)

(3) Unconscious communications from the patient reflecting his or her detection of the countertransference problem and, as a rule, unconscious efforts to cure both the pathological introject and the analyst (unconscious reparation by the patient)

(4) Detection and resolution of the countertransference difficulty by the therapist (implicit benefit from the patient's therapeutic endeavors and a shift to constructive interventions that, as a rule, now serve to distinguish the therapist from the past pathogenic figure)

(5) Rectification of the countertransference influence in the therapeutic interaction with the patient

(6) Interpretation and working through of the patient's responses to the total sequence

The most critical factor in this sequence is the analyst's capacity to recover and to rectify the therapeutic situation. Failing that, destructive countertransference influences will continue to prevail. The main curative possibility in this situation lies in the patient's unconscious appreciation of the therapist's difficulties and subsequent mobilization of his or her own therapeutic resources.

In contrast, when the analyst is capable of restoring noncountertransference-based functioning to the point where it overridingly characterizes the therapeutic work, the patient has the opportunity for an experience—however painful initially—with considerable curative potential. It is this capacity of the analyst to recover and resume valid interpretive work that generates a series of new, constructive introjects in the patient and that provides much-needed cognitive insight.

I must stress, however, that such a sequence includes an interlude during which the analyst's behavior is pathological and destructive (or seductive). And while much is gained by affording the patient an inadvertent opportunity actively to reexperience his or her pathogenic past in the present (Winnicott, 1956), there is nonetheless a significant difference between this type of sequence and one in which the therapist has not behaved pathologically and has maintained both a relatively countertransference-free therapeutic stance and the capacity to manage the therapeutic environment.

While countertransference-based errors are inevitable and reflect the analyst's humanness and limitations, they leave a destructive imprint despite the possibility of considerable ultimate therapeutic gain. This point deserves emphasis since there has been an all-too-ready tendency among analytic writers to accept the type of sequence outlined above as if it were the optimal form—or sometimes, the only possible form—of therapeutic work. There is no sound basis for such a generalization, and a therapist must continue to strive to minimize countertransference expressions and their effects. Therapeutic work that is not unduly traumatic is certainly preferable to treatment situations in which interludes of major pathological expression and recovery are recurrent.

In perspective, then, the type of sequence described here makes the best of a disturbing interlude during which the most significant therapeutic gain takes place when the analyst has regained optimum functioning. Thus, in such situations it is not the countertransference per se that contributes to the curative process, but rather the therapist's recovery from the countertransference disturbance. Let us now turn to situations in which countertransference more directly contributes to curative effects.

Countertransference and Cure

There are several ways in which countertransference can contribute to alleviating the patient's symptoms. As we shall see, some of these effects entail neither positive introjective identifications with the therapist nor sound cognitive insights. They are based instead on an uninsightful curative process that I will discuss below.

First, as already noted, an appreciation of the unconscious communicative interaction leads directly to the recognition of a modicum of *inevitable countertransference* every time the therapist is silent or actively intervenes (Langs, 1979a). Of importance to the present discussion is the realization that the continuous existence of inevitable countertransference implies that patients in therapy always—to a greater or lesser degree—feel the pressure of their own pathological introjects and pathogenic past. Therefore, on one important level, their associations and behavior constitute responses to the therapist's unconscious countertransference fantasies; the latter are communicated in derivative form via the therapist's attitudes, interventions, and silences. As a result, every analytic interaction—including valid interpretations—is influenced by countertransference.

It appears, then, that countertransferences are ever-present in psychotherapy and psychoanalysis. They stand high among the inevitable stimuli for the patient's reactions, and are therefore an integral part of the curative process. We can no longer think of psychotherapy as simply based on efforts to interpret the patient's fantasies and communications. These expressions are stimulated by adaptive contexts—precipitants—within the therapeutic interaction—essentially, the therapist's interventions and failures to intervene—to which countertransference consistently contributes. Countertransference is therefore an essential aspect of the curative process, though it must be recognized that a positive outcome of such effects requires their consistent recognition, rectification, and the analysis of the patient's direct and derivative reactions.

Several curative mechanisms are involved in a patient's responses to the therapist's countertransferences. I have already alluded to unconscious curative efforts directed toward the therapist, which, if successful, lead to ego strengthening in the patient and ultimately to a positive introjective identification with the therapist. When such unconscious curative efforts are thwarted or when the therapist fails to respond to them with a resolution of the prevailing countertransference constellation, however, as a rule there will be an interlude that is quite detrimental to the process of cure. As Searles (1975) noted, the inevitability of offering patients opportunities unconsciously (and quite rarely consciously) to cure the therapist fosters the actualization and reliving of the patient's early childhood efforts to "cure" pathogenic primary objects. Often, such reliving provides an opportunity for a successful resolution of previously pathogenic responses; and thus helps to modify the influence of earlier failures in this regard. It must be stressed again, however, that this type of therapeutic experience must find appropriate limits, so that the treatment does not become the therapy of the therapist, with the negative consequences far outweighing the positive ones. In addition, the therapist must implicitly reveal his or her ongoing struggle against countertransference expressions in order to provide the patient with a critical positive introject; the absence of signs of such a struggle is highly destructive to the therapeutic interaction.

So far, I have discussed the curative potential of countertransference in terms of its ultimately insightful and constructive possibilities. I have stressed the positive potential in the patient's unconscious reactions to countertransference and have detailed how the cycle of expression, recognition, rectification, and interpretation is actually one dimension of every cure. There are, however,

several additional ways that countertransference can lead to symptom alleviation—by contributing to uninsightful symptom relief. Let us now consider
these possibilities.

Unresolved Countertransferences and Symptom Alleviation

It is well known that symptoms may be alleviated without insight and adaptive structural change. I propose that all such "cures" are countertransference-
based.

In 1958, Barchilon specifically described countertransference cures founded
on transference-based patient reactions to the therapist's pathological unconscious need for uninsightful symptom resolution. Such "cures" are based on a
wish to please the therapist; to get well because of love or dependency on the
therapist to maintain his or her omnipotence, and to acquire—through identification—the therapist's modes of conflict resolution. Some time later, to
stress the significant role played by the psychopathology of both patient and
therapist in such an outcome, I coined the term *misalliance cures* for this type
of uninsightful symptom relief (Langs, 1975a, 1976a, 1976c). More recently
(Langs, 1980), I attempted to define some of the specific ways in which countertransferences provide the patient with both defenses and defensive barriers,
as well as with pathological gratifications and superego sanctions, all as a way
of providing symptom relief that involves neither insight nor the development
of new adaptive resources.

To clarify, countertransference expressions invite both projection and projective identifications of the patient's psychopathology onto and into the therapist. More broadly, this loading of the unconscious communicative interaction
with the therapist's psychopathology gives patients an opportunity to place
their own, similar disturbances into the therapist, and thereby cover over their
own illness with that of the therapist (Langs, 1976a). These projective mechanisms may temporarily relieve patients' symptoms. Quite often in such clinical
situations, therapists or their supervisors will find that patients' communications reveal little of their own psychopathology but much of their unconscious
adaptive functioning; the therapists' interventions, on the other hand, show
evident disturbance.

Finally, countertransference-based interventions tried to stir up aspects of
the patient's psychopathology—in addition to the already noted recollections
of his pathogenic past and his adaptive resources. On this basis they may provide the patient with an opportunity to work over actively mobilized conflicts,
fantasies, and memories—conscious and unconscious—which might not otherwise have been activated. Clearly, such interludes will have little positive
effect unless the countertransference is rectified and the proper analytic work
carried out with the patient. It is, however, especially valuable for a patient to

experience with the therapist an initial replay of a past pathogenic interaction, his responsive conscious and unconscious fantasies, memories, and introjects, and then to discover the analyst's capacity to recover and be different, while simultaneously analytically resolving the unconscious pathological constellation so mobilized.

Another type of symptom relief occurs when patients react to the therapist's preponderant countertransferences by firming up their own defenses as a protection against the seductive, provocative aspects of the therapist's expressed pathology. As Searles (1959) has so clearly shown, the analyst's expressions of countertransference not only involve pathological sexual and aggressive needs but also constitute unconscious attempts to drive the patient crazy. Such attempts imply an unconscious wish in the therapist for the patient to be the container of the therapist's psychopathology. Thus, patients may mobilize their defenses in order to justify a termination dreaded on any other basis (the therapist is seen as a terrifying object and introject), as a means of taking protective flight from the overwhelming threat contained in the therapist's pathological behaviors and interventions. Such interludes need not be characterized by gross disturbances in the therapist; repeated communication of more subtle countertransference-based expressions may well have the same devastating effects.

Communicative Style and Countertransference

In a recent study (Langs, 1978, 1978–1979), I attempted to demonstrate clinically three types of communicative interactions between patients and therapists. I defined a Type A communicative mode in which illusions and symbolic expression predominate. The patient expresses himself by representing the significant adaptive contexts in the therapeutic interaction, and by conveying meaningful clusters of associations which serve on an indirect or derivative level as a means of expressing pertinent and coalescible responsive unconscious perceptions and fantasies, and their genetic echoes. The therapist in this type of communicative field proves capable of securing and maintaining the ground rules of therapy and the therapeutic environment, and of responding in an essentially interpretive way to the patient's material.

The Type B communicative style is characterized by the use of projective identification and action discharge, and may exist in the patient or the therapist or both. Finally, the Type C communicative mode is identified by the development of impenetrable barriers, lies, and falsifications, and by efforts to destroy meaningful interpersonal links—efforts that may characterize the communications of the patient or the therapist.

A Type A communicative field implies a relative absence of countertransference, restriction to occasional expressions of preponderant countertransference and the minimum of inevitable countertransference. It also implies the therapist's capacity to recognize, rectify, and interpret the relevant counter-transference difficulty and the patient's responsive material.

Therapists who are inclined to the Type B mode of communication, however, usually have extensive countertransference difficulties and consistently tend to projectively identify aspects of their psychopathology into the patient. Often, insight fails to develop. Under these conditions, the patient may experience periods of symptom relief by functioning as a container of the therapist's pathology, by metabolizing or detoxifying the disturbances involved, and by returning these projective identifications to the therapist in some less disruptive, more benign form. In this way, countertransference may foster the development of a capacity for what Bion (1962) has termed *reverie,* an ability to receive pathological projective identifications and properly to manage and reproject the disturbance involved. Again, however, the risk is considerable that the disturbing elements will dominate and that the patient's resources—even on an unconscious level—will fail to meet the challenge, leading to significant regression. Nonetheless, despite the dangers involved, some degree of symptom relief can occur on this basis.

The Type C therapist is also functioning under the influence of significant—and usually preponderant—countertransferences. To the unsuspecting observer, the pathology often goes unrecognized. Recently (Langs, 1979d, 1980) I proposed that most therapists and analysts present their patients with falsifications of, and barriers to, the disturbing underlying truths within both participants in the therapeutic dyad. I have suggested the term *lie therapist* to describe such therapists in order to emphasize nonmorally the extent to which such therapy is designed to falsify or create barriers against the chaotic truths pertinent to the neurosis of the patient (and secondarily to that of the therapist).

Technically, the countertransference-based interventions of such therapists can be identified through several characteristics: the use of unneeded deviations in the therapeutic ground rules and framework; the use of noninterpretive interventions; and the failure consistently to interpret within an adaptive context that uses the therapeutic interaction as the fulcrum. These deviant responses, many of which are still generally accepted as standard practice, express countertransferences and offer the patient lies and barriers to the truth rather than insight. They may lead to periods of symptom relief by helping patients to seal off their inner disturbance and their threatening unconscious perceptions and introjects of the therapist.

Since the truths of the therapeutic dyad are ultimately terrifying, such barriers provide interludes of welcome relief. But they offer no sense of understanding, they preclude growth and the development of new and constructive adaptations, and they require consistent pathological reinforcement. The expressed psychoanalytic cliché—the use of psychoanalytic concepts and terms

clinically as jargon and as formulations devoid of dynamic interactional meaning—is among the most significant means through which these barriers are
erected. In addition, alterations in the basic framework, ranging from unnecessary changes in hours to deviations from neutrality, confidentiality, and the
like, serve similarly to seal off chaotic truths and to projectively identify into
the patient aspects of the therapist's pathology (as a rule, such interventions
function primarily as both barriers and projective identifications). Elsewhere
(Langs, 1979c) I have used the term *framework deviation cures* for such uninsightful symptom relief based on alterations in the framework.

Thus, countertransference can mobilize or reinforce the patient's defenses or
alleviate the patient's symptoms through the development of shared fictions
created to avoid pathogenic truths. Many of these falsifications cover over
truths related to the immediate therapeutic interaction, and especially to the
therapist's countertransference-based communications. As such, they involve
a pervasive denial of the countertransference; often, they prompt expressions
of negation and denial in the patient's material.

It should be noted, too, that in these conditions we are usually not dealing
with Type A communicative defenses, which ultimately reveal their own derivative meanings and functions, as well as the material defended against. In a
Type C situation, there are relatively refractory and impenetrable nonderiva-
tive lies and barriers through which a view of the truth is impossible. These
fictions can proliferate for long periods of time, generating an extended situation of lie therapy and, at times, symptom relief based on lie-barrier systems.
The detection of these situations requires a careful evaluation of the unconscious implications of the therapist's interventions and a search of the patient's
derivative communications for indications of misalliance, falsifications, non-
meaning, and essential nonrelatedness.

In all, then, there are several avenues through which uninsightful symptom
relief may develop in response to persistent, inevitable, and noticeably preponderant countertransferences. These formulations help to account for symptom
alleviation in nonanalytic psychotherapies and in psychotherapy that focuses
on manifest content (a remarkably common occurrence; see Langs, 1979d) or
on what I have termed Type One derivatives (attempts to interpret the patient's
material through isolated readings of inferences and symbolic implications
divorced from the ongoing adaptive therapeutic interaction; see Langs, 1978).

Of necessity, therapists and analysts must work with what I have termed
Type Two derivatives (material organized around significant, ongoing adaptive
contexts within the therapeutic interaction; see Langs, 1978) for there to be
true, largely countertransference-free, insightful, and positively introjective
modes of cure. Even interpretations cast in this mold, however, may be under
the influence of significant countertransferences, since the form of an intervention does not guarantee its validity. This leads us to the ultimate criterion of

sound, insightful psychotherapy: distinctive, Type Two derivative validation of specific interventions (see Langs, 1978).

Clinical Material

The following clinical vignettes will illustrate and clarify some of the ideas presented in this paper.

Case 1

Mr. A was a young man in psychotherapy once a week with Dr. Z because of periods of depression and difficulties in holding a job. After three months of therapy, in the last session before the therapist was to take an extended winter vacation, the patient began by asking if this was their last meeting before the interruption. He was unsure whether he would continue therapy both because he feared that he was boring the therapist and because he felt somewhat better than he had before beginning therapy. He expressed his need for a woman but felt confused—something in him was trying to come out.

Dr. Z pointed out that this was the last session before his vacation and that Mr. A was talking about quitting, needing a woman, and having difficulty in getting things out—all against the backdrop of his vacation. Mr. A responded that the threat is the vacation and then suddenly mused that his father is the one who is paying for therapy. He guessed that he didn't want the therapist to leave and that he wanted their relationship to be more reciprocal. The patient described his problems with closeness, and then looked at a throw rug on the floor of the therapist's office, stating that it somehow looked like a face. Dr. Z pointed out that the patient had been talking about Dr. Z's vacation and that Mr. A would himself like to leave in response. He added that Mr. A was putting aside his thoughts of closeness by talking about images in the rug.

The patient fell silent for a while and then arose from his chair, walked over to Dr. Z, and shook his hand. Dr. Z suggested that there was something from within Mr. A that was pressing for expression and that by shaking his hand, Mr. A. had changed the way in which they worked verbally. Mr. A stated that he wanted to touch someone and noted that he had never touched the therapist before. He gave the therapist a check and left, describing himself as feeling very confused.

In discussing this session, we might best view the therapist's first intervention as premature and ill-defined. Dr. Z himself felt that he had identified the most critical adaptive context of the patient's material as his own vacation; he stated that he had been attempting to play back some pertinent related derivatives (see Langs, 1978), especially since the patient showed a major resistance in his thoughts of quitting. In retrospect, however, Dr. Z found the intervention wishy-washy and too general, and felt that he should have waited for the patient to offer more specific derivatives. He also felt that perhaps some over-looked and disruptive interventions on his part in the preceding session or two had contributed to the patient's thoughts of termination.

Despite these subjective and objective qualifications, this particular interven-tion does not appear to be basically erroneous, since it is a valid effort to play back some important themes related to the known adaptive context of the ther-apist's vacation, in the therapeutic context of thoughts of prematurely termi-nating the therapy. Since the intervention is indeed quite vague and indefinite, we might best place it somewhere in the middle of the continuum along which interventions are assessed for countertransference and noncountertransference-based input: it has a distinct mixture of validity and error.

The patient's response appears to be in keeping with this evaluation. His conscious comment that the threat is indeed the therapist's vacation is what I have elsewhere termed a *primary confirmation* (Langs, 1979b) and is of little value in assessing the psychoanalytic validity of an intervention. The latter must rely on indirect communications from the patient in the form of Type Two derivatives that coalesce to produce a selected fact (Bion, 1962) that lends new and unanticipated meaning to the material at hand.

In some ways, the reference to the father's payment for treatment meets these last criteria for psychoanalytic validity, since it alludes to a number of modifications in the framework of therapy that were never rectified or explored with the patient. These included a major reduction in the therapist's fee at the initiation of treatment and several self-revelations by the therapist which mod-ified both his anonymity and his neutrality. It may well be that these alterations in the framework—along with the rupture in the therapeutic hold created by the therapist's vacation—created doubts about treatment in the patient's mind, evoked his unconscious need to disturb the therapist, and interfered with the patient's own hold on Dr. Z (see Langs, 1979c).

Without allowing the further development of indirect, derivative communi-cation, the therapist intervened a second time after the patient saw the image of a face in the rug. Here, the qualities of prematurity, generality, and accu-sation are striking, despite the therapist's conscious wish to confront the patient with what he thought was an important resistance. This confrontation disre-gards the critical role of indirect communication from the patient and may well constitute a pathological projective identification from the therapist into the patient, based on the former's guilt and sense of disturbance about his vacation.

There is also evidence that among the patient's unconscious fantasies and responses to the therapist's vacation were intensified unconscious homosexual fantasies and needs (cf. his need for a woman), responses that were rendered especially dangerous in the face of the unanalyzed reduction in the therapist's fee. This modification in the framework had made the boundaries of the ther-apeutic relationship uncertain and had raised questions, expressed indirectly by the patient, about the therapist's management of his own unconscious homosexual fantasies and countertransferences. Thus, there is some suggestion that this second premature intervention—and to some degree, the first comment as well—was designed to create barriers to the emergence of the patient's unconscious homosexual fantasies and perceptions. In all, there is considerable evidence that this second intervention reflects preponderant countertransference, as well as serving as a disruptive projective identification and lie barrier.

It is striking, then, that the patient's handshake some minutes before the end of this session appears to validate the two formulations made here of the therapist's interventions. (In supervision, both assessments were made immediately after each intervention had been described.) The handshake reveals the extent to which the communicative bipersonal field had been disrupted, the boundaries between the patient and therapist rendered unclear, and action discharge and projective identification fostered in lieu of symbolic communication. It also confirms the evaluation that the therapist's disruption of the patient's communication of his image of the face served as an unconscious directive to reject symbolic Type A communication in favor of either Type B action discharge or Type C barriers.

Once symbolic communication failed, the patient turned to the Type B mode of communication. The result is not only direct physical contact, and gratification for both patient and therapist of the underlying, unresolved, pathological homosexual fantasies, but also a disturbing projective identification of this disruptive homosexual constellation. The physical contact probably served magically to undo the pending separation and to convey the patient's unconscious perception and introjection of the therapist's difficulties in managing both that vacation and the underlying homosexual stirrings in himself and in Mr. A. The avowed confusion with which the patient ended the hour is an interactional product with contributions from both participants.

The patient's reference to his father's paying for therapy is filled with unconscious implications, only one of which I wish to stress: the father is the key genetic figure in this therapeutic interaction. Material from earlier sessions suggested strong latent homosexual conflicts in Mr. A's father and a powerful latent homosexual overcast to the father-son relationship. Mr. A's father had also shown a relative intolerance for his son's efforts at play and self-expression, and it seems clear that the therapist's preponderant countertransferences unconsciously replayed the patient's pathogenic experiences with his father.

On one level, the patient's sudden handshake may be viewed as an unconscious effort to stress the unrecognized and uninterpreted homosexual fantasies and perceptions. It may also contain a curative wish directed toward the therapist. For the moment, however, the therapist had failed to recognize, understand, and resolve within himself this area of countertransference. In addition, he did not rectify such countertransference expressions in the therapeutic inter-action; nor did he accept the patient's unconscious curative endeavor or inter-pret his other unconscious responses. The handshake therefore constituted a significant repetition of the patient's—and therapist's—pathogenic past, a neu-rotic vicious circle (Strachey, 1934; Racker, 1957) that would serve only to reinforce the patient's neurosis and his pathological unconscious fantasies, memories, and introjects. The therapist lacked the insight and inner manage-ment to turn the situation into a curative experience—as the premature hand-shake clearly bore witness.

Despite this failing, the handshake may also reflect a mobilization of adap-tive resources in the patient in response to the therapist's unresolved counter-transference. This view is supported by material in the hour after the thera-pist's vacation, in which the patient spoke in some detail of his sexual encounters with women during the previous weeks. The woman with whom he was most involved, however, was too seductive, and he was impotent. Mr. A also spoke of his extensive fears that he would become a homosexual. He had made plans to cancel the next session to be with some friends who were visiting him. He also mentioned that he had begun to paint.

This material, which is of course highly condensed here, reflects the patient's wish for a symbolic communicative space in which he could express and ana-lyze the unconscious aspects of his psychopathology, and his continued concern about the homosexual contaminants that are disturbing the therapeutic rela-tionship. The material does show the mobilization of some adaptive resources but they are ineffectual in the face of the therapist's and patient's unresolved homosexual conflicts.

In summary, then, the therapist's countertransference at this juncture was based primarily on unconscious homosexual fantasies. Their presence afforded the patient an opportunity to experience in the immediate therapeutic inter-action aspects of an earlier pathogenic interaction with his father. However, the therapist's failure to identify, resolve, and interpret his countertransference expressions and their repercussions for the patient ultimately led to an inter-lude of therapeutic failure which culminated in a form of "acting in" by the patient. Still, on an unconscious level, the handshake can be viewed as an effort to make the therapist aware of his unresolved homosexual countertransference and of the need to resolve and rectify it.

For Dr. Z, the handshake had just that effect: he felt seduced by the patient and wondered if he had contributed, and he felt disturbed because the act had taken place before the actual end of the session. In some way, the handshake may represent a compromised metabolism of the homosexual projective iden-tifications of the therapist, including appropriate and nonpathological aspects as well as inappropriate and unresolved ones. The latter aspects deserve emphasis since the patient was unable to deal with his introjective identification with the therapist through a verbal response; his behavioral reaction indicates a significant failure in containing and metabolizing.

There was some indication in the hour after the vacation that the patient had experienced temporary symptom relief through unconsciously perceiving the therapist as having more significant homosexual pathology than himself. This perception had led to his involvement with several women, though ultimately he became impotent and fearful of both his own homosexuality and that introjected from the therapist.

Case 2

Miss B had been in therapy for several years, because of periods of confusion, depression, and instability in her social life. She had spent most of one session discussing whether she should go out on her birthday with a former boyfriend, T, who had disappointed her of late. She decided to ask him to take her out and to tell him where to take her. A girlfriend of the patient wanted to arrange a blind date, but Miss B felt frightened, wondering if it would be sexual and yet feeling it was crazy to back away, so she would try. She talked too about her need for treatment and her feeling that recently she had been getting something from her sessions; she no longer felt disorganized and crazy and was working on her problems with men.

In the next hour, she spoke of her birthday and ruminated about how she should not feel upset because her boss forgot about it. She had been at a bar, but refused to become involved with a queer-looking man who tried to engage her attention. At another bar, she spoke to a man who turned out to be a marriage counselor, but she thought he was crazy and felt that he was pestering her. She had seen T, who slept with her but berated her for being involved with other men. He accused her of being a tramp, and the patient regretted having told him about her other relationships; she felt he had torn her apart. She then ruminated about refusing to feel guilty and being entitled to have relationships. She wished she could analyze things better.

The therapist intervened and suggested that the patient had analysis on her mind and seemed to feel that analyzing things was disruptive. He noted that Miss B had alluded to a crazy therapist and to how T had betrayed her confidence. He suggested that she was struggling with her involvement in treatment and with just how intense she wished that involvement to be. The patient said that this wasn't so, adding that the therapist analyzed everything but never explained why she does what she does; instead, he picks things apart. In the past (referring to an earlier phase of therapy, during which the patient paid a low fee and the therapist offered many noninterpretive interventions), she had felt that the therapist was much more involved in her life. Sometimes she would like more of that, but now she feels that she really doesn't need it and that she's doing better. She feels that the therapist is helpful, though at times she is annoyed with him and thinks about how she could hurt him. Still, she doesn't feel depressed at this time and is glad that she has spoken up.

The therapist suggested that the patient had perceived his comment as confusing, adding that this perception was reflected in her reference to an earlier, perplexing period of treatment. Miss B agreed and said that she wanted to stay in therapy but had mixed feelings that were like those she had had at the bars—as if she were both there and not there. When she first came to treatment she felt crazy, but when she stops she won't feel crazy.

In brief, the therapist's first intervention is an attempt to identify certain ill-defined anxieties and fantasies about therapy and the therapist—an attempt to analyze an unconscious resistance. The comment lacks a specific adaptive context, however, and thus fails to allude to the essential Type Two derivatives—unconscious fantasies and perceptions—necessary for a valid intervention. The intervention is therefore limited to Type One derivatives that lack specificity vis-à-vis the immediate adaptive context, and it does not touch on the convoluted expressions that are the hallmark of neurotic communication.

In addition, the therapist has set aside sexual derivatives in favor of a more deinstinctualized, ill-defined description of the patient's anxieties and conflicts. Such an approach fosters a countertransference-based Type C barrier designed to cover up more specific unconscious sexual fantasies and perceptions related to the therapeutic interaction. Along the me–not-me interface (Langs, 1978)—taking all associations to refer to both the patient ("me") and the therapist ("not me")—this material alludes not only to the patient's sexual conflicts but also to those of the therapist. Similarly, either or both members of this therapeutic dyad may feel threatened and attacked.

In all, then, the first intervention could be placed in the middle of the countertransference-noncountertransference continuum. The therapist makes a valid attempt to identify a resistance and its unconscious basis, but he does not specify its adaptive context and fails to include his own contribution to the resistance (which is actually an *interactional resistance;* see Langs, 1976a). The central unconscious countertransference fantasies, memories, and introjects appear to revolve around sexual matters and to extend considerably beyond inevitable countertransference.

The patient's responses support these formulations in that they emphasize that the intervention is insufficient. The allusions to the therapist's previous involvement in the patient's life suggest possible current infringements on the boundaries and framework of the therapeutic relationship. The patient even seems to feel hurt rather than helped by the intervention.

The therapist's second intervention introduces the idea that the patient is feeling confused, without such a communication in the patient's material. This intervention falls toward the countertransference-dominated end of the continuum: it has definitive qualities of a preponderant countertransference-based expression. Subjectively, the therapist immediately sensed that he was attributing to the patient his own sense of confusion; in retrospect, he was also able to see that he was diverting the patient from the sexual material. This intervention constitutes a projection (the therapist attributes his experience to the patient) and a projective identification (through this erroneous intervention, the therapist actually confuses the patient, and interactionally places his own confusion—and his use of confusion and intellectualization to defend against sexual conflicts and fantasies—into the patient). The intervention may also be viewed as the therapist's attempt to create a falsification that will serve as an impenetrable barrier to the underlying sexual material (especially his own) and the apparent chaos attached to it (Bion, 1977; Langs, 1978, 1980).

The patient responds by experiencing this confusion in her own terms; she communicates her introjection of the therapist's physical presence but emotional absence (lack of understanding) in the session. Her closing comments about leaving therapy in order to avoid feeling crazy in all likelihood reflect her struggle against the therapist's efforts to drive her crazy by confusing her. As a *commentary* on the therapist's interventions, then, her response strongly supports the thesis of the presence of significant preponderant countertransferences. The patient's response also reveals her curative efforts directed toward the therapist. In regard to Miss B's neurosis, the therapist's countertransference-based interventions appear to have provided the patient with defenses and barriers, reinforcing her own tendencies along these lines. Such an interlude could be followed by some degree of momentary uninsightful symptom relief.

The patient began the next hour by describing how she felt depressed and burdened. She planned to go to night school and talked of how hard she was working. She described an incident in which she had planned to sell her present car, which was in need of extensive repairs, and to buy a new one; she had been unable to do so because T had not shown up as promised to take her to the car dealer. Her brother would have taken her. T is uncaring and Miss B should have known. She talked of feeling lonely and let down by her girlfriends, and of lacking goals. T is passive, but she herself lets people take advantage of her; he doesn't know where he's heading, nor does she.

The therapist said that the patient seemed very upset and in a lot of pain. She is talking about people who offer her aid but in the end disappoint her, and of feeling alone and forced to do things for herself—without goals, not knowing where she is going. He added that something more must be stirring up these feelings. After a long silence, Miss B said that the therapist must be talking of therapy. She feels paralyzed and blocked, as if there were a fog in the room between them. She feels that anything she said would be criticized by the therapist, even though she knows this isn't so. Somehow, in the past, when the therapist gave her guidance and talked to her, it was better; now she doesn't know where she's headed and feels no sense of security. Sometimes she feels she doesn't need treatment, but is afraid of leaving—it's like a security blanket. The therapist then said that Miss B was indicating that something in therapy was not satisfying and was evoking feelings of disappointment. The patient responded that it was what she felt in the last session: they hadn't connected and she felt misunderstood.

In this session, the therapist's first intervention took the form of playing back derivatives of the patient's unconscious perceptions and fantasies in an effort to generate surface links and bridges to the therapeutic relationship and to the therapist's specific interpretive failures in the previous hour (Langs, 1978). He had been aware of some of his insensitivities and failings in the previous session—expressions of his countertransference—although he had not defined their relationship to his own sexual conflicts and anxieties. He had struggled to organize the material in this particular session around the adaptive context of his interventions in the preceding hour, and was able to recognize the implications of the realtively valid images of the uncaring insensitivity of the patient's boyfriend, T. He was also aware that the patient's view of T and herself as being alike in their goallessness was a sound and telling commentary on his failure to intervene correctly, and that the patient's depression derived in large measure from her disappointment in him as a therapist. Through his own subjective reappraisal of the unconscious implications of his interventions and a monitoring of the patient's material for valid commentaries on his work, he was able to identify several expressions of countertransference in the preceding hour.

During this earlier session, the therapist had struggled with the decision about whether to remain silent and await clearer, coalescing derivatives, or to play back the derivatives that he had identified. After the hour, he realized that he had again omitted all sexual referents, and that, once he intervened, he should have mentioned the fact that the patient utilized her boyfriend as a means of conveying her unconscious perceptions and fantasies about himself. He also recognized that the patient was feeling burdened with his problems and that this feeling too might have been pointed out in terms of her experience of the situation. In all, then, Dr. Y felt that he might have suggested that Miss B referred to her boyfriend as a means of describing her feelings toward Dr. Y, and added that this undoubtedly had further implications, as did her sense of being burdened by T's problems. Further self-analysis enabled Dr. Y to identify the general nature of his unconscious countertransference-related conflicts and fantasies. Though the working through had not reached the point of full rectification, progress had been made.

Despite these limitations, the therapist felt that his first intervention in the second hour was essentially sound and valid. I agree and would therefore place this intervention toward the noncountertransference end of the continuum, largely in the sphere of inevitable countertransference, though I would note the fragments of continued preponderant countertransference related to sexual matters. Nevertheless, on the basis of the derivatives in the particular hour (and every session should be its own creation; see Langs, 1976a, 1978), the failure to allude to the boyfriend had less countertransference significance in the second hour than the comparable omission in the preceding hour.

There are clear indications here of the therapist's ability to benefit from the patient's unconscious curative (largely derivative) attempts to alert the therapist to the effects of his craziness, his unconscious seductiveness, and his many unsuccessful interventions. Miss B also directed the therapist to some of the hostile and attacking qualities of his earlier interventions, and through a derivative representing a response to an introjective identification, she clearly expressed the wish for a more effective therapist. Benefiting from his monitoring of these derivative communications and from a period of self-analysis, the therapist was in some measure able to resolve his countertransference; to intervene in a more effective, valid manner; and implicitly to accept and benefit from the patient's unconscious curative efforts. Nonetheless, there is evidence of a residual countertransference—an air of unresolved and inappropriate seductiveness—to which the patient will continue to respond.

The above evaluation finds validation in the patient's immediate reference to the treatment situation after the therapist's first intervention. It is also supported by her many comments about her own sense of paralysis and fog, which convey her unconscious appreciation of the recent interactional resistances generated by her and by the therapist. Her comments about the therapist's failure to provide her with enough guidance may, in this context, be taken to allude to those aspects of his intervention that were unsound, while her reference to using treatment as a security blanket conveys an effort to desexualize the unconscious therapeutic interaction—a defensive need expressed by both patient and therapist.

The second intervention, however, addresses the manifest content of the patient's material without an adaptive context, and is essentially countertransference-based. The therapist felt the need to respond to the patient's depression, and proved intolerant both of this depression and of the possible appearance of other derivatives. This intervention reflects the return of preponderant countertransference, and the offer of a seemingly reparative comment that will serve to deaden the communicative field and create a Type C barrier.

This relatively rapid reemergence of countertransference-based expressions reflects the therapist's relative failure to master his own psychopathology. In a sequence of this kind, in which there is an expression of countertransference, a period of resolution, and then an upsurge of new expressions of the therapist's pathology, patients are quite likely to suffer and regress, to become depressed, and to experience a sense of failure.

The patient responded to the second intervention by referring again to her sense of dissatisfaction and of being misunderstood in the preceding hour. In the immediate adaptive context of this intervention, her commentary reveals her introjective identification of the therapist's inability to understand the implications of her present associations. The patient's comment that she felt distant from the therapist is an incorporative introjection of the therapist's use of this last intervention as a means of creating distance between himself and the patient. Thus, his wish to be supportive, however sincere, actually led to an intervention that was experienced either as seductive—thereby requiring a distancing response—or as lacking in empathy and understanding—thereby creating distance rather than implicit support.

While the material in these two sessions is lacking in genetic derivatives, those available from other sessions indicate that the patient had repeatedly experienced failures in empathy in her relationship with her mother, who also was quite intolerant of her sexual needs. It seems likely, then, that the therapist's interventions repeated this earlier pathogenic interaction, which was significant to the patient's borderline pathology and fear of being driven crazy, her depressive propensities, and her difficulties in relating to men. It seems self-evident that as long as the therapist unconsciously behaved in this pathogenic way—as long as he was incapable of any enduring rectification and self-analytic modification of his countertransferences and was unable to interpret them to the patient—the therapeutic interaction would not lead to insightful, introjective identificatory, adaptive inner change.

A more positive, if brief, sequence may be seen in the patient's responses to the therapist's first intervention in this second hour. First, there is the validation of the therapist's silent hypothesis (Langs, 1978) that the patient was unconsciously alluding to her relationship with the therapist. In addition, in the adaptive context of this particular intervention, the reference to things being better in the past can be seen as an affirmation of the therapist's comment. In this context, the allusion to the security blanket has positive connotations (in addition to other meanings discussed above). While the patient's response is certainly a mixed symbolic communication—a *transversal* communication (Langs, 1978)—that embodies both positive and negative elements, it has a distinctly constructive aspect that is lacking in her responses to other interventions.

Unfortunately, the therapist intervened a second time before the patient could continue her associations. We therefore do not know whether the patient would have provided additional communications that would have permitted further interpretation of this unconscious communicative interaction and its genetic components—the essential work that leads to the curative effects of the therapist's inevitable and preponderant countertransferences.

Concluding Comments

This presentation has been an elaboration and clarification of the generally accepted, though often misused, thesis that countertransference in the narrow sense, while detrimental to the process of cure, is nonetheless essential to that very process; that once expressed, it can be significantly modified and ultimately contribute to a positive and insightful therapeutic resolution of the patient's neurosis. It has been necessary to specify, however, that unresolved and repetitive countertransference expressions can destroy insightful therapeutic interactions and generate a stalemated or detrimental therapeutic outcome, significantly fixating the patient's neurotic adaptation so that it becomes virtually unmodifiable. Preliminary clinical indications suggest that these detrimental effects carry over to any new attempt at therapy. Once patients' defenses, barriers, and pathological gratifications have been satisfied by a therapist, they are loath to seek other solutions to their neurosis. Instead, such patients characteristically tend, consciously or unconsciously, to defend their previous destructive therapists and to prefer their own neurotic adjustment to an anxiety-provoking but truthful and sound therapeutic exploration.

The positive effects of analytic work based on the sequence described earlier—that is, a notable countertransference is expressed; then the analyst recognizes it, rectifies its influence, and fully interprets the patient's responses—are now rather well known. Less clearly understood are the important differences between this type of therapeutic experience and those in which the therapist has not expressed himself through repetitive or preponderant countertransferences. While we can make only a rough estimate, a broad review of the clinical psychoanalytic literature suggests that the sequence in which significant countertransferences play a role is far more common than is usually recognized. In terms of present therapeutic techniques, most ultimately valid therapeutic work appears to take place on such a basis (Langs, 1980), though all too often the countertransference elements are not recognized, rectified, or interpreted.

Countertransference expressions do indeed actively mobilize the residuals of the patient's pathological past and his present psychopathology; they afford an opportunity for living analysis and working through in the here and now. Nonetheless, therapeutic efforts in which countertransferences play a lesser role offer a steady, reliable image of the therapist as a sound container with secure holding capacities—a person capable of genuine, extensive, persistently constructive therapeutic efforts in the face of threat and danger. Such an approach implicitly offers a far more therapeutic image of the therapist and clearer, more viable interpretations accurately developed around the main truths of the therapeutic dyad than does therapy in which countertransferences generate repeated disturbances in both the identificatory and cognitive spheres.

There are, of course, many inevitably traumatic aspects to a sound therapeutic experience, and to the inevitable expressions of countertransference that arise in the course of the most effective therapeutic work. In the long run, while both courses—those with and without significant expressions of preponderant countertransference—can lead to constructive inner change in the patient, the latter is less risky and less likely to conclude with negative residuals.

Little attention has been paid to the role of countertransferences in noninsightful symptom alleviation. Many therapists accept the criterion of symptom relief as validation of their interventions and as a sign that countertransferences are in abeyance, failing to recognize the pathological means through which such effects may be realized. The present study of countertransferences has been designed to formulate several such avenues of "cure" as a means of promoting their identification in clinical practice.

We may conclude that countertransference is the single greatest hazard to cure, and yet one of the several essential components to insightful adaptive change. Since countertransference is based on unconscious fantasies, memories, perceptions, and introjects, the possibility that the therapist will fail to recognize countertransference expressions is considerable. For this very reason, the monitoring of the therapist's subjective state and the patient's material for countertransference expressions—for their contributions to cure as well as for their interfering aspects—becomes a first-order requisite for all therapists.

REFERENCES

Barchilon, J. (1958), On countertransference "cures." *J. Amer. Psychoanal. Assn.* 6:222–236.
Bion, W. (1962), Learning from experience. In: *Seven Servants.* New York: Jason Aronson, 1977.
—— (1977), *Seven Servants.* New York: Jason Aronson.
Bird, B. (1972), Notes on transference: Universal phenomenon and hardest part of analysis. *J. Amer. Psychoanal. Assn.,* 20:267–301.
Chediak, C. (1979), Counterreactions and countertransference. *Internat. J. Psycho-Anal.,* 60:117–129.
Cohen, M. (1952), Countertransference and anxiety. *Psychiatry,* 15:231–243.
Freud, S. (1905), Fragment of an analysis of a case of hysteria. *Standard Edition,* 7:3–122. London: Hogarth Press, 1953.
—— (1909), Notes upon a case of obsessional neurosis. *Standard Edition,* 10:153–320. London: Hogarth Press, 1955.
—— (1910), The future prospects for psycho-analytic therapy. *Standard Edition,* 11:141–151. London: Hogarth Press, 1957.
—— (1912a), The dynamics of transference. *Standard Edition,* 12:97–108. London: Hogarth Press, 1958.
—— (1912b), Recommendations to physicians practising psycho-analysis. *Standard Edition,* 12:111–120. London: Hogarth Press, 1958.
—— (1913), On beginning the treatment (further recommendations on the technique of psycho-analysis, I). *Standard Edition,* 12:121–144. London: Hogarth Press, 1958.
—— (1914), Remembering, repeating and working-through (further recommendations on the technique of psycho-analysis, II). *Standard Edition,* 12:145–156. London: Hogarth Press, 1958.

—— (1915), Observations on transference-love (further recommendations on the technique of psycho-analysis, III). *Standard Edition,* 12:157–171. London: Hogarth Press, 1958.

—— (1918), From the history of an infantile neurosis. *Standard Edition,* 17:3–122. London: Hogarth Press, 1955.

—— (1937), Analysis terminable and interminable. *Standard Edition,* 23:209–253. London: Hogarth Press, 1964.

Greenson, R. (1967), *The Technique and Practice of Psychoanalysis,* Vol. 1. New York: International Universities Press.

Heimann, P. (1950), On countertransference. *Internat. J. Psycho-Anal.,* 31:81–84.

Langs, R. (1974), *The Technique of Psychoanalytic Psychotherapy,* Vol. 2. New York: Jason Aronson.

—— (1975a), Therapeutic misalliances. *Internat. J. Psychoanal. Psychother.,* 4:77–105.

—— (1975b), The therapeutic relationship and deviations in technique. *Internat. J. Psychoanal. Psychother.,* 4:106–141.

—— (1976a), *The Bipersonal Field.* New York: Jason Aronson.

—— (1976b), Misalliance and framework in the case of Dora. In: *Technique in Transition,* New York: Jason Aronson, 1978, pp. 231–251.

—— (1976c), *The Therapeutic Interaction,* Vols. 1 & 2. New York: Jason Aronson.

—— (1978), *The Listening Process.* New York: Jason Aronson.

—— (1978–1979), Some communicative properties of the bipersonal field. *Internat. J. Psychoanal. Psychother.,* 7:89–136.

—— (1979a), Inevitable countertransference: Hazardous vehicle of cure (unpublished paper).

—— (1979b), Interventions in the bipersonal field. *Contemp. Psychoanal.,* 15:1–54.

—— (1979c), *The Therapeutic Environment.* New York: Jason Aronson.

—— (1979d), Three modes of cure in psychoanalysis and psychotherapy (unpublished paper).

—— (1980), Truth therapy, lie therapy. *Internat. J. Psychoanal. Psychother.,* 8:35–44.

Little, M. (1951), Countertransference and the patient's response to it. *Internat. J. Psycho-Anal.,* 32:32–40.

Loewald, H. (1960), The therapeutic action of psycho-analysis. *Internat. J. of Psycho-Anal.,* 41:16–33.

Racker, H. (1957), The meaning and uses of countertransference. *Psychoanal. Quart.,* 26:303–357.

Reich, A. (1951), On countertransference. *Internat. J. Psycho-Anal.,* 32:25–31.

—— (1960), Further remarks on countertransference. *Internat. J. Psycho-Anal.,* 41:389–395.

Searles, H. (1959), The effort to drive the other person crazy—an element in the aetiology and psychotherapy of schizophrenia. *Brit. J. Med. Psychol.,* 32:1–18.

—— (1975), The patient as therapist to his analyst. In: *Tactics and Techniques in Psychoanalytic Therapy, Vol. 2: Countertransference,* ed. P. Giovacchini. New York: Jason Aronson.

Strachey, J. (1934), On the therapeutic action of psycho-analysis, *Internat. J. Psycho-Anal.,* 15:127–159.

CHAPTER 8

Identification and Related Psychic Events:
Their Appearance in Therapy and
Their Curative Value

Vamık D. Volkan

A Review of Identification and Related Concepts

The main focus of this chapter is the curative nature of the patient's identification with the representation of his therapist in the course of psychoanalytic psychotherapy. It will become clear that it is no easy task for a therapist
to observe, monitor, and research the sometimes silent healing and growth that
result from such identification. In patients with severe regression in ego organization, identification may be overt and present a "hot" focus for the therapeutic process. Such patients facilitate research on how the representation of
the therapist can become an enriching identification for the patient.

Identifications are the end result of related but different psychological
events. The subject of identification has received much attention in the psychoanalytic literature, but there is no unanimity among the views expressed.
Thus I feel the necessity to clarify my concept of identification as well as
related concepts—i.e., introjection, the introject, imitation, incorporation,
internalization, projection, externalization, and projected identification—
before offering relevant clinical material.

Introjection "signifies an activity": the self-representation takes in an object
representation. The result may be an identification, which "is a more static
term, describing a state of affairs" (Fuchs, 1937, pp. 276–277). In identification, the self-representation resembles the object representation. Introjection
that results in identification can serve to maintain a close tie to an object or its

representation. Freud (1921) spoke of identification as "the earliest expression of an emotional tie with another person" (p. 105). But at the same time introjection (especially when followed by identification) opens the way for relative independence from an object or its representation. When self and model are perceived as one, the self achieves relative independence insofar as it no longer needs the model to function autonomously.

The establishment of relative independence through identification may itself yield different and sometimes contradictory results. For example, identification with the lost object is disruptive in neurotic depression. As Freud (1917) wrote, when love for the lost object cannot be surrendered, identification with the object (representation) takes place. "Then the hate comes into operation on this substitute object, abusing it, debasing it, making it suffer and deriving sadistic satisfaction from its suffering" (p. 251). The representations of the sufferer and of the substitutive object are one in this disruptive identification. In this type of clinical condition, the patient's self-accusations are really reproaches directed at the lost object "that have been shifted on to the patient's own ego" (p. 248).

It is possible, however, for identification to enrich the ego. In describing the structural theory, Freud (1923) explained how identification plays an important role in the development of ego and superego. Following his ideas, Anna Freud (1936) described "identification with the aggressor." In a major contribution, Hartmann (1939) emphasized the importance of taking part of the external world into the internal one: "In phylogenesis, evolution leads to an increased independence of the organism from its environment, so that reactions which originally occurred in relation to the external world are increasingly displaced into the interior of the organism. The development of thinking, of the superego, of the mastery of internal danger before it becomes external, and so forth, are examples of this process of internalization" (p. 40). Hartmann and Loewenstein (1962) later spoke of internalization as the replacement of those regulations that govern interaction with the outside world by inner regulation.

The psychoanalytic study of children played no small part in stimulating interest in introjection, the related concept of projection, and identification (Knight, 1940). Unfortunately, key terms have been used interchangeably and/or for different emphasis in psychoanalysis. Freud himself, during the years when psychoanalytic understanding was being formulated, used the terms introjection, identification, incorporation, and imitation interchangeably. As interest in these concepts grew, attempts were made to clarify them (Fuchs, 1937; Knight, 1940; Greenson, 1954; Brody and Mahoney, 1964; Miller et al., 1968). It was Schafer (1968), however, who made the most telling attempt (other than the contribution of Hartmann and his coworkers) to examine the specificity of these terms closely. He used *internalization* to refer to *all* "those processes by which the subject transforms real or imagined regulating interactions with the environment, and real or imagined characteristics of his environment, into inner regulations and characteristics" (p. 9). Schafer saw introjection and identification as two distinct types of internalization, and he used *incorporation* to refer to a specific wishful primary-process ideation about taking the object in through the mouth or other body orifice.[1]

There is controversy about continuing the use of another psychoanalytic term: *introject.* The act of introjection, which consists of taking an object representation into the self-representation, may fall short of the kind of melding of one into the other that characterizes identification. Instead, the object representation is perceived as an ongoing, discrete phenomenon *within* the patient. It is usual for psychotic patients and children (Schafer, 1968), as well as those suffering from *established pathological mourning* (Volkan, 1976, 1981), to describe such an inner presence, which may also be spoken of as a "frozen" entity (Giovacchini, 1967; Volkan, 1981).

Jacobson (1964, 1971) and Kernberg (1975, 1976) conspicuously refrain from using the term introject in situations where others would find it appropriate. They prefer to use the term introjection instead. I prefer not to use such a broad term to speak of the inner presence patients describe—i.e., the representation of the head, voice, or other aspect of the other that patients feel is lodged inside them—since such a felt presence is a describable, specific clinical phenomenon. But are all object representations that are taken into the self-representation introjects? Schafer (1968) states that objects become introjects in a crisis—for example, when they are urgently needed and are unavailable, or when they are caught up in extreme ambivalence. In his view, both the genesis of an introject and its continued existence represent attempts to modify distressing situations vis-à-vis the external object. Giovacchini (1972a) refers to introjects as "experiences and objects that have become part of the ego but have a structure of their own that distinguishes them from the rest of the ego" (p. 157).

Elsewhere (Volkan, 1976) I have described an introject as a specific kind of object representation that strives to be absorbed by the self-representation in order to achieve a certain degree of identification (although a true melding of self- and object representation does not occur). Introjects are functional in the sense that they influence the self-representation, but they do not lead to structural changes in it—and therefore in the ego organization—as do identifications.

Although most of the frozen inner presences patients describe are *object* rep-

---

[1]It is most interesting that, in 1973 Schafer argued that internalization is a "pseudospatial" metaphor "that is so grossly incomplete and unworkable that we would do best to avoid it in psychoanalytic conceptualization . . . it refers to a fantasy, not to a process" (p. 434). I (Volkan, 1976) have emphasized the importance of Schafer's 1968 contribution, however. Its theoretical formulations provide technical tools for understanding and employing technical maneuvers.

resentations that are needed and/or are established at a time of crisis, there are situations in which patients will describe a frozen, unassimilated *self*-representation that they perceive as "a foreign body" buried in their chest. For example, the latter state of affairs appears in the "little man" phenomenon described by Kramer (1955), Niederland (1956), and myself (Volkan, 1965), in which patients begin referring to part of themselves as "the little man," or sometimes "the little boy," "the little lord," etc. This phenomenon appeared in treatment when patients became aware of the resistance of this part of themselves to treatment. The analysis of "the little man" indicated that the term referred to an ego segment—or, in the terminology of today, a self-representation within this ego segment—that continued its autonomous existence, unchanged and unmodified, throughout the patient's life. The establishment of "the little man" arises from early successive narcissistic injuries; its primary aim is the restoration of the lost infantile omnipotence and its continuing protection and preservation.

Although the literature usually refers to the inner presence of a special and unassimilated object representation as an introject, the "little man" phenomenon reminds us that not all inner presences are predominantly object representations. Indeed, it seems to me that in practice all introjects that are special object representations are to some extent contaminated by corresponding self-representations. For example, when a schizophrenic patient perceives and describes a demoniacal presence in his head, it is revealed by analysis to be both an early perception of an early "bad" part object and condensed aspects of the early "bad" self.

Sometimes a patient will describe the introjection of the therapist's representation and the consequent formation of an introject of the therapist. This introject may be initially distorted by the externalization of archaic introjects and fragmented self-representations on it. At other times the introject of the therapist competes with other archaic introjects for influence over the patient's psychic structure and/or behavior (Volkan, 1968, 1976). Boyer and Giovacchini (1967) insist that the first task in treating patients with severe disorganization of the ego is to modify their archaic introjects. Giovacchini (1972b) goes further in coining the term *analytic introject,* which applies when the representation of the analyst that is taken in is *not* contaminated either by externalization of existing introjects and fragmented self-representations into it or by archaic fantasies, but provides a model of the analytic attitude for the patient. I may add that what is sought here is the depersonification of the analytic introject in order to involve its functions in an identification. In describing "transmuting internalization," Kohut (1971) emphasized that once the psychic apparatus is ready for the formation of structure there is a breaking up of those aspects of the object representation that are being internalized (identification). During this process depersonification of the object representation takes place. The emphasis shifts from the total human context of the object's personality to certain of its specific functions. Thus the internal structure becomes able to perform those functions that the object itself formerly had to execute for the child.

Gaddini (1969) reviews the literature on *imitation*, reminding us that the psychic protomodel of imitation—"imitating in order to be"—instills itself not in the presence of the object but in its absence. Because of this, he says, the aim of imitation "seems to be that of re-establishing in a magical and omnipotent way the fusion of the self with the object" (p. 477); and "In the process of identification imitations and introjections are found and integrated in the service of the aims of adaptation and of the reality principle" (p. 484).

Another concept—that of *projection*—is related to that of identification. It was developed by Freud in 1895, and in his later writings he used five interrelated but differentiated applications under the general heading of projection (Novick and Kelly 1970). Rapaport (1952) described different conceptualizations of projection. He envisioned a continuum "extending from the externalization of a specific type of tension in paranoid projections, to that of any kind of tension in infantile projection, to that of a whole system of attitudes and tension in transference phenomena, to where it imperceptibly shades into the externalization in the form of a 'private world' defined by the organizing principles of one's personality" (p. 463).

Novick and Kelly (1970) use the term *externalization* to refer to a specific type of projection. It is striking that externalization, as Novick and Kelly describe its application in the psychoanalytic literature, is not directly opposed to what would appear to be a contrary concept: internalization. Novick and Kelly use the term externalization as it pertains to the projection of aspects of the self, but differentiate it from projection proper, which is motivated by the sequence of fantasied dangers that arise from drive expression. Projection proper—putting out onto the external world a painful impulse or idea—may, however, be condensed in externalizations. Novick and Kelly believe that as the self emerges from the state of "primal confusion," the child faces the extremely difficult task of integrating the various dissonant components of the developing self. The earliest conflicts that the child confronts relate to attempts to integrate incompatible aspects of the self. Some aspects are valued because they are associated with pleasure—or, more important because they meet with favorable response from parents. Other aspects become dystonic and are externalized. This concept can be enlarged if we include whole or part objects, the ego ideal, or parts of the superego as elements to be externalized (Zinner and Shapiro, 1972).

Knight (1940) pointed out the role of projection (and by implication externalization) in identification. Jaffe (1968) described how this mechanism of projection seeks, on the one hand, to bring about the object's annihilation (when the object is distanced), and on the other hand, to preserve a tie with it (when the object is not sufficiently distanced to be lost but can still be used for identification).

The origin of Novick and Kelly's *externalization*—and its place in object relations—can be traced back to Melanie Klein's (1946) term *projective iden-tification,* which referred to "a combination of splitting off parts of the self and projecting them on to another person" (p. 108). In 1955 she added "the feeling of identification with other people because one has attributed qualities or attri-butes of one's own to them" (p. 58). In this sense projective identification is closely associated with a symbiotic or transitional object relationship (Modell, 1963, 1968; Volkan, 1976). In such a relationship the patient perceives the important other (analyst) as an independent entity but one nevertheless invested almost entirely with qualities emanating from the patient (Modell, 1963).

Zinner and Shapiro (1972) state that projective identification, as an activity of the ego, modifies the perception of the object and in a reciprocal fashion alters the image of the self: " . . . projective identification provides an important conceptual bridge between an individual and interpersonal psychology, since our awareness of the mechanism permits us to understand specific interactions *among* persons in terms of specific dynamic conflicts occurring *within* individ-uals" (p. 523). In view of this interpersonal ramification, it is not surprising that projective identification has been carefully scrutinized in transference and countertransference phenomena by Rosenfeld (1952, 1954); Racker (1968), Giovacchini and Boyer (1975), Kernberg (1975, 1976), Searles (1979), and others.

The Therapist's Representation as the "New Object"

A major attempt at metapsychological understanding of the therapeutic (psychoanalytic) process appeared in Strachey's (1934) now classic paper. He reminded us that the patient's original superego is a product of the introjection of archaic objects distorted by the projection of infantile id impluses. The char-acter of this superego can be altered, he claimed, through the mediation of an auxiliary superego which is the product of "the introjected imago of the ana-lyst" (p. 140). The repeated introjection of the images of the analyst—when not distorted by archaic projections—changes the quality of the patient's harsh superego. Heiman (1956) later stated that what really changes the archaic superego is the modification of the ego during the analytic process. The ego recognizes impulses and projections, and other conditions for setting up the archaic superego, and thus the modification of the ego certainly changes the character of the superego.

In 1951 Hendrick described what he called "ego-defect" neuroses. He maintained that many of these are psychoses and that others resemble the psycho-neuroses, although from a psychodynamic point of view the latter are closer to psychoses "in that the functional incapacities of the individual result from fail-ure to develop some type of essential integrated functioning at some time dur-ing the development of the ego" (pp. 44–45). In general Henrick was referring to borderline and narcissistic personality organization, to use the terminology of today. The symptoms displayed in these cases are not primarily the result of a healthy ego's defense against an unresolved infantile conflict, but the result of a fundamental inadequacy of some essential function of the ego itself.

Hendrick described how the infant provides itself with executant capacities by selecting partial functions from the mother. He referred to this process as *ego identification*. Although identifications leading to superego formation involve the more mature object relatedness of a child going through the reso-lution of the Oedipus complex, ego identifications are chiefly derived from the mother's way of doing things. Ego identifications therefore contribute substan-tially to the child's growing capacity to deal effectively with the external world. They are essential to the development of a useful ego organization; failure in essential ego identification will result in "ego-defect" neurosis in adult life.

Although Hendrick did not specifically refer to the therapeutic process itself, he implied that the main aim of therapy for those with defect in some ego functions is to correct their deficiency through new partial identifications. He noted that the acceleration of the process of identification is commonly accom-panied by abundance of oral—especially cannibalistic—fantasies (which Schafer [1968] would call incorporative fantasies).

More recently, Loewald (1960) has emphasized the importance of changes in the ego in the therapeutic process. He declares that psychoanalytic treat-ment is in many ways like the process of normal personality development, and that ego development is resumed during the therapeutic process of psycho-analysis. Loewald cites Erikson's (1956) concept of identity crisis in support of his view. Although there is marked consolidation of ego organization about the time the Oedipus complex is resolved, ego development does not stop there, but continues indefinitely unless psychosis or neurosis intervenes. Higher integra-tion and differentiation of the psychic apparatus are continuous in the absence of such disturbance. There are periods of consolidation after the Oedipal phase—one toward the end of adolescence and others at different phases of the life cycle. Consolidation occurs after a period of ego regression.

I believe that the notion that ego regression may give way to a new ego organization is best illustrated in mourning. If one looks at the psychological processes involved when a loss by death occurs, one will see that, after the initial reaction of shock, anger, and disbelief and the subsequent work of mourning, there is a disorganization that signals a new organization (unless complications develop) (Bowlby, 1961; Bowlby and Parkes, 1970; Volkan,

1981). Only then can the death be more realistically accepted. Psychologically speaking, the representation of the dead is no longer exaggeratedly needed, and libidinal and aggressive investment in this representation can be withdrawn and directed to new objects. During this time, the bereaved one may be able to experience relative autonomy, and thus ego growth, by identifying fully with the enriching functions of the dead person.

Erikson used the term *identity crisis* to describe ego regression that culminates in disorganization, followed in turn by reorganization. Loewald saw the promotion of transference neurosis in psychoanalysis as a means of inducing ego disorganization and reorganization—in short, ego development. He further suggested that the resumption of ego development in psychoanalysis is contingent on the relationship with a new object—the analyst. The analyst's "newness" consists in:

> . . . the patient's rediscovery of the early paths of the development of object-relating leading to a new way of relating to objects and of being one's self. Through all the transference distortions the patient reveals rudiments at least of that core (of himself and "objects") which has been distorted. It is this core, rudimentary and vague as it may. be, to which the analyst has reference when he interprets transferences and defenses, and not some abstract concept of reality or normality, if he is to reach the patient [Loewald, 1960, p. 20].

Similar descriptions of the analyst as a new object or as a "real person" can also be found in Kernberg's (1972) and Volkan's (1976) writings.

The relationship between child and parent provides a model. Loewald reminds us that when a child internalizes aspects of his mother, he is also internalizing the mother's image of himself—i.e., the way the mother sees, feels, smells, hears, and touches him. Thus, early ego identifications are built not only by absorbing what the mother is like, but also by absorbing how the mother regards her infant. "The child begins to experience himself as a centred unit by being centred upon . . . in analysis, if it is to be a process leading to structural changes, interactions of a comparable nature have to take place" (Loewald, 1960, p. 20).

The process Loewald describes applies to patients who have achieved a cohesive self-representation and corresponding integrated object representations. Patients who are psychotic or borderline, or who lack a cohesive self-concept and integrated object representations, experience the same process on a more archaic level, reminiscent of the early parent-child relationship. "The further we move away from gross ego defect cases, the more the integrative processes take place on higher levels of sublimation and by modes of communication which show much more complex stages of organization" (Loewald, 1960, p. 21).

Other analysts have made similar observations. For example, Cameron (1961) holds that operation on archaic levels, while creating problems, permits the borderline or psychotic patient to use the equivalent of early partial identifications in a way that a person with a more maturely developed psychic system could not. "It may even still be possible ... to introject massively with archaic completeness in adulthood and then be able to assimilate the new introject as an infant might, so that it disappears as such, but some of its properties do not" (Cameron, 1961, p. 95).

However, introjection from the outside world into the ego does not enrich the ego unless there is already clear differentiation between that which belonged to the one and that which belonged to the other (A. Freud, 1936). If the patient is regressed to a level on which self- and object representations are not differentiated, then the therapist's representation is either undifferentiated from, or heavily contaminated by, the patient's self-representation and internalized object representations. Thus the therapist's representation is *not yet* a "new object"; therefore, identification with it will not enrich the patient's psychic structure. With gentle clarification and confrontation the therapist must help the patient to "decontaminate" the therapist's representation in a piecemeal fashion.

With this type of severely regressed patient, primitive relatedness is reactivated once the treatment is under way. The representation of the therapist, whether realistic or not, is going to be included in an introjective-projective relatedness. Any maneuver of the therapist to offer himself or herself directly as a model is a seductive intrusion that will awaken anxiety and reduce the potential for ego building. It is important to monitor the patient's image or representation of the analyst and how it is contaminated by other archaic images or representations. The analyst should also take into account how much competition (Volkan, 1968) or even jealousy (Searles, 1979) is involved between the already existing archaic object representations and the representation of the analyst. Since the therapist is not taken in initially as the "new object" by severely regressed patients, he or she must help such patients differentiate the "new object" from the archaic representations in piecemeal fashion so that they can identify with the new object's observing, integrating, and taming functions (Volkan, 1968, 1976).

Different Levels of Ego Organization in Which Introjective-Projective Relatedness Includes the Therapist's Representation

It is my assumption that *introjective-projective relatedness* (I use this term in a general sense to include all the inner and outer flow as reviewed at the beginning of this chapter) appears in all psychoanalytic therapy but with differing clinical pictures and significance according to the degree of ego organization the patient has achieved. For example, if the patient is neurotic and has a cohesive self-representation, the introjective-projective relatedness is rather silent. It may appear openly in regression, but only temporarily and usually accompanied by an observing ego; the patient does not experience it fully as would the person with low-level ego organization. The main focus of a neurotic's analysis will be the interpretation of unresolved mental conflicts as they are related to drive derivatives and defenses against them and appear in the transference neurosis. In the background of this central endeavor, a "constant series of micro-identifications" (Rangell, 1979) with the analyzing function of the analyst will take place. Rangell refers to them as being the same as Kohut's (1971) "transmuting internalization."

In fact, the introjection of the analyst in a gross and exaggerated way involving a depersonified representation, i.e., one made up of the analyst's penis, nipple, face, or voice, is an unusual phenomenon in the treatment of neurotics (Rangell, 1979) which the therapist should react to as such, seeking to learn the reason for its appearance. However, if the patient suffers from what Hendrick (1951) called "ego-defect" neurosis, i.e., has a psychotic, borderline, and/or lower-type narcissistic personality organization (Kernberg, 1970), one may expect to see in the treatment the open and continued appearance of introjective-projective relatedness. The patient will openly refer to the therapist's representation along with and in competition with the archaic representations. There will be a "therapeutic story" of introjection, projection, imitation, and externalization, accompanied by incorporative fantasies and leading to identifications that will alter the patient's psychic structure and change his self-representation. This process usually includes the development and resolution of therapeutic symbiosis (Searles, 1961, 1963)—in other words, a transference psychosis. I will report such a "therapeutic story" later.

I agree with Boyer (1971) that once such a patient's ego organization matures, and once he or she forms a cohesive self and an integrated internalized object world, an upward-evolving transference relationship will appear. The development of more mature object relations with the therapist will occur in a transference neurosis, and introjective-projective relatedness will fall into the background of this relationship.

Of course, there is the danger that the "ego-defect" patient and his or her therapist may get "stuck" in the cycle of internalization and externalization, producing a therapeutic stalemate. Such a situation may result from: the utilization of such relatedness as a defense against anxiety (Searles, 1951); the fact that such an early mode of relatedness is so strong that moving out of it presents great difficulty; the therapist's lack of experience with such patients; or the therapist's failure to interfere with an endless introjective-projective merry-go-round.

It is well known that projective identifications in the treatment of such patients, which are sometimes accompanied by counterprojective identifications, induce exaggerated countertransference phenomena (see Rosenfeld, 1952; Bion, 1956; Giovacchini and Boyer, 1975; Searles, 1979). Such countertransference occurrences, unless understood and analyzed, result in therapeutic failure. In the "normal" course of events, however, the inclusion of the therapist's representation in the new identification of a patient when it has become an "analytic introject" will initiate integrative function, enabling the patient to mend fragmented and split self- and object representations and to attain a more cohesive identity.

The following vignettes will illustrate these theoretical statements. I will begin by describing aspects of a neurotic patient. One of his dreams reported here graphically illustrates how his introjective-projective relatedness appeared in the shadows of working through his infantile conflicts, most of which centered on an Oedipal theme.

A Ping-Pong Game

A sports-loving college student in his early twenties felt a pain in his chest while playing basketball, after jumping to put the ball through the hoop but missing. He thought this indicated cardiac problems, and thus gave up playing basketball and refrained from sexual intercourse with his wife, to whom he had been married for about a year. After a few months he consulted his family physician, who kept him in a hospital for a week undergoing tests. Since all the tests showed him to be in excellent physical condition, a psychiatrist was called in for consultation. His diagnosis was that the patient had a "cardiac neurosis," and the young man was referred to me for psychoanalysis.

The dominant meaning of his presenting symptom became clear soon after his treatment started. His father was a general in the armed forces, and the family had left their son in this country to continue his college education when the father was given an assignment in Europe. It was while his parents were abroad that he began to date the girl he later married (after she proposed to him). He had not told his family about his marriage. The day before he felt chest pains on the basketball court, he had received a letter from his father telling him of the family's plan to return to the United States within a few months and visit him as soon as they were in the country. Reading this letter made him anxious about the need to inform his parents about his secret marriage, and this anxiety lead to the incident that put a stop to sexual congress with his wife.

The secret of his marriage was connected with a childhood secret. When he was at the Oedipal age, his father left the family for an extended period on a military assignment, and during his absence his young son, who was handsome and intelligent, had become the man of the house and the focus of his mother's attention. The child's Oedipal triumph was short-lived since his father did return, but his mother kept alive in her son's mind a special liaison between them that was to be kept from her husband. While putting the little boy to bed at night the mother would lock his bedroom door and smoke a cigarette—of which her husband disapproved—as she sat on the edge of the bed. She would tell her child every night, "This is our secret. Let's not tell your father!"

This was a ready-made symbolic interaction that kept alive a secret Oedipal triumph. The child was in turn guilt-ridden, and into his teens and his years at college he saw his father as the Oedipal father, whereas in reality the general was a kind, gentle, and liberal man, as became clear only after his son described him to me for two years as a brutal warrior. It took three years of analysis to learn that the general's medals had been given him for some compassionate project concerning refugees rather than for expressing brutal force and bravery in battle, as his son had led me to believe.

As a teenager the patient had been unable to stay alone in the same room with his father without an anxiety attack. When he began to date he kept all knowledge of this activity from his father by going out and coming in through the window of his *locked* bedroom. When, after marriage, he had intercourse with his wife, he would jump off the bed after completing his lovemaking, open the windows, and sit down in front of the television. His fantasy was that any passerby would see him sitting there, and no one would guess that he had been engaged in intercourse, which remained a secret act.

The arrival of his father's letters put an end to his protection of this secret. The Oedipal father would learn about his son's sexuality! He developed symptoms of a cardiac condition to account for the interruption of his sexual activity and to defend himself against anxiety. In a sense, he was castrating himself in order not to be castrated. This formulation was well confirmed once his analysis started: for months he was accident prone, coming to his hours with me with real cuts and bruises that he showed to me so I would not damage him. Paradoxically, as soon as he began his analysis, he left school and became a laborer in order to build up his muscles, and engaged in much physical activity in spite of his fear of cardiac arrest. He showed me his muscles as though his strength were the other side of the coin of his castrated state, to make me hesitant to attack him.

Beginning with the first dream he reported to me, the Oedipal struggle between us appeared in ball games—basketball, volleyball, etc. In such dreams his representation and mine would appear on opposing teams. Although I will not give the details of his analysis, which was terminated successfully, I will focus on a dream of his that occurred when his Oedipal struggle had become "hot" in the transference neurosis. He moved back and forth in the Oedipal contest, facing toward and away from this threat as his analysis advanced. With bravado he would push forward to confront his analyst-father in defiance—as well as in a longing to know him—only to fall back defensively to a pre-Oedipal dyadic relationship with his pre-Oedipal mother. By the latter move he was able to escape the threat of castration that was sometimes associated in his fantasies with the fear of going blind.

In the dream he saw himself approach a building like the one in which I have my office and climb to the floor on which my office is situated. He found the furniture gone and the room empty. Going to the window, he saw a small boy and his mother on the street below. There was a shattering of glass, and small pieces of glass flew into the child's eyes, which then bled. The child clung to his mother's hand. Turning away from the window, the dreamer found a Ping-Pong table in the place of the usual furniture in his analyst's office. At one end of this table stood a man who obviously represented the analyst; he engaged the dreamer in a game of Ping-Pong. The pair played at a normal speed at first, but soon they slipped into slow motion. Occasionally the analyst held the ball for a moment before putting it into play. Although the ball was dark at the beginning of the dream, it got lighter each time it was in the analyst's court.

It became evident that the dream represented the patient's Oedipal fears (blindness) and subsequent defensive regression to a symbiotic tie with his mother. The Ping-Pong game represented a confrontation with his Oedipal father-analyst. The ball, which was laden with symbolic sexual meaning, alternated between the players. By the time he had this dream, the patient had learned much about his psychopathology pertaining to his Oedipal conflicts, but he was still engaged in an Oedipal struggle with me. He was preoccupied with Malcolm Lowry's novel *Under the Volcano,* whose title suggested homosexual surrender to Volkan-analyst. He had fantasies of smashing my office furniture with karate blows, although in his dream the furniture was replaced by a Ping-Pong table. The patient agreed with my suggestion that this dream was related to what was going on between us and was a sort of review dream (Glover, 1955).

I will now point to another theme of this dream that appeared beneath the symbolic representations. The slow-motion exchange of the Ping-Pong ball, and the gradual alteration of its color each time it was in the analyst's court, reflected the fact that at the peak of his Oedipal struggle with me he was able to see that whenever he attacked me in the transference as a brutal Turkish invader (his Oedipal soldier father) I was able to absorb his anger and tolerate the image he had displaced on me without responding harshly. He likened this transaction to the way the other player in the dream—the analyst—would momentarily withhold the Ping-Pong ball and then send it into the other court considerably lighter in color with each volley. He thus referred to the projective-introjective relationship between us that was helping him to tame his affects, and to reduce the heat of his Oedipal struggle and effect its resolution.

The above interpretation calls for a searching return to Freud's (1914) mirror analogy of the analyst's reflecting the patient's view. It is true that the analyst reflects the patient, but as was evident in the dream reported here, the analyst *absorbs* enough of the patient's material to reflect the patient's view "freed of guilt and anxiety" from "an altered perspective." Moreover, the analyst "evaluates what of his own experience with the patient needs to be reflected" (Olinick, 1969, p. 43).

If we call the patient's volleys into the analyst's court transference projections, we assume that the analyst's return volleys and the patient's introjective attempts will include whatever changes occur in the original projections as a result of the analyst's feeling responses. What interests us here is that the slow-motion Ping-Pong game appeared in the background of an Oedipal story. The central focus of the analytic process—and of the dream—was the Oedipal material: the anxiety over and defenses against the Oedipal impulses, the wish to resolve them, and their interpretation. The Ping-Pong game referred chiefly to the directions of the patient's drive derivatives pertaining to the Oedipus complex; self- and object representations flowing in and out between the two players were only implied.

The patient's associations indicated that at this point of his analysis the feeling of homosexual love had been transformed into hatred and was projected onto the analyst, who was seen as a castrator. The patient had seen a postcard on the analyst's table the day before. It came from Turkey and showed two Turkish wrestlers wrestling in the shadow of some minarets. Stimulated by the picture of the wrestlers in one another's embrace, the patient had a homosexual fantasy in which the minarets appeared as phalluses. When he became anxious he mentally "chopped off" the analyst's table into pieces. It was in the place where the table had stood that the Ping-Pong table appeared in the dream. The slow-motion play of the ball and its change of color from dark to light represented my tolerance of the patient's assaults and his subsequent identification with me in becoming able to tolerate his own unacceptable impulses.

With this neurotic patient—unlike "ego-defect" patients—introjective- projective relatedness primarily concerned painful impulses and ideas. In "ego-defect" patients, such relatedness would include a more apparent in-and-out flow of self- and object images contaminated with affect. Projective identification, attempts at identification for the building of a more cohesive self-system, and the integration of object representations might also be included.

The Tin Man

I do not mean to imply that in the analysis of neurotic patients we do not encounter introjective-projective relatedness that predominantly involves an in-and-out flow of self- and object images—that is, introjections, introjects, and identifications on the one hand, and externalization and projective identification on the other. However, such occurrences take place only after much ana-lytic work permits regression to take place, usually under the gaze of an observ-ing ego. The appearance of such introjective-projective relatedness is only a part of the patient's experience with his analyst.

A physician in his midthirties came into analysis after his wife left him. He had been "so good" to her that he could not understand why she had left him; he had a depressive reaction. As his treatment progressed I learned that his mother had been adopted by a rich family, but that when her adoptive parents died she was not provided with financial security in their wills. She married and my patient was her first child. She perceived him as someone whose success in life would ease her pain about being adopted. When my patient was 4½, his mother had a second son, who was sickly. The mother's attention was neces-sarily given to this infant, and the change was a narcissistic blow to her first child. He dealt with the situation by identifying with the "bad aspects" of the new infant in order to keep the nurturing mother near him. For two years in analysis he described the troubles he had had as an infant: he had had x-ray treatment for a thymus problem, and his mother had made him wear a special hat to fend off additional rays from the sun whenever he went outside. It was only after two years of work in analysis, and after his repression lifted and he tested reality by talking to those who had known him when he was a child, that he was able to report that it was not he but his brother who had undergone the x-ray treatment and been obliged to wear a special hat.

The narcissistic blow his mother had dealt him led to his need for an ideal-ized woman who would give him unending attention. The search for such a woman accounted for what he called "The other grass is greener" syndrome, which kept him unsatisfied with any one girl. His jealousy of and murderous rage toward his brother soon found their way into his Oedipal relationship with his father. In reality his father tried to reach him, but the son kept his distance from the Oedipal father. Later, although fiercely competitive with other men, he would symbolically castrate himself when success was at hand. In high school he was elected class president and was just about to take the most beau-tiful girl in school to the prom when when he "accidentally" chopped off one of his toes. As an adult he felt an obligation to "pay dues," as he later expressed it, in order to be successful.

He had married his wife in the belief that she was an ideal woman. She was the daughter of a highly successful man, and the patient fantasized that she would help him successfully resolve his Oedipus complex. Unfortunately, how-ever, he soon found that his wife was far from an ideal person, and he there-upon engaged in activities to improve her so she would become his ideal. Tired of his efforts to change her, she left him.

The first two years of his analysis helped him to understand the influence of his childhood circumstances, fantasies, and impulses on the formation of his character. In the transference neurosis he alternated between the frustrating search for an idealized mother and attempts to deal with his Oedipal father by paying his "dues." After two and a half years of treatment, armed with a great deal of understanding of his relationship with the mother of his childhood, he tried again to get to know his father. His direct interest in me as the Oedipal father became apparent. His father had died from a terrible illness at the time of his own graduation from medical school, and although in reality there was nothing he could have done for his father, he felt such guilt that he could not grieve for him. On the couch he at last became able to grieve fully, and this allowed him to renew work on his relationship to his idealized mother on a deeper level—to grieve over surrendering this ideal. The following material from this period in his analysis shows him revisiting his archaic part-introjects of his mother, and attempting to identify with the therapist's representation— first, as contaminated by these archaic introjects; and later, as a "new object."

As Halloween approached, he decided to make a costume representing the Tin Man in *The Wizard of Oz* for his ten-year-old daughter, who lived with him. It occupied a great deal of his time, and during his therapy hours it became clear that the Tin Man was himself. Its manufacture required putting together a number of different pieces and tying them in place with string. He said that his analysis had been like putting the pieces of a puzzle together and that he was integrating the different things he had learned. He asked me if I had ever seen the film *The Wizard of Oz,* and pointed out that the journey on the yellow brick road to the palace of the Wizard was like his analysis. He said that I looked like the Wizard, having the same color hair, etc. In the film, the Tin Man had expected the Wizard to respond to his wish magically, but neither the Wizard nor I, his analyst, had such magic.

The Tin Man had been able to cry in the end when he realized that he must be separated from Dorothy; I told the patient that I had been observing his attempt to abandon his search for an ideal woman and suggested that he was hesitant to cry for the possible loss of his idealized mother image. After a moment of silence he said that on the way to his hour he heard a story on the radio about a shop that repairs teddy bears, and that many grown people, including businessmen, take the teddy bears they have saved from their child- hood to this shop. The patient said that the bear of one businessman client had lost its hair, and that of another, its voice. Noting that no bear would be quite the same after being repaired in the shop, the patient said sadly, "I have my teddy bear in my mind. It is my mother. She is stuck in my throat!" Then his sadness gave way to anger when he recalled a childhood memory of his mother literally stuffing food into his throat. He understood that she had equated food with love, and that her love had been damaging to him. He had in fact become obese as a child because his mother fed him so much. Images of the loving, pampering, damaging, and smothering mother came and went during this treatment hour.

The next day the patient reported a dream in which the arm of the Tin Man was reaching into a toilet. He then described the floor of the toilet with its water-trap contour, and spoke of the Tin Man's arm starting to pull something out of its opening. It was not feces, but pieces of a human body—hands, arms, legs, etc.—all green. His associations indicated that he was cleaning up different images of his mother that were "stuck in his throat." The green color reminded him of the green witch in *The Wizard of Oz* who melted away when water was poured on her. In his dream the pieces did not melt in the water but had to be pulled out (externalized) piece by piece. The patient then recalled a childhood memory of his mother, who wore odd clothes, going to a department store in a black dress and black hat. She had a prominent nose like a witch's and a little boy pointed to her and screamed, "There's a witch!" hiding behind his own mother. The patient's mother had often told this story herself, but he now realized that she had been more hurt than amused by the incident.

During the rest of this hour, the patient played with different images of his mother. Once more his feelings ranged from sadness to rage. He was reviewing his mother's images as if to say farewell to them, but I sensed that he was afraid to surrender the "bad" images in the fear that the "good" ones would disappear also. It then became clear that he was using externalization (projective identification) to put the "idealized" images into me—for safekeeping, as it were. An item about the prime minister of Turkey had been in the previous day's news, and, knowing of my national origin, he fantasized that I was a relative of the prime minister, his cousin at least. I interpreted this as an indication that he was attempting to give up the archaic images of his mother that had influenced his character organization. He was afraid of losing idealized images with the smothering ones. In reality, his mother had openly discussed her own fantasy that she was the illegitimate daughter of a Spanish nobleman who had visited the state in which she was born!

When the projective identification had been interpreted, the patient went back to the work of integrating the different images of his mother and the corresponding images of himself. He spent his hour the next day talking about his girlfriend, and I could now see his identification with me as the "analytic introject." He was unconsciously using my own terms and analytic approach in describing his girlfriend as idealized, smothering etc. Finally he said, "She is the most put-together person," and added, "I am the one who can put together her different aspects to make her most realistic."

By going back to his previously repressed foundation and seeing the different bricks (introjects) of which it was made, he was able to use his new identification with me to modify and strengthen it. If we apply the same analogy to a patient with severely regressed ego organization, we might say that such a patient is doomed to continuous foundation building. In the therapy of such a patient the main issue is not the repairing of a structure, but the rebuilding of its very foundation.

The following case vignette of a chronically regressed patient is given to compare her "raw" introjective-projective relatedness with the kind of relatedness reported in the two vignettes above.

A Woman Whose Inner World Was Populated by "Aggressive" and "Benign" Creatures

A woman in her twenties began treatment by referring to her inner world, one populated with threatening animals or parts of them as well as parts of human bodies, such as eyes, faces, detached penises, or nipples. Alongside these aggressive images of animals and people were other, "benign" images that moved in and out. She felt that she lived in a world of poltergeists, where objects were moved by some mysterious power beyond her control.

Patients with borderline personality organization (Kernberg, 1967), like the patient above, have a tendency to polarize images into "benign" or "aggressive," "all good" or "all bad." Akhtar and I (1979) wrote that such polarization may also occur in schizophrenia, but schizophrenic images may shift from one camp to the other very quickly. In other words, the primitive splitting of opposing object representations (as well as self-representations) is not a stable defense in schizophrenia. Besides, there is fragmentation of images *within* each camp. In borderline patients, especially those on a high level, the images in one camp can be consonant, can "fit" each other. In schizophrenia, however, images within one camp—e.g., the evil eye, the head of a bloody bull, a detached penis—are in a constellation that is itself fragmented. There is tension or an absence of fit among the images in any one constellation.

In the treatment situation the therapist's image is soon included in the introjective-projective relatedness of patients such as the one under discussion, and it will appear alongside other images with which the patient is preoccupied. Soon after the young woman just mentioned began treatment, she would, while under stress, ask the therapist to look here and there, to move near to or away from the light—then she would blink her eyes as if they were the shutters of a camera. Thus she "took my picture," or introjected a representation of me via her eyes. In a crisis she would in effect create an introject, "developing" a picture in her mind to soothe her when she was away from me. My introject, contaminated by her "all good" archaic introjects, would then be used as a child uses a mother: as an external ego-superego. At this point in her treatment, taking me (my pictorial image) in would destroy me as an object in the external world; thus she could not altogether escape anxiety. Moreover, my soothing image could readily be contaminated with her "bad" image and be quickly shifted from the "benign" camp to the opposite one. She was taking me in in a personified fashion, in terms of my physical appearance. I was not yet being taken in in terms of my functions, but as a somewhat abstract being (or part of such a being).

I do not propose to discuss this case in detail here,[2] except to point to the patient's core difficulty: her inability to individuate fully. She had been born to a grieving mother who had a deformed child 1½ years old, who was not expected to live. When this tragic child did die, it was in the arms of her mother in a car taking them to the hospital, and my patient was with them. The mother's depression continued for some time, and her inability to be a "good-enough mother" dovetailed with the small child's sense of guilt (a form of survivor guilt) to provide the foundation of her psychopathology. Berman (1978) and Volkan (1981) have described patients whose lives were organized around guilt about the death of infant siblings whom the patients had never seen. My patient's sense of guilt was clear when for days during one period of her analysis she acted like a crippled baby, inducing intense "bad feelings" in me through projective identification. Since her mother had been distant from her, her father had tried to reach the child, but unfortunately he sexualized the interaction and overstimulated her, thus leaving her no choice but to be fixated in primitive object relations with their attendant conflicts and primitive defenses.

As the treatment progressed, the unavailable early mother appeared as images of cancerous breasts; the patient had corresponding images of good breasts in her mind. She wanted to save me (Searles, 1975) when I represented the grieving mother, and tried to leave good peaches and apples for me in my parked car. When she found the car locked and felt that she could not save me, she went into a psychotic panic. She felt, for example, that the earth was like an empty eggshell, and that if she stepped on it she would crush it and fall inside the earth. I acknowledged her wish to save me, and conveyed my appreciation of this to her. I then reassured her that I was in control of my faculties, and that her notion that without her efforts we were both without hope was a childhood fantasy. In time, when she could "hear," I also made genetic interpretation of the fact that she was repeating an effort to repair a grieving mother in order to have her mothering.

She then went through a "therapeutic symbiosis" (Searles, 1961, 1963), as was demonstrated by her belief that the couch was a swimming pool. She would lose the sensation of touch in parts of her body. Her body boundaries would disappear, and she would fuse with the analyst-mother (couch). Such fusion with the analyst represented a therapeutic regression from clinging to

---

[2]I have described other aspects of this case elsewhere (Volkan, 1975, 1976; Volkan and Kavanaugh, 1978).

fragmented good and bad images. When, with therapeutic help, she came out of her therapeutic symbiosis, she already seemed to have achieved a different and healthier individuation.

In the third year of her treatment she had a dream that indicated important structural changes that were beginning to take place within her.

> I was in a palace in front of a king. I told him I wanted to get married, and that he could help me. There were monks in the palace looking over old law books, one of which indicated that I could not get married. At this point I turned to the king and said, "*You* are the king; why don't you decide whether or not I can get married?" Then a vent appeared in the floor and drew in the pages of the archaic law books by suction. They disappeared.

This dream came after the patient's attempt to get her cat, Miss Kitty, put to sleep. She had been using this cat as a *reactivated* transitional object (Volkan and Kavanaugh, 1978), a bridge between mother-me and not-me (Greenacre, 1970). I felt at the time that the wish to "kill" the cat was in the service of intrapsychic separation from archaic mother representations. The dream reported above followed a dream of killing her father, which she reported in the same hour. In a sense she was saying, "The king is dead. Long live the [new] king!" The (new) king represented the structural change toward superego characteristics taking place within her. The archaic law books pertaining to archaic representations were disappearing as the (new) king was being established to decide about adult matters like marriage.

The dream report was followed by appropriate weeping, an indication that she could now grieve over what she was leaving behind. Within a few days the patient, who until then had continued to live in her parents' home, found an apartment and moved away from home to try living on her own. Just before having the "new king" dream, and while she was still in her parents' home, she cooked her own breakfast for the first time. In the next treatment hour after she moved into her apartment, she asked me for Turkish recipes. Since I am Turkish, she was in effect trying to internalize the "good therapist" via her incorporative wish. Instead of providing Turkish recipes I helped her understand her anxiety at the separation from her parental home and at the prospect of new relatedness to the world with the achievement of her newly found inner structure.

During her hours throughout the next month I felt comfortably sleepy most of the time. Finally I realized that she was speaking in an unusual, monotonous way. She was symbolically putting me to sleep with "lullabies." She was the "new" mother and I was the "new" baby. She spent hours in the kitchen of her new apartment baking pastries and thought of them as being made for me.

During this time she described her schedule of four hours a week with me as being "like that of a mother nursing a baby on schedule." Who was feeding whom was interchangeable in her mind. Sometimes she "fed" me and put me to sleep, but at other times I would perform these mothering functions for her in her fantasy. But such interactions—introjective and projective—were different from those that had appeared at the beginning of her treatment: they were much less contaminated with the absolutely "good" or "bad" images of her introjective-projective relatedness. She was experiencing new objects in the service of healing and growth.

Soon her interest in me as an element to be introjected (food) changed from the crude and cannibalistic form it had had earlier. She became interested in me in more sophisticated and "grown-up" ways. She was identifying with me on a different and higher plane. She began reading about my homeland and its people, taking a leap from eating to the cultural field. This led to her talking to me about the Middle East and Vietnam, where the war, to which she had previously made no reference, was taking place. She then began paying attention to world news and developed what she called "adult interests."

This patient successfully finished her analytic work with me in a little over six years. She is now married, and, as far as I know through checkups made over the years since her treatment ended, is an excellent mother to her two children, and a happy and supportive wife.

SUMMARY

This chapter deals with the appearance of introjective-projective relatedness in the therapeutic process. I define the terms and concepts that are included in such relatedness. According to the level of ego organization, the manifestation of such relatedness may be "open" or may exist within the shadows of more sublimated and sophisticated manifestations in the transference-countertransference phenomena. Introjective-projective relatedness may lead to identification with the functional representations of the therapist. Such identification enriches the patient's ego functions and serves as an essential part of the curative element in the therapeutic process.

For a patient with a defective ego organization, (i.e., one who lacks a cohesive self-representation and an integrated internalized object world), introjective-projective relatedness will remain the dominant focus of psychoanalytic treatment for a long time—until the cohesiveness of self- and object representations is achieved. The curative elements of an introjective-projective process that leads to new identifications in such patients can then be readily observed and monitored. Such patients provide us with a clinical laboratory for researching how structuralizations are formed and what kinds of curative factors result from structuralization.

REFERENCES

Berman, L. E. A. (1978), Sibling loss as an organizer of unconscious guilt: A case study. *Psychoanal. Quart.,* 47:568–587.
Bion, W. R. (1956), Development of the schizophrenic thought. *Internat. J. Psycho-Anal.,* 37:344–346.
Bowlby, J. (1961), Process of mourning. *Internal. J. Psycho-Anal.,* 42:317–340.
────── & Parkes, C. (1970), Separation and loss within the family. In: *The Child in his Family,* Vol. I, ed. J. E. Anthony & C. Koupernik. New York: Wiley, pp. 197–216.
Boyer, L. B. (1971), Psychoanalytic technique in the treatment of certain characterological and schizophrenic disorders. *Internat. J. Psycho-Anal.,* 52:67–86.
────── & Giovacchini, P. L. (1967), *Psychoanalytic Treatment of Characterological and Schizophrenic Disorders.* New York: Science House.
Brody, M. W., & Mahoney, V. P. (1964), Introjection, identification and incorporation. *Internat. J. Psycho-Anal.,* 45:57–63.
Cameron, N. (1961), Introjection, reprojection, and hallucination in the interaction between schizophrenic patients and the therapist. *Internat. J. Psycho-Anal.,* 42:86–96.
Erikson, E. H. (1956) The problem of ego identity. *J. Amer. Psychoanal Assn.,* 4:56–121.
Freud, A. (1936), The ego and the mechanism of defense. In: *The Writings of Anna Freud,* Vol. II. New York: International Universities Press, 1966.
Freud, S. (1887–1902) *The Origins of Psychoanalysis. Letters to Wilhelm Fliess, Drafts and Notes: 1887–1902.* M. Bonaparte, A Freud, and E. Chris (eds.) New York: Basic Books, 1954.
────── (1914), Observations on transference-love. *Standard Edition.* 12:157–171. London: Hogarth Press, 1958.
────── (1917), Mourning and melancholia. *Standard Edition,* 14:237–258. London: Hogarth Press, 1961.
────── (1921), Group psychology and the analysis of the ego. *Standard Edition,* 18:67–143. London: Hogarth Press, 1961.
────── (1923), The ego and the id. *Standard Edition,* 19:3–66. London: Hogarth Press, 1961.
Fuchs, S. H. (1937), On introjection. *Internat. J. Psycho-Anal.,* 18:269–293.
Gaddini, E. (1969), On imitation. *Internat. J. Psycho-Anal.,* 50: 475–484.
Giovacchini, P. L. (1967), The frozen introject. *Internat. J. Psycho-Anal.,* 48:61–67.
────── (1972a), The symbiotic phase. In: *Tactics and Techniques in Psychoanalytic Therapy,* ed. P. L. Giovacchini. New York: Science House, pp. 137–169.
────── (1972b), Interpretation and definition of the analytic setting. In: *Tactics and Techniques in Psychoanalytic Therapy,* ed. P. L. Giovacchini. New York: Science House, pp. 291–304.
────── & Boyer, L. B. (1975), The psychoanalytic impasse. *Internat. J. Psycho-anal. Psychother.,* 4:25–47.
Glover, E. (1955), *Techniques of Psychoanalysis.* New York: International Universities Press.
Greenacre, P. (1970), The transitional object and the fetish: With special reference to the role of illusion. *Internat. J. Psycho-Anal.,* 51:447–456.
Greenson, R. R. (1954), The struggle against identification. *J. Amer. Psychoanal. Assn.,* 2:200–217.

Hartmann, H. (1939), *Ego Psychology and the Problem of Adaptation*. New York: International Universities Press, 1958.

———— & Loewenstein, R. (1962), Notes on the superego. *The Psychoanalytic Study of the Child*, 17:42–82. New York: International Universities Press.

Heiman, T. (1956), Dynamics of transference interpretations. *Internat. J. Psycho-Anal.*, 37:303–310.

Hendrick, I. (1951), Early development of the ego: Identification in infancy. *Psychoanal. Quart.*, 20: 44–61.

Jacobson, E. (1964), *The Self and the Object World*. New York: International Universities Press.

———— (1971), *Depression: Comparative Studies of Normal, Neurotic, and Psychotic Conditions*. New York: International Universities Press.

Jaffe, D. S. (1968), The mechanism of projection: Its dual role in object relations. *Internat. J. Psycho-Anal.*, 49:662–677.

Kernberg, O. F. (1967), Borderline personality organization. *J. Amer. Psychoanal. Assn.*, 15:641–685.

———— (1970), A psychoanalytic classification of character pathology. *J. Amer. Psychoanal. Assn.*, 18:800–822.

———— (1972), Treatment of borderline patients. In: *Tactics and Techniques in Psychoanalytic Therapy*, ed. P. L. Giovacchini. New York: Science House, pp. 254–290.

———— (1975), *Borderline Conditions and Pathological Narcissism*. New York: Jason Aronson.

———— (1976), *Object Relations Theory and Clinical Psychoanalysis*. New York: Jason Aronson.

Klein, M. (1946), Notes on some schizoid mechanisms. *Internat. J. Psycho-Anal.*, 27:99–110.

———— (1955), On identification. In: *Our Adult World and Other Essays*. New York: Basic Books, pp. 55–98.

Knight, R. (1940), Introjection, projection and identification. *Psychoanal. Quart.*, 9:334–341.

Kohut, H. (1971), *The Analysis of the Self: A Systematic Approach to the Psychoanalytic Treatment of Narcissistic Personality Disorders*. New York: International Universities Press.

Kramer, P. (1955), On discovering one's identity. *The Psychoanalytic Study of the Child*, 10:47–74. New York: International Universities Press.

Loewald, H. (1960), On the therapeutic action of psychoanalysis. *Internat. J. Psycho-Anal.*, 41:16–33

Miller, A. A., Pollock, G. W., Bernstein, H. E., & Robbins, F. P. (1968), An approach to the concept of identification. *Bull. Menninger Clin.*, 32:239–252.

Modell, A. H. (1963), Primitive object relationships and the predisposition to schizophrenia. *Internat. J. Psycho-Anal.*, 44:282–292.

———— (1968), *Object Love and Reality: An Introduction to a Psychoanalytic Theory of Object Relations*. New York: International Universities Press.

Niederland, W. G. (1956), Clinical observation on the "little man" phenomenon. *The Psychoanalytic Study of the Child*, 11:381–395. New York: International Universities Press.

Novick, J., & Kelly, K. (1970), Projection and externalization. *The Psychoanalytic Study of the Child*, 25:69–95. New York: International Universities Press.

Olinick, S. L. (1969), On empathy, and regression in the service of the other. *Brit. J. Med. Psychol.*, 42:41–49.

Racker, E. (1968), *Transference and Countertransference*. New York: International Universities Press.

Rangell, L. (1979), Countertransference issues in the theory of therapy. *J. Amer. Psychoanal. Assn.* (Suppl.), 27:81–112.

Rapaport, D. (1952), Projective techniques and the theory of thinking. In: *The Collected Papers of David Rapaport,* ed. M. M. Gill. New York: Basic Books, 1967, pp. 461–469.

Rosenfeld, H. A. (1952), Transference-phenomena and transference-analysis in an acute catatonic schizophrenic patient. *Internat. J. Psycho-Anal.,* 33:457–464.

—— (1954), Considerations regarding the psychoanalytic approach to acute and chronic schizophrenia. *Internat. J. Psycho-Anal.,* 35:135–140.

Schafer, R. (1968), *Aspects of Internalization.* New York: International Universities Press.

—— (1973), Internalization: Process or fantasy. *The Psychoanalytic Study of the Child,* 27:411–436. New York: Quadrangle.

Searles, H. F. (1951), Data concerning certain manifestations of incorporation. *Psychiatry,* 14:397–413.

—— (1961), Phases of patient-therapist interaction in the psychotherapy of schizophrenia. In: *Collected Papers on Schizophrenia and Related Subjects.* New York: International Universities Press, 1965, pp. 521–559.

—— (1963), Transference psychosis in the psychotherapy of chronic schizophrenia. In: Collected Papers on Schizophrenia and Related Subjects. New York: International Universities Press, 1965, pp. 654–716.

—— (1975), The patient as therapist to his analyst. In: *Tactics and Techniques in Psychoanalytic Psychotherapy. Vol. II: Countertransference,* ed. P. L. Giovacchini, A. Flarsheim, & L. B. Boyer. New York: Jason Aronson, pp. 95–151.

—— (1979), *Countertransference and Related Subjects.* New York: International Universities Press.

Strachey, J. (1934), The nature of the therapeutic action of psychoanalysis. *Internat. J. Psycho-Anal.,* 15:127–159.

Volkan, V. D. (1965), The observation of the "little man" phenomenon in a case of anorexia nervosa. *Brit. J. Med. Psychol.,* 38:299–311.

—— (1968), The introjection of and identification with the therapist as an ego-building aspect in the treatment of schizophrenia *Brit. J. Med. Psychol.,* 41:369–380.

—— (1975), Cosmic laughter: A study of primitive splitting. In: *Tactics and Techniques in Psychoanalytic Psychotherapy, Vol. II: Countertransference,* ed. P. L. Giovacchini, A. Flarsheim, & L. B. Boyer. New York: Jason Aronson, pp. 425–440.

—— (1976), *Primitive Internalized Object Relations.* New York: International Universities Press.

—— (1981), *Linking Objects and Linking Phenomena.* New York: International Universities Press.

—— & Akhtar, S. (1979), The symptoms of schizophrenia: Contributions of the structural theory and object relations theory. In: *Integrating Ego Psychology and Object Relations,* ed. L. Saretsky, G. D. Goldman, & D. S. Milman. Dubuque, Iowa: Kendall/Hunt, pp. 270–285.

—— & Kavanaugh, J. G. (1978), The cat people. In: *Between Fantasy and Reality: Transitional Phenomena and Objects,* ed. S. A. Grolnick, L. Barkin, & W. Muensterberger. New York: Jason Aronson, pp. 289–303.

Zinner, J. and Shapiro, R. (1972) Projective identification as a mode of perception and behavior in families of adolescents. *Internat. J. Psycho-Anal.* 53: 527–530.

CHAPTER 9

Regression:
Curative Factor or
Impediment in Dynamic Psychotherapy?

Saul Tuttman

Many psychoanalytic theoreticians and practitioners consider regression to be among the important factors that may facilitate or impede growth in the process of dynamic psychotherapy. To some it is an inherent, unavoidable aspect of the process. Manifestations of regression may be considered a reflection of the analyst's limitations or of the patient's pathology. On the other hand, regression is sometimes looked on as a crucial factor in the therapeutic process leading to greater mental health.

The premises underlying psychoanalytic thinking are continually subject to question and reexamination (as well they should be). Among psychoanalytic constructs, the concept of *regression* and its ramifications have traditionally generated controversy and perplexity.

First, let us examine the word itself. "Regression" is defined by the *Oxford English Dictionary* (1971) as: "The act of going back; a return or withdrawal, to the place of origin . . . a previous state or condition . . . back in thought from one thing to another; from an effect to a cause; relapse, . . . reversion to a less developed form . . ."

Two opposing implications of this definition seem apparent: first, the undoing

An earlier version of this chapter was presented at the Annual Meeting of the American Academy of Psychoanalysis, Atlanta, Georgia, May 1978, and appeared in the *Journal of the American Academy of Psychoanalysis,* 7:111–131, New York: Wiley, 1979.

of progress, and perhaps a deterioration; second, the return to fundamentals and origins that might facilitate a potential reorganization and better integration. Indeed, there is something highly paradoxical in a process that is often considered a central factor in the most serious pathology[1] and yet is acknowledged by many to be an important means of treatment!

Do our patients really show signs of such a process? Are there observations to be made in practice or in the experimental laboratory which relate to this notion? Does the concept apply to Margaret, a middle-aged married woman, who came to treatment complaining of unbearable self-consciousness and insecurity? Since childhood she has suffered severe chronic constipation and has had great difficulty in urinating. By the time a therapeutic alliance was established, it became apparent that Margaret develops paranoid feelings of being invaded and controlled and that she considers herself the victim of everyone's manipulations and intrusions.

One day in the course of her analysis, she recalled early memories of being an only child in a small town. Her father was a minister and her mother a respected home economist. These educated parents applied with gusto the Watsonian principles so popular in child rearing at that time. Margaret's activities were carefully timed and structured. Mother and father were "pillars of the community," proud of the order and rigor in their lives. They were determined to have their daughter carry on the family traditions. Margaret was continually supervised and scrutinized by her parents, especially those days when she produced no bowel movement by bedtime! These self-sacrificing diligent caretakers would set the alarm clock for the middle of the night, then wake their daughter and place her on the "potty." They awaited dawn together anxiously. All three were exhausted, but the parents unrelentingly required the production of feces. Usually, the pressured child would not or could not produce.

In the following session, Margaret reported that after reexperiencing these memories, she had returned home (husband and son were not expected for several hours), placed a rubber sheet on the bed, removed her clothing and, in private, relaxed her sphincters and let it all out.

Was this "regression"? Was it therapeutic? Is Margaret getting healthier or more ill? Is it significant that this particular instance was not confined to the session and that careful control had been exercised by the patient to avoid harmful practical consequences of her *private* behavior? Was this act a regression or was it a progression toward a capacity to experience and explore her condition, which involved a previously repressed, ongoing regressive state that had been "acted out" in the external world without restraint or understanding?

At times during her sessions, Margaret became very belligerent and accu-

---

[1]E.G., Balint's (1968) "malignant regression" and Arieti's (1959) "progressive teleological regression."

satory toward the analyst; she complained that she was being degraded and controlled. Was this a sign of regression manifested within the transference? Could it be utilized therapeutically? How might such material prove beneficial for the patient?

There are many questions we might consider, among them:

(1) Are there relationships between the content, timing, pervasiveness, reversibility, therapeutic potential, and prognostic value of regression on the one hand, and the particular psychopathological state of the patient on the other?

(2) Are regressive manifestations recapitulations of earlier experiences? How can we know if they are? When are such states exploratory play that is encouraged or facilitated by the treatment? And can such "regressive" trends be useful in the treatment?

(3) When and how does regression lead to therapeutic change?

(4) What types of regression are helpful and what dynamics are involved?

(5) When do signs of regression in treatment represent a healthier flexibility involving enhanced, adaptive reintegrative potential and when are they manifestations of a decompensatory breakdown in control?

Historical Perspectives and Review of the Literature

The notion of regression is considerably older than psychoanalysis. Plato *(Timaeus)* believed that "disease may be due to a reversal of the formation of the structures" (Jowett, Ed., 1937, p. 8) or bodily tissues. Darwin (1871) occasionally employed a concept of "reversion" or atavism somewhat akin to phylogenetic regression.[2] Nietzsche (1909, p. 40) conceived of man, when dreaming, as "brought back to" modes of mentation characteristic of prehistoric times.

Freud proposed several concepts concerning regression (see Arlow and Brenner, 1964; Balint, 1968). His first view, expressed in *The Interpretation of Dreams* (Freud, 1900), was an application of Hughlings Jackson's (1888) hierarchical-evolutionary neurological schema. (Freud [1891] had also applied this schema earlier, in *On Aphasia*.) Freud's concept of "temporal regression" was based on the assumption that the gradual psychological development from simpler, primitive, stages toward more complex, organized levels is undone by regression. The concept of reversal of genetic development became one of the cornerstones of psychoanalytic theory.

Another concept of regression—topographic regression—also appears in

---

[2]Stanley Jackson's (1969) scholarly work offers a more thorough discussion of the intellectual climate that probably influenced Freud's thinking as he developed his regression concepts.

The Interpretation of Dreams. In order to explain the hallucinatory quality of dreams, Freud adapted the reflex-arc model. He proposed that, in waking states, excitation ordinarily begins as a sensory stimulus which passes from unconscious through preconscious to conscious thought, terminating in motor action. The regression toward the unconscious sensory imagery accounts for the hallucinatory nature of dreams.

Originally "borrowed" from biology, regression has gradually acquired meaning as a defensive and adaptive mechanism (e.g., in dreaming, avoiding stress) and as an element in pathogenesis (e.g., in hallucinations, infantile behavior).

Freud (1914) stated that, in retrospect, he had come to realize that during his early studies on hysteria, the turning backward in time found in patients' associations was a characteristic feature of neurosis. "Psychoanalysis could explain nothing in the present without referring back to something in the past and thus analytic technique that neglected regression would render scientific study of the neurosis impossible" (pp. 10–11).

Temporal and topographic regression gradually found their way into theory of psychoanalytic technique. As Freud formulated newer *theoretical* constructs involving progressive developmental aspects, still other forms of "backward movement" could be conceptualized. Consequently, as the psychosexual theory evolved, instinctual or libidinal regression was postulated. Similarly, energic, structural, and ego regressions have been described.

More recently Kohut (1971, 1977) proposed that there is a developmental pathway leading to mature narcissistic self-cohesiveness. Consequently, his treatment for narcissistic pathology involves "working through" the infantile states of narcissism in treatment (Tuttman, 1978).

Peto (1967) goes back to the first case in the history of psychoanalysis (Anna O.; see Breuer and Freud, 1893–1895) to show the dangers and benefits of regression. The problems led to Breuer's abandoning the patient. Only much later did Freud (1912) recognize the Scylla and Charybdis of "good" and "bad" regression. He sensed that the regressed transference could be a most potent resistance. And yet he acknowledged that in the transference certain patients repeated their forgotten past, which was otherwise inaccessible. This repetition was induced partly by the "new" technique of free association in the analytic situation. And so Freud referred to regression as an ally in analytic treatment.

Still later, in 1914, looking back at the earlier Dora analysis, Freud noted that in her treatment direct attempts to resolve the pathological effects of a recent trauma had failed and that Dora had had to make "a long detour, leading back over her earliest childhood" (p. 1); furthermore, he warned against the neglect of regression in analytic technique.

The tragic Freud/Ferenczi controversy more than forty years ago concerning the use of regression in treatment shocked the psychoanalytic community (Balint, 1968; Lorand, 1965). Ferenczi (1930, 1931) had continued his experiments with "active technique," work that Freud (1918) had originally supported. Ferenczi elicited the reactivation of what he considered to be vivid infantile traumas apparently involving significant child-rearing persons; and his patients craved reparation, comfort, and understanding. Ferenczi then experimented further. He wondered if the neutrality of the analyst might not repeat the attitudes of indifferent or neglectful parents. He therefore explored the possibility of reducing the tensions of these longings by responding positively; this new approach he called "relaxation technique" (Ferenczi, 1932).

Freud became distressed about the dangerous possibilities of arousing incessant cravings and frustration rather than "working them through" in accordance with the classical position (Peto, 1967). This clash between the "father" of the field and a brilliant pioneer—who died before the issues were clearly resolved—seems to have deflected conservative analysts from the further study of the potential in Ferenczi's work. Exploration of the therapeutic use of regression in analysis was suspended, especially by "classical" analysts.

Balint (1968) pursued this subject in relative isolation, keeping in contact with several of Ferenczi's former patients. Balint noted Ferenczi's eventual awareness of the hazards and failings in his research; however, there were great theoretical benefits. The data obtained from patients when the analyst did not maintain "classical" neutrality elucidated the effects the analytic attitude can have on the particular transferences that are encouraged. Furthermore, the technical possibilities of countertransference interpretations and the importance of the analyst's reactions opened up a new area for consideration (Ferenczi, 1932).

One of the classical analysts, Kris (1934, 1952), formulated a new and important idea about regression, mainly during his investigations of artistic creativity. He distinguished two forms of regression: in one the ego is overwhelmed by regression; in the other regression is "manifested in the service of the ego." In the latter instance, a well-integrated person has the capacity to regulate and use creatively some of the primary processes. There appears to be a relation between the two forms of regression described by Kris and the work of Balint, yet there is a vital difference in their concerns; namely, Kris was interested in sublimation and artistic creativity as an intrapsychic one-person psychological act, whereas Balint refers to a therapeutic regressive process occurring in a dyadic relationship.

Balint (1968) had carefully studied the value and dangers of regression. He conceived of regression as benign and beneficial in treatment when the analyst provides an accepting atmosphere in which the patient feels safe enough to regress "for the sake of recognition," understanding, and shared experiencing. In contrast, regression is malignant when the aim is libidinal gratification;

which, Balint (1968) proposed, is quite similar to regression that overwhelms the ego (Kris, 1934, 1952).

Although Kris was to some extent concerned with the therapeutic uses of regression, he was primarily interested in its intrapsychic aspects and in brief regressive episodes in a single session with relatively resilient personalities or creative artists. Alexander (1956) differentiated those who regressed to a past trauma from those inclined to regress to pretraumatic satisfactory situations. Knapp (see Guttman, 1959) proposed that "for a psychoanalysis to be possible, an additional capacity must supplement 'regression in the service of the ego,' namely, 'regression at the behest of an object'" (p. 144), and in the analytic dyad that object would be the analyst.

For some years, members of the British school, namely, Little (1960), Winnicott (1960), Guntrip (1969), Milner (1969), and Khan (1974), focused on regression as an important therapeutic tool. In addition, Fromm-Reichman (1950), Sechehaye (1951), Rosenfeld (1965), and Searles (1965) have worked in this area. Most of these therapists have dealt with very serious pathology. In recent years Wangh (Weinshel, 1966), Boyer and Giovacchini (1967), Frosch (1967a, 1967b), Peto (1967), and Wallerstein (1967) have explored the analyst's share in promoting regression, and they question the analyst's technical responses as well. Gerald Adler (1974) and his colleagues conducted a symposium (Shapiro, 1974) at Tufts University that examined these issues impressively. Countertransference factors were given much consideration. Volkan (1976) discusses, among other things, regressive aspects of primitive internalized self- and object representations and how to treat them. This work is, in part, based on Kernberg's formulations (1975, 1976) and therefore relates to important developmental observations and theories of Anna Freud (1965), Mahler (1975), and Jacobson (1964) regarding progression and regression.

I shall not elaborate a long list of theoretical concepts to answer the question: Is regression necessary or desirable? I prefer to present the story of a patient's psychotherapy that I believe and hope will illustrate the importance of the question under consideration and its therapeutic ramifications—for the treatment of at least this type of patient. I shall intersperse relevant theoretical points as they seem applicable to the case.

Case Example and Discussion

Inge,[3] at age forty-seven, believed that she was losing her hair at an alarming rate. In desperation, she consulted dermatologists and endocrinologists. She could not accept their findings that the measured rates of hair loss and natural

---

[3]Niederland (personal communication, 1979) reviewed this case and provided insights relating to his work on obsessional characters (1960) and Holocaust victims (1961).

replacement were within normal limits. She became overwhelmed with despair and panic, and she was referred for psychiatric evaluation.

Inge was a petite woman of German birth. Before World War II, when she was ten, her Jewish parents arranged for their children's release from Nazi Germany to England, where Inge remained until coming to the United States. About twelve years ago, she married a man of similar background. They are childless. He works as a specialized technician and she is an executive in a research organization. Despite limited formal education, Inge is an intellectually developed, cultivated person who speaks with a charming accent combining the grace of English and the precision of German. Her gentle voice approaches the meek and tentative, though she can reach levels of deep tension, sarcasm, and intense rage.

During treatment it gradually became apparent that Inge lived a life of profound emotional isolation. She married her husband *because* she did *not* "love" him. Consciously, she believed her only hope for deep satisfaction in life could come from being uninvolved and "free." Her goal was to exist surreptitiously in a perfect fantasy world uninterrupted by the pressures of the outside world. She went about paying "lip service," conforming to the routines with minimal energy. Aside from fantasy, her only interest was reading. She had never revealed to anyone the details of her secret world, although she does admit that as treatment progresses she lives less and less in fantasy.

This observation is granted grudgingly, with an air of both relief and wistful contemplation. There are indications to support her observation. For example, more effective work functioning resulted in a pay raise, praise, and a promotion to a complex, highly responsible position. Furthermore, an interest in my office plants—initially hampered by expressed feelings of futility and apprehension about her capacity to care for anything—has developed into an elaborate and gratifying hobby. It sounds as though she has become quite expert in the real world, at least as far as caring for exotic temperamental plants is concerned!

Despite these signs of greater participation and gratification via investments in the "outside," it remained difficult to know how Inge felt because of her almost endless guarded qualifications and obsessional "contortions." For example, she often states:

I cannot tell you how I feel because (1) if I do I *may* be unfair or incorrect—I can be vicious and hostile; (2) it will show you how awful I am and you will surely send me away; (3) furthermore, it will hurt you because I can see so clearly how inept and incompetent you are; (4) you may misunderstand and conclude incorrectly that I care for you or need you. In actuality, I am utterly indifferent and unconcerned about you.

She also made it clear that she considered herself stupid, dull, unworthy, and guilty. She was certain that I was critical, hostile, and disgusted with her. Her attitudes and moods were usually submerged, and she appeared bland and indifferent. As she became more comfortable or felt more provoked in treatment, her mood swings and shift in attitudes were indescribably extreme.

Details of her past history emerged slowly. Her father was an accountant and her mother a housewife. Father, as Inge recalled, would become enraged when not obeyed. Mother was "proper" and felt strongly about children's compliance and responsibilities. When Inge was eighteen months old, a sister was born. The little infant was colicky and demanding. Inge became angry and assaultive toward the newcomer and her mother would threaten to leave if Inge misbehaved by expressing anger. There was a brother (the oldest child) two years older than Inge, and the father was particularly harsh toward this son, who was to supervise the younger siblings. When her father was punitive toward the brother, Inge felt especially guilty.

When it was time to buy a pair of shoes, Inge reports, her parents took her to the store and a tight-fitting pair was offered. The child remained silent and suffered the pinching, feeling martyred and secretly enraged despite everyone's inquiries as to the fit; Inge responded that they felt fine.

Within the treatment situation, every time a telephone rang, she became morose. Every time a sound reflecting movement, breathing, or swallowing emanated from the therapist, Inge showed signs of profound tension. She tried to stifle her reactions but it was apparent to her that I could feel her reactions. Along with denial of all feelings, Inge released volcanic rage—despite her gigantic efforts to squelch it. She "accused" me of reading newspapers, preferring telephone talk with others—anything but listening to her! I was a hypocrite, a noncaring, self-centered, sadistic, "phony" doctor feigning an interest; but, then again, who could care for anyone as stupid and worthless as she? I even "cheat" her of time from her sessions; naturally I cannot stand her, but how hypocritical of me not to admit it and let her go, free her from this confusion and contradictory "mess" of our weird, unrealistic, chaotic "nonrelationship"! She pleaded with me to "let her go," but she kept her appointments regularly.

When Inge's rage and fear became unbearable, she would jump up and run out of the office, hurling curse words and shrieking that she would *never, never* come back! Sometimes she would become very morose and silent and then, a few hours after the session, leave a telephone message to the effect that she would have no more sessions as of now—good-bye forever! A few days later she would phone and meekly ask if I could see her immediately. I structured the situation by informing her that I would continue to hold her appointment hours for her—even if she said good-bye—for a while, at least, in case she decided to come back and explore things further. In this way, I reasoned to myself, I could reassure her that I was reliable and would not retaliate or mirror her behavior if she needed to experience "killing me" in rage; that a safe ongoing situation was possible in treatment despite her stormy reactions and harsh attacks.[4]

Inge's intense reactions, manifested gradually in treatment, impressed me as being part of the regressive transference expressions of someone who had developed a false self-organization, someone who had experienced cumulative traumata and a deep-rooted sense of helplessness and distrust. The regressive pull was frightening; Inge especially feared (1) the surfacing of primitive impulses and feelings, and (2) the temptation to take a chance by admitting her needs and emotions. The confusion about which of us (if either) was sincere, genuine, or worthwhile probably reflected a regressive dedifferentiation (of mental self-representations from her mental representations of others) that was further blurred by primitive splitting and projection.

This patient was torn between living a pseudolife—by attempting to bury all self-awareness—and taking the risk of looking back and experiencing and sharing her memories, accumulated pain, hate, guilt, shame, and neediness for emotional support and sensual contact.

Her initial caution—even in the form of negation—and her controls (though somewhat brittle) had reassured me of her ego strength. She had somehow been able to "contain" herself appropriately enough to go through the motions of living. Her dissatisfaction with the status quo was also encouraging. Despite her denial, I experienced the subtle beginning of a working alliance and gradually developing self-observation in the quality of her nonverbal response to my attentive presence. Despite her accusatory rage and craving for gratification, there were signs of hidden pleasure and relief whenever she was able to share feelings, to "be" and to be recognized! These signs indicated a positive prognosis for a therapeutic regression (Balint, 1968) despite Inge's probable borderline status in Kernberg's (1972, 1975, 1976) terms.

From time to time, Inge might say, "I must tell you something, but I cannot—I won't . . . it is so terrible. Surely you'll reject me. I'm so wrong and you will be contemptuous." She would repeat this theme over and over.

As a Jewish schoolgirl growing up in Nazi Germany, she had experienced the Nazi movement as it infringed on daily life. She was forced to leave public school. Every day fathers of her friends disappeared. She recalls running home from school and feeling ritually compelled to touch the stones of a particular government building en route. This magical gesture was her only means of ensuring that the Gestapo had not taken Papa away. The family maid, a loyal "Aryan," had worked for Inge's family for many years. And now the family became frightened of this housekeeper's potential for making serious trouble, so they cautiously avoided making her angry or jealous.

---

[4]Hoedemaker (1967) and Winnicott (1960, 1971) explore the therapeutic use of anger in treatment.

The atmosphere became increasingly ominous and the family tried unsuccessfully to leave the country. Finally, it became possible for Jewish children to leave Germany unaccompanied by their families. Inge felt frightened and happy at the same time. She claims to have been particularly pleased that she was sent to live with a foster family in an English city some distance from her sister and brother. The foster family was kind and accepting. When letters arrived from home, the child diligently replied; however, her parents' plea that their daughter ask the foster family to request visas for her mother and father was something Inge ignored. She felt ashamed and guilty about this, but she so valued being accepted that she wanted to forget the old home relationships in Germany and her foreign roots. She could not bear the possibility of her parents arriving; furthermore, she desperately feared that her request for their visas would be rejected by her foster family. Life was becoming quite pleasant and she felt "at home"; nevertheless, the secret guilt was intense and became even stronger when the letters from Germany ceased. After the war, documentation made quite clear her parents' fate in the concentration camps; and Inge considered herself to be their murderer.

Talking about this subject has been most painful for Inge and is often followed by verbal assaults against herself as well as against me.

Therapeutic Considerations

An understanding of the psychodynamics of severe characterological and early developmental states and fantasies aids the analyst in maintaining a monitoring role and an emotionally appropriate attitude. Despite the patient's provocations, accusations, misperceptions, and projections, a therapeutic sense of proportion becomes possible (Federn, 1952). Perspective about the historical roots of the patient's "acting out" and distortions helps moderate countertransference reactions. Of course, a great deal depends on the personality of the therapist; nevertheless, an understanding of the stereotypic, primitive, polarized introjects and defenses (which imprison and distort the patient's mental life) can help the analyst respond therapeutically.

Shortly after World War I, Ferenczi experimented with regression in treatment. His student, Michael Balint, appreciated the concept that inappropriate stimulation and lack of understanding by the early caretaker impeded the child's psychological growth and resulted in an internal sense of a "basic fault." Balint (1968) stated that these patients experience something distorted or lacking in the mind, producing a defect "which must be put right" (p. 21). Unless there was a "harmonious, interpenetrating mix-up" (p. 66) between significant other and self (at the preverbal, preconceptual stage before differentiation)— unless the parent "fit" the child's needs (as the amniotic fluid "fits" the fetus, the sea "fits" the fish, or the air "fits" the lungs); unless there was an unstructured, need-gratifying, spontaneous nonconscious flowing-between—a "basic fault" and its consequent pathology would result.

Thus, meaningful therapeutic work necessitates an opportunity for the patient to regress to that psychophysiological matrix (Tuttman, 1979) of a time before boundaries and words. Verbalizations or explanations alone are probably meaningless in such a framework.[5] The "pretransference resistance" concept of Sechehaye (1951) and the "dread of surrender to resourceless dependence" of Khan (1974) are concepts based on the following insight: patients who lack the crucial "support systems" established in early life would automatically and inevitably respond with dread and avoidance to the reactivation of their frustrated dependency needs, which have remained deeply unfulfilled ever since early childhood.

Thus, the first task of the understanding analyst who has determined that a therapeutic regression is indicated is to establish a trusting therapeutic partnership that encourages the dissolution of resistances to the regression. Once the resistances have dissolved, the patient must be allowed to experience acceptance and recognition. In this way, the treatment provides what was unavailable during the patient's early life.

Balint (1968), the major advocate of this approach, has been joined by other contemporary analysts who have become proponents of a kind of opportunity for regression in treatment. The focus is on the analytic atmosphere and the crucial dyads of (1) caretaker-child in early life and (2) analyst-patient in treatment. Related concepts are:

The "good-enough" facilitating environment, which involves the holding function of the mother or therapist and the availability of transitional objects and opportunity for play (Winnicott, 1960, 1971).

The "container" role of mother or therapist and the need to help establish links involving thoughts and feelings (Bion, 1977).

The basic unit of caretaker and dependent one (Little, 1960).

The protective shield (Khan, 1974).

The extrauterine matrix and symbiotic phase before individuation (Mahler, 1975).

The mirroring in self-discovery (Lacan, 1949).

The availability of a self-object and the opportunity for idealizing and mirroring (Kohut, 1971, 1977).

---

[5]Could there be some relationship between these concepts and the cerebral-cortical specialization data discussed by Bogen, Mandell, Knapp, and others at the May, 1977, meetings of the American Academy of Psychoanalysis in Toronto, Canada?

The importance of space, presence, and absence in development and treatment (Winnicott, 1960, 1971; Green, 1975, 1978): that is, in treatment, the patient needs an opportunity to experience a sense of self, both within his own psychological space and as apartness from others. Problems in these areas arose in early life in reation to parents who could not allow the growing child psychological space by acknowledging everyone's need and entitlement to be present sometimes and absent at other times.

According to such concepts, the patient's illness developed early in life through "cumulative trauma" (Khan, 1974) related to the unbearable "misfit" between mother and infant-child. The assumption is that, as development proceeds, healthy growth requires fusion, followed by closeness, and finally, space; transitional experiences and play are prerequisites for healthy individuation (Winnicott, 1960; Mahler, 1975).

Green (1975) talks about our failures with such patients as a reflection of present limitations in our therapeutic understanding. We impose too many words too authoritatively on the patient, which may tragically parallel the mother's insensitive intrusiveness. Perhaps patients sometimes need a respectful—rather than intrusive—presence, one that permits a sense of space.

We are too rigid or too idealistic if we think that it is a question of transforming primary processes into secondary ones. It would be more accurate to say it is a question of initiating play between primary and secondary processes by means of processes . . . which have no existence other than that of processes of relationship [Green, 1975, p. 17].

In summary, skillfully accepting regression to the traumatic developmental phases where something needed for growth was missing, and then facilitating understanding and growth from that point forward via an analytic relationship with transitional, mirroring, nonautocratic, nonintrusive, and synthetic qualities are necessary steps in the treatment approach described above.

It should be noted that this approach to regression in treatment is not universally accepted. Another viewpoint challenges the contention that regression is essential if psychodynamic psychotherapy or psychoanalysis is to be more than merely supportive. For example, Gill (personal communication, 1979) doubts that patients need to become more regressed in the course of treatment than they were before. He proposes the possibility that persons who manifested regressive behavior in their life situation before treatment may display such behavior in therapy. The therapist may incorrectly attribute the expression of this regressive state to the influence of treatment rather than appreciating the pretreatment regressive inclination. Gill strongly recommends that the patient's regressive fantasies and wishes be explicitly verbalized in therapy rather than manifested only in behavior. He objects to the viewpoint that a crucial part of treatment must involve a wordless, primitive interaction which is supposed to make up for infantile trauma. He acknowledges the importance of patient-therapist interaction (and he does not equate neutrality with an austere, distant stance). Nevertheless, he also presses for focusing on the meaning of the interaction as it occurs and for making the transference explicit. He rejects the contention that "some mystical silent union is required" (personal communication, 1979). Furthermore, he does not accept Balint's (1968) program involving regression to a psychophysiological matrix before boundaries and words since, in Gill's opinion, regression in treatment to such a time is simply impossible.

Spitz (1965) states that:

[Some of the early life disturbances,] be they psychogenic affections or psychosomatic conditions, bear a striking resemblance to disturbances with which we are familiar also in the adult . . . these resemblances do not make the two, the disturbance in the infant and the psychiatric disease in the adult, either homologous or even analogous [p. 293].

Nevertheless, many ego psychologists (Blanck and Blanck, 1974) reiterate that the more disturbed personalities need to be understood and approached in relation to developmental failure; however, the psychic structure of the adult differs from that of the child and simplistic parallels are of limited value.

Jacobson (1964) summarizes the early-life psychophysiological matrix, the undifferentiated drive energies, and the "physiological discharge toward the inside, i.e., or the self" (p. 9). Schur (1955) refers to such psychophysiological discharge mechanisms that, in accordance with his theory of *somatization,* operate when there is a dedifferentiation of drives and of self- and object representations. Physical symptoms often result from such regressive processes; there may be reactivations of infantile manifestations involving various body organs for affect discharge. Schur proposes using treatment to promote verbalized, neutralized discharge of aggressive and libidinal energies, thereby relieving somatic symptoms with the concomitant progression of ego functioning toward meaningful "structural change."

The "somatization" Schur describes probably involves an archaic, preverbal body language that is "out of touch" with words and interpretations. Such somatic expressions probably refer to pre-ego manifestations that occurred early in life before language developed. Again, this brings up the question, Is preverbal experience retrievable? Somatic channels are probably more primitive and less accessible to speech and ideation than are motoric or "acting-out" phenomena. The issue of "reconstruction of preverbal experience" is debated in the literature (Blanck and Blanck, 1974). Anna Freud (1969) acknowledges the importance of preverbal experience but questions whether it is possible to work therapeutically with such material. She states:

This means going beyond the area of intra-psychic conflict, which had always been the legitimate target for psychoanalysis, and into the darker area of interaction between innate endowment and environmental influence. The implied aim is to undo or to counteract the impact of the very forces on which the rudiments of personality development are based.

Analysts who work for this aim assure us that this can be achieved [pp. 38–39].

But Anna Freud is dubious about working through preverbal issues in analysis. Dealing with such genetically archaic material differs from focusing on the ego's defensive maneuvers. She further questions whether the transference can "transport" the patient back to the beginning of life and concludes:

[It] is one thing for pre-formed, object related fantasies to return from repression and be redirected from the inner to the outer world (i.e., to the person of the analyst); but [it] is an entirely different, almost magical expectation to have the patient in analysis change back into the pre-psychological, undifferentiated, and unstructured state in which no divisions exist between body and mind or self and object [pp. 40–41].

In summary, the ego-psychological position regarding treatment emphasizes the role of ego mechanisms of defense and attempted adaptation. Among the coping measures are: regression to a dedifferentiated state, energic diffusion, and the return to an early-life psychophysiological matrix where internal discharge and somatizations are prevalent. Patients undergoing such manifestations can be very demanding on the therapist. I believe that often a primitive, empathic alliance is necessary, with the therapist's silent, unobtrusive presence and subtle but firm sensitivity providing "phase-specific," symbiotic support (Mahler, 1975) that aids the establishment of forestages of thought, communication, and identification. Some consider such an alliance impossible to achieve; others claim success.

Ego-psychological and object-relations theory may be applied to the patient-analyst dyadic interation in an effort to "work through" ego deficits—or what Federn (1952) called "ego lesions"—which had developed as a result of deficiencies in the early-life child-parent dyad. For example, Mahler's (1975) concept of the infant's initial symbiotic state and subsequent subphases leading to individuation may provide guidelines for treatment approaches.

One hopes that practitioners use analytic interpretation and empathically facilitated regression-reconstruction in appropriate combination when applying the therapeutic framework proposed in this chapter to work with severely disturbed patients. In my opinion, the interpretive-neutral model alone cannot be used in the treatment of severe character disorders, borderline cases, or psychotic patients without generating overwhelming resistances. For example, the therapeutic application of a theory that of necessity focuses on and emphasizes the patient's split-off rage, assaultiveness, and hate would—perhaps inevitably—arouse guilt, resentment, and possibly a masochistic stance or a sadistic "counterattack." Such reactions would be most likely to occur when the patient is projecting unconscious rage while in a state of confusion regarding the "bad" split-off self-objects.

All too often such a patient experiences an interpretation about "split-off" rage as if the analyst were saying, "Patient, you are bad. The hate is in you while I am knowing and good! You, patient, want to devour and kill, and then blame it on me—the good, innocent doctor." Thus, we become trapped in a vicious circle: the patient projects hate, envy, and rage into the analyst; the analyst then interprets these feelings and appears to "deposit" hate, envy, and rage into the patient. Even if such interpretations are accurate, we must keep in mind the difference between explaining and understanding (Kohut, 1977).

Sometimes a less verbal, less interpretive focus might help in such stalemates. For example, one might listen quietly when acknowledging the patient's aggression and interpret—when necessary—with an understanding emphasis. The analyst could empathize with the subjectivity of the patient—with his or her particular historical drama of rage and despair.

Inge was inclined to feel tremendous responsibility and guilt about her early-life rage, jealousy, greediness, and failure to "rescue" her parents. I accepted these feelings as profoundly painful and encouraged her to examine with me, why, given her background and life circumstances, she had reacted as she did.

As a very young child, Inge did not experience a crucial kind of unconditional acceptance—one that transcends issues of right or wrong, guilt or innocence, good or bad—a space in which to feel anything, to experiment and to ventilate; a beginning sense of identity wherein there flows the broad spectrum of human impulses, thoughts, and emotions. It is invaluable for children to have their feelings and thoughts accepted and reflected by their caretakers. Human beings *do* feel jealous and enraged.

Of course Inge experienced such feelings when, as a hungry, unfulfilled young child who craved attention and nurturance, a newcomer suddenly appeared and attracted maternal care with her colicky demands. Parental mirroring and understanding of Inge's feelings, drives, and "selfness" might have helped. But Inge's parents apparently were not able to provide such understanding; instead they overdisciplined her—at least, so it felt to her.

If an atmosphere conducive to exploring regression and recapitulation within the therapeutic alliance is not present, the patient often experiences the analyst as detached, accusatory, hostile, and superior. And yet, unless the projections and split-off impulses and feelings are appropriately interpreted, their contaminating effects may interfere with the patient's developing enough trust in the analyst to risk therapeutic regression, feel nurturance, and gain meaningful understanding.

Were there reasons Inge experienced her therapist as a noncaring hypocrite who rejected her? Were her observations and conclusions accurate? Could she have misperceived his reactions? Was the press of her own overwhelming neediness for more than full attention related to her past experiences? Was her obsession with controlling people and circumstances related to her unbearable early-life feelings of powerlessness (and compensatory fantasized omnipotence)? Did the damming up of a lifetime of rage and guilt contribute to her misperceptions of me and our relationship? Did she fear her need to bring up all of these dreaded unresolved issues of the past again? Did her ill will and nihilism make for a safer situation than daring to hope and revive vulnerable dependency states?

Gradually, Inge dared explore the frightening risks involved in sharing her magical fantasies and self-protective rituals. With great pain and hesitation, she reluctantly admitted secrets. For example, each session she *had* to place her pocketbook on a particular part of the Oriental rug in the office. She disclosed a fear that I or her husband would die unless she engaged in rituals that would somehow "protect" us from harm. It petrified her to admit these rituals, since exposing them verbally might in itself dissipate the protective "magic" of the compulsive act. At the same time she felt humiliated at her irrationality and ashamed of her aggressive wishes.

Finally, she courageously decided *not* to allow herself a particular movement (walking down the curb of a sidewalk in a "special" way while twisting her head so that she could look at a certain signpost). It frightened her to relinquish these protective devices, although she resented the imprisoning effects of such actions, which had dominated her life. It was frightening to contemplate finding that all of this suffering had been unnecessary and ineffective in influencing fate. The positive therapeutic alliance (despite her ambivalences) and her willingness to trust me enough to share her infantile, primitive thoughts and affects served her struggle to overcome lifelong constrictions.

The dramatic interplay of progression and regression developed in a later phase of Inge's treatment which involved risk-taking and the reexperiencing of a most painful early memory.

In addition to caring for her exotic home garden, Inge ventured forth and bought a puppy. She had always wanted a pet and yet dreaded the possibility. From her view, it was an awesome responsibility: she and her husband lived in a small city apartment; both worked all day. How would she "train" this exuberant, impulse-ridden "baby"? He was irrepressible, not even housebroken, teething, quite stubborn and playful. She felt joy along with apprehension;

when the pet barked noisily, scratched, snapped, and soiled the house, all was chaos. Inge was enraged—there was no order or gratification. She blamed the dog, herself, her husband, and me; she attacked herself for wanting the puppy, for loving it, for hating it, for keeping it, and for wanting to get rid of it. Finally, in desperation, she gave up. She arranged for a family who lived in the country to adopt the animal. At this point, Inge assaulted herself—her disloyalty, treachery, irresponsibility, and shallow values. The parallels with her own childhood became apparent.

As a child, none of Inge's instinctual or aggressive expressions were indulged; any such manifestations were greeted with rejection and threats of parental abandonment. It seems that the pup encouraged a regressive reactivation of naïve mental representations of early life. Inge played the role of the harsh, righteous parent toward the instinct-laden child/puppy. At the same time (true to infantile relationships), she manifested a fluidity of boundaries and a lack of self-cohesiveness. Thus, she shifted her role and identified with the fun-loving, self-indulgent, and assertive creature doomed to be abandoned.

This fluidity of boundaries also permitted a regressive transference in which there were confused oscillations. One moment I was the analyst-tyrant and she was the guilty child-patient; the next second she was the attacking, righteous patient-parent and I the condemned, "bad" analyst-child. Her desertion of the beloved and hated dog also paralleled her failure to rescue her parents. Although most painful, such aspects of treatment provide a climate for meaningful ventilation and for exposing and exploring fragmented regressive components. Active mastery and better integration become possible when regression in treatment makes accessible previously repressed and split-off, conflict-laden misperceptions and distortions from early life. These primitive affects and infantile defensive patterns had cheated the patient of a freer, fuller life.

Guidelines for the Practitioner and Conclusion

It has been my experience that regression in treatment affords many patients a new chance to make crucial material accessible to consciousness—to the "observing self" that is developing in alliance with the analyst. As a consequence, a productive experience often ensues. Both participants cope with "the unfinished business" of fragmented percepts and primitive longings, hurt and rage, anxious confusion and early-life maladaptive coping patterns. Here is the opportunity for the "truer self" (Winnicott, 1960) to emerge.

The analyst's sensitivity to countertransference phenomena is crucial in establishing an atmosphere that permits therapeutic regression. The analyst's capacity to accept ambiguity, neediness, and intrusiveness is also important. A patient's "reactivated" craving for fusion, fear of disintegration, and accusatory rage often challenge the therapist's sense of security. The regressive fantasies can involve needs to "kill the object," to play with illusions, to create distance or absence, and to feel murky blending or transitional states. Such behavior may prove disquieting to the analyst, depending on his particular problems and conflicts.

A patient's regressive behavior often evokes strong countertransference reactions. The emotional predicament of the analyst may parallel the caretaker's position, as elaborated by Benedek (1959) in her description of "Parenthood as a Developmental Phase." Like the parent and child, the analyst and patient also make up a dyad. Thus treatment ideally can offer a parallel of the mother-child "facilitating environment" (Winnicott, 1960). This analogous recapitulation may prove therapeutically vital, whether or not the patient precisely reduplicates the specifics of the past in the regressive experience in treatment.

I have stated the reasons why I consider regression to be potentially productive in psychoanalysis; however, I do not advocate a "milk-giving, hand-holding," libidinally gratifying interaction. Such an interaction often leads to more malignant pathology (insatiable and sometimes irreversible regression) rather than achieving our objective, that is, enhancing perspectives, insight, and integration.

I do not maintain complete neutrality *at all times in all cases*. There are some pathological states that require modified technique. For example, sometimes the analyst's overt expression of particular countertransference feelings proves to be essential and productive. Such positions may be observed in the work of Sechehaye (1951), Winnicott (1960, 1971), Searles (1965, 1979), and Hoedemaker (1967).

I did not consider the issue of regression a simple matter. There are serious dangers and many things we do not understand. Our diagnostic and prognostic judgments are somewhat primitive and too often postdictive. Our comprehension of what produces change in the analytic dyad requires further investigation. It is encouraging that consideration is devoted to these issues today. It seems to me that, in the past, all too often an extreme predilection toward either the "intrapsychic" or the "interpersonal" bias created an artifact. In my opinion, human development and psychoanalytic treatment can be most effectively understood via exploration in the therapeutic dyad of the ramifications of the early-life interpersonal *and* intrapsychic interactions which lead to intrapsychic representations and eventual intrapsychic structures and interpersonal relationships.

I hope we will follow Balint's courageous research and investigate more thoroughly those painful examples of failure in treatment where regression took on malignant qualities. We might examine Khan's (1974) hypothesis that a hidden, misunderstood dread of surrender to resourceless dependence often underlies malignant regressions.

It is difficult for those therapists who acknowledge the importance of regression in treatment to deal with the inevitable stresses and demands involved.

It is difficult for our patients to dare to reopen dreaded, hidden areas of indescribable trauma resulting from the unavailability of vitally needed "support systems" in early life.

We imperfect practitioners try to keep prearranged appointments completely regulated by calendar and clock. We do our best to listen patiently and sincerely, although it is inevitable that we listen selectively and defensively. We strive to be open and receptive despite our predilections and prejudices. We do not and cannot provide unconditional love and the superhuman availability our patients often crave. The latter "failing" is probably all for the best, since such "ideal" fulfillment would hardly prepare our patients to become more adaptive to the realities of life. Furthermore, the fear of obliteration through intimacy and fusion is also frightening to many of our analysands. There is more than one Scylla and Charybdis through which we must chart our adventurous dialectical course.

How can we do better? I suspect our theory and technique would benefit greatly from further elucidation of the nature and developmental role of: transitional phenomena and objects, play and illusion, presence and absence, and "facilitation" and "holding." I consider these factors to be crucial in the working through of the therapeutic regressive interaction between patient and analyst—or perhaps we might call this aspect of the dyad "me and not me." Is it too far-fetched to think of the Janus-like unique creation of the psychoanalytic encounter as a dyad and, at the same time, much more than a couple—for, at least at times, we have present in our consulting room a living *triad:* patient, analyst, and patient-analyst.

REFERENCES

Adler, G. (1974), Regression in psychotherapy: Disruptive or therapeutic? Symposium at Tufts University on "Regression in psychotherapy." *Int. J. Psychoanal. Psychother.,* 3:252–264.

Alexander, F. (1956), Two forms of regression and their therapeutic implications. *Psychoanal. Quart.,* 25:178–196. (Reprinted in: *The Scope of Psycho-Analysis.* New York: Basic Books.)

Arieti, S. (Ed.) (1959), *American Handbook of Psychiatry,* Vol. I. New York: Basic Books.

Arlow, J. A., & Brenner, C. (1964), *Psychoanalytic Concepts and the Structural Theory.* New York: International Universities Press.

Balint, M. (1968), *The Basic Fault.* London: Tavistock.

Benedek, T. (1959), Parenthood as a developmental phase: A contribution to the libido therapy. *J. Amer. Psychoanal. Assn.,* 7:389–417.

Bion, W. R. (1977), *Seven Servants.* New York: Jason Aronson.

Blanck, G., & Blanck, R. (1974), *Ego Psychology: Theory and Practice.* New York: Columbia University Press.

Boyer, L. B., & Giovacchini, P. L. (1967), *Psychoanalytic Treatment of Characterological and Schizophrenic Disorders*. New York: Jason Aronson.

Breuer, J., & Freud, S. (1893–1895), Studies on hysteria. *Standard Edition*, 2. London: Hogarth Press, 1955.

Darwin, C. (1871), *The Descent of Man and Selection in Relation to Sex*, 2nd Ed. New York: Appleton, 1899.

Federn, P. (1952), *Ego Psychology and the Psychoses*. New York: Basic Books.

Ferenczi, S. (1930), The principle of relaxation and neo-catharsis. In: *Final Contributions*. New York: Basic Books, 1955.

——— (1931), Child analysis in the analysis of adults. In: *Final Contributions*. New York: Basic Books, 1955.

——— (1932), Notes and fragments. In: *Final Contributions*. New York: Basic Books, 1955.

Freud, A. (1965), *Normality and Pathology in Childhood: Assessments of Development. The Writings of Anna Freud*, New York: International Universities Press.

——— (1969), *Difficulties in the Path of Psychoanalysis: A Confrontation of Past with Present Viewpoints*. New York: International Universities Press.

Freud, S. (1891), *On aphasia*. New York: International Universities Press, 1953.

——— (1900), The interpretation of dreams. *Standard Edition*, 4 & 5. London: Hogarth Press, 1953.

——— (1912), The dynamics of transference. *Standard Edition*, 12:97–108. London: Hogarth Press, 1958.

——— (1914), On the history of the psycho-analytic movement. *Standard Edition*, 14:7–66. London: Hogarth Press, 1957.

——— (1918), Lines of advance in psycho-analytic therapy. *Standard Edition*, 17:157–168. London: Hogarth Press, 1955.

Fromm-Reichmann, F. (1950), *Principles of Intensive Psychotherapy*. Chicago: University of Chicago Press.

Frosch, J. (1967a), Severe regressive states during analysis: Introduction. *J. Amer. Psychoanal. Assn.*, 15:491–507.

——— (1967b), Severe regressive states during analysis: Summary. *J. Amer. Psychoanal. Assn.*, 15:606–625.

Green, A. (1975), The analyst, symbolization and absence in the analytic setting (on changes in analytic practice and analytic experience) *Internat. J. Psycho-anal.*, 56:1–22.

——— (1978), Potential space in psychoanalysis: The object in the setting. In: *Between Reality and Fantasy*, ed. S. Grolnick et al. New York: Jason Aronson.

Guntrip, H. (1969), *Schizoid Phenomena, Object Relations and the Self*. New York: International Universities Press.

Guttman, S. A. (Rep.) (1959), Panel report: Criteria for analyzability. *J. Amer. Psychoanal. Assn.*, 8:1–60.

Hoedemaker, E. D. (1967), The psychotic identifications in schizophrenia: The technical problem. In: *Psychoanalytic Treatment of Characterological and Schizophrenic Disorders*, L. B. Boyer & P. L. Giovacchini. New York: Science House.

Jackson, J. H. (1888), Remarks on the diagnosis and treatment of diseases of the brain. In: *Selected Writings of John Hughlings Jackson*, Vol. 2, ed. J. Taylor. London: Hodder & Stoughton, 1931–1932, pp. 365–392.

Jackson, S. W. (1969), The history of Freud's concepts of regression. *J. Amer. Psychoanal. Assn.*, 17:743–784.

Jacobson, E. (1964), *The Self and the Object World*. New York: International Universities Press.

Jowett, B. (Ed.) (1937), Timaeus. *The Dialogues of Plato,* Vol. 2. New York: Random House, pp. 3–68.

Kernberg, O. F. (1972), Early ego integration and object relations. *Annals N. Y. Acad. Sci.,* 193:233–247.

—— (1976) *Object-Relations Theory and Clinical Psychoanalysis.* New York: Jason Aronson.

—— (1975), *Borderline Conditions and Pathological Narcissism.* New York: Jason Aronson.

Khan, M. M. R. (1974), *The Privacy of the Self.* New York: International Universities Press.

Kohut, H. (1971), *The Analysis of the Self.* New York: International Universities Press.

—— (1977), *The Restoration of the Self.* New York: International Universities Press.

Kris, E. (1934), The Psychology of Caricature. In: *Psychoanalytic Explorations in Art.* New York: International Universities Press, 1952.

Lacan, J. (1949), The mirror stage: Source of the I function as shown by psycho-analytic experiences. *Internat. J. Psycho-Anal.,* 30:203–212.

—— (1977), *Ecrits: A Selection.* Trans. A. Sheridan. New York: Norton.

Little, M. (1960), On basic unity. *Internat. J. Psycho-Anal.,* 41:377–384.

Lorand, S. (1965), Sandor Ferenczi, Pioneer of Pioneers. In: *Psychoanalytic Pioneers.* New York: Basic Books, pp. 14–35.

Mahler, M. S., et. al. (1975), *The Psychological Birth of the Human Infant.* New York: Basic Books.

Milner, M. (1969), *The Hands of the Living God.* New York: International Universities Press.

Modell, A. H. (1968), *Object Love and Reality.* New York: International Universities Press.

—— (1976), The holding environment and the therapeutic action of psychoanalysis. *J. Amer. Psychoanal. Assn.,* 24: 285–307.

Niederland, W. G. (1960), Some technical aspects concerning the analysis of obsessive-compulsive patients. *Bull. Phil. Assn. Psychoanal.,* 10:148–153.

—— (1961), The problem of the survivor. Part I: Some remarks on the psychiatric evolution of emotional disorders in survivors of Nazi persecution. *J. Hillside Hosp.,* 10:233–247.

Nietzsche, F. (1909), Human, all-too-human. In: *The Complete Works of Friedrich Nietzsche,* 6 & 7, ed. O. Levy. Edinburgh: Foulis.

Peto, A. (1967), Dedifferentiations and fragmentations during analysis. *J. Amer. Psychoanal. Assn.,* 15:534–550.

Rosenfeld, H. (1965), *Psychotic States.* New York: International Universities Press.

Schur, M. (1953), The ego in anxiety. In: *Drives, Affects, Behavior,* ed. R. M. Loewenstein. New York: International Universities Press.

—— (1955), Comments on the metapsychology of somatization. *The Psychoanalytic Study of the Child,* 10: 119–164. New York: International Universities Press.

Searles, H. F. (1965), *Collected Papers on Schizophrenia and Related Subjects.* New York: International Universities Press.

—— (1979), *Countertransference and Related Subjects.* New York: International Universities Press.

Sechehaye, M. A. (1951), *Symbolic Realization.* New York: International Universities Press.

Shapiro, L. N. (1974), Introduction and discussion from Tufts University Symposium on "Regression in psychotherapy." *Internat. J. Psychoanal. Psychother.,* 3:249–251.

Spitz, R. (1965), *The First Year of Life.* New York: International Universities Press.

Stone, L. (1961), *The Psychoanalytic Situation.* New York: International Universities Press.

The Compact Edition of the Oxford English Dictionary (1971), London: Oxford University Press.

Tuttman, S. (1978), Kohut Symposium. *Psychoanal. Rev.,* 65:624–629.

——— (1979), Psyche and soma. In: *Integrating Ego Psychology and Object Relations Theory.* Dubuque, Iowa: Kendall/Hunt, pp.134–149.

Volkan, V. D. (1976), *Primitive Internalized Object Relations.* New York: International Universities Press.

Wallerstein, R. S. (1967), Reconstruction and mastery in the transference psychosis. *J. Amer. Psychoanal. Assn.,* 15:551–583.

Weinshel, E. M., rep. (1966), Panel report: Severe regressive states during analysis. *J. Amer. Psychoanal. Assn.,* 14:548–549.

Winnicott, D. W. (1960), Ego distortion in terms of true and false self. In: *The Maturational Processes and the Facilitating Environment.* New York: International Universities Press.

——— (1971), The use of an object and relating through identification. In: *Playing and Reality.* New York: Basic Books, pp. 86–94.

CHAPTER 10

The Unconscious Fantasy as Therapeutic Agent in Psychoanalytic Treatment

Lloyd H. Silverman

What is the psychological process that brings about change in psychoanalytic treatment? The consensus among psychoanalysts is that the *main* agent of change is insight, with the qualifications that the insight must be experienced emotionally as well as cognitively and that it must be "worked through." But as to whether there are other subsidiary agents of change, there is no consensus. Or, at least, there is no consensus on whether other processes that can lead to change during psychoanalytic treatment are "legitimate"—i.e., whether they are compatible with the main agent of change. Thus, in answering this latter question, many analysts would respond with an emphatic "No," maintaining that in properly conducted psychoanalytic treatment insight is the *only* legitimate agent of change; if any other process is in evidence, it should be nullified by subjecting it to analysis. Another substantial group, on the other hand, would legitimize certain other agents of change as long as they do not impede insight.

What are these other agents of change? They include "transference grati-

*An earlier different version of this chapter was presented at the Annual Meeting of the American Academy of Psychoanalysis, Atlanta, Georgia, May 1978, and appeared in the *Journal of the American Academy of Psychoanalysis,* 7:189–218, New York: Wiley, 1979. I am grateful to Drs. Gerald Epstein, Merton Gill, Stanley Grand, Marvin Hurrich, Nathan Leites, David Rubinfine, David Shainberg, and Paul Wachtel for their comments, criticisms, and suggestions.

fications" (Freud, 1915), internalizing the analyst as an "auxiliary superego" (Strachey, 1934), "identification with the analyst" (Sterba, 1934), "corrective emotional experiences" (Alexander, 1954), and the "holding environment" (Winnicott, 1965). Central to the thesis I will propose here is that at least one aspect of the ameliorative process that each of these terms refers to involves the activation of unconscious fantasies.

In this paper I shall proceed in the following way. First, I shall argue that there are certain unconscious fantasies which, when activated, can have a powerful adaptation-enhancing effect on behavior. To support this argument, I will first cite an experimental research program of many years standing that has extensively tested this hypothesis. Then I will describe a variety of instances in real life, including nonpsychoanalytic treatment situations, in which the same fantasies that we have deliberately activated in the laboratory are inadvertently activated, with improved adaptation again being the outcome. Finally, I shall suggest that these same fantasies are often—if not regularly—inadvertently activated during psychoanalytic treatment and that they account for some, if not most, of the change in such treatment that has been attributed to the "non-insight agents of change" referred to above; then I shall discuss the clinical implications of this view.

I

Since the early writings of Freud, the concept of the unconscious fantasy has appeared many times in the psychoanalytic literature. It has been only in the past two decades, however, that it has been given detailed and systematic treatment, with major papers devoted to the subject by Beres (1962), Sandler and Nagera (1963), and Arlow (1969). In the current paper, I shall define unconscious fantasy as an organized configuration of unconscious ideas and images, motivated (to varying degrees) by libidinal and aggressive wishes, anxieties, defensive operations, and adaptive strivings. When a behavior emerges, intensifies, diminishes, or disappears without any apparent conscious instigation (i.e., perception, memory, anticipation, or other cognition), the activation of some unconscious fantasy (or some element thereof) is likely to be causative. Whereas any kind of behavior can be influenced by such a fantasy, almost all explicit references in the psychoanalytic literature have been to the influence of unconscious fantasy on pathological behavior. Most frequently, references have been made to fantasies that generate symptoms—for example, the womb fantasy that Lewin (1936) described as underlying claustrophobia. But as I indicated above, the thesis of this paper is that the activation of unconscious fantasies can also have the opposite effect—i.e., it can lead to the dissipation of a symptom, or in other ways improve adaptation.

When I speak of improved adaptation, let me say at the outset that I am not referring to either a final or a summary judgment. The resulting adaptation-enhancing change may be only temporary; or it may be limited to one area and even be accompanied by a negative change in another area; a careful weighing is necessary to judge its *overall* effect on adaptation. On the other hand, I am not maintaining that adaptation-enhancing changes that come about in this way are *necessarily* temporary or "at a price." As I have detailed elsewhere (Silverman, 1978a) and will touch on later here, this question must be considered an empirical one; its answer requires the accumulation of particular kinds of systematically collected clinical data.

II

The major evidence that I shall present to support the thesis of the adaptation-enhancing effects of unconscious fantasies emanates from the laboratory. Many psychoanalysts will have doubts about a thesis concerning the effects of unconscious fantasy that is based primarily on laboratory experimentation. Thus, let me indicate why I have chosen this focus. First, there is very little in the psychoanalytic literature that addresses this thesis. While, as I will spell out, there is *implicit* evidence in the observations reported by many analysts for the adaptation-enhancing effects of unconscious fantasy activation, there are very few instances of an analyst drawing the *explicit* conclusion that such activation has the power to bring about such effects. Second, there is the matter of how convincing such a conclusion would be to a skeptic if it were based primarily on clinical evidence. For, as I have elaborated on elsewhere (Silverman, 1975), the clinical situation, while providing opportunities par excellence for *developing* hypotheses about unconscious mental processes, does not allow for the necessary controls to be instituted to *test* these hypotheses so that one psychoanalytic clinician can convince another of a clinical proposition about which the latter is skeptical. The clinical situation is too complex, and its ability to test alternate explanations too deficient, for it to serve as a vehicle for resolving controversy. And the proposition under consideration here is clearly controversial, even within the psychoanalytic community.

It is in just such situations as this—when psychoanalytic clinicians disagree—that research on the issue in question is particularly important; and such research requires, among other things, laboratory data that can meet the dual criteria of stringent controls and relevance (Silverman, 1975). I believe these criteria have been met by the research I shall now describe.

In the early 1960s, a method termed "subliminal psychodynamic activation" was developed that allows for the experimental study of the effects of unconscious fantasies on behavior. Using the demonstrations of subliminal registration in Fisher's pioneering studies (e.g., 1954, 1956) and the later investigations stimulated by Fisher's work (summarized in Wolitzky and Wachtel, 1973) as a starting point, this new type of investigation attempted to *utilize* the phenomenon of subliminal registration for stimulating unconscious fantasies in order to make a systematic, precise, and controlled appraisal of their influence on behavior. Over thirty published reports have now appeared documenting the success of this method in achieving its aim (most recently summarized in Silverman, 1976), and several earlier discussions have dealt with the implications of these findings for psychoanalytic theory (Silverman, 1967, 1970, 1972, 1975, 1978a).

The following is a description of the experimental design that has been used in these investigations. Subjects are seen individually for an experimental session on one day and a control session on another, with their order counterbalanced. In the first session the experimenter briefly explains the purpose of the study to the subject and seeks his or her cooperation. Then the subject is told about the tasks that will be administered to assess aspects of his or her behavior and is further informed that several times during these tasks he or she will be asked to look through the eyepiece of a machine (a tachistoscope) at flickers of light that contain extremely brief exposures of verbal and pictorial stimuli. The subject is promised that at the end of the experiment he or she will be told the content and purpose of these stimuli.

The session proper begins with a "baseline" assessment of the subject's propensity for whatever pathological manifestations are being investigated. The subject is then asked to look into the tachistoscope and to describe the flickers of light. There follow four exposures of either a stimulus related to an unconscious fantasy (the experimental session) or a (relatively) neutral stimulus (the control session). Each exposure lasts for 4 msecs. Then the specific pathology is reassessed to determine the effect of whatever stimulus was exposed. The procedure for the second session is the same except that a different stimulus is exposed between the baseline and reassessment task series. Subjects who are exposed to the fantasy-related stimulus in the first session are shown a neutral stimulus in the second session, and vice versa. In each session the experimenter who works the tachistoscope and administers the assessment procedures is "blind" to which of the stimuli is being exposed. Since the subject is also unaware of the stimulus (it being subliminal), the procedure qualifies as "double-blind," analogous to drug studies in which neither the patient nor the person administering the capsule knows whether a drug or a placebo is being ingested. The evaluation of pathological manifestations is also carried out blindly.

In our early work with this method, our interest was in stimulating pathogenic (rather than adaptation-enhancing) unconscious fantasies. Here, it was our intention to subject to rigorously controlled laboratory study the proposition, agreed on in the psychoanalytic community, that certain fantasies lie behind psychopathology. In these earlier studies (summarized in Silverman, 1976) a great deal of data was accumulated supporting our expectation. With many groups of subjects, characterized by a variety of symptoms, *intensifications* of symptoms appeared after the pathogenic fantasy-related condition but not after the control condition. This was the case both for symptoms for which there is a consensus among psychoanalytic clinicians as to the chief conflict involved (e.g., depression, stuttering, and male homosexuality) and for symptoms where no such consensus exists and controversy within the psychoanalytic community abounds (e.g., thought disorder and other symptoms of schizophrenia). I should add that both these results and the ones I am about to describe involving adaptation-enhancing stimuli are dependent on the tachistoscopic presentations being *subliminal*. When the same stimuli are presented in awareness, they typically leave the subject unaffected.

III

After several years of applying our research method in the way that has been described, we moved in a new direction—one that relates to the topic of this paper: the adaptation-enhancing effects of activating certain unconscious fantasies. I became interested in such an effort after reading papers by Limentani (1956) and Searles (1965), who reported that there is often an abatement of symptoms in schizophrenics when *symbiotic wishes* are gratified. A further search of the clinical literature revealed, however, that other psychoanalytic clinicians held the opposite position and maintained either explicitly or implicitly that such gratification would only intensify the pathology—or at least impede the progress—of such patients (Freeman, Cameron, and McGhie, 1958; DesLauriers, 1962). The absence of a consensus on this issue served as a further impetus to our attempt to study it in the laboratory. We reasoned as follows. While it would hardly be feasible to gratify symbiotic wishes in a laboratory experiment, it might be possible to stimulate a *fantasy* of these wishes having been gratified using the subliminal psychodynamic activation method that had been used so profitably in the earlier studies. We then could test a hypothesis derived from the writings of Searles and Limentani, namely, that the stimulation of unconscious symbiotic gratification fantasies could reduce symptoms in schizophrenics.

We proceeded as follows. Schizophrenic subjects were seen for two sessions, experimental and control, in each of which "baseline" and "critical" assessments were made of their symptoms, especially the degree to which they gave evidence of a thinking disorder.[1] Between the baseline and critical assessments,

---

[1]Thinking disorder is defined as manifestations of illogical, unrealistic, and loose thinking, assessed from such tests as the Rorschach, Word Association, and Story Recall using the manuals that have been developed for such assessment purposes (e.g., Holt's 1969 manual for assessing primary-process manifestations in Rorschach responses). The other measure of psychopathology that we have used with schizophrenics is one that we term "pathological nonverbal behavior": peculiar mannerisms, inappropriate laughter, blocking, body rubbing, etc., that emerge during the testing procedures.

they were given four subliminal exposures of a stimulus—either one designed to activate a fantasy of symbiotic gratification (experimental session), or one intended to be neutral (control session). The former consisted of the message MOMMY AND I ARE ONE, presented by itself in some experiments and accompanied in others by a picture of a man and a woman merged at the shoulders like Siamese twins. The control stimulus consisted of a neutral message, such as MEN THINKING or PEOPLE ARE WALKING accompanied by a congruent picture in those studies where a picture accompanied the symbiotic message. To date, nine studies have been carried out with the above-described design, four by us in our laboratory (Silverman et al., 1969; Silverman and Candell, 1970; Silverman et al., 1971; Bronstein, 1976) and five by others trying to replicate our findings (Leiter, 1973; Kaye, 1975; Spiro, 1975; Kaplan, 1976; Fribourg, 1979). In all of these studies the symbiotic condition resulted in a decrease in pathology that was not in evidence after the control condition. This well-replicated finding was subject to the following qualification, however: The reduction in pathology was found only in schizophrenics who could be characterized as "relatively differentiated from their mothers"; this characteristic was assessed by a procedure that is described in detail elsewhere (Silverman et al., 1969).[2] For *less* differentiated schizophrenics, on the other hand, the stimulation of the symbiotic fantasy did *not* reduce pathology and in one study even intensified it (Leiter, 1973). Our explanation of this finding was the following. Fantasies of symbiotic gratification can serve a number of adaptation-enhancing functions, such as the fulfillment of libidinal wishes, insurance against object loss, the restoration of narcissistic equilibria, and as a protection against both destructive wishes and external destruction. Such a fantasy also can pose a threat, however; it can lead to a loss of sense of self, an experience to which schizophrenics are particularly vulnerable. Thus, whether or not a schizophrenic will respond positively to the stimulation of a symbiotic fantasy will depend on the degree to which this threat is mobilized. For schizophrenics who are relatively differentiated, the balance of forces favors an adaptation-enhancing outcome, whereas for those who are highly undifferentiated, this is not the case. We were therefore able to conclude that there is some validity in the position of the clinicians on both sides of the controversy over whether symbiotic experiences are ameliorative for schizophrenics, and that the schizophrenic's initial level of differentiation is the decisive factor in whether his or her response to such experiences will be positive (see Silverman, 1975).[3]

---

[2] We have found that between 50 and 80 percent of the populations of hospitalized schizophrenics score as "relatively differentiated" on this procedure.

[3] This statement should not be taken to imply that schizophrenics are necessarily stable with regard to where they fall on this differentiation variable. We have not yet ascertained the degree to which schizophrenics maintain themselves over time as "relatively differentiated" or "relatively undifferentiated."

This, then, was the first series of experiments to indicate that, at least for some people, the stimulation of a particular unconscious fantasy—in this case a symbiotic-gratification fantasy—could be adaptation-enhancing.

In a second group of studies we investigated whether the adaptation-enhancing effects of the symbiotic fantasy are *limited* to schizophrenics. The data from these studies indicate that this is not the case. In some of the studies we questioned whether symptom reduction would follow the symbiotic stimulation of subjects with particular neurotic symptoms. In one study (Silverman et al., 1973) two groups of male homosexuals were assessed for manifestations of anxiety and defensiveness (as reflected in Rorschach responses) after the subliminal presentation of both the symbiotic stimulus that had been used for schizophrenics and a neutral control stimulus. These manifestations were found to diminish significantly after the symbiotic condition.

In investigations of three other symptoms, the effects of symbiotic stimulation were investigated in a treatment context and thus are more directly relevant to the theme of this paper. The experimental design differed somewhat from the one just described: groups of patients received, over several weeks, a nonanalytic therapeutic intervention designed to help them overcome particular symptoms; subliminal stimulation accompanied the intervention. In each study one group of patients received the MOMMY AND I ARE ONE stimulus and a matched group received a (relatively) neutral stimulus such as PEOPLE ARE WALKING, again in a context of double-blind controls. One of these studies (Silverman, Frank, and Dachinger, 1974) was carried out with insect phobics, and therapy consisted of systematic desensitization. In a second study (Schurtman, 1978), the patients were alcoholics, and an AA type of counseling was involved. And in a third (Martin, 1975), the patients were obese women, and the therapy was behavior modification techniques designed to control overeating. In each of these studies, the patients who received the symbiotic stimulation manifested significantly more symptom reduction.[4]

[4]The following measures of clinical improvement were used: (a) in the phobia study it was the patient's ability to tolerate contact with insects (as revealed in a "behavioral assessment treatment evaluation procedure") and ratings by both the subjects themselves and the investigator of the amount of accompanying anxiety; (b) in the alcoholism study, the indicators of improvement were counselor ratings for patient involvement in treatment; (c) in the weight study, improvement referred to the amount of weight loss four weeks after the behavior modification program ended.

It should also be noted that attempts have been made to replicate the findings from the phobia and obesity studies. The latter replication yielded essentially the same results (Silverman et al., 1978), but the attempt to replicate the phobia findings was unsuccessful (Condon, 1976). With regard to this nonreplication, it may be important that the population used, unlike the original population, did not consist of persons seeking treatment for their phobias. Instead, the subjects were college students who, although manifesting a certain degree of phobic symptoms, entered the study to fulfill a psychology class requirement. It thus may be that for the subliminal symbiotic stimulation to enhance the effectiveness of a treatment intervention, subjects must be well motivated to overcome whatever behavior the treatment is intended to address.

The adaptation-enhancing consequences of activating symbiotic fantasies were also demonstrated for several nonpsychiatric populations (Silverman and Wolitzky, 1970; Parker, 1977; Sackeim, 1977). In one study, for example (Parker, 1977), two groups of college students, matched for academic performance, were given tachistoscopic stimulation at the beginning of a class four times a week over a six-week summer term. For one group the stimulus was MOMMY AND I ARE ONE; for the other group it was PEOPLE ARE WALKING. The students in the former group received grades on their final exam ("blindly" marked) that were significantly higher than those of the controls (average marks of 90.4 percent and 82.7 percent respectively). Thus it can be concluded that, for a wide variety of persons the activation of symbiotic fantasies can have adaptation-enhancing consequences.

IV

What are the particular qualities of the symbiotic fantasy that allow it to be adaptation-enhancing? One of the strengths of laboratory research in general, and the subliminal psychodynamic activation method in particular, is that precise delineations are possible. This advantage is enhanced in the present experiments by the use of *verbal* stimuli to trigger unconscious fantasies, for such stimuli allow for the presentation of variations of a particular fantasy theme to determine the specific characteristics that effect behavioral change.

With regard to the MOMMY AND I ARE ONE stimulus, a number of investigations have yielded relevant data. In each of these, researchers asked whether a particular element of the symbotic fantasy was crucial in producing the ameliorative effects. The conclusion that can be drawn from these experiments is that the fantasy must involve a *sense of oneness* in order for it to be ameliorative. Thus, in a study by Bronstein (1976), the effects of the MOMMY AND I ARE ONE stimulus were compared with the effects of the stimuli MOMMY IS INSIDE ME; MOMMY AND I ARE THE SAME; and MOMMY AND I ARE ALIKE—the latter three implying ways that MOMMY could be internalized other than through a sense of oneness. Bronstein found that, whereas the oneness stimulus produced the same reduction in pathology that it had in the other studies, none of the other internalization messages had this effect. Analogously, Kaplan (1976) compared MOMMY AND I ARE ONE both with a neutral control stimulus and with the following other stimuli, each of which was intended to stimulate some reassuring fantasy involving MOMMY that did not imply a sense of oneness: MOMMY IS ALWAYS WITH ME; MOMMY FEEDS ME WELL; and I CANNOT HURT MOMMY. She, too, found that only the MOMMY AND I ARE ONE stimulus led to a reduction in symptoms.

Finally, mention should be made of four studies (Kaye, 1975; Cohen, 1976; Parker, 1977; Silverman, 1977) that investigated whether the word MOMMY had to be in the message for the outcome to be an adaptation-enhancing one. The results of these studies suggest that, while the word MOMMY need not be in the message, the sense of oneness that is suggested must be with someone who represents MOMMY—the good mother of infancy. Thus, in an experiment by Kaye (1975) with male schizophrenics, an adaptation-enhancing outcome was obtained for the message MY GIRL AND I ARE ONE, as well as for MOMMY AND I ARE ONE, but not for the message DADDY AND I ARE ONE. Apparently, MY GIRL had connotations of the good mother of infancy for these subjects, but DADDY did not.[5]

Let me present one final series of studies in this review of experiments on subliminal psychodynamic activation and adaptation enhancement. In these, a second type of adaptation-enhancing unconscious fantasy was stimulated—one that we term a sanctioned Oedipal gratification fantasy. In seven experiments of this series, five carried out in our laboratory (reported in Silverman and Adler, 1978; Silverman et al., 1978) and two conducted elsewhere (Lonski and Palumbo, 1978; Silverstein, 1978), the performance of college males was enhanced in a competitive situation (a dart-throwing tournament) after the subliminal presentation of verbal messages implying sanction for derivative expressions of Oedipal wishes (DEFEATING DAD IS OK; BEATING DAD IS OK; and WINNING MOM IS OK).[6] As I will soon spell out, these findings can be viewed as paralleling real-life events in which behaviors that have either an explicit or an implicit competitive meaning can be carried out more adaptively if the person experiences a sense of sanction for the Oedipal derivatives hidden in the behavior.

V

Before turning to the issue of the activation of unconscious fantasies as therapeutic agents in psychoanalytic treatment, let me make reference to other situations in which the inadvertent activation of such fantasies can have adaptation-enhancing consequences. With regard to the symbiotic fantasy, as I have

---

[5]The fact that all of the schizophrenics in the study were male was apparently crucial in producing this result. In Cohen's (1977) study, for the first time female schizophrenics underwent the same experimental procedure that theretofore had been limited to male schizophrenics. In contrast to its effect on males, the MOMMY AND I ARE ONE stimulus did *not* reduce pathology for the females, but the DADDY AND I ARE ONE stimulus did. Cohen viewed these results as bearing out the clinical observations of Lidz (1973, p. 47), who has reported that most female schizophrenics, in contrast to males, turn from mother to father as the symbiotic object.

[6]Two of these studies showed that it was specifically the Oedipal sanction in the messages (rather than simply the general sanction in the word OK) that improved the dart throwing of the subjects. In the experiment by Lonski and Palumbo (1978) the message BEATING MOM IS OK did not affect performance whereas BEATING DAD IS OK did. Similarly, in Silverstein's (1978) investigation, whereas WINNING MOM IS OK enhanced performance, WINNING DAD IS OK had no effect.

elaborated in detail elsewhere (Silverman, 1978a), a number of psychoanalytic writers, while not specifically using the term "unconscious symbiotic fantasy," have referred to certain experiences, feelings, and memories that are activated in real-life situations for which our experimental findings are an analogue. Thus, Bergmann (1971) refers to "feelings and archaic ego states that were once active in the symbiotic phase" (p. 32) being revived in the experience of being in love. Winnicott (1958) makes reference to a symbiotic element in experiences of sophisticated aloneness, which he views as a mark of health and as having adaptation-enhancing value. And Rose (1972) has made reference to a more general adaptation enhancement that can result from symbiotic gratification. He writes:

Mastering something by "fusing" with it, temporarily obscuring the boundaries between the self and object representations, recalls the primary narcissism of the infant and the psychotic. But to merge in order to re-emerge, may be part of the fundamental process of psychological growth on all developmental levels. Although fusion may dominate the most primitive levels, it contributes a richness of texture and quality to the others. Such operations may result in nothing more remarkable than normally creative adaptation to circumstance. At the least, it affords what [William] James called the "return from the solitude of individuation" refreshed to meet the moment. At the most, it may result in transcending the limitations of earlier stages of narcissism to simplify, unify anew, and recreate an expanded reality (p. 185).

Moreover, while Searles, Limentani, and others have written about the pathology reduction following the stimulation of symbiotic experiences in the treatment of schizophrenics, others have indicated that for nonschizophrenics, the inadvertent activation of such experiences in a variety of nonanalytic treatments leads to clinical improvement. This conclusion is implicit in discussions of transference improvement by Fenichel (1945) and Oremland (1972); and the role of symbiotic experiences in specific forms of nonanalytic treatment has been explicitly discussed by Gordon (1970) for group-activity therapies of the Esalen and Synanon type, by Shafii (1973) for meditation, and by me (Silverman, 1979) for systematic desensitization and client-centered therapy. It has been suggested that for each of these treatment modalities there are specific symbiotic activators embedded in the therapeutic procedures. For example, in client-centered treatment, it is the therapist continually conveying to the client his sense of the latter's experiential state. This explicitly conveyed empathic focus can arouse in the patient unconscious memory traces of interactions with the good symbiotic mother of infancy in which she was exquisitely in touch with the infant's needs and desires, often explicitly and sympathetically conveyed with such words as "little baby is frightened" or "you want your mommy."

VI

The other type of fantasy that our laboratory results bear on—the sanctioned Oedipal gratification fantasy—is also one that is activated in many real-life situations with adaptation-enhancing consequences. Thus, everyday sexual contact between men and women can contain as a *component* of its meaning the sanctioned gratification of incestuous longings; participation in sports can allow for the expression of sanctioned competitive feelings toward the same-sex parent; and vocational accomplishment can have the unconscious meaning of a sanctioned triumph over the same-sex parent.[7]

As I have elaborated on elsewhere (Silverman, 1979), the inadvertent stimulation of sanctioned Oedipal gratification fantasies also plays a significant role in the therapeutic success of many nonanalytic forms of psychotherapy. Treatments in which such stimulation is most likely to occur are those in which the therapist is experienced as a "superego figure" by virtue of assuming what I have termed a "directive stance" (Silverman, 1974). By this I mean a stance in which the therapist is heavily involved in directing the patient's thoughts, feelings, and/or actions either in or out of the treatment sessions, particularly where patients are directed to engage in libidinal or aggressive behavior. Included here are the Masters and Johnson type of sex therapy, touching and other body-contact therapies, behavior-assertiveness training, and encounter treatment. In all of these, it is easy for the therapist to be unconsciously experienced as a permissive superego figure—i.e., as an external representation of the patient's superego who is giving permission for the fulfillment of wishes that previously have been taboo.

VII

Summarizing the thesis thus far, my focus has been on two types of unconscious fantasies, each of which is associated with early childhood experiences that have been well described in the psychoanalytic literature. But whereas these psychoanalytic writings on unconscious fantasies have focused on their pathogenic potential, my focus has been on a variation of each fantasy that can

[7]In each of these situations, there are particular circumstances that increase the likelihood that the Oedipal fantasies that are activated will be experienced as sanctioned. Thus, the greater sexual activity and more pleasurable experience that many people report after viewing X-rated movies can be seen (in part) as a result of the implicit permission that the availability of such movies conveys. Analogously, the familiar "home-court advantage" in professional sports competition can be viewed (in part) as the result of the cheering of the crowd, which implies sanction for the expression of competitive impulses. And the improved work performance that sometimes occurs in response to the encouragement of an older same-sex person can similarly be seen as reactive to the fantasy that the Oedipal same-sex parent is approving of one's successful performance.

be "adaption-enhancing" (in the limited way I defined earlier). Two types of data were presented to support this thesis. The first came from a series of tightly controlled laboratory experiments in which the activation of these fantasies through the subliminal psychodynamic activation method led to improved adaptation in many varied subject populations. The second came from observation of persons in various types of real-life situations, including nonanalytic psychotherapies, from which it was inferred that the inadvertent activation of these same fantasies also had adaptation-enhancing consequences.

Before going on to the implications of this thesis for psychoanalytic treatment, let me offer the following clarification. The difference between the versions of the fantasies that can be adaptation-enhancing (which have been my focus) and the versions that are more likely to be pathogenic (which earlier psychoanalytic writers have dwelt on) would seem to be the following. In the former, a compromise is attained that simultaneously satisfies unconscious wishes and the countermotivations that oppose these wishes. Thus, for activation of the symbiotic gratification fantasy to be adaptation-enhancing, the fantasy has to involve only partial merging so that the need for individuation as well as the wish for oneness can be satisfied. In this regard it is interesting that in one study of schizophrenics (Silverman, 1970), when we changed the words of the symbiotic stimulus so that they read I AM MOMMY, rather than MOMMY AND I ARE ONE, the pathology level increased rather than diminished. This we understood as due to the fact that the former wording implies a much more complete loss of self-object differentiation than does the latter wording.

Similarly, for the activation of the sanctioned Oedipal gratification fantasy to be adaptation-enhancing, the gratifications that are experienced have to be derivative rather than unmodulated. Or in the words of our experimental stimuli, DEFEATING DAD IS OK in sports competition (and even in heterosexual activity), but not in taking mother as a sexual object.

VIII

Let me turn now to the implications of the above discussion for psychoanalytic treatment. As mentioned at the outset, it has always been the consensus among psychoanalytic clinicians that the main agent of change in psychoanalytic treatment is insight, defined as the working through of the cognitive and emotional realization that particular aspects of one's behavior are the result of specific motives which one previously had warded off. I believe that there also would be a consensus among psychoanalytic clinicians that other agents of change frequently assert themselves in the psychoanalytic situation, as they do in nonanalytic therapies and other real-life situations. Thus, while the analyst's assumption of an "interpretative stance" lessens the likelihood that other processes will be mobilized, it by no means offers assurance against this happening (see Silverman, 1974).

What are these noninsight agents of change? As I indicated at the beginning of the paper, a number of concepts have been used in the psychoanalytic literature. These include, most prominently, "transference gratifications" (Freud, 1915), the analyst as "auxiliary superego" (Strachey, 1934), "identification with the analyst" (Sterba, 1934), "corrective emotional experiences" (Alexander, 1954), and the "holding environment" (Winnicott, 1965).

I shall now argue that each of these concepts can be reconceptualized as involving the activation of unconscious fantasies, particularly the two that I have been discussing. Thus, the holding environment can be viewed as referring to those aspects of the analyst's behavior (and other qualities of the "psychoanalytic situation") that stimulate symbiotic gratification fantasies. The analyst as auxiliary superego can be reconsidered as involving the activation of sanctioned Oedipal gratification fantasies. And transference gratifications, corrective emotional experiences, and identification with the analyst can be seen as involving the activation of both these fantasies. As I noted at the outset, this formulation is not meant to imply that for each of the earlier terms used, the process referred to involves *only* the activation of an unconscious fantasy. Rather, I am suggesting that for each of the concepts the unconscious fantasy activation is one aspect of the underlying process involved.[8]

What is the advantage of my having reconceptualized the other concepts that have been used to describe noninsight-based changes during psychoanalytic treatment in terms of the activation of unconscious fantasies? For one thing, it calls attention to the fact that these other concepts have a core element in common and it specifies just what this element is. This advantage would not mean much, however, if I could not simultaneously maintain that the new conceptualization better fits the available data than do the earlier ones. Thus, let me point out the following. While the old conceptualizations might be perfectly adequate for the clinical data, the same cannot be said for the laboratory data that have been cited. Consider again the experiments that have been described. A subject—patients in some studies, nonpatients in others—enters the labo-

---

[8]With regard to what else is involved, it is explicit in Alexander's concept of the corrective emotional experience and Strachey's concept of internalizing the analyst as an auxiliary superego (and perhaps implicit in the other three concepts as well) that the following element also plays a mutative role. The analysand has a new experience that is contrary to his past experiences, thus contradicting the analysand's expectation of negative environmental reactions. In a recent personal communication, Merton Gill made the following comment, which I would endorse, at least as a working hypothesis: "In my opinion there are at least three major mutative factors [in all psychotherapies]: insight, unanalyzed transference [or the activation of unconscious fantasies], and new experience.... The relative role that these three factors play in any particular therapy differs widely."

ratory and looks into the tachistoscope for a few seconds. He or she receives subliminal exposures both of experimental stimuli (e.g., MOMMY AND I ARE ONE or DEFEATING DAD IS OK) and neutral control stimuli (e.g., PEOPLE ARE WALKING), the former producing adaptation-enhancing changes not produced by the latter. These changes are obviously not due to a "holding environment," an "identification," a "corrective emotional experience," a "transference gratification," or an "auxiliary superego"—processes in which there is an interaction over time with some significant person. In the laboratory the subject's encounter is brief, and even more important, it is no longer during the experimental condition than it is during the control condition. And whatever unconscious importance the experimenter may have for the subject, that remains the same during the administration of the experimental and control conditions. The differential reactions of the subjects under the two conditions, therefore, can only be ascribed to differences in the stimulus content, and to account for these data a different conceptualization is needed. The formulation that something in the external world has activated a latent unconscious symbiotic gratification or sanctioned Oedipal fantasy provides a reasonable fit.[9]

IX

Earlier I noted that noninsight processes of the kind I have reconceptualized in terms of the activation of unconscious fantasies often occur in the psychoanalytic situation. When such processes act detrimentally on the analysand's adaptive functioning, they should of course be nullified. As I will detail, the analyst can accomplish this by: (1) subjecting the noninsight process to analysis—i.e., calling attention to it and exposing its links to the analysand's current motivations and personal history; (2) reflecting on his or her interaction with the analysand so that any aspects of the analyst's behavior that are contributing to this process can be modified.

A more controversial question, however, is what position the analyst should

---

[9]Let me make mention of a third fantasy, the activation of which also may play a role in some of the noninsight agents of change under consideration here; a fantasy involving an internalization of the "Oedipal father's" strength and power, and on a deeper level, his penis. This fantasy, like the two already discussed, is activated in many real-life situations, perhaps most particularly in religious experiences in which God is unconsciously equated with father; and in the placebo effect in medicine in which the physician is so equated. Like the previously discussed fantasies, this one too may be the primary agent of change in nonanalytic therapies, particularly in treatments such as est (Erhard Seminars Training) in which the therapist comes across as authoritarian, mysterious, and potentially punitive. The difference between the version of this fantasy that is adaptation-enhancing (in the limited way defined earlier) and the version that is pathogenic (see Arlow, 1969) lies, I suspect, in whether the father's penis, strength, and power are unconsciously perceived as shared or as stolen. I am proposing this fantasy in a more tentative way than the other two, because it has not yet been studied in the laboratory.

take when the noninsight process appears to be having a *positive* effect on the analysand's adaptive functioning. In the "psychoanalytic community," three positions have been taken (at least implicitly) on this question: (1) noninsight processes are always to be nullified; (2) these processes need not be nullified if they are the means to the end of furthering the insight process; however, to the extent that they are a direct agent of change, they are to be abrogated; (3) noninsight processes need not be nullified even if they are acting as a direct agent as long as they are subsidiary to the insight process, which remains the *main* agent of change.[10]

The major (implicit) point at issue would seem to be the following. Those adopting the first position assume that noninsight processes *always* risk compromising the analysis—if not immediately, then in the long run. Those sympathetic to the second position assume that this danger will materialize only if the noninsight process is producing direct change. And finally, those accepting the third position assume that even when the noninsight process is producing direct change, the analysis is not *necessarily* impeded.

The resolution of the controversy described above would require extensive, detailed, and systematically collected clinical data from both analyses in which attempts were made to nullify these noninsight processes and those in which no such attempts were made.[11] In my opinion, studies seeking these types of

---

[10]Among those favoring positions 2 and 3 above, there would be a further division between those who would allow the noninsight process forever to operate silently and those who, later in treatment, would subject it to analysis. In the opinion of this writer, this latter step (similar to Eissler's [1953] recommendation that "parameters" be analyzed after they are "employed") may well be necessary if the insight process *is* to be the main agent of change.

[11]Such a resolution also would require evaluations made by clinicians other than the treating analysts as to the outcome of each type of analysis. These evaluations should cover all important ego functions (level of object relatedness, frustration tolerance, sublimatory capacity, etc.), as well as the fate of the presenting symptoms, and should include extensive follow-ups. The means that I am suggesting for addressing this controversy may seem obvious to some readers and thus my emphasis on it unnecessary. However, there has been an unfortunate tradition in psychoanalysis for clinicians to react to controversial questions by making theoretical deductions or alluding to their "clinical experience." As I have expanded on elsewhere (Silverman, 1978b), when clinicians disagree, as in the current instance, the clinical experience of either antagonist cannot be given much weight. And as for theoretical deductions, not only are they a less scientific way of resolving controversy, but they often are based on unwarranted assumptions. With regard to the current controversy, for example, some analysts unjustifiably assume that a change based on a gratification experience could only be understood as a catharsis, with the implication that it *necessarily* will be short-lived. But as has been detailed elsewhere (Silverman and Frank, 1978, pp. 135–136), a case can be made for the formulation that, in certain circumstances, a gratification experience can lessen the need for pathological defenses or lead to cognitive restructuring, thus providing an "acceptable rationale" (within a psychoanalytic framework) for anticipating personality change. Lest I be misunderstood, let me make clear that I am not arguing for the validity of this formulation; I am only stating that it cannot be rejected out of hand. The accumulation of data that are systematically and objectively collected and evaluated should be the basis for resolving this controversy.

data deserve high priority and, in carrying them out, I think it important to consider the *degree* to which the unconscious fantasies at issue have been activated. I would hypothesize that, for most analysands, while continuous or even frequent activation of these fantasies will impede the analytic process, their *occasional* activation will have a facilitating effect. More specifically, I would propose that the occasional activation of the symbiotic gratification fantasy leaves the analysand with an increased sense of well-being so that he or she is willing and able to engage in the arduous task of analysis (for related viewpoints, see Stone [1961] and Nacht [1964]). Similarly, the occasional activation of sanctioned Oedipal fantasies can enable the analysand more comfortably to allow himself or herself ideational and affective derivatives of Oedipal wishes so that they are more accessible to analysis.

X

I should now like to return to the matter of nullifying symbiotic and Oedipal gratification fantasies in psychoanalytic treatment. Whatever validity the hypothesis offered above may turn out to have—and more generally, whatever results may emerge from studies investigating the merits of the three positions outlined—I believe there would be agreement among psychoanalytic clinicians that there are instances when these fantasies *should* be nullified in psychoanalytic treatment. (It is only the frequency of these instances that would be at issue.) I am referring to those occasions when these fantasies impede the insight process or when they have a maladaptive effect on the analysand's functioning outside of treatment. My discussion of these instances is based in part on my experiences in conducting, supervising, and discussing with colleagues psychoanalytic treatment; and in part on findings from the laboratory research program, which I described earlier. With regard to the latter I should mention that, while the activation of both the symbiotic and the sanctioned Oedipal gratification fantasies has had a positive effect on the great majority of subjects in our investigations, a few (about 5 percent) have reacted in a paradoxical fashion; and it is what we have learned from these subjects that has relevance for the psychoanalytic clinician in the current context.

First let me note the most frequent circumstances in which the activation of each of the fantasies cited has had maladaptive consequences. With regard to the symbiotic gratification fantasy; the circumstances include: (1) when the fantasy serves a defensive rather than a restitutive function—particularly when it serves to ward off Oedipal wishes; (2) when it reinforces a symbiotic fixation and prevents a person, who is otherwise ready, from developmentally advancing to a stage of greater individuation and separation; (3) when it shades into an experience of total, rather than partial, merging and thus threatens the person with a loss of sense of self; and (4) when, for a male, the fantasy shifts its meaning from one of symbiosis to one of incest. In any of these circumstances, the activation of a symbiotic gratification fantasy can be expected to disrupt the analysand's functioning either within or outside of the psychoanalytic situation.

As for the sanctioned Oedipal fantasy, two negative fostering circumstances have been noted: (1) when the Oedipal gratification that is experienced as sanctioned is not derivative enough—i.e., when the wish involved has not been sufficiently modulated with regard to its original incestuous or aggressive aims; and (2) when the analysand experiences the sanction as carrying with it what can be termed "an unreasonable contingency clause" (Silverman, 1979). I will return to this concept shortly with a clinical example.

Whether the activation of these fantasies will result in maladaptive consequences will depend not only on the psychology of the analysand but on the behavior of the analyst as well. Consider the following example. A female analyst, whom I was supervising, was treating a young woman with a height phobia, a symptom that remitted after several months of treatment. My supervisee and I understood this remission to be less the result of insight and more the consequence of an activated unconscious fantasy in which Oedipal wishes that underlay the phobia were experienced as sanctioned by the analyst, who was the Oedipal mother in the transference. Then, over a year later, the symptom returned shortly after the analysand became pregnant for the first time. The understanding that evolved from her associations and dreams was that the sanctioned Oedipal fantasy, which had been operative, contained a contingency clause in which pregnancy was taboo. Or, to put this somewhat differently, the analyst as Oedipal mother was experienced as permissive only as long as the analysand did not encroach on her territory—i.e., as long as she did not become a mother, as the analyst was, a fact of which the analysand was aware.

What was the contribution of the analyst to this state of affairs? As I "observed" the treatment, I saw no evidence that the analyst actually opposed her analysand's pregnancy. But I was frequently struck by the analyst's manner, which was often subtly restrictive, and which the analysand, on more than one occasion, characterized as "Spartan" and "Prussian." Thus, while the analysand's experience of her analyst as opposed to her pregnancy had an important transferential component, it also contained a grain of truth, a point to which I will return shortly in another context.

XI

What are the means by which the psychoanalytic clinician can nullify the unconscious fantasies under consideration? As noted earlier, he or she can proceed in the following ways: (1) by analyzing these fantasies with the analysand; and (2) by modifying aspects of his or her own behavior that are stimulating the fantasies. Clearly, with regard to the latter step (and as I will soon argue, with regard to the former as well), the analyst must be aware of what behavior is serving as an activator. It is toward delineating these activators that I will now turn my attention.

In an earlier paper (Silverman, 1972) I examined and detailed the real-life analogues of the "subliminal psychodynamic effects" that we have demonstrated in the laboratory. Here I noted that reactions analogous to those produced in our laboratory research usually occur in real life when a person is confronted with an external stimulus of which he is aware, yet *unaware of its psychodynamic relevance*. Consider the following example from a case I described earlier:

A 24-year-old unmarried woman in analysis, who felt exceedingly frustrated over the fact that she was childless, received a birth announcement from an old friend toward whom she had always felt rivalry. She reacted to the announcement with an intensified longing for a child of her own and jealous feelings toward her rival, although not symptomatically. Some time later, however, while reading a book during a train ride, she suddenly, and at the time inexplicably, felt depersonalized. This was a symptom from which she had suffered in the past but which, at that point in analysis, no longer plagued her. She reported that the symptom came on when she began to read a particular article, but she could see no relationship between the article itself and her conflicts and symptom. Suddenly, in the session, she remembered with a laugh that the name of the author of the article was "Rothschild," to which she instantly associated the married name—Roth—of the friend who had sent her the birth announcement a few weeks before. She felt convinced that she was unwittingly reminded of "the child of Roth" and that it was the unconscious hostility this "silently" aroused that brought back her symptom (1972, p. 312).

Keeping this general observation in mind, I have reflected on those aspects of a psychoanalyst's behavior which can inadvertently activate each of the fantasies that have been the focus of this paper. I consider the following to be among the most frequent and potent activators, though whether they will have this effect in a particular instance will, of course, depend on both the analysand's general psychology and the state of the transference at the moment.

With regard to symbiotic gratification fantasies, I would suggest that notable activators include prominent and frequent expressions by the analyst of protectiveness, nurturance, and unconditional acceptance; and frequent *explicit* expressions of empathy (recall my previous discussion of client-centered treatment), as well as the use of the vocalizations "mmm" and "mm-hmm" while listening to the patient (often wrongly regarded as being less "active" than words spoken by the analyst). With regard to the latter I have in mind Greenson's (1954) thesis about the "mmm" sound's link to experiences with the good (symbiotic) mother of infancy.[12]

As for sanctioned Oedipal fantasies, let me suggest that their most notable activator is the analyst who prominently conveys a sense of parental authority, for example, by being directive or by exuding an ex cathedra sense of certainty. Such a stance encourages the analysand to experience the analyst as the same-sex Oedipal parent, as does the adoption of a judgmental approach—for example, the analyst who frequently uses confrontations as an intervention or who makes reference to the analysand's "acting out." While such judgmental expressions obviously cause the analyst to be experienced as the *forbidding* Oedipal parent, they also allow for the opposite experience. It is as if the analysand unconsciously "reasons" that if a previously taboo fantasy is *not* forbidden by the authority, it must be sanctioned.[13]

Knowledge of these activators[14] is important for the analyst not only so that he can modify his behavior when necessary but also for the analysis of these unconscious fantasies. That is to say, whenever an analyst feels that a symbiotic or a sanctioned Oedipal gratification fantasy is having a maladaptive effect on an analysand, the analyst's ability to specify to the analysand just what in the treatment situation triggered the fantasy can help greatly in analyzing it successfully.

This conclusion, which I have tested clinically in my work with analysands, was first suggested to me by the aspect of our research findings alluded to above involving the small minority of research subjects who reacted negatively to the fantasy-related stimuli that the much larger percentage responded to positively. These paradoxical reactions sometimes came to light during the study proper and in other instances during a debriefing interview held at the conclusion of the study. In the latter instances we discovered that when we revealed to the subject the stimulus that he or she had received, encouraged the subject

[12]It is interesting to note that the great majority of mantras--the Sanskrit sounds that meditators in transcendental meditation are instructed to focus on—contain the sound "mmm"; e.g., the prototypical mantra, "om."

[13]This "logic" can be seen more clearly in the Masters and Johnson type of sex therapy where the therapist actually instructs the patient at the beginning of treatment to restrict his sexual interaction with his partner to petting and temporarily to forgo attempts at intercourse. This, I suspect, makes the "go ahead" instructions later in treatment much more likely to be experienced as a sanction for a taboo wish.

[14]If one takes into account the idiosyncratic perceptions and associations of particular analysands, many more activators of the two fantasies under consideration could be added to the above list, including aspects of the analyst's physical appearance and even the analyst's analytic interventions. With regard to the latter, Marvin Hurvich, in discussing an early version of this paper, pointed out that, for certain analysands, those interventions that are designed to further insight (i.e., the offering of interpretations) or to allow for working through can be idiosyncratically experienced and thus stimulate an unconscious fantasy.

to associate to it, and then discussed its idiosyncratic meaning, the paradoxical reaction dissipated.

Extrapolating from the above, as well as from the clinical observations of Langs (1973), who has stressed the importance of helping patients become aware of the aspects of the external world that activate psychodynamically important reactions (which he refers to as the "context" in which these reactions occur), the following recommendation seems in order. Whenever a psychoanalytic clinician views the activation of an unconscious fantasy as maladaptive for a particular analysand, the analysis of the fantasy should include not only the exposure of its content, its dynamics, and its historical roots, but also the activator of the fantasy in the treatment situation.

To exemplify what I mean here let me return to the case vignette cited earlier of my supervisee's analysand in whose treatment a sanctioned Oedipal fantasy contained a disruptive contingency clause. If I was correct in inferring that the analyst's manner was partly responsible for this state of affairs, she might have said the following to her analysand at an appropriate time in treatment:

We have discovered how you experience me as a restrictive mother whose permission you need for feeling good. And we have seen how you have viewed my permission as contingent on your not becoming a mother as I am. While, as we have learned, this view of me is rooted in your earlier relationship with your own mother, I wonder if it may not have been fostered by my manner. You have often characterized me as Spartan and Prussian.

I am not advocating "countertransference confessionals" or even deep revelations to the analysand, but rather, as I hope the example conveys, that the analyst simply avow surface personality characteristics that have been activating the fantasy. While, as in the example cited, analysands (usually) are aware of these characteristics, they tend to isolate them from transference experiences. It is toward countering this defensive operation, and also toward strengthening the analysand's ability to master noxious environmental stimuli, that my technique recommendation is directed

Summary and Conclusions

The following interrelated points have been made in this paper. There is now abundant evidence available from tightly controlled laboratory studies involving the presentation of stimuli outside of awareness that the activation of unconscious symbiotic gratification fantasies and sanctioned Oedipal fantasies can have adaptation-enhancing effects on behavior. These findings can be viewed as a laboratory analogue of real-life situations in which these same fantasies are activated by external events of which the person is aware, yet unaware of their fantasy-related "pull." These situations include psychotherapy encounters in which therapists inadvertently, through their manner or techniques, activate one or the other of these fantasies. In nonanalytic therapies (according to my hypothesis) these fantasies serve as major therapeutic agents. In psychoanalytic treatment, on the other hand, the main agent of change is insight, but these same fantasies are often operative. They play an important role in what have been referred to in the psychoanalytic literature as "transference gratifications," "corrective emotional experiences," "the holding environment," "identification with the analyst," and "the analyst as an auxiliary superego." Reconceptualizing these noninsight agents of change in terms of unconscious fantasies seems to provide a better fit for the available "data"—particularly if one takes this term to cover the results from the laboratory experiments as well as clinical observations.

The hypothesis was offered that the activation of symbiotic gratification and sanctioned Oedipal fantasies in psychoanalytic treatment can facilitate the insight process and thus further psychoanalytic goals if this activation is: (1) occasional rather than frequent, and (2) subject to analysis at some point in treatment. It was noted, however, that psychoanalytic clinicians differ considerably in their views on this matter so that systematic and objective empirical study is clearly in order. The only point on which a consensus can at present be reached is that, in particular instances, the activation of these fantasies can be maladaptive and thus should be nullified. Thus, the position taken here was that when the abrogation of these fantasies is viewed as desirable, this can be effected both by analyzing them and by the analyst modifying aspects of his or her behavior that are inadvertently contributing to their mobilization. It is therefore important for the analyst to be aware of these aspects; toward that end, a listing of some of the more frequent activators was offered. Finally, it was proposed that for the optimal analysis of these fantasies, the analysand should be helped to understand not only the fantasy's content, dynamic function, and origins, but also its activators in the treatment situation.

REFERENCES

Alexander, F. (1954), Some quantitative aspects of psychoanalytic technique. *J. Amer. Psychoanal. Assn.,* 2:685–701.
Arlow, J. (1969), Unconscious fantasy and disturbances of conscious experience. *Psychoanal. Quart.,* 38:1–27.
Beres, D. (1962), The unconscious fantasy. *Psychoanal. Quart.,* 31:309–328.
Bergmann, M. S. (1971), On the capacity to love., In: *Separation-Individuation: Essays in Honor of Margaret S. Mahler,* ed. J. B. McDevitt & C. S. Settlage. New York: International Universities Press.

Bronstein, A. (1976) An experimental study of internalization process in schizophrenic men. Unpublished doctoral dissertation, Yeshiva University.

Cohen, R. (1977), The effects of subliminal stimulation of three symbiotic stimuli on the psychopathology of female schizophrenics. Unpublished doctoral dissertation, Teachers College, Columbia University.

Condon, T. (1976), Systematic desensitization: An evaluation of a psychoanalytic model of its effectiveness. Unpublished doctoral dissertation, University of Connecticut.

Des Lauriers, A. (1962), *The Experience of Reality in Childhood Schizophrenia*. New York: International Universities Press.

Eissler, K. R. (1953), The effect of the structure of the ego on psychoanalytic technique. *J. Amer. Psychoanal. Assn.*, 1:104–143.

Fenichel, O. (1945), *The Psychoanalytic Theory of Neurosis*. New York: Norton.

Fisher, C. (1954), Dreams and perception. *J. Amer. Psychoanal. Assn.*, 2:389–445.

────── (1956), Dreams, images, and perception: A study of unconscious-preconscious relationships. *J. Amer. Psychoanal. Assn.*, 4:5–48.

Freeman, T., Cameron, J. L., & McGhie, A. (1958), *Chronic Schizophrenia*. New York: International Universities Press.

Freud, S. (1915), Observations on transference love. *Standard Edition*, 12:157–171. London: Hogarth Press, 1958.

Friborg, A. (1979), Further studies of subliminal symbiotic stimulation on relatively differentiated and nondifferentiated schizophrenics. Unpublished doctoral dissertation, New York University.

Gordon, L. (1970), Beyond the reality principle. *Amer. Imago*, 27:160–182.

Greenson, R. (1954), About the sound "Mm." *Psychoanal. Quart.*, 23:234–239.

Holt, R. R. (1969), Manual for scoring of primary-process manifestations in Rorschach responses. Draft 10 Research Center for Mental Health, New York University (mimeographed).

Kaplan, R. (1976), The symbiotic fantasy as a therapeutic agent: An experimental comparison of the effects of three symbiotic elements on manifest pathology in schizophrenics. Unpublished doctoral dissertation, New York University.

Kaye, M. (1975), The therapeutic value of three merging stimuli for male schizophrenics. Unpublished doctoral dissertation, Yeshiva University.

Langs, R. (1973), *The Technique of Psychoanalytic Psychotherapy*, Vol. 1. New York: Jason Aronson.

Leiter, E. (1973), A study of the effects of subliminal activation of merging fantasies in differentiated and nondifferentiated schizophrenics. Unpublished doctoral dissertation, New York University.

Lewin, B. D. (1935), Claustrophobia, *Psychoanal.Q.*, 4,227–233.

Lidz, T. (1973), *The Origin and Treatment of Schizophrenic Disorders*. New York: Basic Books.

Limentani, D. (1956), Symbiotic identification in schizophrenia. *Psychiatry*, 19:231–236.

Lonski, M., & Palumbo, R. (1978), The effects of subliminal stimuli on competitive dart-throwing performance. Unpublished manuscript, Hofstra University.

Martin, A. (1975), The effect of subliminal stimulation of symbiotic fantasies on weight loss in obese women receiving behavioral treatment. Unpublished doctoral dissertation, New York University.

Nacht, S. (1964), Silence as an integrative factor. *Internat. J. Psycho-anal.*, 45:299–300.

Oremland, J. D. (1972), Transference cure and flight into health. *Internat. J. Psycho-anal. Psychother.*, 1:61–74.

Parker, K. (1977), The effects of subliminal merging stimuli on the academic performance of college students. Unpublished doctoral dissertation, New York University.

Rose, G. (1972), Fusion states. In: *Tactics and Techniques in Psychoanalytic Therapy*, ed. P. L. Giovacchini. New York: Science House.

Sackeim, H. (1977), Self-deception: Motivational determinants of the non-awareness of cognition. Unpublished doctoral dissertation, University of Pennsylvania.

Sandler, J., & Nagera, H. (1963), Aspects of the metapsychology of fantasy. *The Psychoanalytic Study of the Child*, 18:159–194.

Schurtman, R. (1978), Symbiotic stimulation as an aid in the counseling of alcoholics. Unpublished doctoral dissertation, New York University.

Searles, H. F. (1965), *Collected Papers on Schizophrenia and Related Subjects*. New York: International Universities Press.

Shafii, M. (1973), Silence in the service of the ego: Psychoanalytic study of meditation. *Internat. J. Psycho-Anal.*, 54:431–443.

Silverman, L. H. (1967), An experimental approach to the study of dynamic propositions in psychoanalysis: The relationship between the aggressive drive and ego regression—initial studies. *J. Amer. Psychoanal. Assn.*, 15:276–403.

———— (1970), Further experimental studies on dynamic propositions in psychoanalysis: On the function and meaning of regressive thinking. *J. Amer. Psychoanal. Assn.*, 18:102–124.

———— (1972), Drive stimulation and psychopathology: On the conditions under which drive-related external events evoke pathological reactions. In: *Psychoanalysis and Contemporary Science*, Vol. 1, ed. R. R. Holt & E. Peterfreund. New York: Macmillan.

———— (1974), Some psychoanalytic considerations of nonpsychoanalytic therapies: On the possibility of integrating treatment approaches and related issues. *Psychotherapy*, 11:298–305.

———— (1975), On the role of laboratory experiments in the development of the clinical theory of psychoanalysis, *Int. Rev. Psychoanal.*, 2:43–64.

———— (1976), Psychoanalytic theory: "The reports of my death are greatly exaggerated." *Amer. Psychologist*, 31:621–637.

———— (1977), Experimental data on the effects of unconscious fantasy on communicative behavior. In: *Communicative Structures and Psychic Structures*, ed. N. Freedman & S. Grand. New York: Plenum.

———— (1978a), The unconscious symbiotic fantasy as a ubiquitous therapeutic agent. *Internat. J. Psycho-Anal. Psychother.*, 7:562–585.

———— (1978b), Reply to Theodore Shapiro's discussion of "Unconscious symbiotic fantasy: Ubiquitous therapeutic agent." *Internat. J. Psycho-Anal. Psychother.*, 7:594–601.

———— (1979), Two unconscious fantasies as mediators of successful psychotherapy. *Psychotherapy*. 16:215–230.

———— & Adler, J. (1978), An experimental demonstration of unconscious conflict motivating behavior. Unpublished manuscript, Research Center for Mental Health.

Silverman, L. H., and P. Candell (1970), On the relationship between aggressive activation, symbiotic merging intactness of body boundaries and manifest pathology in schizophrenia, *J. Nerv. Ment. Dis.*, 150:387–399.

Silverman, L. H., P. Candell, T. F. Pettit, and F. A. Blum (1971), Further data on effects of aggressive activation and symbiotic merging on ego functioning of schizophrenics, *Percept. Mot. Skills*, 32:93–94.

———— & Frank, S. (1978), Aggressive stimulation, aggressive fantasy and disturbances of ego functioning. In: *Psychoanalytic Perspectives on Aggression*, ed. G. D. Goldman & D. S. Milman. New York: Kendall/Hung.

——, —— & Dachinger, P. (1974), Psychoanalytic reinterpretation of the effectiveness of systematic desensitization: Experimental data bearing on the role of merging fantasies. *J. Abnorm. Psych.*, 83:313–318.

——, Kwawer, J. S., Wolitzky, D., ' Coron, M. (1973), An experimental study of aspects of the psychoanalytic theory of male homosexuality. *J. Abnorm. Psych.*, 82:178–188.

——, Martin, A., Ungaro, R., & Mendelsohn, E. (1978), Effect of subliminal stimulation of symbiotic fantasies on behavior modification treatment of obesity. *J. Consulting & Clinical Psych.*, 46:432–441.

——, Ross, D., Adler, J., & Lustig, D. (1978), A simple research paradigm for demonstrating subliminal psychodynamic activation. *J. Abnorm. Psych.*, 87:341–357.

——, Spiro, R. H., Weissberg, J. S., & Candell, P. (1969), The effects of aggressive activation and the need to merge on pathological thinking in schizophrenia. *J. Nervous & Mental Disease,* 148:39–51.

—— & Wolitzky, C. (1970), The effects of the subliminal stimulation of symbiotic fantasies on the defensiveness of "normal" subjects in telling TAT stories. Unpublished manuscript.

Silverstein, R. (1978), Studies of subliminal oedipal stimulation and dart-throwing ability. Bachelor's Honors thesis, Brown University.

Spiro, T. (1975), The effects of laboratory stimulation of symbiotic fantasies and bodily self-awareness on relatively differentiated and nondifferentiated schizophrenics. Unpublished doctoral dissertation, New York University.

Sterba, R. (1934), The fate of the ego in analytic therapy. *Internat. J. Psycho-Anal.,* 15:117–126.

Stone, L. (1961), *The Psychoanalytic Situation.* New York: International Universities Press.

Strachey, J. (1934), The nature of the therapeutic action of psychoanalysis. *Internat. J. Psycho-Anal.,* 15:127–159.

Winnicott, D. (1958), The capacity to be alone. *Internat. J. Psycho-Anal.,* 39:416–420.

—— (1965), *The Maturational Process and the Facilitating Environment.* New York: International Universities Press.

Wolitzky, D. L., & Wachtel, P. L. (1973), Personality and perception. In: *Handbook of General Psychology,* ed. B. B. Wolman. Englewood Cliffs, N.J.: Prentice-Hall.

CHAPTER 11

How the Dream Works:
The Role of Dreaming
in the Psychotherapeutic Process

Stanley R. Palombo

Despite the importance of the concepts of incorporation and identification in contemporary object-relations theory, little has been written about the way in which these processes might actually function in the day-to-day setting of psychoanalysis and psychoanalytic psychotherapy.[1] This deficiency is due in part, I believe, to the traditional psychoanalytic view that *dreaming* is primarily, if not exclusively, a *centrifugal* process. For Freud, dreams were a window through which information about the inner workings of the unconscious could be extracted by an outside observer. The topographic model outlined in Chapter Seven of *The Interpretation of Dreams* (1900) seems to take it for granted that the Unconscious is informed effortlessly and with perfect efficiency about the total experience of the person. Freud did not suggest any psychic mechanism to perform this burdensome function, however.

The findings of the sleep laboratory indicate that during most of our dreaming time no inner information is emerging, since dreams cannot be remembered and reported unless we are awakened within five to ten minutes after dreaming

---

[1]Although psychoanalysis must be clearly distinguished from psychoanalytic psychotherapy in many contexts, I believe the phenomena discussed here to be common to both of these treatment methods. The terms *therapy* and *analysis* will therefore be used interchangeably to refer to the broad area where the two methods overlap.

them (Dement and Wolpert, 1958). During the 1960s several investigators independently suggested that in the dreaming state information was being transferred from a short-term memory structure that collected the experience of the previous day to a permanent memory store (Greenberg and Pearlman, 1974). An elaborate process of selection and evaluation would be necessary to sift out the important events of the day and to locate them at appropriate places in the associative network of the permanent memory.

In *Dreaming and Memory* (Palombo, 1978), I proposed a theoretical framework for understanding the role of dreaming in the process through which new experience is incorporated into this associative network. The details of the process were illustrated through an examination of transcribed psychoanalytic hours and sleep laboratory recordings of dreams reported when the patient was awakened after each REM period during a night in the laboratory.

In a similar sequence of analytic hours and sleep laboratory reports presented below, we will see how the associative material that emerges during the analytic hour is worked through in the dreams of the following night and matched with related memories of past events already located in permanent storage. During the matching process the representations of important events of the day are superimposed on the representations of similar events in the past. When the composite image formed by the superimposition has a relatively coherent structure in which common elements of the two experiences are reinforced, an associative link is established between the past and present experiences in the permanent memory. A dream is a series of superimposed images in which such a matching occurs.

A normal dream, in which a successful matching has taken place, does not awaken the dreamer and is therefore unlikely to be remembered. A dream in which the matching is unsuccessful, on the other hand, tends to generate a state of anxiety which awakens the dreamer and thereby introduces the dream into waking consciousness. The typical cause of a mismatched dream, as far as I have been able to observe it, is the interference of the censorship mechanisms in the selection of appropriate items to be matched.

When the dreamer is awakened by an anxiety dream, the contents of the dream are generally remembered on the following day, subject of course to further interference by the mechanisms of defense. The remembered anxiety dream becomes a part of the daytime experience of the dreamer and may be introduced into a new dream as a day residue on the following night. In other words, the original, or *index dream,* is associated with other experiences from the following day, which usually have the effect of revising or correcting the mismatch between the past and present components of the index dream. This is especially likely when the dreamer is undergoing psychotherapy and reporting remembered dreams to the therapist.

The dream of the following night, in which the revised and expanded representation of the index dream is rematched with the contents of the permanent memory, is called a *correction dream*. Because the index dream already contains material from the permanent memory of the dreamer, the day residue of which it forms a part is especially likely to be matched successfully in the correction dream. For this reason the correction dream is not an awakening dream, and ordinarily it is not remembered by the dreamer. In order to study the correction dream directly, therefore, it is necessary to awaken the dreamer in the sleep laboratory after each period of dreaming sleep.

The correction dream is one of the principal agents of therapeutic change. It creates a link in the associative memory structure of the patient between the problem area identified by the mismatch in the anxiety dream and the reconstructive work of the therapeutic hour. This link is essential to the process of incorporating understanding gained in the therapeutic experience into the psychic apparatus of the patient. It is not enough that this experience be taken in. It must be connected with the distorted representations of the self and the object world acquired in the past. We are familiar enough with situations in clinical practice in which patients appear to understand today but are unable to remember or apply what they have learned tomorrow. Without the active assimilation that takes place in dreaming, today's understanding will remain isolated in short-term memory until it is superseded by new accretions of daily experience.

The clinical case material presented in *Dreaming and Memory* was drawn from a single sequence of two consecutive analytic hours with an intervening night in the sleep laboratory. This sequence was sufficiently detailed to permit a demonstration of the full complexity of the process of dream construction and its relation to the cognitive activity of waking life.

The dreams and associative material reported here come from a similar but less complete sequence recorded two months earlier in the patient's analysis. My purpose in presenting this sequence is threefold:

(1) To show that the distinctive pattern of the correction dream is not unique to the example originally described

(2) To give a further illustration of the kinds of defensive interference in the process of free association (or self-examination more generally) that can actually be corrected by the correction dream

(3) To make a beginning assessment of the magnitude of the correction possible during the formation of a single correction dream

The last of these goals is surely the most interesting. We wish to know how far it is possible to distinguish the cumulative effects of psychoanalytic therapy from those that are merely repetitive. If the correction dream represents a cumulative element in the therapeutic process, as I believe it must, then every successful correction dream constitutes an increment of some degree over the accumulated effects of all previous correction dreams during the course of treatment.

Without a program of systematic observation, nothing even resembling a precise answer can be given to the question of magnitude. But by comparing two instances of correction-dream formation which are neither too close together in the course of an analysis nor too far apart, we may be able to form a general idea of the range of possibilities that need to be investigated.

In the sequence reported in *Dreaming and Memory,* we observed what appeared to be a dramatic leap in the patient's self-knowledge. What we are asking now, in effect, is how much of that apparent leap was original to the particular sequence under study and how much of it was a repetition of earlier leaps which may have covered substantially the same ground. Clinical experience indicates that every advance in the patient's self-understanding must be relived in a variety of intrapsychic and interpersonal contexts. We would expect this to be the case in any component system that participates in the therapeutic process.

It is commonplace for a turning point in analytic therapy to be marked by a particular dream that vividly illustrates a new emotional configuration. The traditional psychoanalytic theory of dreams does not help very much in explaining why dreams are such useful indicators of therapeutic progress. If dreams are random expressions of unconscious instinctual impulses, it is difficult to see how they could emerge in an order that reflects the chronological structure of the treatment process. If dreams are created by an essential component of the therapeutic process, however, there can be no mystery about their effectiveness in measuring the changes that take place as that process unfolds.

The "turning point" dream would be one of many therapeutically active dreams, only a small number of which ever reach the patient's waking consciousness. This small number would most likely include those in which the solution of one problem exposes a new problem whose anxiety potential is sufficiently intense to awaken the dreamer.

I have no independent evidence that the previously reported sequence marked a turning point in the analysis of the patient, M. A., a bachelor in his mid-thirties. But the internal configuration of associations and interpretations indicates at least a partial resolution of an important transference theme through the recovery of a series of formative childhood memories. What we would expect to find in our new material is an overlap with the issues dealt with later on, but presumably with less apparent success at this earlier stage of working through. We would not expect to be able to predict the actual content of M. A.'s dreams and analytic hours on the basis of our prior knowledge.

The sequence in question took place on a Monday and Tuesday in January.

After describing an unsuccessful date with a woman who was feeling quite depressed, M. A. reported three dreams. The first and most elaborate of them formed the basis for two new dreams on Monday night in the sleep laboratory. One of these new dreams was clearly a correction dream, supplying two important figures who had been replaced by the dream censor in the original, or index, dream. The second Monday night dream, although not a reworking of the imagery of the index dream, appears to supply new historical material directly related to a theme uncovered by the unambiguous correction dream.

The index dream[2] follows:

I am in an old hotel on the fourth floor, I am trying to picture it as I say it now—with Phyllis Anderson. And what does Phyllis Anderson mean to have gone through that . . . moderately unattractive, kind of dull, who I wanted to marry me—she married someone else—no loss there. Made lots of flowers, I don't know what that means— but I seem to be on a trip—and other unkowns on the floor, and to think there is only one bedroom and a couple of bedrooms across the way—people I know. There is a john to the right. I was supposed to meet, I think, Dennis Bigelow, but then I don't know. Why I put down Dennis Bigelow because I remember the guy was actually supposed to be Arthur Reinhardt—no question about that—so I crossed out Dennis and put down Arthur Reinhardt. Had a date downstairs at a certain time. And Arthur promises great sexual times if I show at a certain time—I am reading now. Phyllis and I leave. I guess we pass through other rooms on the floor. She opens a door and gets out—there is an asparaguslike plant—I call it a bunch of asparagus the size of flowers. Then I catch them on the run. Funny thing, now I remember in the dream— I could not write this out in detail—and she called me silly and immature. What happens—I was waiting in the hall and she was at the other end and I ran full speed down the hall. I think as I was going by I grabbed the plants and I stopped—or else I ran by the plants and suddenly doubled back and grabbed them, you know, like a child would do playing around. I must have run back and suddenly stopped myself in reverse field and came back and grabbed the plants. I remember that she sort of berated me as immature. Well, I am unhappy with being called immature. Then I go down the stairs and I meet Arthur in a weird, all-black costume. I remember he was wearing some kind of a headdress, and the girl was wearing some kind of a loose dress, and she was rather good looking. Another situation of me being with a nothing and a nobody in my eyes, and somebody else with a sex-pot. So that is the dream. I don't know what it means right now. Then upstairs there are other . . . combs, . . . something, I don't know. I go to the bathroom—I can't read it—couples, right. I go to the bathroom and return to a room and return, but I go to the wrong room for some reason. There is a guy sleeping. And other girls are pretty—that is what I wrote down—I haven't looked at this since this morning—other girls are pretty. Here it is again, I got this pig and—she is not a pig really—but an unattractive girl to me—not a pretty girl, all right.

[2]The transcripts have been edited to remove identifying information.

What is striking about this dream is its similarity to the index dreams reported two months later, in March, and described in *Dreaming and Memory*. In fact, several of the associative links that appeared to be uncovered in the working through of the later sequence are already present in the manifest content of the Asparagus Dream just quoted. We have, among many common elements, a setting in "an old hotel" on an upper floor. There are sleeping couples, a bathroom, a man who promises sexual adventures, a woman who ridicules the phallic narcissism of the dreamer. M. A. is in his customary posture as the innocent but very frustrated onlooker. In a second dream reported in the Monday hour, M. A. is building shower stalls in "an old dirt cellar."

Very little imagination is required to reconstruct a primal-scene experience of childhood in the crowded quarters of a resort hotel. What his parents are doing in the bedroom is perceived by the dreamer as something very similar to what he does in the bathroom. In the later March sequence, M. A. was drawn into this theme with intensely conflicting affects and, ultimately, with an excited curiosity. Here, in January, neither the affect nor the curiosity is present. M. A.'s associations drift off in a disorganized tangle.

The analyst asks about M. A.'s considerable efforts to write down his dreams, which is in contrast to his lack of interest in their content. M. A. responds by trying to get the analyst to tell him directly whether or not to continue writing out his dreams. The analyst declines to do so. There is more drifting and complaining about the demandingness of the women in his life. Rather abruptly the analyst asks, "Is that *Playboy* you have there?"

For the first time in this hour M. A. is engaged. He offers a long and elaborate defense against what he takes to be the analyst's accusation that he is a dirty and impotent old man who has to look at pictures because he is incapable of finding a woman of his own. Eventually he becomes aware that this is all his own invention and that he is expressing his own intense doubts about his masculinity. He is afraid of being "a queer" or "a freak." He recalls that his young nephew has no inhibitions about enjoying the pictures in *Playboy*. "He just looked at it and thought it was funny. 'It got big teats,' he said."

There follow two memories, one from adolescence and one from early childhood:

Of course it reminds me of looking at the legs of my mother's friend—a great set of legs—and my mother asking me that question as we were driving up there—Father jumped in—boy, I was caught in the act. Man, did I feel guilty. And I don't mind telling you too that as I was looking at her I had real sexual thoughts that I would like to have some experience with her—she was an older woman and I was hoping she would attack me, or something like that. I didn't know what the hell to do, I was maybe sixteen or fifteen. I was hoping she would make some advances to me, I would not have the guts to do it—and my mother too damn sharp. Boy, you can't scratch your nose without her knowing what you were doing. Come to think of it, that was probably a very traumatic experience in my life. Furtively looking at a woman's figure and then being insulted by your mother—embarrassed to death—almost as if it was public.... That probably did something to me. I will bet your bottom dollar it never happened again—or I never got caught again. My mother is the one that comes and tells me that good looks don't mean anything, and you can . . . and that sort of thing. I wonder what sex means—what passion means to her—or meant to her. I suppose I will be in a better state of mental health when somebody says, "Hey, you buy *Playboy* to look at girls," and I say, "Yes, what the hell else do you think I buy it for?" That is when I start building defenses. [*Silence.*] I am getting the same thing about . . . the glass case with coffee beans in it. Now what does that remind me of? The last time I had coffee beans was at my grandmother's house in Baltimore. She used a coffee grinder—you put coffee beans into it and ground it—made your own coffee. I think of myself in my grandmother's house. I remember my father carried me to bed one night, I was half asleep—very vivid. [Dr.: Yes?] I just remembered. I fell asleep in a chair or on a couch. It was one of these things used—I think it was at Easter. Oh, boy, I fell asleep. They carried me into the maid's room. She had a big spring bed and off I went to sleep. It was a pleasant experience. I still feel bad and guilty about Father dying—I really do. I don't want to break into tears again but I suppose I could if I dwelt on it too long and hit a sore point. I can just see him, you know, withering away and that sort of thing, and I feel guilty.

The hour ends soon after. The analyst has been identified with the pre-Oedipal mother, who was able to read the patient's dirty mind and "embarrassed him to death." This negative maternal transference has defeated the patient's efforts to turn the analyst into an idealized father who both comforts him and provides him with a perfect sexual partner—the good mother who exists only in the dark and in other men's beds. Just so, in the Asparagus Dream, the unattractive ex-girlfriend who ridiculed his masculinity triumphed over his helpful male friend. The dream has been reenacted in the analytic hour in a way that makes its meaning at least partially accessible to the resistant dreamer.

The patient has affectively reexperienced an important childhood event that was represented with little apparent feeling in the Asparagus Dream reported at the beginning of the hour. He does not seem to know as the hour ends that the childhood event (or, more likely, series of events), the dream, and the transference reenactment are all of a piece. The reenactment did not arise from an interpretation of the dream content, but rather, from the analyst's confrontation of the patient with his secretiveness and the fact that he hides his secrets in such a way that they are visible to everyone but himself.

From the analyst's point of view, the important ideas that the patient is keeping from himself are not in the content he is trying to suppress, but in the connections that link his childhood experiences, his dreams, his fantasies, and his transference reenactments. The work of the analytic hour has succeeded in bringing these various elements into the open, but it has not made explicit the fact that they are variations on a common theme. It may be thought that the analyst has missed an opportunity to put everything together for the patient. But we know that the analyst's integrating efforts cannot be effective unless the patient also performs his own act of integration and does so in his own recognizable way.

Let me pose some questions about this typical clinical situation. How much of the analyst's reconstruction is the patient able to assimilate at any given moment in treatment? When and where does this process of assimilation take place: in the analyst's office or outside it, in the patient's conscious thoughts or elsewhere in his information-processing activities? How much is the patient capable of doing on his own, without the direct stimulus of an interpretation? What does he do and how does he do it?

The phenomenon of the correction dream sheds a good deal of light on these questions. It shows how the patient's process of integration results from an enhancement of the normal adaptive mechanisms for evaluating and sorting new experience. The integration takes place not on the level of verbal insight as offered by the analyst, but rather, in the structure of the patient's permanent memory, which is extended through the addition of new connections between the elements of experience brought into juxtaposition by the analytic process. The nature of these new connections is determined not so much by the logical structure of the interpretation as by the *convergence of associative pathways* already present in the patient's memory.

Thus the integrative work of the correction dream may be thought of as acting in parallel with the interpretive activity of the therapist. There is one respect in which the correction dream goes beyond the capabilities of the analyst, however. The successful matching of the correction dream revives a series of related early memories associated in the permanent memory structure with the past component of the index dream. Perhaps one might express this most clearly by saying that the correction dreams results in the transfer of associated early memory representations from the passive structure of the permanent memory to a more directly accessible *working* memory. In any case, these newly revived early memories open up the new associative pathways that establish the direction of further movement in the treatment process.

What, then, can we predict about the correction dreams that will follow the analytic hour in which the Asparagus Dream was reported? First of all, the correction dream should be a composite of the index dream imagery and the new elements of experience uncovered during the hour in which the index dream was reported. In the case of the Asparagus Dream, we might expect to see a repetition of the primal scene translated into an adult party atmosphere. The central characters of the index dream, Phyllis and Arthur, should become more vivid and more directly identifiable with the patient's parents and/or with present-day parent surrogates (especially the analyst).

Second, we should expect to find variations on the primal-scene imagery from other episodes in the patient's early life in which the same emotional configuration was present. We would expect this new imagery to reveal details of the patient's identifications which have not appeared either in the index dream or in the associations of the Monday analytic hour, but which can be seen in retrospect to have influenced the patient's interaction with the analyst. We cannot, of course, predict what the content of these new details will be, only that they will be present.

The following dream was recorded when the patient was awakened after his third REM period in the sleep laboratory on Monday night:

I remember being up in the Marlboro Club. Let's see now—there were groups of people around—a party being thrown somewhere. I guess the people are sort of making out and having a good time, and I am wandering around from place to place, talking to people, really not doing much, and watching and observing, and wishing I was more a participant. There is some kind of a foreign language that has to be spoken. I am not sure what else. Let's see, the dream takes place both in the Marlboro Club and an old home—the party is being thrown in both places. This is a hard one to remember. Actually, the people are making out—the people I know who wanted to make out—and were not able to. There were two guys, and one girl I wanted to be with, and she was more interested in them. There was a party—my mother was at the party, and these girls were much more friendly with her and physically attached too—I looked up and saw my mother [and] said oh, isn't she attractive, and my mother got up and I made a mistake—she looked fairly young, I thought she was wearing a fall, and I went up to her to congratulate her on how well she looked and as I got closer I realized she was not my mother. My mother was over at the other end of the room—she was talking to these girls. That was very strange. The dream ended on the porch of Lake Tahoe. . . . Oh, yes, very strange, in this dream these lovely people suddenly got together and formed some sort of a circle, and there was a very private group that was dressed in sort of dungarees and led by one guy. And it happened that he was showing everybody how they were going to dance and—he was quite professional, and he was dancing to beat the band, and he kept showing them over and over again how they do it. It was almost like group dancing and he was leading. I kept on marveling at him, that he was a professional dancer—unbelievable—he was wearing some kind of high heels. Anyway, at the end of the dream, as I was coming up the steps of the Marlboro Club, a couple was coming out—the girl came out first and the guy was coming out after her and imploring her to wait. They had some kind of words and I watched the thing—I guess they were about to patch up. The dream ended there.

The same dream was reported to the analyst at the beginning of the Tuesday morning analytic hour. The second version contains some additional details that lead to important associations to the major figures in the dream:

I was wandering—in part of a dream where I was at a party—my mother was at this party. A party, a lot of pretty girls there, and guys. I was there all by myself, as usual I should say, at this party I never turn to anybody, and my mother was sitting on a couch and she was looking fairly young, and these girls—a couple of pretty girls that I knew who were friends of mine, said, oh, there is your mother, isn't she good looking, isn't she young looking—something like that—I don't know. She got up and funny thing, I went over there and all of a sudden Mother appeared in a long fall—a phony hairdo. I was going over to congratulate her on how well she looked, I was wondering what she was wearing it for, and as I got closer I realized it was not her, it was a girl that has got a kind of a bad skin complexion. Now here is the side shocker—we used to play this game once, my sister and myself—if I bothered her, one side of her face would break out, and if Alice bothered her, the other side would break out. Maybe that is why I saw the girl with the bad skin complexion. When I got closer I saw it was not her, I don't know who she is. And then she was over in the other part of the room, talking to these girls, and it faded out. I remember one guy, I swear in this group, was in dungarees but he had some kind of cowboy boots with funny little heels on them, almost like little lady's high heels strapped on to the bottom of his boots, and he was showing everybody how it should be done. Now if you ever watch TV and see Dickie DeLillo on—the type of dancing he does, it is very precise, fast, and that tat-a-tat-tat —and he was doing, going through these things. And I looked at this guy and said holy smokes, as an amateur this guy is unbeatable—for supposedly a guy dressed in dungarees going tat-tat-tat, and taking twenty steps, and he is all done. A very pleasant sight to watch.

I think it should be clear by inspection that the Marlboro Club Dream is a reworking of the Asparagus Dream. The physical setting is similar and once again presents a scene in which the dreamer is an unwelcome guest where other men and women are successfully seeking each other out. The unattractive ex-girlfriend who ridiculed M. A.'s masculine pretensions in the Asparagus Dream is revealed as a disguised version of the patient's mother. Interestingly enough, the identifiable mother in the correction dream is also disguised, but the disguise is incomplete and in the end ineffective. Here it is part of a complex of images which represent the mother as deceitful and inconstant, literally two-faced. Her preference for girls corresponds to the mocking of M.A.'s masculine strivings in the index dream, but in the correction dream the emphasis is more on her teasing entrapment of her son.

The fall in the correction dream is particularly interesting. It is a phallic object, like the asparagus, but it is attached to the woman who mocks M. A., unlike the asparagus in the index dream. It is at the moment that M. A. discovers the fall is false that he realizes the woman is not his mother. But the mother immediately reappears elsewhere in the room. This scene strongly suggests that M. A.'s attribution of phallic qualities to his mother has served as a defense against Oedipal guilt, i.e., as a denial that he is attracted to her specifically feminine characteristics. He appears to believe that she has colluded with him in this fantasy, only to drop him abruptly when he asks for more than she is willing to give, shifting her preference and attention to his castrated sister.

We do not know how much of this reconstruction represents the mother's actual behavior and how much is M. A.'s defensive distortion of it. Nevertheless, it reveals a complexity in M. A.'s motives missing from the earlier dream. There he was simply the victim of a castrating woman who disabled him for satisfying relationships with all other women through her disdain. Here we find the mother both tempting and denying, and M. A. willing to be deceived in order to maintain an infantile attachment to her which is relatively free of Oedipal anxiety. His complicity in being rejected by women is confirmed later in the Tuesday hour when he remembers another dream fragment:

There was one girl at one of these parties, I don't know which dream it was at this point, was really attractive, and she was necking with some guy—I think some guy that I had met at Lake . . . with George, a nice fellow, and I was saying, well, he got there first—and that is first come first served. I don't know what it reminds me of right now—back to that in a second—and later on in the evening I came back and there she is on the rug—one guy on the right, one guy on the left—and the guy on the left is just lying with her and holding her, and she is necking with the guy on the right—a new guy, a real good looking guy, and I say to myself, oh shit, jackass again, it could have been you—why, why don't you move—what are you afraid of?

A little later in his associations, he makes this explicit reference to the index dream and to other earlier dreams which must have treated the same theme:

I have got so many dreams running around in my head—the night before I went upstairs to the fourth floor, going from room to room with Phyllis Anderson. Funny thing, thinking back on different dreams that I have had, the one of backing into that parking lot when the caretaker came out—that one still pops into my mind, too. That was three or four months ago. Funny thing, right now most of my old dreams are spilling out, just looking over details, I can recall about four or five of them right now.

Although this passage is not sufficient in itself to establish that the Marlboro Club Dream is a correction dream for the Asparagus Dream (and perhaps other, earlier dreams as well), it clearly indicates that the relationship between the dreams is in some way known to the dreamer. (See *Dreaming and Memory*, p. 121, for a similar recollection during the March sequence.)

Shortly after the reference to his earlier dreams, M. A. has the following association, which appears without apparent connection to the material that immediately precedes it:

I think I am a little guilty about something—going away to Kansas City tonight, not tonight, tomorrow morning, and looking forward to it—a friend of mine, Jim Anderson's mother, is in an oxygen tent, she had a heart attack, she is on the critical list, and Jim is very worried about it and I swear—I am very close to Jim—I am very fond of him—and I like his mother. I am saying to myself, I really hate myself for saying this, that Jesus I hope the old lady doesn't die until I eat already, get back, or she doesn't interfere with my plans, you know. When I catch myself saying that, I feel like a rat, and then quickly it reminds me of my father and I was hoping that he would not pass away this week because something was coming up that week—don't inconvenience me—let him pass away in a convenient week when my private plans are not interfered with—is the least you can do—that sort of thing. And of course catching myself doing this, you do not particularly like yourself, but you seem to be doing it. Which now leads me to the next step—that my mother said I was selfish, and maybe she was right—that I just care about my own selfish interests—so I am a selfish bastard—she didn't use that word bastard—I am throwing it in there. I don't know how to resolve that at all, but that is what happened.

Here we have intimations of a destructive wish toward an idealized father which has been displaced onto the mother, who provides a much safer target. In another of the Monday night dreams in the sleep laboratory, a male friend is killed in a slow-motion racing-car accident. The attack on the mother continues in an association to still another of the Monday night dreams:

That was a popular song—what it was, I don't know—but it was an argument for the most insignificant reason. When I say that I quickly think of my bringing up—about the time my mother used to jump down my throat for the most insignificant reasons, I thought. Boy, what a reason to fight. I don't know what incident I am thinking of but that is what came to mind—or am I just saying that to transfer something or other? I don't know, but it just popped in. I have a feeling—funny thing—right now that there is some big episode in my childhood life with my parents that I have not been able to withdraw—not withdraw, to draw out.

This blockage of memory leads to a halt in the associative flow. The analyst asks about Dickie DeLillo, who is a bisexual figure admired by the patient for his dancing skill and his ability to teach, to demonstrate, and to inspire his student audience. M. A.'s description of him is filled with a kind of manic awe—the parallel to the analyst's role in his life is unmistakable. (The analyst's first name is also Richard.) The references to the study of languages and to dancing in a circle recall a summer camp experience when he developed a crush on a girl but made no attempt to keep in touch with her. This memory brings up a rather unexpected association, which leads, in turn, to another early memory:

I never heard from her or saw her again, or wrote to her, or anything, but [her image] plain stuck as just being a sensual female. And the next . . . of being a sensual female, and the next word came into my mind—I did not say it—was corrupting young boys. I did not say that but that is what came across in my mind—maybe she . . . very well—what I mean, huh? And why I remembered her name—this was back fifteen years ago, and the thing lasted two days and I might have spoken three words to her. It brings another image to mind when I was even younger. I can't remember if it was the same year or a year earlier. I was just about sixteen or seventeen. I was coming down the stairs and a woman named Mrs. Kelley, a friend of my mother, had not seen me for about a year and she said, oh, so Marvin is growing up—look at his legs, they are so manly. I was thin and very muscular—who the hell notices my legs—I remember that—"they are so masculine." Listening to her, I did know what it meant, but again the image stuck. So I was supposed to have what? Feminine legs—maybe the hair was starting to grow, and muscles were growing—I don't know what it was. Females are funny.

This memory is a reversal of the one reported during the Monday hour in which M. A. was admiring the legs of his mother's woman friend. Here it is his own legs that are admired as being masculine, yet he responds to the praise by feeling emasculated. The friend is, of course, a surrogate for his mother, and her sexual "attack" must be seen as a phallic intrusion rather than the generous initiation M. A. had wished for in reporting the similar memory during the Monday hour.

When the analyst directs M. A.'s attention back to his mother, he responds with an intellectualized discussion of the Oedipus complex, which effectively ends the associative work of the hour.

A good deal more could be said about the figure of Dickie Delillo and what it reveals through M. A.'s associations about his view of the analyst at the time this sequence was recorded, but we must adhere to our original purpose. I think we can say with some assurance what the January correction dream accomplished, and we can compare this result with the March sequence.

First of all, we notice that the primal-scene imagery of the index dream has not become more vivid in the correction dream. If anything, this theme is represented more diffusely in the Marlboro Club Dream than it was in the Asparagus Dream. This is in sharp contrast to the March sequence, in which the correction dreams focused directly on the anatomical and psychosocial details of the relationship between M. A.'s parents, details which had been censored from the index dreams. In the March sequence, the success of the correction dreams brought into the open M. A.'s devastating fantasy that marriage and sexual consummation lead directly to the castration and death of the male partner.

In the January sequence, this castration fantasy appears in the Racing-Car Dream in isolation from the primal-scene imagery. Despite the analyst's attempt to recover the associative links between the Racing-Car Dream and another Monday night dream recalling a visit to the Mardi Gras (the two dreams contain some overlapping imagery), M. A. is unresponsive. I think we must conclude that the connection between primal-scene memories and castration fantasies remains under censorship throughout the January sequence. M. A.'s statement that "right now there is some big episode in my childhood life with my parents that I have not been able to . . . draw out" may be literally true. In fact, we might speculate that this "big episode" is precisely the anal impregnation fantasy from very early childhood represented in the imagery of both the index dream and the correction dream of the March sequence; this fantasy was finally recovered in the associations to the correction dream during the second analytic hour of that sequence.

Speculation aside, the comparison of the January and March sequences does show that the primal-scene issue, while clearly represented in the index dreams of both sequences, is only worked through to a significant extent in the correction dreams of the March sequence. This observation tells us that we cannot expect a particular correction dream to resolve all of the significant issues—or even the one most significant issue—its index dream raises. The balance of adaptive and defensive motivations which determines how much leeway the censorship will allow the correction dream is not easily predictable from the content of the index dream alone.

Nevertheless, as we have seen, the Marlboro Club Dream meets the essential criteria for a correction dream. It reverses the defensive substitutions that minimize the relationship of the principal figures in the index dream to parents and contemporary parent surrogates. The static or monovalent attitudes of these figures toward the dreamer become dynamic and ambivalent. The affective tone is raised from dull to lively. New material from the permanent memory is activated and made accessible to waking consciousness, and this new material bears directly on the psychodynamic issues raised by the index dream. Further, the report of the correction dream leads more directly to the associative retrieval of early memories than did the report of the index dream in the previous hour.

The new material brought to light by the Marlboro Club Dream refers to a childhood pattern in which the mother is assigned masculine attributes and the father feminine ones. Although we can surmise with some confidence that this pattern has persisted because it minimizes primal-scene anxiety and Oedipal guilt, the motive for this reversal of parental roles is not represented in the dream. In the correction dreams of the March sequence, we find that when this protective role reversal is removed, the interaction of M. A.'s parents appears to him to be terrifyingly destructive.

In retrospect, we can see that the uncovering of the fantasies of a phallic mother and a nurturant father is a prerequisite for the uncovering of the underlying destructive fantasy, since the former fantasies defend against the latter. The correction dream of the January sequence is therefore a step toward the resolution achieved in the March sequence, a necessary detour on the circuitous path created by the successive interpositions of defensive distortions.

From this comparison of the two sequences, I think we can see that our earlier question about the magnitude of the correction in a particular sequence is badly framed. We have no way of knowing how far the correction dream of the January sequence has carried the patient toward the resolution of the March sequence. We are dealing with shifts in direction which eventually lead to a desired goal. The pathway is crooked and the obstacles manifold. There is no way to discover how much further we have to go except by going.

Nevertheless, the comparison does suggest two important hypotheses. First, the similarities between the index dreams in the January and March sequences indicate that the goal of a reconstruction can be identified in the patient's dreams a considerable time before the patient is ready to reach that goal through his own associative efforts. I think it is useful for the therapist to recognize the goal even though it may be generally impossible and often undesirable to communicate this knowledge to the patient directly.

Second, when a dream meeting the criteria for a correction dream produces associative material that is not clearly relevant to a reconstructive goal visible in its index dream, I think we can assume that the new material presents an intermediary problem that must be worked through before the original goal can be reached. If this assumption is correct, the therapist should be alert for signs of an associative convergence between the material of the correction dream and the issues raised in the index dream.

But if the correction dream is not likely to be an awakening dream, as I have suggested, then what is the relevance of the data from the sleep laboratory to the usual clinical situation? In the material presented here, the contents of the correction dream enter the waking consciousness of the dreamer through the artificial awakening provided by the lab technician. In everyday life, however, the correction dream is not accessible in this way.[3] Yet we find that new associative pathways do open up in normal practice following a successful dream interpretation. (*Interpretation* may be too strong a term. What I refer to is actually the successful juxtaposition of fantasies, memories, or transference reenactments with the contents of the reported awakening dream.)

The fact that the correction dream has taken place—even if it is not actually recalled by the patient—seems enough to make the new associative material accessible in subsequent therapeutic hours. This observation calls for an

[3]This statement must be qualified. The successful correction dream is not ordinarily remembered, but it may be remembered if it is interrupted by an external stimulus, as dreams during the final cycle of REM sleep often are. Patients thus may report only a small proportion of their correction dreams, but certainly *some* of the dreams brought to the therapy hour are correction dreams. In such cases we may or may not have heard the index dream that is being corrected. In addition, hybrid dreams, which contain successfully matched composite images as well as a mismatch leading to an anxiety signal that awakens the dreamer, are not uncommon. As I mentioned earlier, "turning-point" dreams often appear to be hybrid correction dreams.

amendment to the description of dream construction proposed in *Dreaming and Memory*. In that work (p. 55), I suggest that dreams are not ordinarily remembered because dreaming is an intermediate stage in the computation of appropriate locations in the permanent memory for representations of new experience. The purpose of such computation is the efficient storage of information about the real world.

The composite imagery of the dream provides information about the *relationship* between current and past experiences. It does not add directly to the information about the *world* contained in the representations of experience it brings together for matching. Hence it is the new experience itself—rather than the dream that associates it with past experiences—that is stored in the permanent memory.

Although I think this view is accurate as far as it goes, it appears to me now that I incorrectly inferred from it that the *entire process of dream construction* is excluded even from short-term storage unless an anxiety signal awakens the dreamer and brings the dream directly into the realm of waking consciousness. If this inference were valid, it would be impossible for unremembered dreams to contribute in an immediate way to the therapeutic process. They would still provide the permanent memory of the dreamer with a more complete and accurate picture of the world to match with further new experiences in therapy and in life. In the long run, of course, this effect is the most significant result of theraputic work because it enables the patient to retain something of permanent value from the treatment.

If this were the only way the successful correction dream influenced the treatment process, however, such influence would be visible only in the patient's associations to later remembered dreams. Although it is conceivable that a train of associations extending over a period of weeks or even months might be attributable to the stimulus provided by a single dream, on reflection this seems highly unlikely. The patient's associative pathway could be explained much more simply if the past memories evoked in the matching process were stored in a short-term memory structure from which they could be recalled *without* the stimulus of a remembered dream.

This conception would be closer to Lowy's view (1942) that dreaming has the function of restoring important items in the permanent memory to a state of heightened accessibility to consciousness. The memory structure responsible for holding these reactivated memories might be included either in the short-term memory, which collects the significant day residues, or in the working memory, which maintains items needed for immediate recall for relatively long periods. But the memory structure might be quite distinct from these two, with a mode of access that follows its own separate and less direct pathways.

Such a short-term memory structure would be necessary to explain yet another clinical observation that is incompatible with the idea that the entire process of dream construction is excluded from access to consciousness. I have observed that the early memories which contribute their imagery to manifest dream content are often directly accessible to the dreamer if he or she is asked to supply them. Because these memories are only occasionally recovered in the spontaneous associations of patients in analytic therapy, I was rather surprised to discover that they could be elicited by a direct question after the patient's spontaneous associations appeared to be exhausted. Such a response is not simply a transference phenomenon, since I have found that it can be reproduced with nonpatients in nontherapeutic settings.

In the March sequence reported in *Dreaming and Memory,* it appeared to me that M. A.'s recall of the critical early childhood memory at the Burgundy Hotel had been brought about by the retrieval of the correction dreams during the sleep-laboratory awakenings. I may have been right in this particular instance, since the index dreams had been heavily censored. But with many dreams reported in therapy, the censorship is only partial. The early memories included in the uncensored portion of the dream appear to be deposited in a short-term memory structure where they can be retrieved with relatively little difficulty.

Why the directed interest of another person should be so much more effective than the dreamer's own curiosity in eliciting the early memories incorporated in a dream is not so easily explained. Resistance in the usual Freudian sense certainly plays a part. But something else seems to be involved. My guess is that we are seeing another indication of the mother's importance as the original interpreter of dreams. She is the one who assures the infant that the dream world is not "real," i.e., not a report about the state of the world. The awakening anxiety dream breaks through the psychophysiological mechanisms that normally preserve this distinction by keeping the dream out of conscious awareness. The child must be taught to restore the distinction to the anxiety dream through conscious effort.

It is necessary to make clear to young children that what they experience is "only a dream." But "only a dream" merely tells the child that the dream doesn't matter without shedding any light on what the dream *is*. Young children are not yet ready to learn that the dream is a report about their own internal state of mind. Despite the Freudian revolution, our culture remains rather ambivalent about preparing children to understand that dreams are meaningful in this way. Nevertheless, adult dreamers seem to have this information on the tip of their tongue, as it were; they could recall it if only someone would ask them for it—if only someone would take up where mother and culture have left off.

The psychotherapist's recognition that the dream is not merely a secret message but also a record of the patient's experience of self, which cuts across many developmental levels, is more important than any set of rules for interpretation. Secrets emerge during the reconstructive process, to be sure. The censorship mechanisms do, indeed, actively obscure the conflicted areas of life experience for which no stable resolution has been found. But the dream may be opaque for its own good reasons. It has its own job to do, a job which involves connecting rather than explaining, and methods of computation not easily transformed into linguistic or logical structures.

Therapists may be able to improve their performance by working with dream material more in its own terms, by emphasizing the relationships between past and present implied by the composite dream imagery. When we "interpret" we are often substituting an approximate universal developmental history for the actual facts about the patient's early life. This may be a very useful procedure, but it should be reserved until we are sure that the facts themselves are really inaccessible. M. A.'s analyst seems to get the best results by observing the differences between what the patient says and what he does, and by tying together the many loose ends of the associative work. There is very little of the explanatory effort that we ordinarily think of as "dream interpretation."

The phenomenon of the correction dream allow us to see how the dreaming cycle provides its own linkage between the reported dream and the overall experience of the therapy hour. The success of the correction dream seems to me a more reliable measure for the effectiveness of the therapeutic work than any criteria based entirely on what happens in the hour during which the index dream is reported. In both the January and March sequences of M. A.'s analysis, it would have been difficult to determine how the reported dreams had been incorporated into the therapeutic process if we had had only the first hour of each sequence to examine.

Freud's oft quoted remark (1911) that the dream report should be treated like any other association and not singled out for special attention has often been interpreted as a downgrading of the role of dreams in the analyst's technical repertoire. I think we can see now that the issue is far more complex, and that analysts may "use" a patient's dreams to guide their interventions in a way that is both more subtle and more inclusive than an attempt to explain their "meanings." Dreaming is not only grist for the therapeutic mill. It is the mill itself.

Freud was most likely warning against the therapist's temptation to tell patients what a dream means before the patients could tell what it meant to them. I suggest that if we understand how the dream works on the patient's behalf during the therapeutic process, we may be able to ask him or her for more relevant information in a way that does not intrude on the autonomy of the patient's self-examination.

Summary

For the psychotherapist, dreams have been an invaluable source of information about the patient's unconscious. Experiences of early childhood, repressed because of their connection with forbidden wishes, often emerge in the extended working through of a reported dream. This information may then be fed back to the adult patient's waking consciousness for more effective reprocessing.

My concern here has been to show that the process of dreaming acts both to incorporate the new material of the dream interpretation into the patient's permanent memory structure and to retrieve otherwise inaccessible memories of early life. Dreaming is a segment of the larger process through which information about the events of the day, including the therapeutic interaction, is conveyed to and linked up with the dreamer's store of significant memories. As such, it functions to establish an enhanced continuity between the patient's infantile self- and object-representations and his or her current experiences as an adult.

This double movement of information into and out of the associative memory structure results from the necessity to match the current experience, or *day residue,* with a related memory representation from earlier in the dreamer's life, by superimposing the day residue on the earlier memory. The coherence of the composite image formed by this superimposition is the criterion for establishing a permanent associative link between the experiences of present and past.

In the clinical example presented here, we have seen how a reported dream is typically reworked after a therapeutic hour into a new dream that incorporates the experience of the hour in its day residue. This new dream, which I have called the *correction dream,* will in turn evoke a new set of memories of related past events. These earlier memories, activated in the construction of the correction dream, become accessible to the process of free association in the subsequent course of therapy.

The dream sequence takes place without the therapist's making a special effort beyond pursuing the usual methods of clarification and interpretation. Nevertheless, I believe that the therapist's role as correction-dream facilitator may be improved in two ways. The first is shifting the emphasis from *explaining* the patient's reported dream to *assembling* the widest possible network of associative connections. The latter would include related configurations in the patient's early history, external life situation, and current transference reenactments.

A second technical modification would be to *ask* the patient what early events are recalled by the specific imagery of the dream whenever spontaneous associations fail to provide this information. These early memories, whether of actual events or of fantasied elaborations of events, are the focal points in the patient's maladaptive mapping of experience. They mark those gaps in his world view that must be filled by the unfolding therapeutic process—during both the treatment hour *and* the nocturnal reorganization of the correction dream that follows.

REFERENCES

Dement, W., & Wolpert, E. (1958), Relation of eye movement, body motility, and external stimulation to dream content. *J. Experiment. Psychol.*, 55:543–553.

Freud, S. (1900), The interpretation of dreams. *Standard Edition,* 4 & 5:1–627. London: Hogarth Press, 1953.

——— (1911), The handling of dream interpretation in psycho-Analysis. *Standard Edition,* 12:89–97. London: Hogarth Press, 1958.

Greenberg, R. & Pearlman, C. (1974), Cutting the REM nerve. *Persp. Biology & Medicine,* 17:513–521.

Lowy, S. (1942), *Foundations of Dream Interpretation.* London: Keegan Paul, Trench & Trubner.

Palombo, S. (1978), *Dreaming and Memory: A New Information-Processing Model.* New York: Basic Books.

CHAPTER 12

On "Working Through" as a Form of Self-Innovation

Edrita Fried

It is a remarkable fact that ever since Freud introduced the term "working through," it has remained a vaguely and variously defined therapeutic activity. If one were to ask therapists what they mean by working through, one would receive many different versions of the concept and the therapeutic processes involved. Working through is central to the achievement of change. But, whereas other aspects of psychodynamic treatment have been defined with precision (e.g., "insight," "the transference neurosis," "transference," "counter-transference"), the essence of working through has remained relatively obscure. The kind of therapeutic efforts that working through calls for are described in hazy and unintegrated terms (Blanck and Blanck, 1979).

To this author, working through has as its primary objective the *accomplishment of change,* not only in cognitive but also in structural, emotional, and behavioral terms. Working through is largely the achievement of *self-innovation* (Fried, 1980). New structures are gradually built that allow for the flow of fresh and varied emotions and thoughts. This means that new bridges (Spitz, 1965) are established between mind and body; that the self becomes more authentic; that self-esteem derives from the inner condition of the self and depends less and less on external praise; that the range of ego functions is extended; that the superego is modified and the id-ego-superego balance is changed.

Working through calls for a broad assemblage of processes related to insight, some preceding and promoting insight, and others following in its wake. Insights are essential to working through, though they are looked on and treated primarily as forerunners of subsequent psychological experimentation and the active search for new directions. What counts, after experiential insight, is: learning a new outlook on the self and the world; modulating the superego; trying out new structural balances; acquiring the capacity for object love; and the like.

The objectives and processes of working through are always undertaken jointly, by the therapist and patient together. As a rule, the therapist moves first, showing the patient how experiential insight alone is not enough. The emphasis in the working-through phase is on new modes of feeling and thinking, especially within the transference situation. The need for innovations following interpretations is highlighted. Patients learn not just to tuck away insights but to find and try out new ways of living. Eventually, the patient assumes the lead in the search for self-innovation and no longer settles for insights alone. I often prefer to call experiential insights "active insights," because they create an urge to try out new forms of psychological activeness, which is not identical with action, but constitutes an emotional-cognitive state. Working through, as I conceive of it, provides the fuel for change and leads to an emphasis on doing something about one's pathological inclinations and structures. I believe that working through is the most time-consuming aspect of dynamic psychotherapy, and indispensable to the achievement of change.

The vagueness about what constitutes working through seems to me due to the continuing belief that one central reparatory approach—rather than an assembly of approaches—can accomplish the therapeutic objective. The task of working through is often seen as limited to the removal of resistance to insight: rendering the resistances conscious, circumventing them, or puncturing them. This definition is too narrow if we accept the proposition that working through has as its main objective the building of new psychic structures and comprehensive personality changes. At the least, we have to aim not only at the removal of resistance to *insight* but at the removal of resistance to *change*. Anyone who collects insights step by step but does not do anything with them—that is, does not *use* them by casting around for and adopting behavioral change—is not engaged in the serious labor of working through.

In order to effect structural and subsequent behavioral changes, does the patient need new parameters, which have to be added to the established techniques of dynamic psychotherapy? As Eissler (1955) saw it—and he concerned himself in detail with the problem of parameters, particularly in the treatment of borderline cases—parameters are special, temporary alterations of the psychoanalytic process, and their use is not always totally legitimate. My own position is that the use of parameters to accomplish the objectives of working through is legitimate. To be sure, this approach calls for some restraint, since we cannot simply assume that any deviation from established therapeutic process is commendable because it has worked in certain other cases. But such caution should not lead to rigidity.

To help us discern the essence of working through, and to decide whether we need new parameters to pursue its primary objective, namely, structural and behavioral change, let us describe in greater detail the different purposes of working through.

The Objectives of Working Through

(1) Working through, as already stated, consists of a wide variety of processes. Some of them cannot be described directly. It is possible to gain access to their nature, however, by focusing on their *function.*

(2) To work through has come to mean that the therapist makes interpretations, now from one angle, now from another. For instance, at one point the therapist highlights the secondary gains accruing from the existence of the pathology; at another time, the anxiety resulting from existing conflicts and ego deficits; or the therapist may focus on the still obscure past that is responsible for the patient's disturbances. In this sense, working through calls not for a purely sequential approach but for a multipolar one.

(3) To work through means to further both *reflective* and *experiential* insight (Kris, 1956b).

When you have an "experiential" insight, you do not just say to yourself, "this is interesting," but often—perhaps invariably—you wish to express new feelings in some concrete way. These changes need not be spectacular: some patients walk more determinedly or hold themselves more erect; others sit down right after the session and write that important letter they have put off for so long, or have that first frank talk with the spouse.

A different way of putting it is to speak of "spectator" (reflective) and "active" (experiential) insight. By itself, spectator insight adds as little to a person's emotional well-being as spectator sports add to a person's physical musculature. Active insight, just like active sport, brings concrete improvement. Via active insight, patients go about the chores and gratifications of life in a different way. They now have some *novelties* at their disposal—not only cognitive but also emotional and concrete, practical novelties. Since the production of psychological novelties has much to do with creativity, dynamic psychotherapy emphasizes creativity as an essential contribution to, or indeed precondition for, emotional well-being (Kubie, 1958). We unlock the patient's creativity as we work through.

Artists have no monopoly on creativity. People who consider themselves "ordinary" employ creativity when they are at their happiest. The other day a businessman told me that he had hit on a plan for solving a promotion problem by joining together three previously unrelated groups of employees. When I remarked that this plan was creative, he replied in his self-depreciating way, "I think of myself as quite ordinary." Although he was proud of his plan, he did not realize that he had taken a leap, that he had moved beyond his customary tight, static, hostile passivity. He had accomplished a piece of characterological working through, at least for the time being. Working through proceeds bit by bit, leading up to some seemingly sudden innovations.

The "experiential" or "active" insights that lead to solid self-innovation and an active state of mind are rarely the result of logical reasoning. Genuinely creative and integrative insights are likely to surface in loose states of consciousness, related to but not identical with Freud's state of free association. They are not "willed" but "found." It is therefore not the neat pigeonholing of facts that produces the genuine understanding which, in turn, leads to an activist, creative state of mind. Instead, receptiveness and the temporary relinquishment of established order are the prime prerequisites. To assemble the preliminaries for certain forms of working through, the patient needs to realize that the issue of being "right" or "wrong" is beside the point. What matters is that he become increasingly open in the psychotherapeutic interchange; that he stop trying to please the therapist; that he allow repressions and self-imposed restraints gradually to lessen; in short that he loosen the "brakes" or, to use another metaphor, that he lean less and less on, and finally throw away, encumbering neurotic crutches.

(4) Working through means correcting the ego malformations and distortions that have accumulated as result of hampered psychic development. The patient must gradually give up counterproductive efforts to control outside events and forces. An example of such efforts is found in clinging behavior. These distorted efforts may be accompanied by magic thoughts, avoidance patterns, obsessive repetitions, and eventually, domination through power and money. Such *archaic ways* aim at installing the person as dictator over the environment, but they backfire in the end. Working through means gradually replacing such cumbersome and intrusive power methods with *genuine strength*. Genuine strength consists of a rich flow of emotions, realistic perceptions, careful anticipation and organization, and other life skills. As therapists, we work from the inside out, and from the outside in. Some ego distortions correct themselves spontaneously as conflicts are resolved. Others are gradually corrected in deliberate ways that we will explore later.

(5) Working through means that in addition to the *correction of ego malfunctions,* we aim at *ego completion.* Psychological faculties that have been missing in the existing ego structures can be built up. Genuine self-love,

authentic identity formation, the energy derived from taming destructive aggression, the ability to anticipate, and the integration of opposites are some of the ego functions that can be shaped to a considerable extent through specific measures of working through.

(6) Working through invariably presupposes the staking out of a *time continuum*. Past, present, and future become connected in new and meaningful ways. Thus far, dynamic psychotherapy has too frequently neglected the future dimension. The purposes of establishing a time continuum are manifold: the patient is gradually weaned away from outdated mental and emotional processes of the past, many of which are too magical, simplistic, and rigid to be of service in the present and future. Establishing the time continuum helps patients give up faulty connections between causes and effects. It alerts them to the realization that many existing behavior patterns, established to cope with events of the past, are both senseless and changeable. Above all, the time continuum makes it clear that we must grope for an existence in the future.

To envisage, prepare for, and move toward the future must, I believe, be a part of all working through. We need to keep in mind that through this process the patient realizes his threefold existence in time. Until now, working through has *not conjured up references to the dimension of the future*. Rather, the term has come to suggest an excessive preoccupation with psychological leftovers from the past.

Freud discovered that the past can have a strong adverse effect on the present, especially for disturbed persons who are victims of the repetition compulsion. This discovery shifted attention to the inhibiting, unconscious connections between past and present. Therefore, the working-through phase used to deal preponderantly with the past, especially the recapture of repressed impulses. Ego psychology has, in some measure, shifted attention to present-day functioning. It is certainly true that the here-and-now transference phenomena reveal the twisted, distorted, or fractional functioning that has to be repaired.

We know that disturbed personalities repeatedly reestablish relationships with persons whom they do not fully accept. What they search for and eventually resent are alliances through which they can borrow the powers they themselves do not possess. The only real solution, however, is to evolve their own strength. Working through in the present means to dispense with the reliance on complementary figures that permits the neurosis to continue.

Establishing the future part of the time continuum by means of working through proves to be highly productive. Few aspects of therapy are as likely to pull disturbed persons out of their old ruts as the trying out and practice of experiences that are perceived as just emerging on the horizon.

The working-through theme is likely to become a major focus of future psychoanalytic debates and conceptualizations. This prospect does not mean that dynamic psychotherapists must abandon established basic principles, but rather, that they *expand* such principles. We will continue to rely on insight into and interpretation of patients' unconscious desires in order to help them recognize the inner pulls that cause anxiety and other symptoms—this is the first step. But, *in addition,* we will explore the structural defects and developmental deficits that handicap patients in settling their conflicts even when these have come out into the open. For working through, in the true sense, depends on insight *accompanied by* self-enrichment. The ego and self innovations that are gradually acquired enable the person to take the second step. To put it simply, the first step is to *discover what is wrong.* The second step is to acquire the psychic wherewithal—as a patient said, the new plumbing—to *set right what has been wrong.*

That second step poses its own tasks. Among other things, we discuss with the person which external (and, as the case may be, internal) circumstances are unalterable and hence call merely for a rearrangement of defenses, and which call for much more.

Altogether, we see as a primary goal of working through a gradually widening achievement of activity, spontaneity, and creativity, which means flexible and renewable forms of relating, loving, working, and living. Fundamental changes in the external conditions of life call for new forms of educating and modifying people. Dynamic psychotherapy gives consideration not only to basic currents in human nature but also to the possibilities existing in a world that is, in this period of history, constantly and visibly in a process of fundamental change.

The Role of the Transference Object in Working Through

The individual is not a closed system but a product of interchanges between self and environment (H. E. Durkin, 1975; J. E. Durkin et al., in press) that take place from birth until the end of life. This reciprocity between self and environment is one foundation of our belief in change. Distortions, arrests in ego development, and gaps in the range of ego skills are correctable. So are limitations in the capacity for object relations. As we shall see, even the condition of the passions and of energy (the id), as well as imbalances between the id and the rest of the psyche, can be altered by weaving experiential insights and other therapeutic experiences into actual and immediate functioning. Fresh objects, new situations, and unexpected challenges—I call them the "therapeutic startlers"—set off processes of interaction and kinds of functioning that spur the psyche on to reach out for, discover, and practice new emotions and ego capacities. A significantly expanded range of object-relations skills, a fresh self-image, and other new structures surface in the patient-therapist setting. The patient enriched by the resumption of ego development in the experience of the transference delves into the world instead of pulling away from it.

When a new central object, the therapist (in group therapy, the other group members), behaves differently from what the patient expects, the rug is pulled out from under his set reaction patterns. Eventually these new realities, in conjunction with the interpretations offered, convince him that better "fits" have to be found and used. The treatment situation becomes a laboratory where psychological experimentation is necessary. Old reactions are rendered bizarre by new stimuli, such as therapeutic interpretations combined with respect and care (Loewald, 1960). Even the basic roster of old stock emotions and ideas finally becomes unusable. This is especially true of the transference expressions, which are among the most noxious imprints of the past and must gradually be shed.

If the formulations I have just used appear simple, it is because I have merely outlined the skeleton of rather complex efforts. In order to produce the patient's first signs of improvement, overcome relapses, and increase the improvement, much encouragement and many interpretations are necessary.

When patients venture to reveal their mistrust, depreciation, and anger toward the therapist, they fear that they will be deserted. The airing of such feelings within the treatment situation accomplishes a good deal of reparation. The therapist's reaction gives the patient the opportunity to ascertain whether his basic fear that he will be abandoned if he is critical and angry is justified.

As a man told me after he had shouted at me in the therapy hour, "It's good to be angry with you in your presence. Having you listen makes the anger less threatening. I'm coming to believe that you can take it, that my anger won't break or kill you. Holding my anger in gives me self-sufficiency and power. But it is also very painful."

Direct exchanges in the transference situation create experiential insight and fresh beginnings. They go beyond cognition into the world of affect and psychological action (which is not identical with acting out). To illustrate, let me discuss a specific case.

Karen, a twenty-five-year-old woman who had just broken up with the man who had been her lover and companion for three years, remarked: "I feel I really did not deserve him. I never went along with him, though I never opposed him either. I was as anxious with him as I am with everyone. The minute I try to speak truthfully to a person, my thoughts elude me. I stammer and then go under. I am never sure what I really feel or think; maybe it's one thing, maybe it's the opposite."

In subsequent sessions, we clarified some important aspects of her relationship with her mother, which had been central in her life. The hard-working, depressed mother had taken every expression of disagreement by Karen, who was her only child, as a sign of ingratitude and lack of love. Karen never felt free to exercise that degree of self-assertion that is necessary to become a person in one's own right—to individuate. She rebelled in muted ways whenever she felt squelched, for example, by going off to a girlfriend's house, where she would sit with a book in a little spare room. She was usually silent, with an air of mild truculence. Not daring to think her own thoughts and pursue her own interests, she more or less ceased to go in any direction at all. It was a case of pervasive passive hostility. Karen's anxiety-producing loss of thoughts and words when she was about to engage in a dialogue was one expression of her hostile passivity: hardly had she thought something, hardly had she started to formulate it, when her oppositional spirit took over and eradicated what she was about to put forth. As words failed her, the ideas behind them also vanished. The anxiety was largely the result of a certain ego disintegration. The patient experienced a gradually growing vacuum of object connections and ego processes. Her unconscious rage was born of the feeling that she was *compelled* to act the way she did. She lost herself in vague fantasies.

The exploration of her passive-hostile condition and of the many processes resulting from it in relation to her mother and girlfriends was merely a prelude. It was when Karen began to weep bitterly over the parallel aspects in the transference situation that she discovered and practiced a form of self-help. Her insights became meaningful and eventually enabled her to resume her ego development through identity formation and individuation.

When she lost her thoughts and words with me, as she did with others, I interpreted this sudden cessation of interchange as a way of expressing her reluctance to comply with the requirements of communicating, since, after all, this meant giving in and suffering a form of self-extinction. After some such remark, Karen became furious with herself. "I know," she said, "that you are different and not really forcing anything on me. So why should I get antagonistic?" I suggested that she find a special way of speaking designed to fit our relationship. Karen then proposed being deliberately silent as often as she wished. "Maybe that way I will sense that it is *me* who determines what I say and when," she remarked. Her design worked. She felt free to pause at crucial moments and to speak when she chose. My acceptance of her self-determined silences helped her to individuate in a less guilty, more constructive way.

By the fifth month of treatment, the patient was smiling, teasing me, and showing in various ways, both within therapy and outside of it, that her anxiety was significantly reduced. What I have called the three-dimensional time orientation began to develop, a sign of growth and development. Karen said, for example, "I now think about the future. It has become a bright spot, and the past is getting less important. I have more energy. I am experiencing considerable changes. Tell me, how did this come about?"

It is not enough to identify patients' problems and to help them comprehend their uses of destructive behavior; or to show them how the symptoms originated and where they pop up and interfere with truth, superior functioning, and creativity; or to point out that patients are fighting to maintain their resistance to behavioral change, and to pinpoint how they are waging that battle. To tell patients that they are narcissistic, that they withdraw, and readily fill up with guilt—either in outside life or in the patient-therapist relationship—is tantamount to a static F type of labeling and is often experienced as a scientific, polite form of name-calling.

Over and above insight into the existence of resistance and the major forms it takes, patients need to recognize and to alter—preferably within the transference—the minutiae of the strategies they use to escape truth, to avoid awareness of a conflict, and to perpetuate an ego arrest. It is true that such strategies must first be perceived by the patient, through insight, as destructive. But simultaneously, new visions of reparatory experimentation and of a better way to pursue life must be constructed. These reparatory experiments will at first consist of very small steps—what I call *ministeps*. But they are, in the true sense of the word, stepping stones; and they are highly important.

There are transitions that lead one from insight into what is wrong toward the discovery of ultimate alternatives of feeling and acting. The therapist listens to the description of the problem, points out the patient's invariably transferred fears, and—most important—highlights precedents or possibilities of alternative, more constructive behavior that have been tentatively emerging in treatment. Alternatives, creative solutions, fresh perspectives, and neglected affects are among the chief concerns of the new human team, patient and therapist.

The usually impatient patients often ask on the heels of an insight, "And what should I do now?" Such questions—usually asked to get immediate, "big" solutions—need to give way to satisfaction with constructive ministeps. But the questions should also be understood as a reaching-out for delineations of new behavior; thus they do not necessarily indicate a regression toward renewed dependency. Many patients ask them because they are steeped in ignorance, rather than because of resistance or regression.

Gaining insight into a conflict and taking an inventory of ego deficits do not by themselves constitute working through. The ego does not unfold spontaneously when conflicts are understood and removed. Often new structure-building must be mobilized in patients through fresh images of themselves. These fresh images are obtained from the therapist, who is holding them in safekeeping for the patient (Loewald, 1960) and who supplies them by evoking fresh responses. The potentialities of new structures—and thus new object relations—are kept alive in the transference. I do not mean role playing, as Alexander (Alexander and French, 1946) is accused of having proposed, but mobilization of higher structures because of the patient's wish to communicate and deal with a person of more mature self-organization.

I shall describe an episode from a group session to illustrate how ministeps help, and how the demand for higher-level behavior—which groups articulate vividly and individual therapists make by implication—mobilized a patient.

The most striking symptoms of a highly intelligent man, whose career was in politics, were his arrogance and his immediate withdrawal whenever a small demand of his was not met. In three consecutive fruitful meetings, the groups members helped Rick to confront his strategies of evasion, to abstain from using them, and to discover new ways of coping, at least during the sessions. Having been told many times that he was as quick to withdraw as a mouse, group members traced his strategies of resistance step by step. When asked to come out of his shell, Rick's first reply was that, after all, he had avoided personal issues for the better part of his life. Group members told him that that was no reason to continue extricating himself by withdrawal.

Rick's next stance was to tell us that he was not able to use the group's confrontations because he lost interest in the pressures exerted on him and could not remember what was said. Again this evasive strategy was repudiated; he was asked to refrain from using it and instead to call on his extraordinarily fine memory, which never let him down when he dealt with abstractions. Thereupon the patient said that he wished a group member from the previous year was present to protect him. Everyone smiled at Rick and teased him. "Now you are trying to get away by taking on the role of the poor little boy. You should stop this. Don't you see how lucky you are to have us confront you and insist that you give up your hiding maneuvers, which drive you and your teenage son crazy?"

Such well-meant miniexaminations and miniattempts to dislodge resistance make transformation of behavior possible in the transference. For a profound cognitive-emotional reorientation to occur, the impatient patient has to come around to the idea that "slow is beautiful." Although sudden flashlike "aha!" experiences do sometimes occur, they are not the events that herald and bring about change. Working through the minutiae of resistance strategies—the pinpoint work—is much more important.

Ego Repair and Ego Completion

Every society in every period of history has made heavy demands on the psychic apparatus of its members. In the fluid society of today, for example, manners and courtesy no longer suffice to carry a person along, and rigid work habits, while they bring their own rewards, do not equip the person to cope with work demands that, in this era of constantly growing automation, call for greater creativity even in relatively simple work performances. There is a growing and often uncomfortable awareness that the ego and the self have to be put on the line. The twisted or incomplete ego and synthetic self cannot do the job of relating to others, finding a sense of identity within the existing loose social structure, and coping with ever shifting economic conditions. Real capacities and genuine authenticity are needed. In many instances it is just those structures that psychotherapy helps to build (Winnicott, 1965).

The ego psychologist who is psychoanalytically anchored assumes that many problems in the present are the unfortunate result of interference and neglect by the prime parental caretaker of the past; because the required developmental sequence was neither encouraged nor facilitated, deficits became woven into the fabric of the personality. As a result, the psyche had to use make-believe, psychological bypaths, and clumsy, primitive modes of conduct. In turn, this makeshift existence made storms of anger and rage an ever more frequent occurrence, interfering with the currents of energy and love.

The unfortunate connection with the past, then, consists of severe cripplings and deficits. One objective of working through is to bring development up to date. To accomplish this, therapy has to be corrective and reconstructive. It has to invent ways of raising the level of functioning from primitive to more skillful performances. All people, not just borderline cases and schizophrenics, suffer from ego deficiencies that have to be repaired through belated growth experiences.

Reparatory experiences are comprehensive and numerous, and by no means limited to the kind of overprotection that is not unjustly described as "chicken soup therapy." There are many other positive experiences that are more likely to help build good ego functioning. Contact with the therapist mediates these experiences and helps the patient make his way out of the shadows. Often, when the immediate reactions preceding, within, and following the therapeutic session are examined, it becomes possible to devise technical ways and means to alter the ego (Kris, 1956a). I consider such alteration an absolutely essential part of working through.

An example of ego repair is the following. A narcissistic young woman suffered guilt and depression because of the open jealousy and antagonism with which she treated her stepchild. Sondra was fearful, erratic, and impatient, as evidenced by her constant demand for a quick and magical personality change. She also lacked proper ego boundaries, often confusing her own daughter with the stepdaughter, and her own self with that of other women. To improve her self-image, Sondra would sacrifice her boundaries. When she felt inadequate, she frequently sought some form of nearness with a competent female—often a certain cousin who was two years older and had a solid personality.

The patient used a method of "coupling up": she would have long telephone talks with her cousin; she would ask the cousin to spend part of the day with her; the two women went to fine restaurants and ordered identical meals. The "coupling up" also occurred, of course, in the transference. Sondra would call up with some frequency to ask for an extra session. On such occasions I regularly inquired what she wanted to accomplish through the extra appointment, and, whenever she seemed able to tolerate refusal, I recommended that we not schedule an additional meeting. Instead, I encouraged her to stick out an anxious day or weekend without resorting to the magical union with me.

In subsequent sessions I expressed interest in any behavior that showed Sondra was beginning to draw on her own strength. I explained that borrowing strength from the therapist or close friends through her "coupling up" strategies actually delayed her growth. After all, did she not have to forfeit her own selfhood (ego boundaries)? As a result, Sondra's ego expanded as she began to call on her own resources for sustenance.

A ground rule of the analytic process, namely, not gratifying the patient, essentially aims at exactly the kind of ego strengthening mentioned above. Not to answer patients' questions is one aspect of nongratification. I believe the quoted example also has some other reparatory aspects. Nongratification was used specifically to add solidity to Sondra's inadequate ego boundaries, which she tried to bolster through identification. Furthermore, frustrations were combined with a technique of positively cathecting the self by emphasizing the patient's own strength in demarking her own boundaries. It is my conviction that when it comes to ego repair and ego enrichment, frustration must be combined with acknowledgment of strength and progress. Both are part and parcel of working through.

The individual's self-representation (or self-image, to use an older term) is put together gradually. It has to be reaffirmed and continually revised from infancy on. The self-representation starts out as the body image (Freud, 1923). What is called "mirroring" (Mahler, 1968; Kohut, 1977) is one of the early foundations for the body image and hence for self-representation. As the mother affectionately follows her child's movements with her eyes and exclaims at his or her body, the first layers of self-representation are laid down. When later the family or friends applaud the teenager who builds a fence or repairs a faucet, the growing youngster is encouraged to perceive himself or herself as a functioning person who can *accomplish things*. The beginnings of self-representation have been firmly laid down.

Because the self-representation, which is an intrapsychic phenomenon, develops largely through interaction with others, we are dependent on *the ways in which others react to us*. If an important system that we depend on for our self-representation and the affirmation of our own reality is unresponsive or highly idiosyncratic, then our self-representation becomes fuzzy and bizarre. The self-representation bounces off others, so to speak. Their responses round out and correct the first skeletal representation of the self. The therapist (in group psychotherapy, the group members) becomes the open and active system from which a patient with a fragile self-representation can expect strengthening and enrichment. Thus, responsiveness is an essential ingredient of working through.

Samuel was a middle-aged patient who found it very difficult to be alone because his fragile and sketchy self-representation dissolved easily; he lacked both a picture of who he was and the necessary certainty that he existed at all. As a result, he never came home to his bachelor quarters before late in the evening, just in time to make eight or nine frantic phone calls to friends in order to get reassurance of who he was. One day Samuel remarked in the treatment session: "My existence becomes nebulous when I am by myself, but I have discovered that disagreement helps me to discover who I am. When I get to your door I sense my anger rising because I want to fight with you. I'll start right away and say that you are responsible for my troubles during the last two years."

Clashes with others and outbursts of aggression against persons to whom the patient normally submits assist not only in forming the previously mentioned ego boundaries but also in delineating and emphasizing the processes that form the self-representation (Fried, 1956). Aggression prepares the way for individuation and, in Samuel's case, for the building of a solid self-representation. It is in clashes with the therapist that patients discover who they are. While therapeutic soothing is a necessary reparatory experience for patients who are restless and irritable because they have never had their fill of symbiotic gratification (Modell, 1976; Winnicott, 1965), there are other cases in which the formation of solid self-representations is greatly facilitated by the therapist's acceptance of the patient's hostile stances.

On the other hand, absolute neutrality is easily construed by patients as indifference (Dewald, 1976). A continuously neutral attitude in the therapist fails to repair and complete the ego. I hasten to add that, in my opinion, appropriate expressions of acknowledgment, close attention, and warmth from the therapist are just as important as acceptance of the patient's hostility. Indeed, the willingness to share the patient's outbursts of hostility, even with occasional humor, is an important form of acceptance.

The number of ego functions that need to be enriched and anchored in dynamic psychotherapy is unlimited. For instance, patients with strong dependency leanings tend to engage in relatively little anticipatory thinking, which is one reason changes in the status quo are likely to arouse anxiety. Anxiety is a reaction to situations in which the helplessness engendered by ego deficiencies threatens to take over. Expanding the range of anticipatory thinking is one goal of working through in order to accomplish self-innovation. The following incident will illustrate the point.

A borderline patient, who had never gone beyond the symbiotic stage of development, moved far away from home to avoid the mother's continuous attempts to envelop him. Despite the patient's move, the mother called her son long distance almost nightly. Conversely, the patient was drawn daily to the telephone, that lifeline of the dependent person. He meant to call some acquaintance in town to help him with even slight frustrations. But more often than not he found himself dialing his mother's long-distance number to obtain consolation from the customary source. By the afternoon, he rarely knew how he was going to spend the evening.

One day he had a chance to sign a lease for a low-rent apartment, and quite against his habit he committed himself. As the date for moving came closer, he grew anxious. The therapist asked questions about the layout, the lighting, the arrangement the patient foresaw for his bookcases and furniture. The young man exclaimed in surprise: "Those are interesting questions you are asking. I'll remember them. I suppose some people ask such questions of themselves, and this would help them to plan. I need someone else to do the asking." The young man had hit upon a central problem. At an age when healthier people have internalized and integrated both question asking and question answering, he still needed a partner if this dual activity was to be performed. He was able to anticipate problems and come up with answers only if another person supplemented his ego.

A low degree of anticipatory thinking is a source of anxiety and weakness. We have to help dependent people to ask pertinent questions of themselves and to cast about for answers. In this last case, the expansion of anticipatory thinking began with questions asked by the therapist. Did this patient hesitate to ask questions because question asking was frowned on in his parental home? Did he hesitate to ask questions because of their aggressive, devouring nature? Were questions associated with once-forbidden sexual curiosity? Did he hesitate to ask questions because as long as they remained dormant, he could stay passive? Such queries, along with the therapist's expectation that anticipatory thinking would be used in the sessions, enhanced the patient's ego. Working through was begun and the inventory of ego skills was enlarged in such rather direct ways.

Mobilizing, Expressing, and Processing Aggression

In many ways, dynamic therapists are the allies of aggression. With the proviso that aggression should be expressed but not acted out, they look on it as a potentially constructive force that reestablishes contact following extreme withdrawal, that fortifies boundaries, that promotes individuation, and that supplies energy, provided the aggression is worked through and processed. In dynamic psychotherapy, the patient is helped to become aware of his aggression. Inklings of aggressive thoughts, feelings, and impulses ready to break through defensive barriers are heeded and welcomed. The direct expression of aggression is encouraged in the therapeutic setting. I consider dynamic group therapy an ideal medium in which to work through aggression. This is due partly to the existence of certain forms of splitting that the group situation allows. The patient can express anger without having to be afraid that he will lose all support and love. He attacks the therapist more readily if he feels assured of some goodwill from one or several group members (Fried, 1977).

The emergence of somatic defenses—for instance, in the form of muscular tensions—helps to make the person aware of anger. Areas of the human body where nervous excitations to strike or kick are located, such as certain spots between the shoulder blades, are subject to muscle contractions which are meant to inhibit the contemplated motions. Patients can become aware of such muscle tensions and retroactively, as it were, get hold of their aggressive impulses. A thorough working through includes the following steps: (1) awareness of aggression; (2) expression of aggression, preferably in the patient-therapist relationship; and (3) receiving and processing, or refining, aggression. The term refining alludes to the processes that convert the crude oil that spurts from the well into the products that produce energy. It has been mentioned that aggression shores up ego boundaries and promotes individuation, two developmental accomplishments that the disturbed person urgently needs. Moreover, the patient who finally ventures to express aggression resuscitates primitive forms of energy that have been closed off because of past taboos.

By working through their aggressive feelings in the three-step way described, although not necessarily always in that rigid order, patients gradually become ready to allow their loving feelings to surface. More and more clearly the listening and observing self, as well as the world, hears "those titanic melodies," as the Freudian school calls them, "that play on the power of the drives."

When previously repressed aggressive drives venture forth, they are accompanied by the need for nurture and reassurance that their expression will not be punished by abandonment. Unless we recognize these needs, great waves of anger, desires for revenge, and attempts to withdraw will again arise. But if these needs are understood, then the aggressive drives can emerge from their hideouts. The person becomes more animated and energized because aggressive drives are more effective "uppers" than amphetamine pills.

The expression and processing of aggression must take place together. Otherwise, the working through is dangerously incomplete. A woman I treated erroneously believed, as many patients do, that expressions of anger were all that was called for in therapy. Bettina slammed my door and attempted to humiliate me. After one such confrontation she dreamed that she was about to set fire to her (actually my) apartment and was going to drop a new type of green bomb over Germany (that was the land from which her autocratic father had come, but was located near Austria, my country of origin). She felt both guilty and proud of her gradually acquired ability to show rage; this previously timid patient considered such an ability the essence of therapy. It took two years to complete the processing of her rage—in other words, the working through of it—which was not too long considering her deep-seated problems. The first result was that Bettina stopped drinking. Then she stopped wasting weekends in bed to prevent her rages from exploding against others. Eventually she became a rather caring, firm, and effective person.

Freud (1914) remarked that working through is a trial of patience for the analyst and that it is related to the patient's "psychic inertia." This remark is very true, of course, but it is equally true that it is working through which brings in its wake the changes in personality and life which patients so desperately need. And these changes, after all is said and done, are the purpose of any psychotherapy.

REFERENCES

Alexander, F., & French, T. M. (1946), *Psychoanalytic Therapy.* New York: Ronald.

Blanck, G., & Blanck, R. (1979), *Ego Psychology II.* New York: Columbia University Press.

Dewald, P. A. (1976), Transference regression and real experience. *Psychoanal. Quart.,* 45:213–230.

Durkin, H. E. (1975), The development of systems theory and its implications for the theory and practice of group therapy. In: *Group Therapy 1975: An Overview,* ed. L. R. Wolberg & M. L. Aronson. New York: Stratton Intercontinental Medical Book Corp.

Durkin, J. E., et al. (in press), *Living Systems.* New York: Brunner/Mazel.

Eissler, K. (1955), The effect of the structure of the ego on psychoanalytic technique. *J. Amer. Psychoanal. Assn.,* 1:104–143.

Freud, S. (1914), Remembering, repeating and working-through (further recommendations on the technique of psycho-analysis). *Standard Edition,* 12:147–156. London: Hogarth Press, 1958.

——— (1923), The ego and the id. *Standard Edition,* 19:3–67. London: Hogarth Press, 1961.

Fried, E. (1956), Ego-strengthening aspects of hostility. *Amer. J. Orthopsychiat.,* 26:179–197.

——— (1977), When "splitting" occurs in the group. *Group,* 1:26–32.

——— (1980), *The Courage to Change: From Insight to Self Innovation.* New York: Brunner/Mazel.

Kohut, H. (1977), *The Restoration of the Self.* New York: International Universities Press.

Kris, E. (1956a), The recovery of childhood memories in psychoanalysis. *The Psychoanalytic Study of the Child,* 11:54–88. New York: International Universities Press.

——— (1956b), On some vicissitudes of insight in psychoanalysis. In: *Selected Papers.* New Haven: Yale University Press, 1975, pp. 252–271.

Kubie, L. (1958), *Neurotic Distortion of the Creative Process.* New York: Noonday.

Loewald, H. W. (1960), On the therapeutic action of psychoanalysis. *Internat. J. Psycho-Anal.,* 41:16–33.

Mahler, M. S. (1968), *On Human Symbiosis and the Vicissitudes of Individuation.* New York: International Universities Press.

Modell, A. (1976), The holding environment and the therapeutic action of psychoanalysis. *J. Amer. Psychoanal. Assn.,* 24:2–12

Spitz, R. A. (1972), Bridges: On anticipation, duration, and meaning. *J. Amer. Psychoanal. Assn.,* 20:721–735.

Winnicott, D. W. (1965), *The Maturational Processes and the Facilitating Environment.* London: Hogarth Press.

CHAPTER 13

Turning Points in Psychotherapy

M. H. Stone

Turning Points: The Phenomenon

Therapists often resort to the words *turning point* when describing sudden and dramatic improvement in a patient's clinical course. "Turning point" is reserved for revolutionary, not evolutionary, change. As a precondition to the experience of a turning point, the patient's presenting symptoms must deviate widely enough from the norm to lend an air of drama to their subsequent dissolution. Furthermore, the term is reserved for clinical conditions of at least moderate severity.

Patients whose conditions are predominantly characterological tend not to change via turning points. They change, instead, through small increments of improved adaptation in their interpersonal world. "Character," and by extension, "character disorder," imply habitual patterns of behavior that are highly resistant to change. One does see rapid fluctuations in the outward self during adolescence, but these occur *before* the final solidification takes place in the attitudes and behavior that we refer to, collectively as character. Character is, in a sense, *chronic*.

Many chronic schizophrenic patients undergo, at best, slow, evolutionary change. One often speaks of chronic schizophrenics as having a disturbance in their "synthetic" or "integrative" faculty. Whatever the origins of this defect

An earlier version of this chapter was presented at the Annual Meeting of the American Academy of Psychoanalysis, Atlanta, Georgia, May 1978.

may be, the clinician recognizes that, at least in the social field, the chronic schizophrenic is a slow learner. From a diagnostic standpoint, dramatic changes seem to be confined to acute reacions (psychotic or otherwise), suicidal tendencies, phobias, and the like. Among the better integrated patients capable of classical psychoanalysis, presenting complaints usually center on matters of intimate relationships rather than on survival or separation. Hence, if an analysand comes to a turning point, it usually involves some quantum leap in the capacity to sustain and derive gratification from a love relationship. As such, the turning point will be less dramatic than that we encounter among the severer, more acute disorders.

If my understanding of the term's usage is correct, I believe its application is reserved for those treatment situations in which the therapist's verbal interventions were considered instrumental in effecting the rapid improvement. Thus, one seldom hears the swift recuperation from an acute psychosis following the administration of a neuroleptic drug spoken of as a "turning point." Whether a particular example of dramatic improvement really did derive from our psychotherapeutic, as opposed to psychopharmacologic, interventions is not the focus of the presentation. The answer to the latter depends on the solution of a complex probabilistic equation whose variables we can scarcely enumerate in their entirety, since they depend on both the analysis of randomized studies (which thus far have almost never been carried out) and the subtraction of all those dramatic "recoveries" in persons who never even enter psychotherapy (whose numbers we can only crudely estimate). My purpose is not to elaborate a mathematics of the turning point, but merely to refine our impressions about this important clinical phenomenon. It is of interest that, despite the frequent references to turning points in discussions with one's colleagues, the term does not occur in the index of analytic writings (Grinstein, 1966) nor do there appear to be articles devoted to the subject elsewhere in the literature. Occasional reference to the phenomenon is found in papers devoted to psychotherapy (see Crewdson, 1977).

Discussion of turning points requires a careful analysis of the goals of psychotherapy. These are often characterized in such terms as the "relief of symptoms," "happiness," "maturity," or—as Freud more conservatively put it—the conversion of neurotic misery into ordinary human suffering. Apart from relief of symptoms these goals are difficult to measure. It is possible, however, to compare the number and nature of strategies both for survival and for gratification available to a patient *before* and *after* therapy. An increase in the number of adaptive strategies can serve as a reasonable measure of successful treatment. Forrest (1978) has recently introduced the concept of "play"—in the sense of increased freedom of action or movement—as a crucial ingredient of successful adaptation. A prominent feature of neurotic behavior is that it seriously limits one's choices. The following example (taken from a psychoanalytic patient in the second year of treatment) will illustrate: A young man of twenty-five was in bed with his fiancée; it was eleven o'clock in the evening. His mother phoned him at this hour, as she had been in the habit of doing every night since he left home four years before. She spoke with him—as was also her custom—for a full hour, despite his having quite other matters on his personal agenda. During his analytic sessions he presented this situation to me as one in which he felt powerless to take a different course. Though fully aware of his fiancée's irritation, he could not bring himself to interrupt his mother and shorten their conversation. This he could only conceive as an expression of disloyalty to the woman who had brought him into this world. Besides, she would, in his opinion, become tearful and depressed if he imposed any limits on their phone time. Thus he could either endure the call and risk alienating his fiancée, *or* he could gratify his own needs and those of his fiancée and risk "destroying" his mother. He could see no alternatives.

As an outgrowth of his analysis he began to grasp that many other choices were open to him besides the two to which he had for so long remained slavishly fixed. Eventually he was able to take his mother aside and get her to see the wisdom of less frequent and briefer calls. To his amazement, she was not shattered by this confrontation. As a result, he gained respect in the eyes of his fiancée, and saw himself as a man with full entitlements rather than as a boy. In this case the expansion through analysis of his repertoire of behavior vis-à-vis mother coincided with a turning point in his treatment. From this moment forward he took bold and rapid steps to advance his career, dealt more assertively with his superiors at work, and set a wedding date, about which he had been procrastinating for some time. This patient, a well-integrated and intelligent man with only a mild neurosis, was also able to translate the experience of finding additional alternatives into other problem areas, where, in the past, he had tended to behave in a rigid "either/or" manner.

If neurotic adaptation is characterized by limitation and ineffectiveness of strategies, borderline and psychotic adaptations show these defects in an even more blatant—at times grotesque—fashion.

Patients who are less well integrated operate as though "programmed" to issue only sharply polarized messages and to experience stimuli from the external world as though they invariably belonged to pairs of opposites.

Suicidal patients are notorious for construing life in antinomical terms. One may hear, for example, "Either my boyfriend must marry me, or I'll kill myself"; or "Either my boss gives me that promotion or I'll quit my job." Not only do suicidal patients narrow their view down to two alternatives, but one of these is incompatible with life. They live life on the brink and often make their therapists experience their choices in a similarly narrowed way. The therapist of such a patient, especially one who is hospitalized, is confronted with such awesome quandaries as "If I allow this patient a weekend pass, he may go home and jump out the window"—but—"if I forbid any passes, he may languish forever in the hospital."

Many schizophrenic patients, even if they are not suicidal, live life on the razor's edge, so neatly divided is their ambivalence. In this state, the patient will be tilted precipitously toward one extreme or the other with only the slightest provocation. Often, the schizophrenic who harbors two diametrically opposite feelings toward important others remains cognizant only of one. Ironically, the feeling that seems to lie outside consciousness will be the one most strongly governing his outward behavior. The view that is more readily accessible to consciousness is usually the more socially respectable one, though it exerts little influence on behavior. Certain manic-depressive or schizophrenic women with "postpartum psychoses," for example, claim to love a baby whom, at least temporarily, they cannot abide. One hears only of suicidal feelings ("I am unworthy to occupy the same house with so beautiful and unsullied a creature"), when what is really preoccupying them is murder.

I am not speaking here only of "splitting," as the term is conventionally applied to the contradictory and unfused "all good" and "all bad" images of such patients. I also have in mind the unusual pairs of opposites encountered in borderline and psychotic patients that seem completely foreign to one's work with analyzable neurotics. The success of psychotherapy may hinge on one's ability to enter the Alice in Wonderland world of the schizophrenic and to recognize dynamic factors that have no counterpart in the fantasy life of the average "well-analyzed" therapist.

For example, I have worked with a number of female patients who fancied themselves to be ugly even though they were uncommonly attractive. Each was avowedly distressed at her illusory ugliness. In two instances a surprisingly psychodynamic factor was unearthed, consisting of an intense fear of envy (experienced as "murderous" by the patient) by a (truly) unprepossessing sister. Another patient harbored the secret fear that her father would envy her beauty—that he would prefer the hopelessly (for him) unattainable comforts so readily accessible to an attractive woman to the rigors of competition with other men.

I am indebted to Harold Searles for suggesting to me the unusual mechanism at work in this last example; it was through his teaching, in fact, that I learned to suspect the *opposite,* when working with severely ill patients, no matter how far from the beaten path such suspicions might lead me. In several of these women, a turning point in therapy resulted from the exposure of the reasons behind their convictions of ugliness. Once their special and long-buried fears could be confronted, they no longer anticipated being "struck down" if they acknowledged their personal assets. They then became assertive and grew much more comfortable in social situations.

There are a few hospitalized patients selected for long-term intensive psychotherapy who improve dramatically only on being sent, many months after admission, to a chronic-care hospital. The transfer of such patients is never effected with this hope in mind, but represents an act of desperation on the part of the hospital staff. The recovery, when it occurs, is unexpected. Every therapist and staff member seems to know of several cases of this sort, but none seems able to predict which patient will actually improve in the new setting. Some patients, for example, develop "hospitalitis" in an intensive-therapy milieu. The more attention devoted to the crisis they stir up, the more "secondary gain" they accumulate—and the less motivation they have for cooperating with the treatment program. Tension mounts; the therapist and the supporting staff reach a crisis point of their own, and, in an atmosphere of commingled relief and regret, will, with seeming suddenness, finally extrude the patient from the milieu.

One such patient, a young woman with whom I had worked for some two and a half years during my residency training, had come close to death on three or four occasions following suicide attempts around the time of my vacations. She had progressed to the point where she was able to work, and live, albeit precariously, outside the hospital. Changes in my own life—specifically, the birth of my first child—made it impossible for me to live out the promise I once foolishly made to her of a "lifetime" of care, if that was what she "required." I no longer experienced the demandingness, the frequent midnight phone calls, etc., as "challenging"; they had become an intolerable burden.

Unable to work or to tolerate being alone in her apartment, the patient once again required hospitalization. This time she went to a large state hospital, with a very low staff/patient ratio and few amenities. After two weeks in this uncongenial setting she came to a turning point of her own. She reasoned, staring at the bare walls around her, that three paths were open to her: suicide, a miserable existence in this hospital, or a miserable existence outside the hospital. Her recent, although meager, success in managing a life outside was sufficient to render the first option less enticing than it had always seemed in the past. And there was no one in this understaffed facility who would have given her much sympathy if she swallowed pills or scratched her wrists. Of the two possibilities that remained, life in the real world now seemed preferable. She then marshaled her resources and shifted rapidly into a more assertive and much less whiningly dependent posture. Within six weeks she was back at work and living in her own apartment.

We kept in touch through letters once or twice a year, and some eight years after the second hospitalization we met for a "follow-up" session. She had by then achieved the status of a junior executive in a large organization and had weathered several brief, rather gratifying, romantic relationships. Depressive symptoms recurred episodically but with less intensity. When I asked what, in her view, had contributed to that turning point in her recovery, she stressed that our work during the intensive phase of therapy helped her to feel more positive about life. Life became better than death, but only if I was readily available. She could not at first distinguish between wanting me and needing me. In the other hospital—where there simply was no therapist and no "environment" to manipulate, the second lesson suddenly entered consciousness: namely, that however desperately she had wanted me, it was no longer realistic to claim that she could not get through her daily chores without me. Others could help and she had capabilities of her own. It was this realization, finally brought home to her by harsh experience, that galvanized her personal resources and efforts, making possible a "turning point." The interpretive work that had gone on in the first hospital was, by itself, insufficient to catalyze such a change. Placement in the chronic-care hospital, if premature, might have had disastrous results. The two types of intervention, however, fortuitously arranged in the proper sequence and with the proper timing, led to a dramatic, and quite unanticipated, recovery.

Turning points in psychotherapy are often heralded by a dream. The dream need not be confined to the patient. It may happen, for example, that some unresolved conflict in the *therapist* constitutes the chief impediment to therapeutic progress. But the resolution of this "countertransference" difficulty may itself be crystallized and pictorialized in a dream. After laboring for some time in obscurity, the therapist is suddenly able to grasp the essence of the patient's "complexes," or, in other instances, may suddenly be able to extricate himself from some neurotic posture (e.g., boredom, romantic overinvolvement, contempt) that has brought treatment to a stalemate. Whitman et al. (1969) have described how the analysis of therapists' dreams about patients has enhanced the therapists' comfort and effectiveness.

In the more usual situation, the patient struggles for some time without much obvious change, accumulating knowledge about his condition slowly and incrementally until he achieves—with what often seems like a quantum leap in understanding—an insight whose impact transforms his life. Events of this sort are often accompanied by a dream that is unusually vivid and storylike in its completeness. The patient will tend to attribute the insight to the dream, although it may be nearer the truth to say that work was being performed in his mind all along—only it took place outside of consciousness. As this work neared completion, the result was suddenly thrown onto the patient's mental oscilloscope in the form of a dream—in much the same way that the answer to a complex equation is all at once displayed by the crystals of a computer after some minutes of frantic but invisible calculations. The dream may indeed facilitate the translation of this otherwise imperceptible mental processing into the logical language of everyday life. To this extent it may be fair to say the dream "caused" the insight and the gain in adaptive behavior. But beyond this, it is best to think of the "mutative" or heralding dream as a culmination, an epiphenomenon, of complex problem-solving operations already nearing completion.

In the course of psychoanalytic treatment, meticulous analysis of dreams may lead to the sequential uncovering of anxiety sources related to some major inhibition or other symptom. The symptom may persist, seemingly unaffected, throughout this process, until the final element is made conscious. What follows is an "aha experience," accompanied by a dramatic spurt in the patient's coping capacity. I have reported on a case in which a severe sexual inhibition was relieved following the exposure, through dream analysis, of over a dozen separate fears (Stone, 1977a).

How a turning point in the patient's evolution may be facilitated by a turning point in the therapist's own personal growth is illustrated in the following vignette. The rapid change in both participants was set in motion by the analysis of a countertransference dream. The patient had entered treatment because of severe depression following the departure of his homosexual partner. He functioned at the borderline level. Initially he showed little psychological sophistication and was, behind his ingratiating façade, contemptuous of both therapy and therapist. After four months of casuistical argumentation about the efficacy of "mere words" in the treatment of depression, therapist and patient had become quite bored and discouraged with one another. At this juncture the therapist had the following dream:

I am walking in the lobby of a hotel with this patient on one side of me, my wife on the other. The patient tells me, "I have to stop at the pharmacy for a minute to get a prescription filled; I'll meet you shortly." I walk with my wife in a different direction, and purposely "lose" the patient.

The meaning seemed clear to him at once: he had been anxious about the patient's homosexuality. In the dream he underlines his heterosexuality by the conspicuous inclusion of his wife; the two ditch the patient, leaving him to fend for himself with medications. After this "revelation" in dream form, the therapist's fears seemed exaggerated and silly. He grew more comfortable with the patient and spontaneously adopted a more compassionate and accepting attitude. The patient, sensing this change, quickly became more relaxed, candid, and positive about his therapy. The impasse was followed by a turning point: the patient's depression lifted, and he suddenly showed himself as having an excellent capacity for introspection and insight.

The following example concerns a turning point facilitated by dream analysis in a borderline patient. A single woman of twenty-two had been hospitalized because of a suicidal gesture consisting of burning her initials in her forearm with a cigarette and then taking an overdose of Valium. She had been seriously depressed on several occasions since the age of eighteen, when she graduated from high school and left home for the first time. The second of four children, she had been raised in an outwardly Victorian household by an alternately prudish and seductive father and a shy but tender mother.

The patient was shy herself, and painfully self-conscious, but also sulky and impulsive. Exquisitely sensitive to imagined rejections as well as to even brief separations, she would make a bit of progress in treatment only to become suicidal and erratic during any of her therapist's absences. From a psychodynamic standpoint these severe separation reactions had been hard to understand, since her parents seldom left her alone and always took her along on their vacations. Following her therapist's summer vacation during the eleventh month of therapy, she went into an unusually long slump. For several weeks she was uncommunicative and restless, at times threatening to discontinue treatment, at other times reluctant to leave at the end of her session. Despite the obvious "transference" nature of her reaction, it was difficult to broach the subject, because in the past even the gentlest transference interpretations met either with intense resistance or with impulsive suicide gestures similar to the ones that had precipitated her hospitalization.

Just as the situation was becoming desperate, she opened up enough to relate the following dream:

I am sitting alone by the railroad tracks near the little station [of the small Connecticut town where she grew up]. No one is in sight. The train comes by and has some kind of design on the engine which at first I can't make out. As the train approaches, I see that the design was actually my mother's face. Then the train speeds past me and I am alone again.

Although there were strong allusions to loneliness, to longing for the mother, and to a sense of being bereft, suggestions that she might be in the grip of a strong reaction to having been left by someone of importance to her met only with denial. But a few days later, she reported another dream:

Mother was in the hospital. I was trying desperately to get to see her, but as I rush along the streets leading to the hospital, several racy-looking men accost me and try to get fresh with me. I'm so delayed by their interference that when I get to the hospital, mother has already gone.

With this dream, the nature of her dilemma was spelled out unmistakably, so much so that a more forceful interpretation seemed permissible. The connection between the therapist's vacation, her overwhelming reaction of grief and devastation, and something (but what?!) to do with her mother was no longer stated to her in tentative terms but as a fact. This at first brought forth tears, then the recollection of something she had never revealed.

When she was about ten her mother had to go to the hospital for a laparotomy. Her father told her, with particular bluntness, that mother had a "bad ulcer" and might not live more than a year. All through her adolescence, the patient lived in a constant state of dread, expecting any day to come home and hear the news of her mother's death. She became inordinately apprehensive about the most minor illness or briefest separation from her mother—who recovered completely from whatever illness she had and has been well ever since. The pattern of catastrophic reaction to separation was now firmly entrenched, however, unaltered by her mother's continuing good health. Following this sequence of dreams, however, she was able to work through much of the old separation anxiety, and within a few days, became cheerful, more self-reliant, and better able to discuss transference themes without the usual apprehensiveness. Not long afterward she was able to begin an intimate relationship with a young man—her first—and to return to graduate school.

The following example concerns a turning point catalyzed by a dramatic change in the therapist, brought about by a particularly helpful experience in supervision.

A twenty-one-year-old college student had been hospitalized because of severe agoraphobia. She had spent the previous six years in a residential setting for emotionally ill adolescents, following the breakup of her family. During the first year of hospitalization she had made little progress. On several occasions she became mute for long periods of time. The working diagnosis had been "pseudoneurotic schizophrenia," though she did not exhibit a formal thought disorder. One parent had paranoid schizophrenia and had been incapacitated for years. The patient's anxiety was minimal so long as she remained in the hospital. She received no medication.

Her treatment consisted of analytically oriented psychotherapy, but initially she did no more than come to the office three times a week at the appointed hour, curl up in her chair, and remain silent. As the therapist assigned to her case at the beginning of the new academic year, I soon began to feel powerless in the face of her immobility. I became impatient and exasperated. These fruitless sessions continued for four months, at which time I began to receive supervision on the case from Harold Searles. After listening to my lengthy and garbled presentation of this patient's complicated history, Searles commented, "Well, I find, as happens about twenty percent of the time, that I have nothing to contribute about your patient. I have also found, whenever this happens, that there is usually something about the patient the therapist would just as soon leave unchanged. Maybe you cherish her the way she is."

Searles's comment enabled me to recognize a number of feelings this patient engendered in me, feelings I had hitherto been only dimly aware of: a genuine "paternal" affection for this, in my eyes at least, childlike and kittenish woman; at the same time, envy of her ability (through illness) to get others to provide for her needs, while I had to work hard to provide for my own. My supervisor's remarks rendered my own feelings toward her—both the warm and the hostile ones—more acceptable. I now felt neither constrained to suppress such emotions nor reduced to making hollow and pedantic interpretations.

I told her one afternoon, "If one of us doesn't say something pretty soon, I think I'm gonna explode." To which she replied—uttering her first words of meaningful communication to me—"You too, huh!?" After this exchange, she became as verbal as she had been silent before. Almost at once we began to explore what seemed to be the central dynamic behind her mutism: namely, her apprehension that I would be like the sicker of her two parents, the one who was phobic like her, and who was unwilling to part with her or let her grow up.

It developed that she was indeed "cherished just as she was" by this parent; the similar feeling induced in me was both the transferential replica of this earlier paradigm and a stumbling block to further progress. The turning point in my own grasp of the case was brought about by Searles's comment. The patient's subsequent turning point proved to be authentic: she made rapid strides in overcoming her agoraphobia (even without the use of special behavior modification techniques), married some eight months later, and has remained well for the past fourteen years.

Emotional illness is seldom the outgrowth of a solitary major trauma, even though patients will often assign the "cause" of their condition to some memorable event from childhood. Usually such an event is seen, in retrospect, as the symbol for a whole pattern of repeated pathogenic interactions with some important early figure. There are, however, exceptional situations where, over and above the background noise of neurotic family interaction, one pathogenic event of such magnitude occurred that it did derail in some important way the person's subsequent development. The most often cited examples of single major traumata include the suicide of a parent, adoption, or the loss of a close family member through death or divorce (Stone, 1975: Watt and Nicholi, 1978). In children who have narrowly escaped death from felonious assault, serious illness, or injury, psychiatric disturbances may also arise that for the most part, seem to hark back to the one traumatic experience. The resolution of these disturbances through psychotherapy will in some instances be accompanied by a dramatic "abreaction." The long-repressed memory, with all the attendant emotion, suddenly bursts forth during a session—followed by a tremendous sense of relief, and, in the more fortunate cases, a restored capacity to resume the normal path of development.

Such an abreaction occurred in a case reported by Kestenbaum (personal communication, 1978) concerning an adolescent suffering from depression, recurrent nightmares, listlessness, and poor concentration at school. When he was six his mother had committed suicide by hurling herself off the ledge of a building in front of his very eyes. The truth of what had happened was vigorously denied by his whole family. By the time he was sixteen, he scarcely knew which version was correct. He had never dared broach the subject with anyone in the family. When he had been in treatment for about three months, however, he suddenly came to recognize the validity of his original impressions. As the last piece of the puzzle fell into place during one of his hours, he sobbed uncontrollably and nearly fainted in his therapist's office. Shortly thereafter several members of his family were confronted by the therapist, who obtained from them a reluctant admission of what had taken place. This sequence of events constituted the turning point in his therapy. His depression lifted, his schoolwork returned to its previously good level, and he was able to complete the work of mourning so long delayed by the atmosphere of taboo and denial in his family.

At times turning points in therapy may come about in strange ways that are not readily classified into any of the categories thus far outlined. For example, a schizoid man in his twenties had for years felt painfully isolated, because, unlike ordinary people, he seemed not to share in any way the ability to give vent to the usual range of human emotions. He had been in analytically oriented treatment for several years when he heard the news that one of our country's most revered leaders had been assassinated. Not only was he shaken by the tragedy, but he found himself tearful for the first time in his life. When asked what his reaction was to the events of the preceding day, he told his therapist only that he had been "happy." Further inquiry into this seemingly repugnant response led to his revelation that he had been so moved and saddened at the news that tears had come to his eyes, which then, paradoxically, had led to a feeling of joyousness. He too, after all this time, was becoming a full-fledged member of the human family, able to love and to cry, no longer condemned to lead the freakish, robotlike existence that had for so many years alienated him from his fellow human beings.

Some Remarks on Psychotherapy in Relation to Turning Points

The chronically suicidal patient represents one of the most challenging situations in psychotherapy. The patient struggles to die; the therapist struggles to free the patient of self-destructive tendencies. We feel we have succeeded when patients no longer see life as "hopeless" but begin to view their suicidal urges as a hostile and maladaptive game that they have used to tyrannize others. When suicide no longer seems so necessary or so attractive as an "alternative," we have effected a turning point.

In the past, considerable emphasis was placed on getting suicidally depressed patients to ventilate their rage. The depression was viewed as rage turned inward; redirecting it outward must then be the curative step. There are many depressed patients who show evidence, via dreams and verbal productions, that their anger has indeed been turned inward on the self. Yet the mere expression of this anger may not even lift the depression, let alone lead to a turning point in therapy.

It is often more meaningful to observe the sudden drying up of choices in such patients. The executive who gets fired, even if he remains consciously angry at his superior and does not lapse into self-blame, may still become seriously depressed if he reasons (correctly or incorrectly) that he has no hope of quickly finding a similar post elsewhere. If intense self-recrimination is present, expression of the underlying rage is only a first small step toward recovery. It is much more effective to help patients to find alternatives they may have overlooked and to seize opportunities of which they were unaware. This holds true for depressed patients who are reacting primarily to loss as well as for those of the particularly suicide-prone hostile-manipulative type (described by Weissman et al., 1973).

Sometimes a turning point will occur after patients have grasped and assimilated the psychological meanings attached to their suicidal behavior. But, in other cases, the dramatic turnabout will occur only after we have reeducated patients, expanded their range of options, and realistically enhanced their maneuverability. Forrest's (1978) emphasis on helping patients gain a sense of greater spatial "play" (as opposed to sense of confinement or entrapment) is an analogous concept.

Whether patients with borderline or psychotic structure (Kernberg, 1967) ever arrive at a turning point depends greatly on the therapist's ability to instill hope. But hope cannot be dispensed like pills from a vending machine. Hope arises out of a combination of many factors, some of which may, at first glance, seem highly irrational. Often, a measure of good luck must be added to good technique. The therapist should eventually (if not from the beginning) enjoy working with the patient; the therapist must see the patient as having sufficient assets to make lasting recovery possible and to tide him or her over the long period of painful exploration. Treatment may flourish only if there is a certain "chemistry" between therapist and patient (see Stone, 1971) or if the therapist feels toward his patient the kind of parental, desexualized love of which Sacha Nacht (1962) has so movingly written. Sometimes a turning point in the treatment of a severely ill, hospitalized patient will occur after the therapist has taken extraordinary measures to rescue the patient, as in the following example:

A schizophrenic women of twenty-two had been hospitalized because of a psychotic episode following the breakup of a romantic relationship. She continuously vilified her therapist for "not caring" about her, as though there were no distinction between the therapist and the departed lover. One day, in a fit of pique, the patient escaped from the hospital. The therapist, upon hearing the news, got into her car and canvassed all the bars and social clubs in Greenwich Village which her patient was known to frequent. At about midnight, she found her patient and drove her back to the hospital. From that day forward, the patient grew calmer, less impulsive, and made rapid progress in treatment. Later, after making a substantial recovery, she told her therapist that all the interpretations during the first few weeks in the hospital meant very little to her. But after the "midnight rescue mission" it was clear, even to her, how concerned and sincere her therapist had been from the beginning.

Happily, not every borderline or psychotic patient requires this sort of vivid demonstration in order to get on with the business of recuperation. Some do, however, and it is here that the element of luck becomes so relevant. A felicitous mixture of personalities in the therapist-patient dyad may be the magic ingredient in one case; in another, it may be a matter of finding a particular therapist whose professional and life experience enable him or her to impart genuine hopefulness to an unusually great degree. I have dwelt on this matter at some length in order to make clear that, in discussing the matter of turning points, therapist factors are just as critical as patient factors.

Close attention to the phenomenon of the turning point may eventually enhance our capacity to predict which patients are most likely to experience such an event and when in the course of treatment it is most likely to occur. Something is already known about the attributes of the "good prognosis" patient, or, more specifically, about those who will go on to make a dramatic recovery. For example, patients who show borderline structure when first evaluated and who exhibit the more favorable characterological subtypes are more prone to show dramatic improvement (often after a turning point is reached) than are patients with psychotic structure or those with the less favorable characterological subtypes (Stone, 1977b).

It is a regular feature of patients whose recovery begins with a turning point that, for some amount of time beforehand, they were absorbed in the task of learning how to improve and expand their repertoire of coping strategies. Much of psychotherapy may be construed as a tutorial program in which the patient is given individual lessons concerning hitherto problematical life situations. Ordinarily, each lesson centers on some highly specific event, often one that took place within a few days of the therapy session. The best "lessons" concentrate on an event occurring in the dyadic therapeutic relationship, i.e., on a transference phenomenon. Because the latter has been witnessed by the therapist, the lesson that evolves out of its exploration will have a freshness and reality not always present in material derived from extramural life.

Obviously, the learning that occurs during psychotherapy, especially if it has centered on the transference, is of no utility unless the patient is able to apply it to analogous real-life situations. The degree to which learning can acquire this wide applicability will vary inversely with the patient's level of concreteness. The concrete patient is poor at translating lessons into contexts that were not directly discussed. This may help explain why certain schizophrenic patients progress so slowly in psychotherapy. The therapist's vacation this year, for instance, is just as traumatic as the one last year and the year before; the schizophrenic patient seldom arrives at the level where "suddenly" separations are no longer anxiety-provoking. There is no turning point.

In contrast, the patient who thinks less concretely operates as though a lesson in one conceptual cell can be communicated laterally, and rather quickly, to all similar cells. If such a patient was upset during the first interruption in psychotherapy, he or she will usually take the next separation better. By the third or fourth separation, the patient will have derived enough from the therapeutic encounter and will have applied it widely enough to be able to say, "There is really nothing to be so upset about any more." It is usually a realization of this kind that underlies a turning point in therapy. Two examples, chosen from the extremes of the concreteness continuum will illustrate this point.

The first concerns a highly intelligent but chronically schizophrenic mathematician who had been in psychotherapy for many years. During the ninth year of treatment he fell into the habit of eating an apple before his session, leaving the core and some peel lying about on the anteroom table. After quite a few tactful reminders about this from his therapist, he was finally persuaded to put the uneaten portions in the basket. Several months later, he took to eating a banana before the session and would put the banana peel on the table with the same nonchalance as before. When the therapist once more tactfully reproved him about leaving fruit on the furniture, the patient retorted, quite dumbfounded, "You never said anything about bananas."

The second example concerns a depressed professional woman in her twenties, who, when first seen, was considerably sicker than the mathematician (even though she functioned at the borderline level). She abused barbiturates, was frequently suicidal, panicked when alone, and became involved in one brief relationship after another as an antidote to her intense loneliness. The men she sought all conformed to a certain "type": they treated her poorly and predictably soon left her. The course of psychotherapy was initially stormy. At one point, before the therapist's vacation, she had to be hospitalized for several months. While in the hospital, her care was entrusted to a different therapist. Out of loyalty to the first, she assumed she would not get along with the second. But this patient showed very little of the concreteness that was so marked a characteristic of the other patient. She was able to grasp quite clearly, on resuming work with the first therapist, (1) that she *was* able to make a new attachment, (2) that the strength and quality of the first therapeutic relationship were not diminished by the separation, and (3) that the separation itself had not been "fatal," as she had fantasized it would be.

The lesson "taught" her by her experience in the hospital was like a bolt out of the blue. Whereas before, separations of any sort had almost always led to feelings of panic, shortly after this turning point, she was able to tolerate evenings alone. Concomitant with this improvement was a sudden shift away from her old pattern of seeking instant gratification toward a healthier pattern involving sublimation. She became immersed in a wide variety of interests and hobbies and had the patience to seek out more appropriate partners. She was no longer anxious at the thought of not having a boyfriend. Her work as well as her romantic relationships continued to improve so dramatically that after two years of therapy she had become engaged to a very suitable man, had been offered a prestigious post in her profession, and was able to handle several separations—from therapist and financé—with a minimum of anxiety.

Turning Points: Some Theoretical Considerations

(1) Turning points in psychotherapy may be viewed as one of a large class of phenomena characterized by rapid shifts from one state to another. Living organisms are said to possess innate drives, whose expression is governed by an intricate system of reciprocal mechanisms for inhibition and release. In addition, organisms seek an equilibrium state or "homeostasis." But in complex organisms such as human beings, homeostasis remains for the most part a hypothetical construct, approached asymptotically but never actually realized, as the person is buffeted this way and that by a host of simultaneous competing impulses. Human behavior observed at any given moment expresses the temporary balance struck between various drives relating to thirst, hunger, and sexual appetite, and such needs as warmth and freedom from pain. Appetitive drives concerning thirst, hunger, and sex are characterized by rhythmic fluctuations and thus are said to rely on feedback mechanisms that dictate the person's corresponding state of hunger or satiety.

Finally, human behavior involves more complex equations relating to such "abstract" matters as self-esteem and hierarchical position.

On the plane of emotion, one notes that the more "primitive" emotional states have in common with the stronger drives the qualities of urgency and extremeness. They are categorical and possess an "all or none" quality. Objectivity is totally abrogated, as can be seen in such expressions as "engulfed in self-pity," "enveloped by rage," and "blind with infatuation."

Among borderline and psychotic patients, emotional life swings toward the extremes—a tendency noted by psychoanalytic writers over several generations. Rado (1956, p. 343) spoke of the "emergency emotions" (fear, rage, guilty fear, and guilty rage) operative in a less dramatic fashion in psychoneurotic persons. Kernberg (1967) has emphasized the primitivity of emotions in borderline patients; Gunderson and Singer (1975) have drawn attention to the predominance of rage in borderline patients.

Similarly in the sphere of object relations, sicker patients are noted to exhibit childlike and unassimilated views of other people, as though the world were inhabited only by bad guys and (to a far lesser extent) good guys. The higher we ascend the scale toward healthy adaptation, the more we encounter complex, integrated, flexible conceptions of self and others. The more we approach the psychotic end of the continuum, the more we encounter poor integration and widespread splitting of self- and object representations (the all-good/all-bad dichotomy), with the attendant rigidity of attitude and maladaptiveness of response.

Corresponding to the primitive, polarized attitudes and object representations in the more dysfunctional patients are primitive defense operations. Denial, for example, is a pathological on-off mechanism: some attribute or feeling regarded as "on" by those who know him, the patient vehemently asserts to be "off." This is in contrast to the relatively healthier defense of rationalization, in which the person essentially pleads guilty "with an explanation"—acknowledging ownership of the unacceptable attribute or emotion, but dressing it up to look presentable.

At the level of interpersonal conflict, seriously dysfunctional patients have a complex system of two or more simultaneous urges of a competing or contradictory nature. The comparative strengths of these urges—some are active only momentarily, others are more persistent—will determine the patient's relative comfort or discomfort as well as his or her subsequent behavior. Consider the possibilities inherent in the courtship situation: if a woman is strongly enamored of a particular man, and if he returns her affection but is somewhat aloof or insensitive, she may decide that "the good outweighs the bad" and remain with him. (If the same woman is treated with tremendous respect and attentiveness there will, of course, be no conflict. She may even experience elation.)

But if the man should become more aloof or treat her shabbily . . . she will find herself caught in an intolerable state of "strain" between the two opposing emotions of love and resentment. She is now in what one might call a metastable state: tiny additions or subtractions of either emotion may suddenly precipitate a drastic change in behavior. Everyday language is full of metaphors for this unstable condition: an extra measure of shabby treatment, for instance, may be experienced as the "last straw," after which something "snaps," and the relationship is hastily broken off.

Each person works out the calculus of his or her own tolerance. But as we descend from those at the normal end of the spectrum to the distinctly neurotic and on down to the borderline and (chronically) psychotic levels, we note a progressively heightened proneness to switch suddenly to intense and highly maladaptive emotional states—often in response to progressively weaker stresses. An hour's delay in her husband's returning home will, if it is an exceptional event, be written off by a healthy woman to unusual traffic or to some urgent bit of last-minute work. A delusionally jealous woman may be frantic after only five minutes of comparable stress.

The limits of our tolerance are shaped by the intensity of any one stress or emotion as well as by the cumulative effects of concomitant stresses. The "snapping" or sudden breakdown in one's capacity to cope with a set of circumstances may occur after a solitary but major stress (the death of a loved one) or after the last of several less severe but serially occurring stresses (spouse in a bad mood, car had a flat tire, boss was critical, *and* the child brought home a poor report card) has exerted its additive effect to push the person beyond his or her limit.

(2) Recently the French mathematician Réné Thom (cited by Zeeman, 1976) developed a series of models for topological representation of sudden changes of state in physical and animate systems. These models embody what their originator has called "catastrophe theory," because of its focus on certain common "catastrophes," such as the outbreak of war, the onset of assaultiveness in an angered animal, or, in the physical realm, the breaking point of a stressed metal beam. Within the context of Thom's theory, the word "catastrophe" is used to denote any sudden changes in state, not just negative ones.

A number of typical situations in which catastrophe theory appears relevant have been discussed and illustrated by Zeeman (1976). His examples include such "negative" catastrophes as stock market crashes, wartime surrender, or, in the case of anorexia nervosa patients, fasting. There is an opposite "catastrophe" to each of the above, i.e., the bull market, the moment of attack, or an episode of gorging. Zeeman also invites us to contemplate, as an exercise in thought, the predicament of a frightened but angry dog being approached by a man. If the fear and anger are both minimal, no matter what their mix, abrupt behavior will not occur as the man comes nearer. But if these emotions are near maximal, then, depending on their delicate balance, there will be a critical distance between the two creatures such that one additional step closer on the man's part will precipitate either the dog's flight or its sudden attack.

In this relatively simple situation the catastrophe theory model could be embellished by a crude quantification, relating, say, to the maximal degree of encroachment (as a function of distance) before the dog takes action, and to the size of the approaching man. Adherents of Thom's theory have expressed the hope that such quantification could be developed for the vastly more complicated human situations involving individual or group phenomena. The ultimate goal would be the prediction of catastrophic changes in individual and mass behavior. A number of mathematicians have criticized catastrophe theory as being quite far from achieving such quantitative, let alone predictive, goals (Kolata, 1977). It may be more reasonable, at least for now, to adopt the stance taken by Paulos (1978), who regards the theory as a useful analogy for describing a variety of events characterized by sudden change.

Thom describes a number of "elementary catastrophes" named in accordance with the shape they assumed as he attempted to represent them graph-

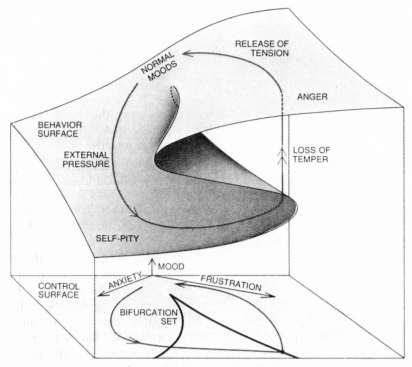

Cathartic release from self-pity is described by a cusp catastrophe in which anxiety and frustration are conflicting factors influencing mood. Self-pity is induced by an increase in anxiety; it can be relieved by some event, such as a sarcastic remark, that causes an increase in frustration. As the control point crosses the cusp the mood changes catastrophically from self-pity to anger; the resulting release of tension gives access to calmer emotional states.

ically, such as "cusp," "butterfly," "swallowtail" (see Zeeman, 1976). A salient characteristic of the catastrophe models, especially of the "cusp" diagram used to depict various psychological "catastrophes," is the existence of a sharply curvilinear region, which shades into a much gentler, nearly planar surface.

In Figure 1, for example, marked increases in anxiety or frustration (shown along the lower, or "control," surface) are correlated with catastrophic changes in mood (self-pity versus anger), the latter being mapped onto the sharply curved "cusp" region of the upper (or "behavior") surface. Toward the rear of the behavior surface, corresponding to low states of anxiety/frustration, is a smooth and slightly inclined region designated "normal moods."

The catastrophe theory model is closely allied to the psychological concept of vulnerability (see Zubin and Spring, 1977). The latter may be construed as a heightened tendency of the person to break down under stresses not ordinarily associated with gross dysfunction. Borderline and psychotic patients appear to exhibit such vulnerability—we often infer it from their behavior—and we assume that in many cases genetic influences play an important role in predisposing them to this lowered tolerance for stress (Stone, 1977b). Put another way, patients require hospitalization at various points in their lives because of an acute ("catastrophic") episode, which may be conceptualized with the help of Thom's models. This is particularly true of the suicidal patient, the severe anorectic, the agoraphobe, and those who suffer from acute and crippling attacks of panic.

Well before the elaboration of catastrophe theory, the emotionally ill were described in everyday language as "edgy," "on the brink," "labile," and "walking a tightrope." These phrases capture both the affective instability so often noted in certain categories of psychiatric disturbances and the tendency toward rapid shifts of state in others. Reconsidered in the light of this theory, psychiatric patients may be visualized as perched on, or near, the most curved portion of one or another "catastrophe" diagram, where a minor change of intensity in one or more emotional states is associated with a drastic change in ideation or behavior.

From the standpoint of available strategies, the more distressed the patient, the fewer his or her perceived options. The patient may reach the point where none of these options is at all compatible with successful adaptation. For the suicidal patient, death itself may be the only acknowledged "option." In seeking to minimize anxiety, the psychosis-prone patient may fall precipitously into delusion, where comfort is all at once reestablished—but at the price of a diminished sense of reality. Occasionally one encounters schizophrenic patients for whom psychosis is experienced quite consciously as a refuge—and the only one known to them—from intolerable anxiety. As one such patient poignantly told me, after having developed a rather enviable reputation among her hospital mates on account of the poetic manner in which she expressed her deslusory ideas: "Why should I be a cipher *out there,* when *here* I can be Queen of the Crazies?!"

As therapists, we try to foster such goals as reduced vulnerability and an expanded repertoire of coping mechanisms. In the terms of the catastrophe theory model, our aims will have been accomplished when we have helped the patient move from the catastrophe-prone portion of a behavior surface to the more planar portion that corresponds to less intense degrees of the "emergency emotions" and that therefore allows greater access to nonstereotyped responses.

In this context, the turning point in psychotherapy may be viewed as a kind of reverse catastrophe, where we have facilitated the patient's rapid leap upward—*away* from the "region" of suicidal, phobic, or other grossly dysfunctional states—toward the low-anxiety "region" of normal moods and behavioral flexibility.

Summary: Guidelines for Practitioner

In psychotherapy, we use the phrase "turning point" to signify moments of sudden and dramatic improvement in a patient's clinical course, related, as far as can be determined, to our therapeutic (particularly, *verbal*) interventions. Since dramatic improvement is scarcely possible in patients whose conditions are very mild to begin with, the term is ordinarily confined to cases of at least moderate severity. Patients who are severely and chronically ill, especially certain schizophrenics whose thinking is characterized by concreteness, tend to improve in a slow, incremental fashion at best, and hence seldom experience a "turning point." One often does see a turning point, however, during the course of psychotherapy with patients showing either moderately severe affective (especially depressive) symptoms or certain dystonic and easily noticeable symptoms such as phobias.

Turning points may occur as abreactions to early traumata (including early object loss that may have been insufficiently mourned), as the sudden conquest of a hitherto crippling phobia, or as a sudden lifting of anxiety or depression. Often the clinician cannot be sure that a particular therapeutic event constituted a turning point until enough time has passed to prove that the initial improvement was not only dramatic but sustained.

Turning points often appear to hinge on unpredictable factors, such as the "chemistry" between therapist and patient, the therapist's capacity to instill hope in an otherwise discouraged patient (who may have had several unsuccessful courses of treatment with other therapists), and the therapist's skill in confronting difficult (i.e., "borderline") patients with the proper timing and proper mix of firmness and compassion. Sometimes a turning point will be heralded by a *dream*—either in the patient or the therapist—in which the answer to a previously "insoluble" conflict is simply and obviously stated.

In many instances, turning points are characterized by the sudden transition from highly maladaptive coping styles to a more integrated state, where patterns of thought and behavior are realistic and adaptive. Examples would include the chronically suicidal patient who, having assimilated some particularly useful interpretation or confrontation, no longer resorts to suicide attempts or gestures in life situations that formerly evoked such responses. The abrupt cessation of other types of impulsive and self-destructive behavior would likewise qualify as turning points.

From the metapsychological standpoint, the "turning point" is analogous to a situation in Réné Thom's "catastrophe theory" model in which there is sudden movement away from an all-or-none (i.e., aggression versus capitulation), two-alternative behavior pattern to one in which more desirable options become available to the patient.

REFERENCES

Crewdson, F. (1977), Separation-individuation: Indicator of change for therapy of borderline patients. Paper presented at the 30th Anniversary Symposium, Society of Medical Psychoanalysis, New York, March 11.

Forrest, D. V. (1978), Spatial play. *Psychiatry,* 41:1–23.

Grinstein, A. (1966), *The Index of Psychoanalytic Writings.* Vol. 9. New York: International Universities Press.

Gunderson, J. G., & Singer, M. T. (1975), Defining the borderline syndrome: An overview. *Amer. J. Psychiat.* 132:1–10.

Kernberg, O. F. (1967), Borderline personality organization. *J. Amer. Psychoanal. Assn.,* 15:641–685.

Kolata, G. B. (1977), Catastrophe theory: The emperor has no clothes. *Science,* 196:287.

Nacht, S. (1962), The curative factors in psychoanalysis. *Internat. J. Psycho-Anal.,* 43:194–234.

Paulos, J. A. (1978), The *New York Times,* March 21st, p. 20.

Rado, S. (1956), *Psychoanalysis of Behavior.* New York: Grune & Stratton.

Stone, M. H. (1971), Therapists' personalities and unexpected success with schizophrenic patients. *Amer. J. Psychother.,* 25:543–552.

—— (1975), The role of loss in borderline and psychotic conditions. *J. Thanatol.,* 3:207–222.

—— (1977a), Dreams, free-association and the non-dominant hemisphere. *J. Amer. Acad. Psychoanal.,* 5:255–284.

—— (1977b), The borderline syndrome: Evolution of the term, genetic aspects, and prognosis. Paper delivered at the 17th Emil Gutheil Memorial Lecture, Association for the Advancement of Psychotherapy, New York City, November 21st, 1976. *Amer. J. Psychother.,* 31:345–365.

Watt, N. F., & Nicholi, A., Jr. (1978), Death of a parent as an etiological factor in schizophrenia. Unpublished paper.

Weissman, M. M., Fox, K., & Klerman, G. L. (1973), Hostility and depression associated with suicide attempts. *Amer. J. Psychiat.,* 130:450–455.

Whitman, R. M., Kramer, M., & Baldridge, B. J. (1969), Dreams about the patient. *J. Amer. Psychoanal. Assn.,* 17:702–727.

Zeeman, E. C. (1976), Catastrophe theory. *Sci. Amer.,* 234:65–83.

Zubin, J., & Spring, B. (1977), Vulnerability: A new view of schizophrenia. *J. Abnorm. Psychol.,* 86:103–126.

CHAPTER 14

Change Factors
in the Treatment of Depression

Jules R. Bemporad

Most depressed persons seek psychotherapy following some major upheaval in their lives that has forced them to reconsider the ways they derive meaning, esteem, and gratification from their everyday existence. For some, this psychological upheaval resulted from the loss of a significant relationship with another person. Others may have experienced a loss in social or economic status such as loss of a prestigious career position. Still other depressed persons complain not of an actual loss but of a realization that a very important goal which they have set themselves will never be achieved. In this case, the loss appears to be of a fantasied or expected status or accomplishment that cannot be obtained. Finally, some depressed persons have not suffered any loss—real or fantasied—and so their depression may appear without any apparent precipitant. With treatment, however, it becomes clear that the exacerbation or onset of their depression can be traced to a time of psychological crisis and readjustment. In such a case, some seemingly trivial experience—reading a certain book or seeing a certain play or movie or having a conversation with a friend—has caused a reevaluation of the meaning and satisfaction of one's whole existence, leading to the conclusion that one is inexorably caught in a frustrating and nongratifying lifestyle.

These are the three major types of clinical presentations that are usually found in patients presenting with a primary depressive disorder.[1] Despite manifest difference in the immediate causes of the depression, those who suffer all three types share similar personality characteristics, patterns of child rearing, and irrational systems of beliefs about themselves and others. The superficial differences are really variations on a more basic theme. It is this more fundamental attribute of the personality that is responsible for the production and maintenance of clinical depression. For everyone becomes depressed at one time or another; yet for most of us this painful affect lasts for only a short time and occurs only after an appreciable, realistic loss or frustration. In some persons, however, this initial depressive reaction does not pass and intensifies with time. Furthermore, the precipitants of the depressive episode do not appear commensurate with the extent of the reaction. Most people who feel depressed mobilize considerable psychic effort to combat their dysphoria and find activities or psychological mechanisms to alleviate their mental pain. Depressives, on the other hand, seem to collapse under their melancholic state, to give up and become hopeless and helpless, often expecting others to relieve them of their painful burden. Finally, healthier people become saddened or depressed in response to an *external* deprivation, whereas depressives, in contrast, experience an alteration in their conception of themselves. This is an extremely significant characteristic of the depressive, as Freud (1917) astutely noted in his differentiation between grief and melancholia. He stated that in grief there is a sense of an environmental loss whereas in melancholia it is the ego—one's own self—that is impoverished.

This inner cause of depression was also eloquently described by Kierkegaard (1849) over a century ago. He wrote that "when the ambitious man whose watchword was 'either Caesar or nothing' does not become Caesar, he is in despair thereat. But this signifies something else, namely, that precisely because he did not become Caesar he cannot endure to be himself" (p. 152). As for those depressions that follow a loss, Kierkegaard describes them as follows: "A young girl is in despair over love and so she despairs over her lover, because he died or because he was unfaithful to her. . . . No, she is in despair over herself. This self of hers, if it had become 'his' beloved, she would have been rid of in the most blissful way . . . this self is now a torment for her when it has to be a self without him" (p. 153).

It would seem that there is a predisposition in some people to repeated and severe episodes of depression which exists before the onset of a clinical episode. It is this premorbid personality pattern, this way of living, that psychotherapy must ultimately alter to effect lasting change.

---

[1]Manic-depressive psychosis or bipolar illness is excluded from this group. Although this disorder has many psychodynamic and historical features in common with unipolar depression, the course of the illness appears to be influenced by unidentified physiological factors.

Patterns of Depressive Personality Organization

Perhaps the most conspicuous feature of the depressive's personality is an extreme reliance on limited external sources for maintaining self-esteem. Arieti (1962) has commented on this characteristic, noting that in contrast to the schizophrenic in whom decompensation results from a failure subjectively felt to be of cosmic magnitude involving the patient's involvement with his entire interpersonal world, episodes of depression often follow the loss of a relationship with only one person. Arieti therefore termed the object of this lost relationship "the dominant other," suggesting that the depressive had excessively relied on him or her for nurturance. When one loses this dominant other, one feels deprived of one's source of meaning and self-esteem; such a person cannot independently reinstate avenues of psychological support and lapses into depression.

This extreme reaction to a loss is best appreciated in the context of the depressive's premorbid mode of conceiving of the self and others. Slipp (1976) found that depressives are trained from childhood to shun autonomous means of gratification, i.e., obtaining esteem directly through their own efforts. Rather, their sense of worth was derived from the parent, who constantly judged their merit. The rewards of hard work or public achievement therefore become meaningless in themselves and are used only in the attempt to secure praise from the powerful parent. The parent also punished the child severely by inducing shame and guilt for any attempt to derive extrafamilial gratification. All of the child's successes were perverted so that they brought no joy in themselves but were accepted as just repayment for the parent's love or one's proper duty to the family. All other means of obtaining worth or a positive sense of self were derided as silly or unproductive or seen as signs of disloyalty.

As a result of this orientation, which stresses that love can be obtained only by abstinence and hard work, depressives often achieve considerable success in later life and, from afar, seem to be highly competent, well-adjusted people. Yet their success means little and they use it only to wrest praise from some dominant other who has transferentially replaced the parent. If this relationship with the dominant other is disrupted, such people suddenly find themselves without sources of pleasure or meaning, and depression ensues.

Episodes of depression sometimes follow job promotions. In such cases, depressives have worked so well under benign or rewarding superiors that they are appropriately promoted. Yet after a few weeks, they find that their work is no longer interesting, that they are uncertain of its worth, that they feel empty and lonely. The depressives have lost their needed relationship with their old superiors and find they cannot function without the old reassurance and feedback. A more obvious example is those depressions that follow the loss of a spouse or loved one. Here again, one finds that the lost other seemed to bestow meaning and worth; he or she actually supplied a needed sense of self that the depressive is incapable of achieving alone.

In addition to the "dominant other" depressives described above, there are also "dominant goal" types who are similar in that they too have precariously limited their avenues of esteem to one external source: that of fulfilling some great ambition. These depressives shun gratification and involvement in everyday life—except for what is related to their goal—for fear that other activities will interfere with their all-encompassing objective. They lead essentially anhedonic lives, taking no pleasure from daily life and avoiding alternative sources of esteem. When this monomaniacal quest for the goal is closely examined, however, it is found that the goal, per se, also has little inherent meaning. What is important is the fantasied transformation of the self that is supposed to occur when the goal is achieved. These depressives attach all sorts of surplus meaning to the end of their quest: they will finally be loved, they will be worthy, they will at last "show the world" how talented they really are. Without this goal, however, they feel unworthy and inferior.

"Dominant goal" depressives were pushed to achieve as children but were not allowed to enjoy the *process* or the inherent aim of their achievements. Their accomplishments were to be used to redeem the family or to prove themselves in the world's marketplace, but not to bring meaning in and of themselves. All other possible areas of esteem and meaning were ridiculed or discouraged through shame and guilt. It is their narcissistic use of an external event (the achievement of a goal), as well as their lack of alternate sources of meaning, that predisposes such persons to clinical depression. When they come up against situations which force them to realize that their goal cannot be attained, they lose all sense of purpose. They believe themselves to be forever unworthy or defective, a view that cannot be tolerated. As Kierkegaard wrote, when the man who has to be "Caesar or nothing" cannot become Caesar, he senses himself to be nothing.

The "dominant other" and "dominant goal" types of depressives suffer from constant apprehension and periods of mild dysphoria for fear of losing their external means of achieving worth, but usually can function without impairment as long as they believe their sources of esteem are intact and realizable. There are some people who are unable to achieve even this pathological mode of obtaining transient satisfaction. These depressives share many characteristics with the previously described types—self-inhibition, anhedonia, and limited means of esteem. They differ in that they derive what little gratification they are capable of by following a rigid code of conduct. They live by a set of strongly adhered-to taboos which allows them little pleasure or involvement. Superficially, they may appear to be highly moral, but in reality their standards are neither rational nor motivated by a conscious sense of ethics. Rather, these people are still blindly following the strict dictates which were inculcated in childhood. Such persons become clinically depressed when faced with certain adverse life circumstances. Some may realize that their mode of life brings them little pleasure, but they find they cannot alter their ways: they are caught by their own beliefs, and any attempt at change brings terrifying anxiety or shame.[2] Others would gladly behave differently and live a more satisfying life but believe it is too late. They feel they are too old to have the romantic love affair they secretly desired or to choose a more rewarding vocation. From an objective standpoint, these people may appear to have become depressed without a discernible cause; their depression seems to be "endogenous." However, close scrutiny, usually after an extensive period of psychotherapy, will reveal that some experience, or series of experiences, has caused them to reevaluate their way of life and to have found it wanting.

Although such evaluations usually occur in middle, or even advanced, age, this form of depression is not infrequent among adolescents or young adults who find that living by the childhood standards of their parents is not applicable, or not satisfying, in the extrafamilial world. Anthony (1975) writes that John Stuart Mill underwent just such a depressive episode in early life when he perceived that abiding by his family belief system would doom him to unhappiness. According to Anthony, Mill asked himself if he would be happy if he accomplished all that his father had asked of him. Mill was forced to answer no, and of that moment of self-confrontation, Mill later wrote, "At this, my heart sank in me; the whole foundation on which my life was constructed fell down . . . I seemed to have nothing to live for." Anthony comments: "He fell ill when he became aware that the realization of his father's aims in life would not satisfy him, and he regained his mental health (to the degree that this was possible) when he understood that the death of the father brought with it the growth of identity, autonomy, and responsibility for the son" (p. 448). Not all such people are as fortunate as young Mill. Many cannot detach themselves from the parental ideal, or cannot concretely change their ungratifying existence.

Psychotherapy

Initial Stage: Course and Confrontation

The first phase of psychotherapy aims at achieving two major objectives: setting a proper course for the remainder of the therapy and helping the patient to become aware of the pathological mode of living which predisposed him to

---

[2]Obviously, these depressed persons are to be differentiated from those who are realistically trapped by external circumstances, such as a chronic or fatal illness or severe socioeconomic deprivation. The latter do not deprive themselves by choice, nor do they suffer from distortions which perpetuate their dysphoria. Finally, while certainly unhappy, they exhibit neither the loss of self-esteem nor the narcissistic need so characteristic of pathological depression.

depression. In most cases, these objectives are immediately threatened by the patient's acute emotional discomfort and persistent requests for magical relief from his dysphoric state. The patient will not consider looking inward but wants only to reiterate his miserable plight. Levine (1965) writes about the patient's "broken-record response"—repetitive complaints which therapists must actively interrupt by introducing new topics. Spiegel (1965) describes how the patient can wear out the therapist by limiting verbalizations to the recounting of symptoms and negative preoccupations. At the same time, the acutely depressed patient will us every means to induce the therapist to offer reassurance and nurturance. The patient will appear so grateful for a message of hope for the future or a word of encouragement that the therapist may believe that such ministrations will cure the patient's depression. However great the temptation may be to comfort a fellow human being, the therapist who offers reassurance or adopts an excessively sympathetic role is setting up a therapeutic relationship that is doomed to failure. Although adopting an initial nurturing role may achieve temporary symptomatic improvement, it will detour the proper course of therapy. The patient will subtly demand more and more until the therapist finds himself in the unrealistic position of shouldering the burden of the patient's everyday life. The therapist feels trapped into giving more and more support without being able to explore the reasons for the patient's behavior. If the therapist then attempts to reinstate a more constructive therapeutic relationship in which the patient assumes responsibility for cure, the patient may become resentful or intensify depressive complaints.

Jacobson (1971) has commented on the pitfalls of allowing an unrealistic preoccupation with and idealization of the therapist to develop. She writes of her therapy with one such patient: "There followed a long, typical period during which the patient lived only in the aura of the analyst and withdrew from other personal relationships to a dangerous extent. The transference was characterized by very dependent, masochistic attitudes toward the analyst, but also by growing demands that I display self-sacrificing devotion in return" (p. 289). Kolb (1956) had also noted that the beginning of treatment with depressives "bears upon the therapist heavily because of the clinging dependency of the patient. The depressed patient demands that he be gratified. He attempts to extract or force the gratification from the therapist by his pleas for help, by exposure of his misery, and by suggesting that the therapist is responsible for leaving him in his unfortunate condition" (p. 589).

In light of these observations, the therapist must communicate a willingness to give full attention and expertise to help patients help themselves without being manipulated into giving reassurances or sympathetic comfort. Nor should the therapist become the focus of the patient's life. From the outset, patients should understand that feeling better is their own responsibility and not an obligation of the therapist. On the other hand, it would be equally counterproductive for the therapist to remain silent and assume a strict analytic posture. That would allow the patient to go on endlessly complaining or, perhaps, to create a grossly distorted transference relationship in which the therapist is seen as a magical, omnipotent helper, an image which will later cause a negative therapeutic reaction when the therapist does not live up to these idealized expectations. Rather, the therapist should be active in the sessions and introduce new themes so as to break the monotonous reiteration of complaints. Also, since most depressives have been raised in an atmosphere of deceit and hypocrisy, it is most important for the therapist to be forthright and honest about his or her own limitations and expectations.

Finally, the therapist should accord patients an expectation of mature behavior and treat them with dignity and respect. Interpretations should represent a shared and equal discovery of relevant information rather than the transmission of insight from a sage to a novice. Patients have to learn to look within themselves by themselves rather than waiting to be told what their difficulties are. Accordingly, transference material is best aired immediately, especially as it embodies patients' attempts to idealize the therapist and to resist acceptance of therapeutic responsibility.

The other major objective of the initial stage of therapy concerns confrontation, meaning that patients are to be helped to become consciously aware of how they had previously structured their belief systems about themselves and others so as to predispose them to depression. This aim is achieved through the interpretation of dream material, timely comments about patients' reconstructions of present and past daily activities, and the analysis of fantasies, hopes, and fears. The therapeutic situation itself may force patients to confront some of their distortions when they unsuccessfully try to turn the therapist into a needed transference figure. This last process is perhaps the crucial one, for it will allow patients consciously to realize their distortions as they are concretely living them out with a person who, in contrast to others, will neither acquiesce to them nor reject them out of hand, but will submit the distortions to analysis.

Eventually, the picture of a basically anhedonic person will emerge, one who, often despite considerable public achievement, has never been able to enjoy any activities or accomplishments. All the talents of the depressive have been harnessed to the need for recognition from selected others endowed with imagined power; or have been centered on some distant goal; or have been stifled for fear of appearing self-indulgent, foolish, or sinful. Human contacts have similarly suffered from the patient's self-inhibitions; others are feared as potential judges or condemned as silly or childish. Interpersonal relationships have usually been characterized by subterfuge, manipulativeness, and control rather than by a free and open exchange of feelings and ideas. The basic theme is clear and repetitive: to dare to be spontaneous or joyful will result in punishment, whether by loss, abandonment, shame, or criticism. The atmosphere is heavily pervaded by sin, accountability, and self-denial, sometimes complicated by a feeling of helplessness and aloneness and a longing for external structure and direction.

As patients are confronted with these basic personality patterns, the hope is that they will begin to understand that their depressive episodes were the result of a pathological lifestyle. As Bonime (1960) has commented, depression should be seen as a *practice* rather than as an episodic illness with healthy intervals. Patients should recognize that if they wish to stop their suffering, they must radically alter their way of constructing their experience and activities. Within the therapeutic relationship patients must identify and confront the underlying causes of their dysphoria before they can begin the difficult process of altering those fundamental systems of beliefs, modes of relating, and manner of experiencing their world that culminated in their depression.

Second Stage of Therapy: Resistance and Change

The patient's realization that his irrational beliefs and distortions of everyday life are ultimately self-defeating or counterproductive does not automatically ensure that his inner self or previous activities will change. Neurotic behavior is never easily relinquished, for these older, well-ingrained patterns have for years offered security, predictability, and even some gratification, albeit transient and inappropriate. To remake one's personality is frightening and involves risk, so it is not surprising that patients will resist change even when they know that it is in their best interests. This process of "working through" is the real battleground of therapy, with frequent advances, retreats, and stalemates. This conflict occurs in the psychoanalytic treatment of almost all pathological conditions but perhaps especially in the therapy of depression, since this disorder so permeates the person's entire being.

The resistances that are seen in depressed patients take the following forms. Some despair over giving up their dominant other or their dominant goal, for they believe that if they eliminate this powerful system of gratification and esteem life will have no meaning whatever. Others fear terrible retribution for deriving genuine, autonomous pleasure from their activities, as evidenced in fantasies of being abandoned, humiliated, or shamed, or fantasies in which others get hurt. For all, enjoyable activities are burdened by guilt and anxiety. For example, a depressed young woman was asked to go on an expense-paid trip as a reward for excellence at her job. She was constantly afraid that her family would die or that some other catastrophe would occur in her absence. This belief was clearly irrational for she often traveled on business without apprehension. Since the latter trips were not for pleasure, she did not feel that they would result in harm to others. It was not her absence, but the fact that she was daring to enjoy herself, that was the root of her anxiety. This magical connection between pleasure and disaster will be found again and again in the dreams and fantasies of depressives. One depressed young man, whose case has been reported in detail elsewhere (Arieti and Bemporad, 1978), started to date as a result of his progress in therapy. However, when he was out enjoying himself with a woman or with friends, he was overcome by the conviction that his father was dying. So strong was this belief that he had to excuse himself and call his parents to see if his father was really all right.

Those patients who complain that their lives are meaningless unless they receive external praise or work toward some grandiose accomplishment may nevertheless find that they can begin to enjoy doing things that they used to forbid themselves. They may begin to read novels, go to movies, spend time with friends, or start hobbies, activities which had once been condemned as unproductive and shameful. These new activities should be encouraged because they represent a change, however small, in the perception of one's self and how one should behave. Often this new conceptualization of the self is first tested in the safety of dreams, sometimes to the alarm of the dreamer.

Such a dream heralded the readiness for change in a depressed young woman after she had realized that it was her whole lifestyle that left her vulnerable to repeated episodes of depression. This woman had been raised by grandparents who were strongly religious and puritanical, and who felt that they were superior to their neighbors (and to people in general). As a child she was not allowed to play with other children after school but had to return home, do her homework, and then receive instructions from her grandmother about the ways of the world. Essentially, these "lessons" stressed that people were evil and dangerous, that temptation lurked everywhere, and that hard work was the only salvation from sinfulness. The patient remembered her childhood with ambivalence: her grandparents' house was big and gloomy, the atmosphere was sterile, she was always afraid of doing something "wrong" that would make her grandparents ashamed of her, yet there was love and acceptance if she obeyed their dictates. Later, there was also a sense of prideful superiority in not being silly or lazy like other children.

It was not until this woman attended college that she began to suspect that her view of life was limited and inappropriate. Away from home, she began to question the family's values as she saw fellow students having fun or enjoying purely creative endeavors. Despite these doubts, she could not bring herself to alter her strict code of conduct and continued to spend almost all of her time studying, at times secretly envying the casual freedom of her peers. She graduated with honors and also won other prizes, but her achievements were perverted by her grandfather, who literally took her diploma, saying that *he* had really earned it since he had paid the bills and she had merely done what was to be expected of anyone who was being supported by someone else. She went along with this line of thinking, even feeling proud that she had pleased him.

After college, this woman got a good job in her field and continued to work hard at her career. But her life consisted of nothing except her work. After a hard day, she would return to her apartment and go over the events of the day, deciding whether she had done a good job, much as she had replayed the day for her grandmother as a child. And like her grandmother, she usually found something she had done "wrong" and berated herself. This was her Monday-through-Friday schedule. On Saturday she ran errands, and on Sundays she spent the day planning the next week's work. In addition, every Sunday she called her grandparents, who somehow managed to "ruin" her day by complaining about their ill health or her lack of gratitude. These calls always left her feeling guilty and worthless.

She became increasingly depressed as she sensed that her life was devoid of gratification. She was desperately lonely, but her fear of what others might do to her prevented any real social involvement. She did have some acquaintances who were dependent on her and used her as a "mother figure" or wise counsel; she thus avoided exposing her own needs, remaining in a superior, if isolated, position. Her work, which was supposed to be her salvation, was becoming a nightmare, as she always expected failure and humiliation. She knew she got little satisfaction from life but felt incapable of changing on her own.

After some months of therapy, during which she was confronted with the basis for her ungratifying lifestyle and pervasive fear of pleasure, she reported the following dream: She was in her grandparents' dark, gloomy house, adjusting a shade so that it would let in more light. Suddenly she was transported to another, unfamiliar house where she was lying on a bed wearing a frilly dress with her hair long and pulled back (as she had worn it as a teenager). She was so startled at seeing herself in this way in the dream that she awakened abruptly with a sense of anxiety.

Obviously, the whole range of associations to this dream cannot be fully reported here. What is important is the sequence of images leading from "childhood self" to "shedding light" (which would make the house less gloomy) to a new (or perhaps old, but repressed) sense of self. In therapy too she was "shedding light" on her earlier self-image and its perpetuation into the present, accompanied by gloom and despair. Therapy revealed the possibility to be someone completely different, a self that may have been secretly desired. The woman on the bed represented sexuality, femininity, dependency, and vanity: all of the terrible "should nots" of childhood. These attributes so frightened the patient that she abruptly awoke. The fact that she was able to see herself in this new light in the dream, however, enabled her to apply the dream content to waking life, and to integrate this estranged self (albeit in a less extreme and pejorative form). Finally, depressives often dream of or recall themselves as adolescents during the initiation of change. During adolescence there may be a normal developmental tendency to rebel against family strictures and define a new identity for oneself. In most depressives, this adolescent rebellion was short-lived and the person quickly fell back into the older pattern of obedience. This transient sense of freedom has not been forgotten, however, and is reactivated in symbolic representations when the patient once again tries to shape an independent self.

Another type of dream which indicates change in the depressed person is one in which a parent dies. In contrast to the Freudian interpretation of such dreams (Freud, 1900), which centers on Oedipal rivalry, for the depressive this type of dream appears to indicate a sense of freedom from the powerful parent. The dominant parent (rather than the same-sexed parent of the Oedipal triad) is disposed of in the dream. Thus, for both male and female patients, it is usually the father who dies in the dream. The following example may be seen as typical of these "death" dreams.[3] A depressed woman in her late thirties dreamed that two women were in a beautiful room. One woman was thin, downcast, and unattractive; the other was beautiful and voluptuous, with intricate tattoos on her body. The voluptuous woman said, "Use my body and I'm happy," and then went into a luxurious bathroom, exuding a great sensual aura. Suddenly, this beautiful woman did something "disgusting," which could not be specified. Then the scene changed to a hospital room where the patient learned from a teenage boyfriend that her father was dying. She felt "sad and horrible" as well as guilty and abandoned; but she could not prevent the death. The boyfriend consoled her and finally told her, "I've always loved you," whereupon the patient awoke in a state of apprehension.

This dream portrays the usual dichotomy between the "good" ascetic image and the "bad" hedonistic self as well as the aforementioned return to adolescence (in the figure of the teenage boyfriend). The dream also conveys that, if pleasure is to be obtained, the father (and the self that was created in relation to him) must cease to exist. In this dream, the woman regains love from an extrafamilial figure, the boyfriend, showing that the father's loss does not mean eternal abandonment but, perhaps, a chance to find intimacy outside the family circle. In real life, the patient's father had actually died years before, but she remained tied to him by following his dictates and by searching for alternate "dominant others" to structure her life as he had in childhood. It is significant that the boyfriend did not fulfill this role; her relationship with him was remembered as a brief interlude of true mutuality that had to be given up out of a sense of duty and shame.

Some of these death dreams portray the futility of continuing to serve the dominant other; in others, there is open rebellion; in still others, there is simply

---

[3]This vignette has been reported previously (Bemporad, 1976).

a sense of resignation—a recognition that the older order has passed and the former authority has been dethroned.

A similar realization may occur in waking life if the dominant other is still alive or if his or her role has been transferred to a new authority figure. An example of the former case occurred during the therapy of a middle-aged executive. He had a "dominant other" type of personality organization and had functioned well in the context of a favored status relationship with his boss. However, he had been transferred to another department where his new boss was aloof and gave his colleagues little feedback. This new superior simply expected everyone to do their jobs and was not concerned with personal niceties. The patient found himself becoming more and more depressed when he failed to elicit the needed reassurance from his new superior. He vacillated between seeing no meaning in his work and getting furious at the company's usually trivial errors, which he now magnified. In therapy, he was able to connect his current plight to his childhood experience of devoting himself to pleasing his father. The latter rarely gave praise and was harshly critical of all the children, but the patient remembered feeling euphoric and important when the father did acknowledge some achievement.

The patient's father was still living and in a nursing home, where the patient visited him regularly. On one occasion, he went to see his father full of high expectations, as he had concluded a very successful business transaction. As he began to describe his accomplishments to his father, however, the latter completely ignored his son's remarks and viciously berated him for wearing a pink shirt, which he considered unprofessional. Such a response from the father was not unusual, but this time, as a result of the work that had been accomplished in therapy, the patient could objectively analyze his initial sense of disappointment and deep feeling of failure for not pleasing the older man. Although this experience led to a transient state of depression, it also revealed to the patient his whole dependent lifestyle—his use of others to supply him with a feeling of worth. This experience added a dimension of immediate reality to the insights that had been achieved in therapy and gave the patient the motivation to change radically his childhood system of perceiving himself in relation to paternal transference figures. This clinical vignette illustrates one of the major objectives of the working-through process: one must perceive usual situations in a new way and then use such insights for the purpose of change.

Actually, most of the process of change is not so dramatic, but occurs in a gradual interplay between the gaining of insights in therapy and the application of this knowledge to everyday life, which in turn leads to new material that serves as a source of fresh insights. The treatment of a young lawyer will illustrate this lengthier and more common type of working through.

This young man's symptoms were chronic episodic depression, migraine headaches, insomnia, and fatigue. His history was typical of most depressives: his father was a tyrannical person who dominated the household but whose love could be temporarily obtained by very hard work; his mother was a childish and ineffectual woman who lived in her husband's shadow; the father stressed achievement and induced shame and guilt for failure or "laziness." The patient's two siblings were also professional men and high achievers.

This young man aspired to be either the United States Attorney General or a Supreme Court Justice. There is nothing inherently wrong with setting one's sights high, but for the patient nothing except his ambition seemed to matter. He worked about seventy hours a week, performing his job in an exemplary manner but deriving little gratification from it. He was extremely critical of himself and others: he had periods of despair when he thought of himself as not smart enough to ascend the ladder of his profession or when he believed he might have alienated someone who could block his rise to success. He was constantly angry at others for not noticing him enough or for not repaying what he believed were obligations to him because he worked so hard. At home, he reprimanded his wife for not appreciating him or pouted in order to elicit care and concern. He genuinely loved his young children but unrealistically expected that they too should show gratitude for his long hours of labor. In essence, he expected everyone both to share in his aspirations (as did his father) and to render privileges and praise for his work (as did his father). He had no idea that other people had their own interests and careers and were not constantly focusing their attention on him. Finally, he had no hobbies or pursuits aside from his legal career. Any diversion from his work had to be repaid by extra studying or writing. He believed that others were keeping a mental tally sheet of his activities and, in the manner of his father, looked on his time away from work with displeasure.

Initially, this patient was confronted with his monomaniacal quest for a lofty goal, which was really his father's goal. He gradually realized that in his pursuit of his ambition he enjoyed fantasies of its achievement but not the process of getting there. His work was drudgery for him because he saw it as only a means to an end and not as an end in itself. Work was also a source of apprehension, as he feared that trivial mistakes would doom his career plans. Finally, he erroneously perceived work as a way to barter for love and force positive reactions from others. This line of inquiry led to an exposure of his distorted view of human relationships: that one extorted obligations from others through hard work, and that everyone judged everyone else.

He began to make some changes in his job by resolving to be less directly involved in the work of his subordinates (possibly much to their relief) and, to his surprise, found that they functioned just as well without his paternalistic meddling. He found that they still respected him and liked him without his having to "take care" of them. He also realized that others in his firm were only peripherally aware of his labors and that, although he was justifiably regarded highly, he could not be angry with others if they did not conspicuously praise his every transaction. Others were simply not his father, nor would they assume that role. He had to learn to reward himself for a job well done.

The implementation of these insights led to a release of tension and an amelioration of his headaches and insomnia. He began to understand how he unwittingly recreated his childhood situation in all of his relationships, therapy included, and connected his periods of depression to occasions when others did not react to him in a predictable, reassuring manner. At the same time, he protested that he was losing control of his life, that he would never achieve his destiny. The therapist interpreted that he was learning a new way of relating to others and a new way of seeing himself, which understandably made him feel vulnerable and anxious since he was giving up the security of his well-worn (if inappropriate) system of obtaining meaning and esteem.

With some trepidation, he began to work less, and was surprised, as well as relieved, to find that his superiors did not really notice if he did not stay late or work weekends as long as his output was satisfactory. On one occasion, he had to pick up his four-year-old son from nursery school, and the young boy, accustomed to seeing his mother, began to cry and protest that he wanted his mommy. The patient felt that the child was ungrateful, since he had had to rearrange his schedule so as to pick him up. After recounting this vignette in therapy, he came to realize how he inappropriately expected gratitude from everybody, even a tired four-year-old, whenever he went out of his way for them. His whole method of setting up situations so that he felt victimized and righteously indignant was explored and applied to his marriage as well as his career. He realized that he used work to blackmail others into fulfilling his needs and related this insight to how his father exploited him as a child by using work to excuse himself from many parental responsibilities.

Eventually, he said that for the first time in memory he felt he had a choice about what he wanted to do with his life. He had always done what was "expected" and never what he really desired, so much so that he had no idea what he actually wanted from his life. He rethought his grandiose career plans and confessed that even being a Supreme Court Justice would give him little pleasure if he continued to structure his existence along the lines of doing for others (namely, his father and his substitutes) and not for himself. Concurrently, he was able to empathize genuinely with others rather than seeing them only as sources of praise or criticism. He enjoyed working and being with others more since he stopped viewing these activities as means to enhance or impede his great quest. At this point, he was free of symptoms, and—free of the many childhood "shoulds"—was on the way to deriving esteem and pleasure directly from a multiplicity of gratifying new activities that would, it was hoped, protect him from depression in the future.

Final Stage: Consolidation

The problems encountered during this phase of therapy may have more to do with external obstacles than internal ones. As patients alter their behavior as a result of therapy, they may find that others in their immediate environment will resent such changes. This conflict is to be expected in most instances of psychotherapeutic change, but perhaps is more deeply experienced by depressives since so much of their illness has been embedded in pathological modes of relating to others. Significant others will unconsciously try to undo what they perceive as irritating and threatening changes that have so transformed what had been, to them, a comfortable relationship. This unconscious resistance may be found in the parents or colleagues of the depressive, but it is most commonly seen in the spouses of older, married depressives. These marital partners truly want the patient to get better and detest the frequent episodes of clinical depression that the patient has had to endure. Yet they do not want to give up the premorbid style of relating which actually predisposed the patient to these depressed episodes. The spouses must become aware of the unfavorable result of their former marital equilibrium to help create a healthier interpersonal system. During this stage of treatment, the therapist may wish to refer the spouse for individual therapy or may wish to see both partners for conjoint therapy. If the latter course is selected, obviously the therapist must be careful not to become the advocate of the patient but must allow the sessions to be used for expression by both partners. This interlocking reinforcement of depression in married couples is so frequent that Forrest (1969) suggests combining marital therapy with individual sessions from the start for optimal results.

Another task of the final stage of therapy is a coming to terms with the ghosts of the past. Too often there is a rapid transition from an idealization of past authorities to a bitter resentment of these same people. The patient should understand that the pathogenic actions of parents (or other childhood influences) were a result of their own pathology and that these childhood idols were just ordinary people with the usual limitations as well as positive attributes. It is most important that the patient appreciate his own willful participation in recreating his childhood situation in adult life, regardless of how he was treated as a child.

The overriding goal of this stage, however, is the consolidation of the changes that have been achieved. Certain superficial characteristics that are indicative of deeper change may help the therapist gauge the patient's improvement. Almost all of these manifestations revolve around the patient's new independence and ability to derive meaning and pleasure directly from everyday activities. For example, creativity bespeaks the confidence to try new things. Spontaneity also reflects an ability to act with assurance—without constantly having to appraise how others will view one's behavior. The ability to take one's failures (and the failures of others) philosophically and with a sense of humor indicates an end to the hypermoral coloring of all events as "good" or "bad." Being able to take failure in stride indicates that the patient does not feel himself evil or worthless if he does not achieve his every objective and, in turn, that his self-esteem is realistically independent of life's vicissitudes. A most important indicator of change is that the patient no longer works only to obtain praise or to master some remote goal, but instead gains satisfaction from everyday life.

Another manifestation of change is a growing interest in others, not for what they can supply to one's self-esteem but because they are important and interesting in themselves. In losing their mainpulativeness, patients may experience true empathy for the first time, seeing others as similar to but separate from themselves. Therapy is then seen as a endeavor which involves sharing and learning, rather than as a constant struggle to obtain needed feedback from a transferentially distorted other. Therapy should remain *the* place where patients can express themselves without fear or shame until they are able to form other such relationships in their everyday life.

Summary

In closing, it may be worthwhile to offer some guidelines for the psychotherapy of depressives.

During the initial phase of treatment, therapists should be careful not to let themselves be set up as a new dominant other or an excessively idealized figure. These transferential distortions will obviously detour the therapy. Nor should they offer undue reassurance despite their natural inclination to help a fellow human being in distress. Finally, therapists must be wary of being worn out by the repetitive complaints of the depressive and should interrupt the patient's litany of misery by introducing new topics that will direct the patient to fresh material that is more likely to lead to insight. Therapists have to be active, forthright, and most important, honest about their own fallibility as well as the limitations of therapy. Patients must understand that they will have to assume responsibility for their own improvement, guided by the professional confrontations and interpretations of their therapists.

Patients must learn to look inward for the reasons for their depression rather than expecting magical relief from external sources. Patients should realize that the painful episodes of depression are a direct result of a pathological lifestyle that must be altered. Once this connection is appreciated, therapists can begin to confront depressive patients with their distorted systems of beliefs, interpersonal relations, and self-inhibitions.

Guidelines for the second phase of therapy involve the handling of resistances and the enhancement of change. The therapist should not be threatened by patients' protestations that giving up pathological modes of obtaining esteem will result in a total lack of meaning from life. Nor should the therapist accept patients' convictions that disaster will ultimately follow any attempt to derive an independent sense of meaning or pleasure. Novel (or previously repressed) beliefs and activities are to be encouraged, as are new ways of viewing the self. Often a healthier state of self is initially formulated only in the safety of a dream. Such self-conceptions can be used to demonstrate to patients their own inner resources for change, if patients will allow themselves to apply the wisdom of their dreams to their waking lives.

More frequently, a reported vignette from everyday life can be used to illustrate that patients have a choice in continuing to adhere to a depression-prone mode of being—that they can begin to make changes that will ultimately lead to a healthier and happier existence. In summary, patients should eventually consider the renunciation of their former mode of being not as a loss but as a liberation. This profound change is gradual and time-consuming and often tests the patience of the therapist. Optimally, there will be a self-reinforcing process: therapeutic insights will lead to changes in behavior outside the office that, in turn, will create new experiences which, when reported to the therapist, will form the basis for newer insights, thus repeating the cycle.

The ultimate aim of therapy is to liberate depressive patients from their rigid belief systems and to allow them to be receptive to the genuine novelty of life. In essence, their everyday lives can be curative if they can learn to experience themselves and others without the crippling distortions that have for so long robbed their lives of true meaning and authenticity.

REFERENCES

Anthony, E. J. (1975), Two contrasting types of adolescent depression and their treatment. In: *Depression and Human Existence,* ed. E. J. Anthony and T. Benedek. Boston: Little, Brown.

Arieti, S. (1962), The psychotherapeutic approach to depression. *Amer. J. Psychother.,* 16:397.

——— & Bemporad, J. (1978), *Severe and Mild Depression.* New York: Basic Books.

Bemporad, J. (1976), Psychotherapy of the depressive character. *J. Amer. Acad. Psychoanal.,* 4:347.

Bonime, W. (1960), Depression as a practice. *Contemp. Psychiat.,* 1:194.

Forrest, T. (1969), The combined use of marital and individual psychotherapy in depression. *Contemp. Psychoanal.,* 6:76.

Freud, S. (1900), The interpretation of dreams. *Standard Edition,* 4 & 5:1–627. London: Hogarth Press, 1957.

——— (1917) Mourning and melancholia. *Standard Edition,* 14:243–260. London: Hogarth Press, 1957.

Jacobson, E. (1971), *Depression.* New York: International Universities Press.

Kierkegaard, S. (1849), *The Sickness unto Death.* New York: Anchor Books, 1954.

Kolb, L. C. (1956), Psychotherapeutic evolution and its implications. *Psychiat. Quart.,* 30:1.

Levine, S. (1965), Some suggestions for treating depressed patients. *Psychoanal. Quart.,* 34:37.

Slipp, S. (1976), An intrapsychic-interpersonal theory of depression. *J. Amer. Acad. Psychoanal.,* 4:309–410.

Spiegel, R. (1965), Communication with depressed patients. *Contemp. Psychoanal.,* 2:30.

CHAPTER 15

Curative Factors
in the
Psychotherapy of Schizophrenic Patients

Theodore Lidz and Ruth W. Lidz

The editor of this volume has confronted us with the challenging task of presenting the curative factors in the psychotherapy of schizophrenia—a disorder that many psychiatrists consider incurable, and certainly untreatable by psychotherapy. We believe that schizophrenic disorders are primarily psychogenic (see Lidz and Lidz, 1949, 1952; Lidz, Fleck, and Cornelison, 1965), and have learned from our work with patients and our supervision of younger therapists that psychotherapy can foster critical changes in schizophrenic patients' understanding of themselves and ways of relating to others so that many can thereafter lead reasonably normal and sometimes highly successful lives. Cure? Well, we know a number of chronically schizophrenic patients who have recovered more completely than have many severely neurotic analysands. This woman who had been delusional, paranoidally fearful and antagonistic for several years while in excellent psychiatric hospitals is now a tenured professor in a leading university. This young woman who became psychotic shortly after starting college was transferred to the Yale Psychiatric Institute from another private hospital after her condition deteriorated. Now, after three or four years of psychotherapy, she is far more capable of leading an independent and well-organized life than she was before she became psychotic. Enrolled in a leading conservatory, she is again on her way to becoming an outstanding musician. Those who have followed the transformation of withdrawn, disorganized, and delusional patients into well-functioning persons know that psychotherapy can accomplish what no other treatment of schizophrenic patients has even approached.

We have not started the chapter with these paragraphs simply as a profession of faith, but because in the tradition of William James we consider that when we cannot know in advance just how much is determined by circumstances beyond our control and how much by our effort and will, the belief in the possibility of succeeding is one of the factors that can produce success: the antecedent belief in the possibility can be important in bringing about the actuality (James, 1907). The therapist's confidence in the potential efficacy of his efforts is an essential ingredient in the treatment of schizophrenic patients, particularly as psychiatric tradition is weighted heavily against psychotherapy. Belief in the efficacy of psychotherapy is not the curative factor, but without it psychotherapeutic efforts have little chance of success.

The Revision of Psychoanalytic Approaches

The increase in our understanding of the nature and origins of schizophrenic conditions has altered our psychotherapy considerably and provided clear goals and guidelines toward achieving those goals. Psychotherapy no longer consists of efforts to bestow unconditional love to offset the hypothesized maternal rejection; or providing symbols of nurture in the manner of Sechehaye (1951), or making early and constant interpretations of the patient's supposed projective identifications as carried out by Rosenfeld (1965) and others of the Kleinian school; or making intuitive "direct" and "deep" interpretations in the style of John Rosen (1947); or permitting the patient to live through the psychosis with minimal interference as Laing has taught (see Boyers and Orill, 1971; Evans, 1976) in the belief that the patient will emerge more imaginative and complete than before the psychosis.

Indeed, although the psychotherapy of schizophrenic disorders has derived largely from psychoanalysis, it has had to free itself from certain constraints of psychoanalytic theory and technique. Of course, without an understanding of unconscious processes and primary-process cognition, pre-Oedipal development and the crucial importance of the Oedipal transition, as well as of repression, fixation, regression, and projection, the psychotherapy of schizophrenics could only have been carried out in a rather simple and primitive way. However, both the theory and practice of psychoanalysis were derived largely from the analysis of neurotic patients and are not fully suited to the understanding of schizophrenic patients, or even to many of the seriously disturbed persons who currently are grouped together in the diffuse and ill-defined category of "borderline disorders."

Freud's concept that schizophrenics' narcissistic withdrawal of libido prevented the formation of transference relationships which made their analysis impossible kept most analysts from working with schizophrenic patients. It took many years and a willingness to disregard the opposition of psychoanalytic colleagues for Sullivan, Fromm-Reichmann, Lewis Hill, and others in the Baltimore-Washington area (aided by the influence of Adolf Meyer and John Whitehorn) to demonstrate that even though a schizophrenic patient could not develop a transference, a therapeutic relationship could be formed. The theory that schizophrenic disorders were due to fixations at the early oral phase of development led many analysts to try to compensate for the hypothesized early infantile rejection or deprivation. Although most analysts who have worked with schizophrenic patients modified classical techniques, most have found it difficult to free themselves of some techniques that are not simply of little value but are actually countertherapeutic. Psychoanalytic technique with its relative passivity, waiting, maintenance of anonymity, fostering of free association, emphasis on interpretation by the analyst, the search for the sources of distortions only within the patient, and the analyst's isolation from the patients' relatives can all impede, if not prevent, the development of a productive therapeutic experience, for reasons we shall examine.

The new guidelines that permit the psychotherapy of schizophrenic patients to become increasingly successful derive from the development of theory based on work with schizophrenic rather than neurotic patients, and particularly from studies of the families in which schizophrenic patients grew up (Lidz and Lidz, 1949, 1952; Reichard and Tillman, 1950; Frazee, 1953; Bateson et al., 1956; Wynne et al., 1958; Alanen, 1960, 1966; Lidz, Fleck, and Cornelison, 1965). Here we can only indicate the modifications in theory that have so greatly influenced the understanding and therapy of schizophrenic patients.

A Conceptualization of Schizophrenic Disorders

It is necessary to grasp how this disorder which virtually eliminates ego functioning—the ability to direct one's life—need not be the result of neural dysfunction but can be a type of personality maldevelopment. We consider schizophrenic conditions to be types of withdrawal from living with others; from responsibility for making decisions concerning unsolvable problems; from the incestuous or murderous impulses toward a parent who blocks movement toward individuation and individuality; and particularly from experiencing the unbearable pain, disillusionment, emptiness, and hostility of being deserted or betrayed by those one needs and has sought to love. Schizophrenia is not simply a withdrawal into a fantasy world; also it is an escape by breaking through the confines set by the language and meaning system of the culture without which one is scarcely human. When these essential constraints (upon which paradoxically the human potentialities depend) are disrupted, the screening functions of categories and concepts dissolve and the patient is flooded by inappropriate associations, deeply repressed intercategorical polymorphous perverse childhood fantasies, and regressions to childhood preoperational or preconceptual magical and egocentric thinking. It is an orientation that does not consider the origins of schizophrenic disorders to be unknown, but rather that such disorders are anticipated anomalies in the developmental process of humans who depend so greatly on those who raise them for their security, socialization, gender identity, superego formation and to guide their learning of language upon which persons depend so greatly to be able to think clearly, reason, direct their own lives, and collaborate with others.

The Family in Human Development

As psychoanalysts, our orientation to human development and its pathology has been greatly modified by our psychotherapeutic work with schizophrenic and borderline patients and their families. In contrast to the explicit and implicit assumptions of psychoanalytic theory and the so-called "medical model," the emergence of an individuated, reasonably integrated adult at the end of adolescence depends on far more than proper physical and emotional nurture and freedom from physical and emotional traumata. Humans are unique among all living organisms in that most of their basic adaptive techniques are not inborn but must be acquired from those who raise them. Homo sapiens emerged essentially by the selecting out of mutations that progressively increased the capacity for tool bearing and language. Language enabled humans to convey what they learned to future generations so that knowledge became cumulative and cultures developed. Unless we realize that humans are born with a dual endowment—a genetic inheritance and a cultural heritage—we can never understand their functioning and malfunctioning correctly. We must also recognize that human beings' capacities to think, make decisions, and plan toward future goals depend on the proper acquisition of a language. People everywhere learn the basic techniques for survival and for living with others within a family or some planned substitute for it. For such reasons the family is an essential concomitant of the human biological makeup. In order to develop into a reasonably integrated adult, the child must receive considerable positive input from the family. We cannot in this chapter concerned with psychotherapy enter upon the family's requisite functions for rearing children, and must refer the reader to previous writings. The family's child-rearing functions can be categorized under the headings of (1) nurture, (2) the structuring of the offspring's personality, (3) basic socialization, (4) enculturation, including the proper guidance of language development, and (5) providing models for identification for the child to internalize (Lidz, 1963).

Deficiencies of Families of Schizophrenic Patients

Careful studies of the families in which schizophrenic patients grew up (Lidz et al., 1965; Alanen, 1966) have shown that these families are incapable of carrying out adequately any of the requisite functions, which results in many serious deficiencies in the offsprings' personalities which leave them vulnerable to both disorganization and regression.

Moreover, the families that produce a schizophrenic offspring are found to have particular characteristics that interfere with the final stage of the separation-individuation process at the end of adolescence. Schizophrenia is essentially a disorder of mid- and late adolescence; when the onset occurs later in life, it is found the patient had never adequately surmounted the critical developmental tasks of adolescence. Adolescence is the critical period when individuals undergo a marked change in their relationships with their parents and should virtually complete the lengthy process of separation from them to achieve individuation as reasonably well-integrated, self-sufficient, and self-directed persons capable of relating intimately with someone outside the family. It is a time when parental directives become self-directives but modified by the ways of other idealized figures. Persons who become schizophrenic have been unable to accomplish such developmental tasks, not simply as a result of maternal rejection or oversolicitude in early childhood, or because of some innate incapacity to develop stable object relationships, but because the family transactions throughout their formative years were seriously disturbed and distorting, and failed to provide them with the essentials for development and individuation by the end of adolescence or early adult life. The basic difficulties seem to derive from the egocentricity of one or both parents, who could not relate to the child as having feelings, perceptions, and wishes discrete from the parent's, but rather who needed the child to remain an adjunct who could complete and give meaning to the parent's life (Lidz, 1973a).

In one type of family (Lidz et al., 1957) that is particularly characteristic of families of male schizophrenics, one parent, usually the mother, cannot properly differentiate her own feelings, needs, and perceptions from those of her child; she expects the child to remain a part of her and provide a sense of completion to her life which is unsatisfactory largely because she has little regard for herself as a female. The mother's ways of relating to her children and rearing them are not countered by the father who is passive or ineffectual within the family. Children, especially sons, raised in such families may be unable to overcome the symbiotic tie to the mother, have problems with gender identity, and fear their incestuous impulses when they reach adolescence. They lack an adequate male figure with whom to identify and follow into adulthood.

In another type of family that is more common among female than male schizophrenics, the parents have been caught in an irreconcilable conflict, compete for the loyalty of the child, undercut one another's worth, and provide opposing directives to the child. The child is caught in continuing binds (Weakland, 1960), as satisfying the directives of one parent provokes rejection by the other. In each of the above family types, as well as in admixtures of the two, parental gender roles are reversed or confused, generational boundaries are broken, Oedipal attachments are fostered rather than resolved, and the intrafamilial communication fragmented, amorphous, and in some respects irrational. Further, the atmosphere of the home is pervaded by a sense of futility, a hopelessness about ever gaining any real satisfaction from marriage or family life (Lidz et al., 1958; Wynne and Singer, 1963a, 1963b; Singer and Wynne, 1965a, 1965b).

Developmental and Regressive Schizophrenic Disorders

Some patients have grown up within families that were so seriously disturbed, so lacking in essentials, and communicated so vaguely or aberrantly that the patients have never been able properly to emerge from the family nexus as independent children or adolescents and may be considered *developmental* schizophrenics akin to "process" schizophrenics. It seems likely that when the onset is in early or mid-adolescence, the mother has had particular difficulties in fostering the patient's individuation from her, and because the father fails to stand between the child and the mother, the Oedipal ties burgeon into incestuous ones. However, many schizophrenic patients function reasonably well within the family while dependent on parents for making decisions and are sheltered within the family, but become perplexed, lost, and unable to cope with independent living. When unable to surmount the developmental tasks of late adolescence, they not only regress to an anaclitic or symbiotic dependency but also return to preoperational, egocentric, magical forms of thinking in which the filtering functions of categorical cognition are lost (Lidz, 1973b). These patients my be termed *regressive* schizophrenics, akin to "reactive" schizophrenics. In addition to the serious problems that existed in their families throughout the patients' lives, the parents may be particularly "binding" (Stierlin, 1974) when their adolescent child needs to move beyond the family. Developmental and regressive schizophrenia are not separate entities but polar paradigms. Most schizophrenic patients fall somewhere on the continuum between these poles.

The Central Therapeutic Task

A therapist gains definitive guidelines for therapy when he recognizes that schizophrenic patients' inabilities to overcome their symbiotic ties to a parent to become individuals with firm self-boundaries and capacities to direct their own lives derive primarily from parental difficulties in releasing them and from the deficiencies and distortions of the families in which they grew up. The central therapeutic task—perhaps in view of the title of this volume we should say, the essential curative aspect of therapy—lies in releasing these patients from the bondage of completing a parent's life, or of bridging a parental schism to enable the patients to invest their energies in their own development and to develop boundaries as distinct persons capable of making decisions and accepting responsibility for their decisions. The therapist consistently and persistently seeks to foster patients' latent desires for individuation; and through the therapeutic relationship counters their fears of rejection if they assert their own needs or express the hostile side of their ambivalent feelings. The therapist needs to provide support when these patients face their fears of independence and the unbearable emptiness they suffer if they become responsible for their own lives. The therapist confirms the patient's worth as an individual through considering the patient's feelings and perceptions as potentially useful guides to living. This usually means that the patients must come to realize that their parents—whom the patients believed knew the way and why of living—were themselves struggling to retain their emotional equilibrium and had rather aberrant ways of perceiving and relating. When schizophrenic patients become capable of regarding their parents and the intrafamilial environment differently from the ways their parents needed and required of them, and begin to trust their own perceptions and feelings instead, they will have moved a long way toward emergence from their psychoses.

We have stated the crucial objectives that the psychotherapist strives to achieve and keep in mind through the many vicissitudes in his relationship to the patient; but how to pursue them with a patient who has withdrawn into his own world, who has no interest in therapy or a therapist, who pays more attention to voices the therapist cannot hear than to what the therapist says or does, whose words no longer adhere to conventional meanings, and whose understanding of his or her experiences is delusional? Even when some sort of relationship is established, therapeutic efforts are beset by difficulties in communication, sudden reversals in attitudes toward the therapist, inordinate expectations and demands that can dishearten the therapist sufficiently to drop psychotherapy in favor of neuroleptic drugs or to turn the patient over to a therapist more masochistically inclined than himself.

Establishing a Therapeutic Relationship

The first task is to establish a therapeutic relationship with the patient. As it became evident that a therapeutic relationship could be established with schizophrenic patients, some analysts insisted that the schizophrenic did not form a transference relationship but rather, a dependent, anaclitic one. We believe that this argument is essentially correct and leads to some of the basic problems encountered in working with schizophrenic patients. The therapist's recognition that the patient, despite fear of engulfment and desire for an independent existence, also seeks to become dependent again on an omniscient and omnipotent person who can solve his problems and provide nurture and protection in an alien world, provides guidelines both for establishing a relationship, as well as for maintaining and for developing it into a more mature relationship. The understanding clarifies why a therapist's overcommitment—including efforts to provide all-encompassing love and to make interpretations for the patient rather than finding them together—can be detrimental. A basic task confronting the therapist is that of transforming the patient's anaclitic relationship into a proper object relationship, or at least into a relationship in which the patient can examine his life together with the therapist and begin to assume responsibility for himself.

Gaining Trust

Thanks to the moderate use of neuroleptic agents—the dosage must be kept moderate for heavy dosages interfere with cognition—as well as improvements in milieu therapy, the therapist today is only rarely faced with a patient who is mute, unresponsive, or wildly excited for months. The essential problem is to gain the trust of a patient who has—because of disillusionment with significant persons, despair over the present, and hopelessness about the future—withdrawn into a private world and regressed to childhood ways in which preoperational magical thinking seems to bestow power to control events. When patients can tentatively trust the therapist not to desert when needed or use them for the therapist's prestige or self-esteem, patients will once again take the chance of suffering the pain of disillusionment because the loneliness of their self-imposed isolation is difficult to endure.

Trust is established through the therapist's interest, thoughtfulness, and efforts to understand the patient's dilemma and grasp what the patient seeks to convey even as he or she seeks to hide thoughts and feelings. Human relationships rest on communication, verbal and nonverbal, and the therapist often faces the difficult task of finding a way of establishing communication with a person who is using an idiosyncratic language. This is not the time for the therapist to remain aloof and, following analytic technique, act as a passive screen against which the patient can react. The patient is lost, and hope and trust must be rekindled. The anxiety provoked by a therapist's relative unresponsiveness is more likely to paralyze than energize. The schizophrenic patient is ever alert to pretense, which may include the therapist's hiding behind a prescribed role. These patients will usually respond only to a real person who is interested in them as individuals—as individuals who are confronted by problems that seem insurmountable, but which the therapist and patient are trying to understand together. The therapist must differentiate between being kindly and being condescending; remembering that even when a psychotic patient acts like a child or infant, he is not a child, and much less an idiot. There is also need to differentiate between being tolerant and understanding and being indecisive and weak. The patient usually needs the security of a firm and assured therapist. Although the patient has withdrawn for self-protection, the therapist must assume that, like all persons, he or she wishes to be understood, respected, and able to share again with another.

Avoiding an Omniscient Role

The therapist's recognition of the patient's symbiotic or anaclitic ways of relating can help establish a relationship that will not collapse because the patient becomes disillusioned. Even though the patient may have attained some degree of independence, when regressed, he or she will seek an omniscient figure who will provide answers, make decisions, and omnipotently provide security in a dangerous world. Therapists who take charge and direct the patient's life, as well as those who make striking intuitive interpretations of the patient's unconscious processes, may achieve brilliant initial results, but they base the relationship on means they cannot sustain, and sooner or later the patient will once again become disillusioned and withdraw. These patients, like the small preoperational child, are incapable of ambivalence (rather than suffering from ambivalence as Eugen Bleuler [1930] believed). They tend toward "splitting," considering a satisfying person "good" and a depriving or punishing person "bad"; and when the omniscient therapist does not understand or fails to protect, he is "bad." Although the schizophrenic patient initially may relate well to a therapist who presumes to know the answers, who directs, and who provides the greatly needed affection, it plays into the patient's belief that someone else knows the way and will care for him magically. Indeed, the need is usually so great that the patient places the therapist in this role even when efforts are made to avoid it. Ultimately, frustration turns the benevolent therapist into a malevolent figure, for the omnipotent figure fails to protect. The therapist must try from the very start to avoid being considered omnipotent, on the one hand, and being like the parents in needing the patient, on the other. Overprotecting, or giving the impression of intuitively or mystically understanding the patient, fosters one need, while masochistically accepting the patient's unbridled demands or condemnations fosters the other. The therapist must be ready to go a long way and even inconvenience himself to help the patient, but must avoid controlling as well as being controlled by passive measures. The strength that a therapist must convey to the patient may well derive from having sufficient integrity not to need to be infallible. The therapist does not insist or even imply that he is "right" and the patient is "wrong," for the therapist's willingness to consider that he may be wrong, annoyed, or may have inadvertently hurt the patient helps the patient become aware that more than one meaning can be placed upon an incident and prepares the way for the patient to overcome his cognitive egocentricity.

The Therapist as Participant Observer

Examining life situations and the therapeutic relationship together *with* the patient, as Harry Stack Sullivan taught, rather than making interpretations *to* the patient is important for several reasons beside avoiding being placed in an omniscient role. The patient had in all likelihood been told how to think and feel by his parents, and the patient must be encouraged to think for himself. The patient is likely to agree with an interpretation but pay little heed to it, or he may disagree in an effort to preserve his autonomy. Examining the therapeutic relationship as well as the patient's past experiences together indicates the therapist's consideration of and respect for the patient's opinions and abilities, which may be a very novel experience for the patient. This approach is especially helpful with paranoid patients, who can participate in analyzing situations but cannot let others tell them what something means or trust another to direct their lives. Above all, the therapist seeks to work in an alliance with the patient, and to avoid an adversary role despite provocation.

Clarification of Schizophrenic Communication

The patient's communications are likely to be vague and confused by magical thinking and intrusive associations. The therapist is under no obligation to understand, but he is obligated to listen and try to hear what the patient seeks to convey or to conceal. Rather than interpret, the therapist tries to clarify what the patient says in a way that the patient can follow. The psychiatrist may comment, "From what you have been saying, do I understand that you mean—" or "Yesterday you said so and so but today you say— Are you uncertain about how you feel?" As progress is made, firmer means of clarification may be warranted: "You have said this—and this—and this. It seems to me that this all means—"

In general, the therapist does not shy away from topics mentioned or even hinted at by the patient because they seem too touchy at a particular stage of therapy. Schizophrenic patients are likely to assume that the therapist hears everything, and if the therapist avoids a topic, it must be completely unacceptable. The topic or concern is at least acknowledged and the patient told that they can consider the matter when the patient feels ready to do so. Knowing how to make comments that will be meaningful to the patient who is ready to discuss a certain topic but can be passed over by the patient who is not ready is a therapeutic skill that one must cultivate in work with seriously disturbed patients. Thus, when a patient talks of the craziness and confusion of the hospital unit without showing any indication of being upset by it, his therapist comments, "You seem to feel quite at home here." The patient accepts the phrasing and goes on to discuss the disorganization of his home—a topic he had sedulously avoided a week earlier.

Free association has little if any place in the treatment of schizophrenic patients, as least not until the patient has clearly emerged from the psychosis and is continuing therapy better to understand his life. The patient who is likely to be flooded by extraneous egocentric associations and primary-process material, and to regress to preoperational cognition, needs first of all to regain the filtering function of categories and the use of shared meanings and syntax. The therapist seeks to strengthen the patient's ego functions rather than to encourage nebulous fantasy or rumination. For related reasons, anxiety is not fostered to gain therapeutic movement, for stimulating the sympathetic nervous system lowers the neurophysiologic stimulus barriers which can increase cognitive disorganization. When the patient becomes anxious or hostile when discussing or thinking about something, it is taken as a sign that he must decide what to do to alleviate such feelings. Feelings of anxiety and hostility are welcomed as directives that indicate a need to examine a circumstance so that the patient can find ways of changing it, or his attitude toward it.

Further, in contrast to the analysis of neurotic patients, the therapist does not analyze patients' defense mechanisms so much as the distortions imposed by the parents' defenses of their own tenuous egos. Efforts are made to imbue in patients trust in their own ideas and feelings, while questioning those that are essentially the parents' feelings and percepts that patients offer as their own. Patients are usually sensitive and responsive to the therapist's ability to differentiate the two. "I don't understand why I had this breakdown," the patient said. "I've a good family, loving parents and a fine, healthy brother and sister." "I wonder who told you that," muses the therapist. The therapist seeks to foster patients' self-esteem and trust in their own ideas and feelings, which they have been taught to eschew in favor of what their parents projected onto them.

Finding a Working Distance

It is essential for the therapist to find and maintain a suitable distance for working with the patient, to be friendly and supportive and at the same time counter the patient's tendency to conceive of him as an ominiscient and all-powerful protector. It is almost impossible, however, to find a distance that is satisfactory to the patient that will not also lead to some difficulties. Many patients who have a desperate need for closeness have at the same time an extreme fear of it, and become panicky over fears of fusion, engulfment, and loss of the self. At times any deep interest may be considered a promise of all-protective love, and earlier incestuous wishes can turn into an expectation of a sexual relationship or marriage with the therapist. On the other hand, patients may believe that their own basic malevolence, or the negative side of their ambivalence can kill the therapist they need so desperately, and therefore fear closeness. The "How are you?" with which a patient opened each session was not a casual greeting; it was accompanied by a haunted, scrutinizing look to see if the psychiatrist was surviving the danger of the patient's sucking neediness.

The difficulties in finding a proper distance involve countertransference as well as transference problems. Therapists require firm self-boundaries to avoid confusing their own needs with those of the patient and to resist being over-whelmed by the patient's hopelessness, despair, and demands. Therapists can-not, like the patient's parents, need fulfillment through the patient, or convey that their well-being or future depends on their patient's recovery. There is a critical difference between the therapist's being warm, giving, and highly inter-ested, and letting the patient become significant on a personal rather than professional level—a difference that can be difficult to maintain when the patient demands love and throws out the challenge, "You don't love me; I don't mean anything in your life, I'm just a patient to you." Therapists properly have other sources of love, persons other than patients who provide meaning and solidity to their lives; and in the long run the patient gains security from know-ing it. In any long-term therapy with a patient who gives evidence of being reborn because of the therapist's efforts, the patient is almost certain to become very important to the therapist. The relationship is far from casual for the ther-apist, but the "love" should be "parental" in the sense of pleasure and even pride in the patient's growth and increasing independence, and should convey that the therapist will be pleased when the patient can emerge from the rela-tionship with, and need for, the therapist, and thus counter the earlier "bind-ing" and "engulfing" love of the patient's parents.

Closure of the Therapeutic Relationship

The therapist necessarily becomes extremely important to the patient. In general, the desire for an intense anaclitic or symbiotic relationship modifies over the course of therapy, and the therapist becomes a model for identifica-tion, a stable model with clear boundaries and clear thinking, in contrast to the parental models. This is one reason why the patient needs the therapist to be a real person. Eventually, the patient internalizes the therapist as something of a superego figure with whom to carry on imaginary conversations to reach decisions or to gain support, even long after therapy has ended (Rubenstein, 1972). In some respects the transference is not worked through completely, as is attempted with neurotic patients. Patients may need to retain the belief that, if serious difficulties arise, the therapist will be there to help extricate them. Some former patients write or telephone from time to time simply to be certain that the therapist is still alive and potentially available.

Working with the Patient's Actual and Tangible Problems

One of the most important contributions that family studies have made to the psychotherapy of schizophrenic disorders is simply that therapists can be certain that schizophrenic patients face very real problems in their current life situation, problems that either concern the long-standing difficulties in the family transactions or rather clearly derive from them. It is on these very real and tangible problems that the therapist seeks to focus as soon as feasible. It is here, rather than with the interpretation of delusional material, or the patient's projective identifications, or other intrapsychic processes, that the therapist starts as soon as feasible. An awareness of what sorts of difficulties confronted patients when they became psychotic helps the therapist hear what they may be wishing to convey even as they seek to conceal, and provides suggestions of how best to respond in order to foster a therapeutic relationship. The keys to such awareness derive from several sources: material from studies of the transactions in the families of schizophrenic patients; knowledge of the preoccupations, fears, and conflicts common to many schizophrenic persons; awareness of the characteristic times of onset; and how these can all interrelate.

Characteristic Times of Onset

There are several critical junctures in development at which schizophrenic disorders are likely to appear. When the onset occurs shortly after puberty, the patient is apt to be so deeply enmeshed in a symbiotic relationship with the mother that relationships outside the family are precluded. The first remark of one such patient to her therapist was, "I can't walk without my mother." Further, the symbiotic bond leads the new sexual impulses into incestuous channels, a direction fostered by one parent's incestuous proclivities and the inability of the other parent to stand between the patient and the seductive parent. The frequency of onset shortly after the patient leaves home for college or the armed forces is related to the parents' inability to consider that their child can manage on his own and make decisions by himself, much as in school phobia; to the lack of adequate integration to replace the structuring provided by the family; and the lack of capacities to relate to and communicate with strangers. Another time of onset—so common that it is difficult to realize that it had not been recognized until rather recently—is when the parents divorce or are seriously considering divorce. The patient then feels hopeless about ever becoming free of the obligation to complete the life of a parent, panic-stricken because the divorce fans the incestuous fantasies fostered by the nature of the parent-child interaction, and, in some cases, feels torn between the parents but also hostile about being deserted. The precipitation of the psychosis by the later loss or threatened loss of a needed person usually reflects an earlier, poorly integrated desertion by a parent.

The therapist can be certain that some such precipitant has occurred and that serious intrafamilial situations exist that are central to the patient's dilemma. Moreover, the therapist can feel confident that the problems are neither beyond the reach of a psychotherapeutic approach, nor that they can only become accessible after prolonged analysis. Such confidence is essential because the therapist must arouse some hope in a patient who has given up coping with life and the important persons in his life. From family studies and our own extensive experience, we feel warranted in saying that the therapist can be certain that serious intrafamilial problems always exist. Further, the nature of the difficulties may become apparent to the heedful at the initial interview with the parents. It is on such tangible problems that the therapist seeks to focus as soon as feasible—which, of course, may be many months. The therapeutic effort is directed toward bringing the patient to consider the life situations from which he or she has been fleeing and not to foster flight from them by working with delusions, fantasies, and "free" or random associations. As intriguing as the patient's bizarre communications, delusional contents, or polymorphous perverse fantasies may be, the therapist is apt to be tapping a bottomless well that enriches the therapist but does not much benefit the patient unless the material is used to clarify current real dilemmas. As Freud taught, delusions are restitutive measures and are needed by the patient until the serious life impasses have been examined and understood, if not overcome; delusions are rarely resolved by uncovering their unconscious meanings. However, patients cannot be expected to face the life situations that precipitated a psychosis until they can again trust someone—usually the therapist—not to desert them in their need and can believe that the therapist will not reject them after learning the nature of their impulses and fantasies, but will be able to understand, will be able to survive their malignant feelings, and support them in their despair. The remark a patient made when her therapist sought to have her face the impact of the turmoil that preceded her parents' divorce is critical. The patient said, "You must be even crazier than I am if you think I'm going to let myself experience that despair again."

Preparedness to Hear Primitive Material

On the basis of experience with other patients as well as the collective experience of other psychotherapists, the therapist is prepared to hear material which schizophrenic patients initially may allude to in veiled ways to find out if the therapist can accept the dark, forbidden feelings that the patient has been unable to accept but which keep intruding and disturbing him or her. As therapy progresses material is likely to emerge that is far more primitive and bizarre than that produced by neurotic patients. Fantasies or delusions of sex change are frequently present in schizophrenic patients; incestuous ideas seem to verge on emergence into action rather than have the quality of fantasy, for actual or near incestuous relationships are common in these families; murderous hostility toward a parent makes the patient seek to avoid the parents; polymorphous perverse fantasies, including cannibalistic notions or desires to drain a supportive figure by fellatio, emerge and may need to be heard lest the patient believe he is beyond help if not beyond consideration. Such material involving the therapist, if unanticipated, can lead the therapist to take distance from the patient. On the other hand, if it can be used as a guide in therapy rather than as an indication of abnormality, it can provide the patient with new motivation. Thus, a young woman's fantasy of being locked in a tight embrace with her therapist with each biting into the other's jugular vein and sucking blood from it led to a clearer understanding of the intertwining of her aggressive rage with her need for fusion, of how the fantasy arose before the therapist's vacation, and thence back into a new understanding of her feelings toward her symbiotic mother who fed on the patient while feeding her. A much more focused therapeutic relationship could then follow.

Utilization of Information from and about the Family

It is important that the therapist does not limit the content of talks with the patient to what he learns from the patient, or act as if that is all he knows, for in the treatment of virtually all schizophrenic patients information is also obtained from relatives. Patients do not know the customs of psychoanalysis and properly assume that the therapist knows a good deal about them, and that the therapist's failure to talk about such matters is part of the mysterious conspiracy against them. The therapist needs information from the family and about the family, including impressions of the parents and how they relate to one another and their children. Some therapists prefer to gain an impression of the parents themselves, but others feel more comfortable having a social worker see the family. Of course, the patient must be informed that the family is providing information, but that the therapist is interested in the patient's version of events which, at least in many ways, has greater pertinence. Openness and directness are a therapist's major protection against being included in a patient's delusional system. If the patient is also in conjoint family therapy, as is often the case, what happens in family sessions should be considered grist for the mill in individual therapy. There is no reason, for example, why the therapist should not say to a patient who talks primarily about her delusions that her parents believe her troubles started after they forbade her to visit her boyfriend's home.

Patience

In the course of trying to establish a relationship with patients who are unwilling or unable to discuss their life situations, the therapist may usefully talk of a relatively neutral topic of known interest to the patient, and preferably a topic that permits a patient to utilize an asset. Patients who block or become incoherent when they try to talk about their problems may become interested and chat meaningfully about a relatively impersonal topic. Their talk or behavior during a bridge game or at a football game may be entirely different from that during a therapeutic session. A therapist spent several months discussing Renaissance painting with a withdrawn and flagrantly delusional graduate student of art history—discussions that became increasingly animated and focused and which gradually turned into the patient's talking about the frustrations caused by her mother's efforts to push her into another field and then about how her mother had always intruded into her life.

Understanding the Patient's Life

In general, the therapist seeks to understand the patient's life; what blocked the patient's individuation and integration; what interfered with his capacities to overcome the problems of adolescence or to cope with one or more critical problems. The therapist's curiosity about filling the gaps that interfere with understanding makes the therapy a very active—that is, a mentally active—affair. The therapist not only listens and lets his own unconscious meet the material, as Freud taught, but also formulates to himself various alternative meanings to be verified, modified, or discarded in the future. The therapist puzzles over how a patient's remark fits in with earlier material and conjectures; what comment or query can lead the patient to amplify, make connections, or clarify; what comment might counter the patient's egocentric understanding of an event or help foster ambivalence (as opposed to splitting); what comment might increase the patient's self-esteem, and so forth. Once the patient also becomes curious and puzzled, both patient and therapist are likely to do a good deal of work between sessions, and then silent or sterile therapeutic sessions become rare as both await an opportunity to clarify a bit more of what has been perplexing. When the therapist finally understands, the patient also will have gained understanding along with the therapist, and in the process will have learned much about thinking things through independently. The patient who has avoided thinking for fear of unbearable anxiety, hostility, disillusionment, or depression learns that such emotions can be used as signals that something is deeply troubling; that their source must be sought and an effort made to change the troubling situation or relationship. By helping patients sort out problems and possible ways of coping with them, the therapist helps them learn to make decisions—a critical aspect of ego functioning—but the decisions are to be made *by* the patient, not *for* the patient, except in emergencies.

Anticipating Disruption of Therapy

The therapist who appreciates the patient's anaclitic or symbiotic needs can anticipate various setbacks that might disrupt therapy. Commonly, just as the patient seems to be forming an attachment to the therapist and the therapist dares to feel hopeful, the patient flees—sometimes from treatment, sometimes into a more regressed condition. Therapists can become profoundly discouraged and give up in actuality, or through losing their commitment to such patients, or by deciding to rely on pharmacotherapy. If, however, the therapist expects patients to flee because of fears that his or her growing attachment will again leave the patient vulnerable to disillusionment and despair, and the therapist refuses to be discouraged or pushed away, a major hurdle will have been passed and a firmer relationship will almost always follow.

Conversely, after a firm therapeutic relationship has been established, when the time comes for the patient to take a step toward increased independence—for example, when a hospitalized patient is permitted greater freedom or anticipates discharge—a resurgence of anxious emptiness occurs and the anaclitic depression that had been covered by the psychotic symptoms becomes apparent. The regressive flare-up of symptoms, and perhaps the efforts to find protective closeness or fusion by sexual acting out, can set back the therapeutic process unless anticipated and focused on in psychotherapy, with the therapist temporarily providing increased support. The appreciation of the anaclitic core of these patients' problems also permits us to understand the admixtures of schizophrenic reactions with amphetamine and LSD psychoses, anorexia, and nymphomania that have changed the phenomenology of adolescent schizophrenic disorders so greatly in recent years.

It is at such times of movement toward increased independence that the therapist must be prepared to provide the patient with greater support. Support does not mean showing affection, or directing the patient's life, or making decisions for the patient. Rather, the therapist may let patients know in advance that they may become anxious or feel deserted, while reassuring them that the therapist believes they can take the step and that the therapist will be available to talk about what is happening. The therapist supports by firmness in expecting the patient to confront the difficulty, look at the anxiety or depression as a sign that something is amiss, and together with the therapist explore possible ways of dealing with it. The therapist further supports by seeing to it that the patient does not undertake more than he or she can reasonably expect to accomplish. The psychiatrist is also aware that it is at such times when the renewed insecurity may lead patients to recall matters that had been troubling them at the time they became psychotic, that critical problems can be worked through.

Anticipating Parental Disruption of Therapy

An understanding of the family situations of schizophrenic patients can help overcome a common major impediment to successful treatment: the parent's premature and often abrupt removal of the patient from the hospital or from psychotherapy. Here the parents rather than the patient need help, and a therapist who feels that his contact with parents must be minimal requires a collaborator to cope with the parents' concerns. The symbiotic mother is very likely to believe that the patient cannot survive without her care and may suffer from such intolerable anxiety that she will take the patient home unless someone understands her predicament and helps alleviate her anxiety. A second cause of parental disruption of therapy has to do with a parent's fear that the patient's attachment to the therapist will disrupt the child's dependent relationship with the parent. A third occurs when the patient begins to show overt hostility to one or both parents, which they rather naturally regard as an indication of a worsening condition rather than as a move toward improvement, particularly if the therapist has avoided the parents or been hostile to them. Then, too, the parents may need to have a sick child at home to serve as a scapegoat—the apparent source of the family's unhappiness who masks the parents' incompatibility—or to provide some meaning to the parents' life.

Understanding Parents' Problems

The therapist's recognition that the parents' egocentricities, narcissism, attitudes, and ways of relating to the patient are important determinants of the patient's schizophrenic disorder sometimes leads him to regard the parents as villains who have ruined the patient's life. The patient's illness is far more tragic to the parents than to the therapist; and the therapist must realize that their noxious influences were not malevolent, but the outcome of their own personal tragedies and emotional instabilities. They are no more to blame for their inadequacies than the patient is to blame for being schizophrenic. One or both parents requires support in order to be able to release his or her retarding hold on the patient. Neglect or hostile exclusion of the parents often leads to aggravation of the patient's condition even though the psychiatrist may believe such action protects the patient from their malignant influence.

Treating the Thought Disorder

The thought disorder is the critical attribute of schizophrenic conditions and requires specific psychotherapeutic attention. The thought disorder has usually been considered to result from primary-process intrusions, a concomitant of regression, and that with resolution of the patient's emotional problems, the primary-process thinking would subside. The thought disorder is a far more complex process, however, and involves regression to childhood precategorical forms of magical thinking, the paranoid mistrust taught in the home, the parents' failure to inculcate a solid grounding in the culture's system of meanings and logic, paralogical efforts to elude double-binding situations, intrusions of intercategorical polymorphous perverse material, egocentric misunderstandings, an inability to feel ambivalently, projection of unacceptable impulses, and extrojection of poorly integrated parental introjects.

Therapists seek to be consistent and clear in what they say and attempt to clarify patients' vagueness. They help counter patients' overinclusiveness and enhance their focal attention by establishing definite boundaries between patient and therapist and foster such boundary formation between the patient and others. The patient's egocentric interpretations are countered by suggesting other ways of understanding events, and the capacity for ambivalence is fostered by working with the patient's shifts from love to hatred, and from acceptance to rejection to enable the patient to grasp that feelings about others are commonly ambivalent. We have focused specifically on finding ways of freeing patients from distorting their perceptions and meanings to fit their parents' aberrant ways of experiencing. As we have already emphasized, it is a difficult but vital aspect of therapy, and once accomplished, the patient is out of the mire and on more solid ground.

The Need for a Comprehensive Therapeutic Approach

This chapter has been concerned with the curative aspects of psychotherapy, and we have focused on individual psychotherapy. However, the treatment of most schizophrenic patients does not rest on psychotherapy alone but is much more comprehensive (Lidz, 1973a). The chance that these persons can change profoundly to become integrated individuals capable of leading satisfactory lives has been greatly improved by the development of neuroleptic drugs, modern milieu therapy, and family therapy. Tranquilizers and milieu therapy have not made psychotherapy unnecessary but have made it more feasible and often more successful. To treat schizophrenic patients without considerable attention to the family in actuality, particularly in youthful patients, and to the internalized parental figures in all patients, is to neglect the essence of the problem.

Family Therapy

One very substantial advance has been the advent of family therapy, which may take many forms. Those who have conducted conjoint family therapy with the families of schizophrenic patients soon become aware of how closely intertwined are the distorted personalities and relationships in these families, and that often little movement can be expected in the patient's therapy unless there are shifts in the family's equilibrium or disequilibrium. With older patients, conjoint family therapy may not be necessary or possible, but individual therapy should focus on how the disturbed family transactions have affected the patient. Unless the therapist is alert to the fact that serious family problems exist, as they always do with such patients, they may never be brought into therapy because patients may not recognize the abnormalities of the transactions in the families in which they grew up, or because they need to preserve a positive image of their parents.

The Therapeutic Community

Understanding patients against their families' background leads to an appreciation of the importance of the modern psychotherapeutic community in providing the necessary facilities. The common current practice of brief hospitalization and discharge of the patient on heavy tranquilization derives either from the belief that schizophrenia is basically incurable or from an awareness that widespread patient neglect in institutions fosters permanent regression. The proper traditional role of the mental hospital has been to provide a "retreat" from the life stresses that contributed to the psychosis. We now realize that the youthful patient also needs to be removed from the distorted and distorting family setting. Patients who have been unable to find an ego identity or to function as reasonably autonomous persons are granted a moratorium during which they are relatively free from parental intrusions and the need to make critical decisions, and during which they can marshal their inner resources and utilize therapeutic guidance. Hospitalization provides opportunities for patients to learn to relate more readily to others; to see other points of view and thereby modify their own egocentricity; to gain social skills that have not been learned in the family; to be in group therapy where they may see problems similar to their own in others before they can see them in themselves and from the group processes become more capable of making decisions; and through family therapy gain a new orientation toward their parents as well as having the opportunity for the parents to modify their attitudes and the family transactions.

Young patients need to continue their schooling in a special school that takes into account their limited attention span and the intrusion of hallucinations, egocentric thinking, and their conceptual difficulties. When patients are hospitalized, therapists are no longer working alone. Others share the problem of delimiting the patient while at the same time improving the patient's socialization. The intensity of the anaclitic dependency is modified by the presence of other significant therapeutic figures, and the opportunity to relate to persons of the opposite sex from the psychotherapist can be very helpful.

Neuroleptics

The use of tranquilizing drugs can be a major factor in recovery when properly used, but it can also be a major impediment when overdone. The acutely psychotic patient whose anxiety and agitation are quieted by drugs may not need to find delusional answers to his perplexity; the disorganized patient is less overwhelmed by extraneous stimulation and distraught ideas. But it is virtually useless to try to conduct meaningful psychotherapy with a patient who is receiving heavy doses of tranquilizers, and using drugs to enable seriously disturbed and delusional patients to leave the hospital interferes with their chances of developing, socializing, and overcoming the psychotic state.

The studies of patients against the family backgrounds in which they grew up have increased appreciation of the need for a comprehensive program of treatment, particularly for socializing experiences and for modifying parental attitudes as well as the patient's attitudes toward the parents. However, we believe that psychotherapy, and usually individual rather than group or family psychotherapy, forms the core of the treatment. The therapeutic relationship enables patients to emerge from disillusionment and despair to dare to trust and relate again—then to rework their intrapsychic relationships to the significant persons in their lives in order to separate from them and gain the ego strength to direct their own lives.

REFERENCES

Alanen, Y. O. (1960), "Uber die Familiensituation der Schizophrenie-Patienten. *Acta Psychother.*, 8:89–104.

Alanen, Y. O. (1966), The family in the pathogenesis of schizophrenic and neurotic disorders. *Acta Psychiat. Scandin.* (Suppl. 189), 42.

Bateson, G., et al. (1956), Toward a theory of schizophrenia. *Behav. Sci.*, 1:251–264.

Bleuler, E. (1930), Primare und sekundare Symptome der Schizophrenie. *Z. ges. Neurol. Psychiat.*, 124:607–646.

Boyers, R., & Orill, R., Eds. (1971), *R. D. Laing and Anti-Psychiatry.* New York: Harper & Row.

Evans, R. (1976), *R. D. Laing: The Man and His Ideas.* New York: Dutton.

Frazee, H. E. (1953), Children who later become schizophrenic. *Smith Coll. Stud. Soc. Work,* 23:125–149.

James, W. (1907), *Pragmatism: A New Name for Some Old Ways of Thinking.* New York: Longmans, Green.

Lidz, R. W., & Lidz, T. (1949), The family environment of schizophrenic patients. *Amer. J. Psychiat.*, 106:332–342.

—— & —— (1952), Therapeutic considerations arising from the intense symbiotic needs of schizophrenic patients. In: *Psychotherapy with Schizophrenics,* ed. E. B. Brody & F. C. Redlich. New York: International Universities Press.

Lidz, T. (1958), Schizophrenia and the family. *Psychiat.*, 21:21–27.

—— (1963), *The Family and Human Adaptation.* New York: International Universities Press.

—— (1973a), *The Origins and Treatment of Schizophrenic Disorders.* New York: Basic Books.

—— (1973b), Egocentric cognitive regression and a theory of schizophrenia. In: *Psychiat.*, Vol. II, ed. R. de la Fuente & M. Weisman. Proceedings of the Fifth World Congress of Psychiatry, Mexico City, 1971. Amsterdam: Excerpta Medica International Congress Series.

—— et al. (1957), The intrafamilial environment of schizophrenic patients, II: Marital schism and marital skew. *Amer. J. Psychiat.*, 114:241–248.

—— et al. (1958), Intrafamilial environment of the schizophrenic patient, VI: The transmission of irrationality. *AMA Arch. Neurol. Psychiat.*, 79:305–316.

——, Fleck, S., & Cornelison, A. (1965), *Schizophrenia and the Family.* New York: International Universites Press.

Reichard, S., & Tillman, C. (1950), Patterns of parent-child relationships in schizophrenia. *Psychiat.*, 13:247–257.

Rosen, J. (197), The treatment of schizophrenic psychosis by direct analytic therapy. *Psychiat. Quart.*, 21:3–25.

Rosenfeld, H. A. (1965), *Psychotic States: A Psychoanalytic Approach.* New York: International Universities Press.

Rubenstein, R. (1972), Mechanisms for survival after psychosis and hospitalization. Presented at the Annual Meeting of the American Psychoanalytic Association, Dallas, Texas.

Sechehaye, M. (1951), *Symbolic Realization.* New York: International Universities Press.

Singer, M. T., & Wynne, L. C. (1965a), Thought disorder and family relations of schizophrenics; III: Methodology using projective techniques. *Arch. Gen. Psychiat.*, 12:187–200.

—— & —— (1965b), Thought disorder and family relations of schizophrenics; IV: Results and implications. *Arch. Gen. Psychiat.*, 12:201–212.

Stierlin, H. (1974), *Separating Parents and Adolescents: A Perspective on Running Away, Schizophrenia, and Waywardness.* New York: Quadrangle.

Weakland, J. H. (1960), The "double-bind" hypothesis of schizophrenia and three-party interaction. In: *The Etiology of Schizophrenia,* ed. D. D. Jackson. New York: Basic Books.

Wynne, L. C., et al. (1958), Pseudo-mutuality in the family relations of schizophrenics. *Psychiat.*, 21:205–220.
———— & Singer, M. T. (1963a), Thought disorder and family relations of schizophrenics; I: A research strategy. *Arch. Gen. Psychiat.*, 9:191–198.
———— & ———— (1963b) Thought disorder and family relations of schizophrenics; II: A classification of forms of thinking. *Arch. Gen. Psychiat.*, 9:199–206.

CHAPTER 16

Toward the Resolution of Controversial Issues in Psychoanalytic Treatment

Lloyd H. Silverman and David L. Wolitzky

Our aim in this chapter is to consider four controversies that are either explicit or implicit in the previous chapters and to outline research strategies that might be used to help resolve them.[1] The four issues are the relative therapeutic efficacy of a focus on: (1) problems of the "self" versus conflicts over libidinal and aggressive wishes, (2) Oedipal versus pre-Oedipal conflicts, (3) transference versus nontransference interpretations, and (4) the therapeutic atmosphere versus insight.

These issues are encountered frequently, whether explicitly or implicitly, in current writings on the theory and technique of psychoanalysis and psychoanalytic psychotherapy. They are issues that, as we shall argue below, cannot be resolved adequately through further case studies based on psychoanalytic treatment as it is typically conducted.

I

Psychoanalysis probably has been more preoccupied than any other scientific discipline with its status as a science. Its self-consciousness in this regard

---

[1]Since dealing with all the issues raised in the preceding chapters would be an impossible task, we have selected those that, in our judgment, are most central to psychoanalytic treatment and are sufficient to illustrate the research strategies discussed later.

can be inferred from a couple of simple observations. First, a steady flow of articles through the years (e.g., Brenner, 1968; Joseph, 1975; Gaskill, 1979; Kaplan, 1979) has proclaimed that psychoanalysis *is* a science. And second, the "paper sessions" listed in the programs of psychoanalytic conventions and meetings of local psychoanalytic societies typically contain phrases such as "scientific papers" or "scientific sessions"—designations that undoubtedly would be unnecessary at a convention of physicists. We suggest that assertions of this kind simultaneously reflect the intense desire of psychoanalysts to obtain greater scientific status for psychoanalysis (in our opinion an admirable goal) and a kind of illusion based on wishful thinking that this status already has been achieved (hardly admirable).

We think it likely that these "demonstrations" by pronouncement have been resorted to because, as analysts, we have underlying doubts about "our science" (as Freud called it). Recent years have seen a number of cogent attacks on the seemingly scientific concepts of Freudian metapsychology (e.g., Gill, 1976; Holt, 1976; Klein, 1976; Schafer, 1976). These developments, in the context of the proliferation and increasing popularity of other schools of therapy (especially behavior therapy) over the past two decades, have made many analysts sensitive to the question whether psychoanalysis can properly be called "scientific."

We believe, however, that it *is* possible to adopt an effective scientific approach to the validation of psychoanalytic hypotheses. We share the view of such writers as Klein (1976) and Gill (1976) that metapsychology is not the essence of psychoanalytic thinking. We can therefore grant credence to the criticisms of metapsychology, note that its assumptions are untestable, and concentrate on developing and testing the data-generated "clinical theory" (Klein, 1976) of psychoanalysis. And whatever the complex factors underlying the increasing popularity of other systems of therapy, there is no evidence that their approaches are more efficacious, particularly with regard to the kinds of emotional problems typically dealt with in psychoanalytic treatment.

In our judgment, where psychoanalysis can be legitimately faulted is in its failure to develop theory and practice in accord with existing scientific principles and procedures that it is possible to follow. The minimal requirements for any discipline that aspires to be a science include: (1) making the "raw data" of observation accessible to all interested observers; (2) stating clear and falsifiable hypotheses; and (3) establishing rigorous methods of testing these hypotheses as the means of resolving disagreement. Unfortunately, these standards have been ignored by most psychoanalysts.

The first two standards are easier to meet than the third, and in recent years a few psychoanalytic investigators actually have taken steps toward meeting them (see Gill et al., 1968; Wallerstein and Sampson, 1971; Sampson et al., 1972; Rubinstein, 1975). The third requirement poses many thornier difficulties, so it is not surprising that it has received relatively little attention. What has made such avoidance possible is a deeply ingrained attitude among many analysts that, in conducting a psychoanalysis, one is concurrently carrying out research. Since Freud spoke of psychoanalysis as simultaneously a method for investigating the mind, a theory, and a treatment technique, it became easy for psychoanalysts to avoid the distinction between "search" and "research." Stated otherwise, they failed to make the distinction between the "context of discovery" and the "context of justification" (Reichenbach, 1938), and have maintained that in their clinical practice they are not simply generating hypotheses about patients but also testing these hypotheses.

While the main thrust of Freud's writings suggest that he believed that the clinical hypotheses of psychoanalytic theory could be tested within the analytic situation, on at least one occasion he acknowledged the limitations of the psychoanalytic method as a scientific procedure. In his introductory remarks to his discussion of Little Hans (1909) he wrote:

It is true that during the analysis Hans had to be told many things that he could not say himself, that he had to be presented with thoughts which he had so far shown no signs of possessing, and that his attention had to be turned in the direction from which his father was expecting something to come. This detracts from the evidential value of the analysis; but the procedure is the same in every case. For a psychoanalysis is not an impartial scientific investigation, but a therapeutic measure. Its essence is not to prove anything, but merely to alter something. In a psychoanalysis the physician always gives his patient (sometimes to a greater and sometimes to a lesser extent) the conscious anticipatory ideas by the help of which he is put in a position to recognize and to grasp the unconscious material. For there are some patients who need more of such assistance and some who need less; but there are none who get through without some of it [p. 104].

Freud's comment can be viewed as casting doubt on the assumption that a patient's productions are a reliable means of judging the correctness of an analyst's interpretations and understanding.

Brenner (1976), in elaborating the opposite position, introduces distinctions between "conjecture," "interpretation," and "understanding." The term conjecture refers to "an analyst's formulation in his own mind about a patient's psychic conflicts," whereas interpretation is "what an analyst tells his patient about his psychic conflicts" (p. 3). Brenner reserves the term understanding for conjectures that are "strongly enough supported to seem quite certainly correct" (p. 3).

But how does an analyst know when he has moved from a conjecture to an understanding? Brenner states, "Psychoanalysts, like other scientists, must have some way of putting their conjectures to test" (p. 41), and he properly rejects the view that awareness of a conjecture is equivalent to proving it. But to what, then, can the analyst turn to validate or support a conjecture? Brenner suggests four types of evidence: (1) the patient repeats the same behavior on which the initial conjecture was based; (2) the patient confirms a prediction the analyst makes based on an earlier conjecture; (3) the patient convincingly acknowledges the analyst's interpretation; (4) a heuristic reconstruction from a source outside the analysis confirms the interpretation—this last, according to Brenner, a relatively rare event. In addition to the four main criteria listed above, Brenner also refers to other indices of validity: the emergence of new analytic material (e.g., memories); expressions of surprise and other affective reactions; parapraxes; "confirmatory associations"; and "confirmatory actions."

If Brenner had presented these guidelines in the spirit of a *proposal,* i.e., suggesting criteria that could be used in the treatment situation to validate conjectures that psychoanalysts make about patients, we would view his paper as a significant step forward. For such a spirit would imply that one should develop operational definitions for the various criteria and propose ways in which the reliability and validity of analysts' judgments could be tested. However, Brenner seems to be saying that his criteria have already proved to be reliable and valid, and that a method is now available that allows psychoanalysts to operate scientifically in the clinical situation.

By taking such a view, Brenner seems to be glossing over the complex issue of validating analytic hypotheses, as is clear in his inclusion of "confirmatory" associations and actions in his criteria of validity. The very use of the word "confirmatory" begs the question. Even if we set aside for the moment such thorny issues as suggestion and patient compliance, it is not at all clear how associations come to be regarded as confirmatory. For example, how does one decide whether to accept at face value the emergence of pre-Oedipal content following an interpretation of a defense, or whether to view such content as a further defensive reaction to underlying Oedipal issues? It is too easy to "find" supporting evidence for a conjecture, particularly if an analyst is invested in a particular hypothesis—a not uncommon occurrence (see Spence, 1976).

To consider a more topical example, would it really be a cut-and-dried matter, as Brenner's thesis implies, to decide whether a reported pattern of masturbatory behavior expresses a conflict over particular wishes or an effort to experience greater cohesion of the self? In short, one has to ask, "What is an observed fact during psychoanalytic treatment?" It is not the behaviors per se (and we include here the verbal productions of patients), but rather, the *meaning* the analyst assigns to the behavior, that validates a conjecture or interpretation.

Brenner's position that the treatment situation has proved itself as a vehicle for testing and validating psychoanalytic clinical propositions is contradicted by the following evidence. First, the many longstanding controversies among psychoanalytic clinicians strongly suggest that psychoanalytic clinical observers have great difficulty in agreeing on how the productions of patients are to be "read." Second, in the few formal studies (e.g., Seitz, 1966) of this "consensus issue," the results have been most discouraging. Thus, in Seitz's study, when a group of analysts (trained at the same institute, which, if anything, should have increased the chances of their arriving at a consensus) were presented with the same material from a patient's analysis, the degree of reliability in their judgments of what unconscious conflicts were being expressed was disappointingly low.

The available data seem instead to support the view of Kubie (1952), who maintained that the data generated by typical psychoanalytic practice "give rise to controversies, but they are hardly the stuff out of which fundamental scientific advances can be fashioned" (p. 118). It is important to note that Kubie did not regard the validation of psychoanalytic propositions as impossible in principle, but only as impossible within the usual treatment situation. He thus advocated setting up a research institute for the study of psychoanalysis that could devote itself to correcting deficiencies in gathering and assessing clinical data (e.g., establishing a better data base than notes taken after sessions, and improving clinical follow-up studies) and devise other research methods to test clinical psychoanalytic propositions. The present chapter has been written in the spirit of Kubie's proposal.

II

What are the treatment issues that divide psychoanalytic clinicians? Many could be listed, but we will limit ourselves to the four stated at the outset, about which differences are particularly sharp and clear.

(1)   In interpretation, what weight should be given to "self problems" in contrast to conflict over unconscious wishes? This question has been a major divisive issue among psychoanalytic clinicians since the publication of Kohut's first book (1971), and controversy has greatly intensified following the publication of his second book (1977). The substantive point in question is the following. Traditionally, psychoanalytic clinicians have viewed conflict over libidinal and aggressive wishes as the central problem in all nonpsychotic psychopathology. Kohut has challenged this view, at least for one (substantial) group of patients—those he refers to as "narcissistic personality disorders." For this group, according to Kohut, the pathogenic agent is not conflict over unconscious wishes, but rather, deficiencies in the sense of self (or what Kohut terms "self structures") resulting from early experiences of unempathic parenting. (Problems in the sense of self have been recognized before by psychoanalytic clinicians, but they have been viewed as the result of conflict over unconscious impulses.)

The response to Kohut in the psychoanalytic community has been very mixed. On the one hand, there are those (e.g., Stein, 1979) who reject his central thesis entirely and maintain that conflict over impulses is no less central in the psychopathology of narcissistic personalities than it is in the psychology of other (nonpsychotic) persons. Others (e.g., Wallerstein, 1979; Stolorow and Lachmann, 1980) accept Kohut's formulation but view its applicability as limited. Here, the criticism of Kohut is that, whereas his thesis legitimately applies to one group of patients, he has overextended it and sees too many patients as suffering from a deficient sense of self. At the other end of the continuum are some followers of Kohut (Goldberg, 1978) who seem to have extended the applicability of Kohut's formulation to an even larger group of patients than Kohut has applied it to.[2]

(2) What weight should be given to Oedipal versus pre-Oedipal conflict in the analyst's interpretions? Putting aside the question whether, or to what degree, self problems should be viewed in Kohutian fashion, where it is agreed that interpretation of libidinal and aggressive wishes should be the focus of treatment, there is considerable divergence about whether Oedipal or pre-Oedipal conflicts are more deserving of attention. At one end of the continuum are clinicians like Fairbairn (1952) and Guntrip (1961), who view virtually all behavior from a pre-Oedipal perspective. Thus Fairbairn has written:

I have departed from Freud in my evaluation of the oedipus situation as an explanatory concept. For Freud, the oedipus situation is, so to speak, an ultimate cause; but this is a view with which I no longer find it possible to agree ... I now consider that the role of ultimate cause, which Freud allotted to the oedipus situation, should properly be allotted to the phenomenon of infantile dependence [p. 120].

Note that Fairbairn is not speaking here of particular patients or particular conditions but is completely rejecting the view that psychopathology can be rooted in Oedipal problems.

There are some clinicians who accept Fairbairn's characterization of infantile dependence (or other pre-Oedipal wishes) as the predominant pathogenic agent, with the amendment that Oedipal wishes act as an occasional agent. Others believe that there are substantial numbers of both Oedipal and pre-Oedipal patients, and still others claim that in many, if not most, patients, *both* Oedipal and pre-Oedipal conflicts are centrally involved. Finally, at the other

---

[2]Kohut himself appears somewhat ambiguous concerning the explanatory scope of his self psychology. On the one hand, he advances the view that self psychology is better suited to explain certain phenomena (e.g., varieties of narcissistic disturbance) while traditional Freudian theory offers a better explanation of other phenomena (e.g., Oedipal conflicts). At the same time, he suggests that concepts from self psychology offer superior explanations even of phenomena (e.g., masturbation) explained by traditional Freudian theory.

end of the continuum are clinicians like Brenner (1974), who view Oedipal conflict as the crucial issue for the vast majority of patients.

Some of the Oedipal versus pre-Oedipal controversy is focused on particular types of patients. For example, among those who reject the Kohutian understanding of "narcissistic personality disorders" and view conflict over unconscious wishes as the pathogenic agent, there is a further split between those who implicate Oedipal conflict and those who view pre-Oedipal conflict as causative. Representing the former position is Wangh (1974), whereas Kernberg (1975) describes these same kinds of patients as struggling with pre-Oedipal "oral envy" and "oral rage." Similarly, while most analysts view most depressions as of pre-Oedipal origin, Brenner (1974) writes: "in my experience, the clinical facts contradict the prevalent view that unconscious conflict associated with depressive affects in later life must be pre-Oedipal. For most [depressed] individuals it is the Oedipal phase that is crucial" (p. 30).

(3) What weight should be given to nontransference as opposed to transference interpretations? This issue has been explored in detail by Leites (1979). He notes that in recent years many analysts have been tending to limit themselves to "transference interpretations," a term that has come to refer "not so much to the genetic interpretation of the current transference attitude as . . . of an attitude toward the analyst which is at the moment active but unconscious or . . . preconscious" (Stone, 1967, p. 48), referred to by some as interpretion of the "here and now" transference. The position of the most extreme segment of this group (with Merton Gill [see Chapter 6] their most articulate spokesman) is well-captured by Leites in two sections of his book entitled, "Is All Transference?" and "Is Transference All?"

With regard to the first question, the group of analysts just referred to assume that virtually all patient productions are dominated by, if not exclusively the expression of, veiled references to the analyst. Their second assumption, which follows from the first, is that the *only* effective (i.e., mutative) interpretations in psychoanalytic treatment are (here and now) transference interpretations—i.e., those exposing the hidden meanings behind the veiled references to the analyst. Other interpretations are, according to this school of thought, at best ineffective and at worst damaging to treatment. In the words of Gitelson (1962), "the analyst plays into . . . resistance by directing interpretations [to other things] rather than to the [here and now] transference" (p. 266).

On the other hand, Leites cites other clinicians who believe there is considerable value in nontransference interpretations (i.e., those referring to the patient's past or present life outside of treatment). Leites cites papers by Rosen (1955), Neiderland (1965), Heimann (1977), and Schafer (1977), in which nontransference interpretations appeared to elicit important material from patients. Whereas this latter (more inclusive) position probably characterizes the practice of most psychoanalytic clinicians, there is wide variation in the *degree* to which nontransference interpretations are made. For some they are clearly the exception, for others they are the rule, with all points in between represented by different segments of the "psychoanalytic community."

(4) What weight should be given to fostering a therapeutic atmosphere in psychoanalytic therapy in addition to offering interpretations? Let us spell out this issue in some detail.

There is no disagreement among psychoanalytic clinicians that the chief role of the therapist is to offer interpretations and make whatever other interventions are necessary (e.g., clarifications, confrontations, and questioning) to pave the way for interpretations.[3] Moreover, there is no dissent from the view that in offering interpretations, the psychoanalytic clinician should be objective and nonjudgmental, an attitude that is part of the "interpretive stance." But there is disagreement about whether maintaining this interpretive stance is enough, or whether something more has to be done either to make interpretations more effective or to supplement them.

Again, differences among psychoanalytic clinicians can be viewed on a continuum. At one end are those who clearly believe that for all patients something more is needed—the "something" most often having been conceptualized as a "working alliance" (Greenson, 1967), a "therapeutic alliance" (Zetzel, 1956), or a "holding environment" (Winnicott, 1965; Modell, 1976). These conceptualizations are not identical but they share the view that something additional must be created in the therapeutic atmosphere if the analyst's interpretations are to have maximum effect and if patients are optimally to "work through" their conflicts.

Other psychoanalytic clinicians believe that special attentiveness to the therapeutic atmosphere is important only for certain types of patients. Fleming (1975), for example, notes that with patients who have experienced "early object deprivation" it is important to provide some symbiotic gratification and, toward that end, "how useful wordless sounds of response from the analyst can be" (p. 754).

Nacht (1964) also suggests that the analyst help such deprived patients experience a degree of symbiotic satisfaction. He writes that "It seems necessary to me when this [symbiotic] need is too strong ... that the [analysand] should be enabled to experience it at least fleetingly in analysis. ... [If gratified] the patient will find ... a new peace and strength which will prove valuable for achieving normal relationships" (p. 301).

While changes achieved in this way might be viewed by some analysts as resulting from a "corrective emotional experience" rather than from the psy-

---

[3]See Levenson, Chapter 5, for an exception to this statement.

choanalytic process as it is usually conceived, Nacht makes clear his belief that the symbiotic experience can stimulate the analytic process as well.

From [then] on, the explanations and the interpretations of the analyst will be accepted and experienced altogether differently . . . verbal interventions will . . . be received in a different manner . . . the words will form roots in [the patient's] deepest being and will bear fruit, whereas before they were virtually lost, almost as soon as they were heard [p. 302].

At the other end of the continuum are clinicians (Arlow, 1975; Kanzer, 1975; Brenner, 1979) who view any behavior by the analyst that goes beyond the adoption of an interpretive stance as not only unnecessary but as likely to interfere with the analytic work. Brenner, for example, after reviewing Zetzel's (1956) and Greenson's (1967) concepts of the therapeutic and working alliances, concludes: "I am convinced by all the available evidence that the concepts of therapeutic and working alliance that have been current in the psychoanalytic literature since 1956 are neither valid nor useful" (1979, p. 149). On the basis of his reading of Zetzel's and Greenson's cases as well as Leo Stone's (1961) widely cited book, *The Psychoanalytic Situation,* Brenner believes that any departure from a strictly interpretive stance is likely to provide gratification to patients that will interfere with the analysis.

III

The issues we have outlined not only bear on various aspects of psychoanalytic theory but are crucially involved in determining the fate of psychoanalytic treatment. A psychoanalyst's position on the first two questions—self problems versus conflict over impulses, and Oedipal versus pre-Oedipal conflict—will obviously influence the kind of interpretations he or she makes. If we accept the psychoanalytic assumption that treatment outcome depends in large measure on the insights a patient develops into the specific psychodynamic and genetic roots of his pathology, and if we agree that such insights are based on analytic interpretations, the accuracy of these interpretations is obviously important.

Similarly, with regard to transference versus nontransference interpretations, Rangell (1978), Gill (Chapter 6), and Leites (1979) make it clear that in their minds the degree to which each type of interpretation is made (a point on which they disagree) plays an important role in determining the effectiveness of treatment. And clinicians such as Zetzel (1956), Stone (1961), Greenson (1967), Arlow (1975), Kanzer (1975), and Brenner (1979) believe that one's conception of the proper atmosphere for psychoanalytic treatment (about which they disagree) plays an equally important role in outcome.

Since these issues are important ones for psychoanalytic clinicians, it is appropriate to ask what systematic investigations have been brought to bear on them. In a word, extremely few. With but a few significant exceptions (see Luborsky and Spence, 1978), psychoanalytic clinicians operate as if their theoretical and clinical differences will resolve themselves in time without any special effort beyond carrying out more analyses. The fact of the matter is, however, that three of the four issues under consideration (all but the first) have been dividing psychoanalytic clinicians for six decades.

It should not be surprising that the continued use of the conventional case study method has not brought these issues any closer to resolution than they were sixty years ago. For this method, as productive as it has been in generating meaningful hypotheses about the causes and treatment of psychopathology, does not allow for the controls necessary to test these hypotheses so that one psychoanalytic clinician can convince another of a clinical proposition about which the latter is skeptical. (See Silverman [1975, 1978] for an elaboration of this point.) Gill (Chapter 6), in reflecting on why psychoanalytic findings have failed to "become solid and secure knowledge instead of being subject to erosion again and again by waves of fashion" attributes such failure to "the almost total absence of systematic and controlled research in the psychoanalytic situation."

IV

We will now suggest some research approaches that could yield reliable knowledge relevant to the controversial treatment issues outlined above.[4] In presenting these approaches we will outline them in a somewhat schematic, idealized fashion, neglecting for now the fine points of method and issues of feasibility.

We shall present five "research paradigms," ranging from most to least "naturalistic" on a continuum that reflects the degree of departure from the typical psychoanalytic treatment situation. The dilemma that investigators in this area must confront is that, the greater the methodological rigor of a study, the more the situation will depart from the typical treatment situation, making generalizations about typical treatment situations more hazardous. On the other hand, the closer the researched situation is to treatment as it is typically conducted, the fewer the controls that can be instituted and the more tentative the inferences that can be drawn. This is one reason why data generated from different approaches are useful in providing converging lines of evidence.

---

[4]For a presentation of various research approaches to psychotherapy in general, rather than psychoanalysis in particular, see Garfield and Bergin (1978).

Paradigm 1: Naturalistic Design with Interclinician Comparisons

In this paradigm, the data come from psychoanalytic treatment as it is ordinarily conducted, by groups of analysts representing two contrasting approaches. In terms of the issues that have been outlined, treatment results could be compared for clinicians as follows: (1) those who approach self problems in a Kohutian fashion versus those who do not; (2) those who focus on Oedipal issues versus those who emphasize pre-Oedipal issues; (3) those who largely limit themselves to transference interpretations versus those who do not; (4) those who make a special attempt to foster a therapeutic atmosphere versus those who do not.

For this paradigm to advance knowledge substantively, the following steps should be taken: (1) Each of the positions being compared should be represented by a sizable number of clinicians (twenty or more). (2) The clinicians representing the positions being compared should be equated for years of experience, sex, and whatever other variables are judged pertinent to treatment outcome. It would be desirable if in each group there were clinicians at different levels of experience and of both sexes. (3) In selecting cases of the participating clinicians, an attempt should be made to match the groups being compared for relevant patient characteristics. At the very least, such matching should be done for degree of pathology, character type, and the presence of personality characteristics that are generally viewed as conducive to successful outcome in psychoanalytic treatment. It would also be desirable if, in each group, patients were represented at different levels of pathology, with different character types, and with varying resources available. (4) Evaluations should cover the fate of the presenting problem, the status of various ego functions (object relationships, adequacy of defenses, sublimatory capacity, etc.), and other important considerations such as the degree to which transferences—particularly the transference neurosis—have been resolved. (5) The evaluations should be carried out by independent clinicians who do not have knowledge of the characteristics of the psychoanalytic treatment that each patient received.

Paradigm 2: Naturalistic Design with Intraclinician Comparisons

This paradigm proceeds in the same way as the first except that, instead of comparisons being made between two groups of clinicians, they are made between pairs of cases from one group of clinicians, each clinician conducting treatment from the two vantage points being contrasted. This has an important research advantage over the first paradigm, but it poses a practical problem. The advantage is that it holds constant (or at least more constant) many aspects of the clinician's behavior that could influence outcome, other than the treatment variable that is being evaluated. Put simply, it is much more likely that two cases will be handled in a similar way with regard to such extraneous variables if they are treated by the same clinician than if they are treated by two different ones. The practical problem is that the clinicians involved have to be both willing and able to conduct treatment from the two vantage points. For this to be feasible, the participants could either be neophyte clinicians, not set in their ways, or seasoned clinicians who are receptive to the two approaches being compared. In addition to the evaluation "instruments" needed in paradigm 1, this paradigm also would require the development of a questionnaire or a structured interview that could assess the potential clinicians' openness to the two approaches being contrasted so that the above criterion could be fulfilled.

Paradigm 3: Modified Naturalistic Design with Interclinician Comparisons, and Paradigm 4: Modified Naturalistic Design with Intraclinician Comparisons

In these paradigms things proceed in the same way as in the first two paradigms except that the psychoanalytic treatment sessions are taped. The taping is the "modification." Whereas some psychoanalytic clinicians have voiced discomfort at the idea of taping treatment sessions, a number of those who have done so (e.g., Gill et al., 1968; Dahl, 1972) have reported that neither the treatment process nor the outcome need be adversely affected.

Without taking sides on this issue (only systematic investigation will provide data that will allow a substantive resolution), our point is only that this paradigm has important research advantages. For one thing, characterizations of how clinicians conduct treatment would no longer be dependent on prospective and retrospective self-reports, but could be judged directly by noting the actual content and delivery of interventions. Thus, this information would serve as a way of verifying that the clinicians are actually representing their selected positions.

Such information is also relevant to the first two issues under consideration, which deal with the clinician's understanding of what underlies particular forms of psychopathology. Is a "narcissistic personality" struggling with a "self problem" in Kohut's sense, or with conflict over impulses? Is a depressive beset by primarily Oedipal or pre-Oedipal conflict? A question could be raised about whether the differences of opinion on these issues are due to the fact that clinicians are exposed to the same clinical material but view it differently; or whether by virtue of their particular personalities and interventions they elicit different kinds of material. For example, there may be a personality difference between clinicians who focus heavily on Oedipal problems and those who focus on pre-Oedipal problems. A reasonable hypothesis might be that the former come across as more authoritative, which in turn leads to their more often being experienced as the same-sex Oedipal parent in the transference. This transference experience could lead in turn to the frequent activation of Oedipal conflicts in patients, with the result that they "produce" more Oedipal material than the patients of less authoritative clinicians.

All of the above, of course, presupposes that the psychoanalytic clinician can play a significant, if often unwitting, role in determining the kind of material that emerges in treatment. This supposition will no doubt be challenged by many, but it is precisely this issue that could be put to the test. Clinicians' interventions could be evaluated not only for the degree to which they represent a particular approach, but for the way in which they are conveyed.

Another important research advantage of recording sessions is that it allows for the objective observation of the immediate reactions of patients to particular kinds of interventions (see Gill et al., 1968; Sampson, Horowitz, and Weiss, 1972). Such observations would nicely complement the observations of the more distal effects that are observed in posttreatment and follow-up evaluations. Whereas these latter observations reflect on the important question of how a particular therapeutic approach influences the way a person emerges from treatment, it leaves uncertain just which aspects of the approach are having which effects. Viewing the patient's behavior immediately after a treatment intervention allows the observer to be much more certain of the intervention's specific short-term consequences. One could address questions such as the one just alluded to, i.e., Is an intervention that is conveyed with an air of authority more likely to stimulate Oedipal rather than pre-Oedipal material?

Other questions one might address are: (1) Do transference interpretations elicit more intense emotional reactions than other kinds of interpretations? (2) Does a comforting tone of voice (as a concrete manifestation of a "holding environment") allow a patient to address anxiety-arousing material that he or she might otherwise avoid? (3) Under what conditions does focusing on conflict about impulses in a narcissistic personality stimulate nonproductive rage and a further narcissistic withdrawal? Obviously, one would have to look at a number of instances from the treatment of any one patient before arriving at a judgment of the effect of a particular intervention on that patient. Similarly, one would have to evaluate the reactions of many patients (in a diagnostic grouping) before one could generalize about the value of a particular therapeutic intervention for that type of patient.

Paradigm 5: Experimental

We use the word "experimental" in its strict sense here, referring to research in which there is an experimental manipulation designed to affect behavior in a particular way, the effect of which is compared with a "control" manipulation, with all other variables held constant. This paradigm is viewed as alien by many psychoanalytic clinicians, yet it is as necessary in investigating clinical psychoanalytic issues as it is in medical research. The obvious advantage of the experimental method is that it provides controls that cannot be exercised in the clinical situation and thus can complement the clinical paradigms that have been outlined. (See Silverman, 1975, for elaboration).

Is there an experimental method available that can effectively address the controversial issues under discussion? We think that an affirmative answer can be given for at least some of these issues. The method has been termed "subliminal psychodynamic activation" and is described in Chapter 10 of this volume.

Over fifteen years ago, an interesting discovery was made that paved the way for the development of this method and for the study of psychodynamic processes in the laboratory. The discovery was built on earlier work on subliminal perception by Fisher (e.g., 1954) and others stimulated by Fisher's research (summarized in Wolitzky and Wachtel, 1973). In this earlier work, it was demonstrated that stimuli exposed tachistoscopically at a speed so great that nothing more than a flicker of light could be consciously perceived would nevertheless register in the brain and affect behavior. Thus, when subjects were asked to free-associate or "free-image" (i.e., draw whatever comes to mind) immediately after such subliminal exposures, aspects or derivatives of the stimuli would often appear in their productions.

The new discovery (Silverman, 1967) was that if the stimulus has "psychodynamic content" (i.e., content related to unconscious wishes, anxiety, or fantasies), in addition to its content becoming retrieveable, the person's level of psychopathology would be affected. That is, the subliminal input would silently stir up psychodynamic motives congruent with the particular stimulus, and symptoms rooted in these motives that the person was vulnerable to would emerge or become intensified. (See Silverman, Lachmann, and Milich [in press, Chapter 4] for a detailed account of this discovery.) This then made possible the systematic experimental study of the effects of psychodynamic processes on psychopathology. We have detailed the procedure that has been used in these experiments in Chapter 10, but we repeat it here to refresh the reader's memory.

Subjects are seen individually for an experimental session on one day and a control session on another, in counterbalanced order. The first session begins when the experimenter briefly explains to the subject the purpose of the study and seeks his or her cooperation. Then subjects are told about the tasks that will be administered to assess aspects of their behavior and are informed that several times during these tasks they will be asked to look through the eyepiece of a machine (a tachistoscope) at flickers of light which contain extremely brief exposures of verbal and pictorial stimuli. Subjects are promised that at the end of the experiment they will be told the purpose and content of these stimuli.

The session proper begins with a "baseline" assessment of the subject's propensity for whatever pathological manifestations are being investigated. Then the subject is asked to look into the tachistoscope and to view and describe the flickers of light. There follow four exposures of either a psychodynamically relevant stimulus (the experimental session) or a (relatively) neutral stimulus (the control session). Each exposure lasts 4 msec. The specific pathology is then reassessed to determine the effect of whatever stimulus was exposed.

The procedure for the other session is identical to that just described except that a different stimulus is exposed between the baseline and reassessment task series. Subjects who are exposed to the psychodynamic stimulus in the first session are shown a neutral stimulus in the second, and vice versa. In each session the experimenter who works the tachistoscope and administers the assessment procedures is "blind" to which of the stimuli is being exposed. Since the subject is also unaware of the stimulus (as it is subliminal) the procedure qualifies as "double blind" in the same sense as in drug studies where neither the person administering the capsule nor the person ingesting it knows whether the capsule is a drug or a placebo. The evaluation of pathological manifestations is also carried out blind.

In almost fifty studies that have been completed to date (summarized in Silverman, 1976, 1980), the psychodynamically relevant stimulus effected behavior changes not brought about by the neutral control stimulus. For example: (1) in twelve groups of schizophrenics (detailed in Silverman, 1971), indicators of ego disturbance (particularly thought disorder) significantly intensified after a stimulus with oral-aggressive content was exposed; (2) this same kind of stimulus content also was found to intensify dysphoric feelings of depressive persons (Miller, 1973; Rutstein and Goldberger, 1973; Varga, 1973); (3) in three groups of stutterers (Silverman et al., 1972; Silverman, Bronstein, and Mendelsohn, 1976) speech disturbance intensified after the subliminal presentation of anal content; and (4) in three groups of male homosexuals (Silverman et al., 1973; Silverman, Bronstein, and Mendelsohn, 1976) indices of homosexual interest intensified after the subliminal introduction of content suggesting incest. (It is of interest to note that, in a number of these studies, when the same stimuli were presented supraliminally—i.e., in the subject's awareness—the level of pathology was unaffected.)

Can this type of study yield data that have bearing on the treatment issues under consideration? We think that for the first two issues discussed (self problems versus conflict over wishes, and Oedipal versus pre-Oedipal conflict), the answer is "yes"; for the third issue (transference versus nontransference interpretations), "probably not"; and for the last issue (the importance of the therapeutic atmosphere), "to some extent." Let us detail each of these answers.

Issues one and two relate to the psychodynamic content of interpretations. To what degree should interpretations address "self problems" in Kohut's sense and to what extent should they address conflict over Oedipal and pre-Oedipal impulses? This question can be recast as "What kind of psychodynamics underlie particular types of psychopathology?" The results from the studies just cited bear on this question, but for such studies properly to address these issues, a modification of the experimental design is called for. What is needed are experiments in which patients with a particular kind of pathology are given *three* experimental conditions: one in which a neutral control stimulus is subliminally introduced, and two in which the stimuli have been designed to tap each of the two positions that are the subject of debate.

A series of experiments has already been carried out in which the experimental design approached the one just described, and which yielded data that have some bearing on one of the issues under discussion. In these experiments, four groups of subjects were seen: hospitalized male schizophrenics, hospitalized female depressives, stutterers of both sexes from an outpatient speech clinic, and male homosexual nonpatient volunteers from the community. The question that was addressed was one of "specificity"—i.e., whether the identifying behavior of each of the groups (thought disorder in the schizophrenics, dysphoric reactions in the depressives, stuttering in the stutterers, and the homoerotic interests of the homosexuals) was tied only to conflicts about which psychoanalytic clinicians have written or to other types of unconscious conflict as well.

Each group received three (counterbalanced) conditions in which the following stimuli were exposed subliminally: (1) a "relevant" conflictual stimulus that had been implicated for the behavior at issue in the psychoanalytic clinical literature and which had intensified the relevant behavior in previous research using the subliminal psychodynamic activation method (i.e., an oral-aggressive stimulus for the schizophrenics and depressives, an incestuous stimulus for the homosexuals, and an anal stimulus for the stutterers); (2) a conflictual stimulus that was "irrelevant" for the group in question but had been shown to intensify the symptoms of one of the other groups (i.e., an incestuous stimulus for the schizophrenics and stutterers, an oral-aggressive stimulus for the homosexuals, and an anal stimulus for the depressives); and (3) a neutral control stimulus. The findings for these different groups were consistent (Silverman, Bronstein, and Mendelsohn, 1976). Although further support was obtained for the original psychodynamic relationships studied, in no instance did the irrelevant conflictual condition influence the symptom under consideration.

We have cited these experiments not only because they exemplify the kind of design that we are suggesting for the first two issues under discussion, but because for three of the groups (all but the depressives), both an Oedipal and a pre-Oedipal stimulus were used. Interestingly, for two of the groups—the schizophrenics and the stutterers—the pre-Oedipal stimulus affected the behavior studied while the Oedipal stimulus did not. On the other hand, for the third group—the homosexuals—the reverse was the case, with only the Oedipal stimulus affecting behavior.

These findings suggest that pre-Oedipal and Oedipal conflicts are pathogenic for different kinds of pathology, a conclusion that contradicts the exclusionary view that only one or the other kind of conflict can play a pathogenic role. These results, however, amount to only a drop in the bucket. Before such findings could be viewed as substantially bearing on the point of controversy, several additional steps would have to be taken. First, whereas in each of the experiments cited the comparisons were between but one type of Oedipal and pre-Oedipal stimulus, several types would have to be compared.

Second, in addition to sampling the effects of different Oedipal and pre-Oedipal stimuli, various groups of persons manifesting the psychopathology under investigation would have to be studied. For example, it is possible that in the experiments cited above, the homosexuals' responsiveness to the Oedipal stimulus and their nonresponsiveness to the pre-Oedipal stimulus, with the reverse pattern found for the stutterers, were a function of a sampling artifact. The homosexual sample happened to be composed of nonpatients whereas the stutterers were patients from a speech clinic. It is thus conceivable that those in the former group had available greater personality resources, which could account for their differential responsiveness to the Oedipal and pre-Oedipal stimuli. Only if varied groups of homosexuals and stutterers were studied could this possibility be ruled out.

Finally, more than one research laboratory should be involved in experimentation on each issue. This arrangement would not only provide more facilities to ensure that all the necessary experiments are carried out, but it would also enable the reliability of one laboratory's findings to be checked by another. The model would be that of laboratory experimentation in medicine, in which no single type of experiment and no single laboratory is viewed as providing enough data for drawing meaningful conclusions.

V

Could the subliminal psychodynamic activation method be of help in addressing the other two issues under consideration? We think this unlikely with regard to the issue of transference versus nontransference interpretations because, in contrast to the first two issues, this issue is entirely "treatment bound." That is, whereas we were able to translate the technique controversies over "self problems" and Oedipal versus pre-Oedipal interpretations into broader questions about the unconscious motivations for particular forms of psychopathology, no such translation seems possible with regard to the third issue. Whether or not patients in psychoanalytic treatment could benefit more from a singular focus on transference interpretation, or from a variety of interpretations of which transference interpretations are only one part, does not lend itself in any way that we can think of to a meaningful translation.

With regard to the fourth issue—the importance of creating a therapeutic atmosphere—there is a good possibility that the experimental method described above would yield relevant data. In fact, data are already available that we believe have some bearing on the issue.

Several years ago, the subliminal psychodynamic activation method was put to a new use. Whereas previously the stimuli were designed to stir up unconscious wishes and thus (temporarily) exacerbate psychopathology, interest now focused on providing a fantasied wish gratification that might be expected temporarily to reduce pathology. As has been detailed in Chapter 10, the main stimulus chosen for this purpose was one intended to activate a fantasy of symbiotic gratification. It consisted of the verbal message MOMMY AND I ARE ONE, sometimes used alone and sometimes accompanied by a picture of a man and a woman merged at the shoulders like Siamese twins.

When the effects of this stimulus were compared with the effects of a control stimulus, such as MEN THINKING or PEOPLE ARE WALKING (accompanied by a congruent picture in those studies where a picture accompanied the symbiotic message), the following was found: (1) in ten studies carried out with "relatively differentiated" schizophrenics (summarized in Silverman, 1980), the symbiotic stimulus led to reduced thought disorder and otherwise more adaptive ego functioning;[5] (2) in twelve studies carried out with various types of nonschizophrenic groups (including "normal" college students, phobics, alcoholics, overweight persons, depressives, and character disorders), there also was increased adaptive behavior after the symbiotic condition.

In several of these studies, the subliminal stimulation accompanied a therapeutic intervention and was found to increase the effectiveness of the intervention. For example, in studies by Silverman, Frank, and Dachinger (1974) involving phobic women, by Martin (1975) involving overweight women, and by Palmatier (1980) involving cigarette smokers of both sexes, various nonanalytic treatment modalities were used to deal with the problem behavior (phobic symptoms, overeating, and cigarette smoking, respectively). In each study, subliminal stimulation accompanied the treatment intervention, with the participants randomly assigned to an experimental or a control group—the former receiving the symbiotic stimulus and the latter a neutral control stimulus. In each instance, there was significantly greater symptom reduction for the former group.[6]

What bearing do these findings have on the issue under consideration—the importance of establishing an optimal therapeutic atmosphere? It may be remembered that Fleming (1975) and Nacht (1964) have characterized this atmosphere (at least for certain kinds of patients) as one that provides a mod-

[5]See Chapter 10, for a discussion of the relevance of the "differentiation level" on schizophrenics' responsiveness to the activation of symbiotic fantasies.

[6]See Silverman (1980) for a listing of all studies—with both positive and negative results—that have used the subliminal psychodynamic activation method.

icum of symbiotic gratification, which they maintain can improve adaptive functioning. (See also Marmor, Chapter 3, this volume; and Winnicott, 1965.) Thus, the research findings that have been cited on the pathology-reducing effects of the MOMMY AND I ARE ONE stimulus can be seen as supporting Fleming's and Nacht's position.

Those who disagree with this position might argue, however, that the therapeutic effects of activating symbiotic fantasies may well be at a price, especially when they are activated during psychoanalytic treatment. According to this argument, though such fantasies may produce symptomatic improvement, they can impede the analytic process and interfere with the attainment of the more ambitious goal of "structural personality change." Although we can hardly discount such a possibility at this point, some studies already carried out have yielded data that are consistent with the contrary view (explicitly stated by Nacht) that symbiotic gratification can *further* the analytic process as well as reduce symptoms.

Specifically, in three such studies, the focus was on "treatment facilitating behavior" rather than on symptom reduction; in each instance, more of the facilitating behavior appeared after the symbiotic condition. The findings were as follows: (1) in one study (Silverman and C. Wolitzky, 1972), subliminal symbiotic stimulation, when contrasted with subliminal neutral stimulation, led to an increased willingness in the research participants to own up to wishes, feelings, and other personal motives; (2) in a study by Schurtman (1978), a group of alcoholics who were receiving subliminal symbiotic stimulation became more involved in their AA counseling sessions than did a control group receiving subliminal neutral stimulation; and (3) in a study by Linehan (1979), the same symbiotic condition, when compared with a control condition, was found to increase the degree to which college students were willing to disclose things about themselves in group counseling sessions.

If symbiotic gratifications could lead to the behaviors just described, they might well have a facilitating effect on psychoanalytic treatment. Of course, many more data are called for—data from studies that attempt to replicate the findings just cited, and data from related experiments. For example, new studies similar to those described above should be carried out, but using research subjects with various kinds of personality structure. Then we could determine whether the adaptive behaviors that follow the activation of symbiotic fantasies characterize people generally, or only those with particular personality types. (It might turn out, for example, that for certain kinds of people, the activation of such fantasies leads to *less* acceptance of responsibility, involvement, and willingness to disclose things about oneself.)

It might also be possible to carry out an experimental study in which a method is first devised for tapping a person's potential for developing insight into his or her motivations; then the effects of subliminal symbiotic stimulation on this potential would be investigated—again, optimally for persons of different personality types.

Finally, one could study the behavioral effects of other fantasies that bear on the "therapeutic atmosphere." For example, a message such as MOMMY HOLDS ME CALMLY could be viewed as creating (in fantasy) the kind of holding environment that Winnicott (1965) and Modell (1976) view as facilitating psychoanalytic treatment.[7]

Of course, data from studies such as those just described would have only indirect and circumstantial bearing on the "therapeutic atmosphere" issue in psychoanalytic treatment. When considered together with data from our clinical research paradigms, however, the experimental data could be of considerable value. In the next section, we will attempt to demonstrate the complementary roles that clinical and experimental paradigms can play in addressing a psychoanalytic treatment question.

VI

Let us suppose that the question to be researched is: What are the merits of each of the major psychoanalytic approaches to the treatment of narcissistic character disorders? If we delineate the major approaches as those of Kohut (1971, 1977), Kernberg (1975), and the classical school of thought (for example, as described by Rothstein, 1979), this question can be seen as touching on both the first and second treatment issues outlined earlier—i.e., self problems versus intrapsychic conflict, and Oedipal versus pre-Oedipal pathogenesis.

Before undertaking such a study, one would have to deal with a series of preliminary matters relating to definitional and measurement problems. First, the "representatives" of the three positions would have to agree on how to define the term "narcissistic character disorders" and on which specific behaviors to include in an operational definition. Second, the representatives of the three positions would have to spell out in concrete detail the defining characteristics of their approaches. And third, a consensus would have to be reached about which behaviors would be targeted—that is, which changes in treatment sessions and at termination would be viewed as bearing on the merits of the different approaches.

Addressing these preliminary matters would be important for two reasons. The obvious one is that the research procedures would require that these matters first be addressed. (For example, if one implements the paradigm in which each therapist uses the three different approaches on a trio of matched patients, one must be able to specify to the therapist, in concrete detail, the defining characteristics of each approach.)

---

[7]Dr. Susan Farber, our colleague at New York University, suggested this experimental possibility.

But equally important is the fact that addressing these preliminary matters would allow for a determination of the extent of *substantive* disagreement among the adherents of the three approaches. Thus, when the question of defining "narcissistic character disorders" is addressed, it should become clear how much of the disagreement among these adherents is based on the fact that their clinical experience has been with different kinds of patients. As Stolorow and Lachmann (1980) have suggested, it is possible that the proponents of the different approaches have been treating very different kinds of patients even though all have been given the same diagnostic label.

Similarly, with regard to the second preliminary matter—eliciting from the representatives of the different positions a concrete detailing of the defining characteristics of their respective approaches—we might find that the representatives do not differ as much in practice as one might suppose from reading their papers. (One could get an even better answer to this question by studying the transcripts of treatment sessions from a paradigm 3 study.)

And finally, in addressing the question of what changes one would look for as a result of treatment, it might turn out that the adherents of the three different approaches have very different things in mind when they assert or imply that their approaches have been successful with narcissistic patients.

VII

Assuming that a consideration of the results of these preliminary discussions leaves one convinced that substantive differences do exist among the proponents of the different positions (a likely possibility in our opinion), and assuming also that the proponents can achieve a working consensus on an operational definition of "narcissistic character disorder" and on the kind of patient changes that are to be viewed as germane to evaluating the three treatment approaches, we can now return to the question of the place that experimental data could play in addressing the research question.

In order for us to make our point here, we will consider two hypothetical sets of findings that might emerge from the use of the four clinical paradigms. First, let us suppose that these findings consistently indicate that one of the three treatment approaches is superior to the other two. More specifically, let us suppose that a study using paradigm 1 reveals that, in examining the pre-, post- and follow-up evaluation material of patients who have been treated by clinicians representing each of the three approaches, the narcissistic patients in one of the groups have shown a greater degree of positive change than those in the other two groups. Let us further suppose that when the same evaluation material was examined using the second paradigm we outlined, parallel findings emerged. That is, when the same clinicians treated matched patients with the three approaches, the treatment approach that was found to be superior in the first study emerged as superior in the second study as well. And finally, let us suppose that similar studies using paradigms 3 and 4 revealed that recorded sequences in sessions produced results consistent with those found using the previous paradigms.

Despite their consistency, such findings would still leave unclear which aspect of the "most effective" approach was responsible for its greater effectiveness. Since the treatment approaches of Kohut, Kernberg, and those who are more traditionally oriented are multidimensional, it would be hard to determine which aspect of each approach was responsible for its particular effects. For example, Kohut not only advocates addressing a particular kind of psychic content—the underlying deficiencies in "self structures"—but maintains that this content should be addressed in particular ways with regard to the timing and ordering of interpretations, the relative weight given to transference and nontransference interpretations, and most important, the manner in which interpretations are given. Thus, if one wishes to know whether the superior approach succeeded because the relevant content area was dealt with, some other kinds of data would be needed.

The "other kinds of data," in our view, could be obtained from the subliminal psychodynamic activation method. More specifically, the following type of experiment could be undertaken.

Nonpatients who met the criteria for "narcissistic character disorders" could serve as research participants and could be evaluated for changes in the degree of narcissistic pathology that they manifested after being exposed to different subliminal conditions. Extrapolating from the writings on each of the three approaches, stimuli could be devised that would be expected either to intensify or to reduce narcissistic pathology if the particular approach is correct in its understanding of such pathology. For example, it would follow from the classical approach that a stimulus message that intensifies Oedipal conflict—e.g., DEFEATING DAD IS WRONG (for male subjects)—should exacerbate narcissistic pathology, whereas a message reducing such conflict—e.g., DEFEATING DAD IS OK[8]—should have the opposite effect.

Analogously, from Kernberg's theory, it might be expected that the message MOTHER'S BREASTS ARE EMPTY would exacerbate the pathology, whereas the message MOTHER'S BREASTS ARE FULL would have a diminishing effect. And from Kohut's theory, it might be predicted that the message I AM NOBODY would intensify narcissistic pathology, whereas the message I AM STRONG AND ABLE would have the opposite effect.

Following the research strategy described earlier, in later experiments other stimuli that tapped the same psychodynamics with different messages could be introduced. If the messages related to one approach consistently had a greater effect on the research participants than those related to the other approaches, and if the former approach was the same one that the clinical studies found to

---

[8]For a discussion of studies that have used this particular message and their bearing on psychoanalytic treatment, see Chapter 10.

be superior, the following conclusion could be drawn. Since the experimental data would have been collected under tightly controlled conditions, one could reasonably infer that the superior experimental approach also produced the best therapeutic outcome because the content of its interpretations was most on the mark in addressing the psychodynamic issues at work in the type of patient studied.

Let us now consider the role that experimental findings could play in different hypothetical circumstances. Let us suppose this time that the clinical paradigms have produced discrepant results: that the findings from the first two paradigms (where treatment outcome is evaluated) indicate that one approach is superior, whereas the results from the paradigms that evaluate changes within a session indicate no difference among the three approaches.

There would be at least two ways of understanding such discrepant results. It could be that the approach fared better only when posttreatment results were the point of focus because the working through of insights required time. Thus, when short-term changes were looked at, it erroneously seemed as if the interpretations had not had an effect.

But another possibility is that the absence of changes within sessions mirrored the fact that the interpretations were incorrect, and that the superiority of the approach in the outcome studies was due to the therapist's manner or other aspects of what we have referred to as the therapeutic atmosphere.

What could be helpful in deciding between these possibilities would be the results from the type of experiment described above. If the psychodynamic messages related to the approach that produced the best treatment results were found to have a greater effect on subjects than the messages related to the other two approaches, this finding would be a strong argument for the validity of the first explanation. But if one of the other sets of psychodynamic messages turned out to have as much or greater effect, the second explanation would be supported.

It is the complementary use of clinical and experimental data that we are stressing here. Experimental data by themselves could be justifiably viewed as too artificial and removed from clinical reality to be given heavy weight in their own right. Conversely, clinical data could be legitimately criticized as too poorly controlled to be taken seriously by themselves. But when both kinds of data are considered together, the weaknesses of each are compensated for by the strengths of the other, so that conclusions can be drawn with greater confidence.[9]

---

[9]Our discussion of the use of the subliminal psychodynamic activation method to investigate controversial issues is not meant to imply that experimental research always yields results that are replicable and clear in their implications. Often the road to obtaining reliable data that have (relatively) unambiguous meaning is a rocky one. (See Silverman, Lachmann, and Milich, in press, Chapters 4 and 7, for some examples.) What *can* be said for experimental research is that when findings are inconsistent or unclear, there are accepted ways of resolving these ambiguities.

VIII

Concluding Comments

In his article "The Future of Psychoanalysis and Its Institutes," Holzman (1976), commenting on the use of clinical reports in the psychoanalytic literature, writes:

It is noteworthy that our 80-year-old discipline never developed further canons for research or for judging the worth of contributions. . . . New ideas in psychoanalysis provoke some essays for and against, but these are not sufficient. Unlike . . . literary criticism, we require more than such essays. We need proposals to test ideas systematically, and unfortunately there are too few calls for such tests [p. 269].

We are sounding one of these calls for the development of reliable empirical evidence relevant to the clinical theory of psychoanalysis, particularly regarding controversial treatment issues such as the four that have been the focus of this paper. In so doing, we emphasize our agreement with George S. Klein (1976), who stated, "Among the sorriest clichés I have heard in psychoanalytic circles are the views that doing therapy *is* research and . . . that treatment *is* experimentation" (p. 64).

One of the major difficulties for clinicians who maintain the view that Klein criticizes is that when they disagree among themselves, the citation of clinical evidence rarely changes the minds of those on the other side. In this regard, one of Rapaport's (1960) conclusions in his systematic evaluation of psychoanalysis twenty years ago is equally valid today: "The extensive clinical evidence which would seem conclusive in terms of the system's internal consistency, fails to be conclusive in terms of the usual criteria of science, because there is no established canon for the interpretation of clinical observations" (p. 113).

Given the absence of clearly specifiable rules of evidence and the necessity of heavy reliance on clinical inference in attributing meanings, motives, and intentions to the patient's behavior and utterances, it is not surprising to observe the persistence of controversies such as those we have discussed. How clinicians understand pathology generally—as well as for particular patients— and how they conduct treatment can be too readily influenced by subjective factors, as the following report bears out.

For several years, one of us (D. L. W.) was engaged in a collaborative study with a group of colleagues from a psychoanalytic institute.[10] A major aim of the study was to explicate the underlying logic and implicit assumptions of

[10]The group was led by Drs. H. Dahl and B. Rubinstein. The study is currently being prepared for publication.

clinical inferences made by trained analysts. The guiding hypothesis was that this task could be accomplished most readily when analysts agreed that a clinical segment constituted strong evidence for a given clinical hypothesis.

After considerable trial and error, the following procedure was adopted. Hypotheses about a patient were generated by reading aloud the typed transcripts of the first six sessions of a tape-recorded psychoanalysis. Any member of the group was free to interrupt to offer a hypothesis and state the observation on which it was based. In this way, about two dozen hypotheses were formulated. Then nine subsequent sessions were selected at random, with the restriction that they cover a sizable time span in the analysis. The transcripts of these sessions were read for evidence that would support or refute any of the initial hypotheses. When a member of the group came upon material that he regarded as having evidential value, the others paused and made independent ratings of the evidence item. Ratings were done on a scale of -4 (a judgment that the evidence went against the hypothesis) to $+4$ (when the evidence supported the hypothesis). The higher the rating, the stronger the evidence, pro or con.

A number of interesting findings emerged from this study, but we will focus only on the following one. The judge who first called attention to an evidence item consistently rated it higher than the other judges. That is, whereas at other times any given judge may have seen evidence as more or less positive than the other judges, when introducing a piece of evidence, he typically rated the evidence as more compelling.

This finding strongly suggests that clinicians overvalue evidence that they themselves find. A reasonable extrapolation to the clinical situation would be that there is a danger that therapists will have a vested interest in "confirming" their favorite hypotheses. Their threshold for "finding" supporting evidence will be lower, and conversely, their threshold for finding disconfirming evidence or evidence for another hypothesis will be higher. We therefore need additional methods of accumulating a body of responsible clinical knowledge. In this paper we have outlined some of the methods that might be used.

REFERENCES

Arlow, J. A. (1975), Discussion of Kanzer's paper. *Internat. J. Psychoanal. Psychother.*, 4:69–73.

Brenner, C. (1968), Psychoanalysis and science. *J. Amer. Psychoanal. Assn.*, 16:675–676.

—— (1974), Depression, anxiety and affect theory. *Internat. J. Psycho-Anal.*, 55:25–32.

—— (1976), *Psychoanalytic Technique and Psychic Conflict.* New York: International Universities Press.

—— (1979), Working alliance, therapeutic alliance and transference. *J. Amer. Psychoanal. Assn.* (Suppl.), 27:137–157.

Dahl, H. (1972), A quantitative study of a psychoanalysis. In: *Psychoanal. & Contemp. Sci.*, 1:237–257. New York: Macmillan.

Fairbairn, W. R. D. (1952), *Psychoanalytic Studies of the Personality*. London: Tavistock.

Fisher, C. (1954), Dreams and perceptions. *J. Amer. Psychoanal. Assn.*, 2:389–445.

Fleming, J. (1975), Some observations on object constancy in the psychoanalysis of adults. *J. Amer. Psychoanal. Assn.*, 23:743–760.

Freud, S. (1909), Analysis of a phobia in a five-year-old boy. *Standard Edition*, 10:5–149. London: Hogarth Press, 1955.

Garfield, S. L., & Bergin, A. E. (1978), *Handbook of Psychotherapy and Behavior Change*. New York: Wiley.

Gaskill, H. S. (1979), Bridges to the future. *J. Amer. Psychoanal. Assn.*, 27:3–26.

Gill, M. M. (1976), Metapsychology is not psychology. In: *Psychology versus Metapsychology* (*Psychol. Issues*, Monogr. 36). New York: International Universities Press.

———, Simon, J., Fink, G., Endicott, N. A., & Paul, I. H. (1968), Studies in audio-recorded psychoanalysis. I. General considerations. *J. Amer. Psychoanal. Assn.*, 16:230–244.

Gitelson, M. (1962), The curative factors in psychoanalysis. I. The first phase of psychoanalysis. *Internat. J. Psycho-Anal.*, 43:194–205.

Goldberg, A. (1978), *The Psychology of the Self*. New York: International Universities Press.

Greenson, R. R. (1967), *The Technique and Practice of Psychoanalysis*. New York: International Universities Press.

Guntrip, H. (1961), *Personality Structure and Human Interaction*. New York: International Universities Press.

Heimann, P. (1977), Further observations on the analyst's cognitive process. *J. Amer. Psychoanal. Assn.*, 25:313–333.

Holt, R. R. (1976), Drive or wish? A reconsideration of the psychoanalytic theory of motivation. In: *Psychology versus Metapsychology* (*Psychol. Issues*, Monogr. 36). New York: International Universities Press.

Holzzman, P. S. (1976), The future of psychoanalysis and its institutes. *Psychoanal. Quart.*, 45:2   .

Joseph, E. D. (1975), Psychoanalysis—science and research: Twin studies as a paradigm. *J. Amer. Psychoanal. Assn.*, 23:3–31.

Kanzer, M. (1975), The therapeutic and working alliances. *Internat. J. Psycho-Anal. Psychother.*, 4:48–68.

Kaplan, A. H. (1979), From discovery to validation: A basic challenge to psychoanalysis. Presidential address to the Plenary Session, American Psychoanalytic Association, New York City, December.

Kernberg, O. F. (1975), *Borderline Conditions and Pathological Narcissism*. New York: Jason Aronson.

Klein, G. S. (1976), *Psychoanalytic Theory: An Exploration of Essentials*. New York: International Universities Press.

Kohut, H. (1971), *The Analysis of the Self*. New York: International Universities Press.

——— (1977), *The Restoration of the Self*. New York: International Universities Press.

Kubie, L. S. (1952), Problems and techniques of validation and progress. In: *Psychoanalysis as Science*, ed. E. Pumpian-Mindlin. Stanford, Ca.: Stanford University Press, pp. 46–124.

Leites, N. (1979), *Interpreting Transference*. New York: Norton.

Linehan, E. (1979), A study of the effects of subliminal symbiotic stimulation on self-disclosure during counseling. Unpublished doctoral dissertation, St. John's University.

Luborsky, L., & Spence, D. P. (1978), Quantitative research on psychoanalytic therapy. In: *Handbook of Psychotherapy and Behavior Change*, ed. S. L. Garfield & A. E. Bergin. New York: Wiley, pp. 331–368.

Martin, A. (1975), The effect of subliminal stimulation of symbiotic fantasies on weight loss in obese women receiving behavioral treatment. Unpublished doctoral dissertation, New York University.

Miller, J. (1973), The effects of aggressive stimulation upon adults who have experienced the death of a parent during childhood and adolescence. Unpublished doctoral dissertation, New York University.

Modell, A. (1976), The "holding environment" and the therapeutic action of psychoanalysis. *J. Amer. Psychoanal. Assn.*, 24:285–307.

Nacht, S. (1964), Silence as an integrative factor. *Internat. J. Psycho-Anal.*, 45:299–308.

Neiderland, W. G. (1965), The role of the ego in the recovery of early memories. *Psychoanal. Quart.*, 34:564–571.

Palmatier, J. (1980), The effects of subliminal symbiotic stimulation in the behavioral treatment of smoking. Unpublished doctoral dissertation, University of Montana.

Rangell, L. (1978), Discussant on panel on Psychoanalytic Classics Revisited. American Psychoanalytic Association, New York City, December.

Rapaport, D. (1960), *The Structure of Psychoanalytic Theory: A Systematizing Attempt* (*Psychol. Issues,* Monogr. 6). New York: International Universities Press.

Reichenbach, H. (1938), *Experience and Prediction.* Chicago: University of Chicago Press.

Rosen, V. H. (1955), The reconstruction of a traumatic childhood event in a case of derealization. *J. Amer. Psychoanal. Assn.*, 3:209–221.

Rothstein, A. (1979), Oedipal conflicts in narcissistic personality disorders. *Internat. J. Psycho-Anal.*, 60:189–200.

Rubinstein, B. R. (1975), On the clinical psychoanalytic theory and its role in the inference and confirmation of clinical hypotheses. *Psychoanal. & Contemp. Sci.*, 4:3–58. New York: International Universities Press.

Rutstein, E. H., & Goldberger, L. (1973), The effects of aggressive stimulation on suicidal patients: An experimental study of the psychoanalytic theory of suicide. *Psychoanal. & Contemp. Sci.*, 2:157–174. New York: Macmillan.

Sampson, H., Horowitz, L., & Weiss, J. (1972), Defense analysis and the emergence of warded-off mental contents: An empirical study. *Arch. Gen. Psychiat.*, 26:524–532.

Schafer, R. (1976), *A New Language for Psychoanalysis.* New Haven, Ct.: Yale University Press.

——— (1977), The interpretation of transference and the conditions of loving. *J. Amer. Psychoanal. Assn.*, 25:335–362.

Schurtman, R. (1978), The effect of psychodynamic activation of symbiotic gratification fantasies on involvement in a treatment program for alcoholics. Unpublished doctoral dissertation, New York University.

Seitz, F. D. (1966), The consensus problem in psychoanalytic research. In: *Methods of Research in Psychotherapy,* ed. L. A. Gottschalk & A. H. Auerbach. New York: Appleton-Century-Crofts.

Silverman, L. H. (1967), An experimental approach to the study of dynamic propositions in psychoanalysis: The relationship between the aggressive drive and ego regression—initial studies. *J. Amer. Psychoanal. Assn.*, 15:376–403.

——— (1971), An experimental technique for the study of unconscious conflict. *Brit. J. Med. Psychol.*, 44:17–25.

——— (1975), On the role of laboratory experiments in the development of the clinical theory of psychoanalysis: Data on the subliminal activation of aggressive and merging wishes in schizophrenics. *Internat. Rev. Psycho-Anal.*, 2:43–64.

——— (1976), Psychoanalytic theory: "The reports of my death are greatly exaggerated." *Amer. Psychol.*, 31:621–637.

────── (1978), Reply to Theodore Shapiro's discussion of "Unconscious symbiotic fantasy: Ubiquitous therapeutic agent." *Internat. J. Psychoanal. Psychother.,* 7:594–601.

────── (1980), A comprehensive report of studies using the subliminal psychodynamic activation method. Research Center for Mental Health, New York University, New York City. (Unpublished.)

──────, Bronstein, A., & Mendelsohn, E. (1976), The further use of the subliminal psychodynamic activation method for experimental study of the clinical theory of psychoanalysis: On the specificity of relationships between manifest psychopathology and unconscious conflict. *Psychotherapy: Theory, Res., & Prac.,* 13:2–16.

──────, Frank, S., & Dachinger, P. (1974), Psychoanalytic reinterpretation of the effectiveness of systematic desensitization: Experimental data bearing on the role of merging fantasies. *J. Abnorm. Psychol.,* 83:313–318.

──────, Klinger, H., Lustbader, L., Farrell, J., & Martin, A. (1972), The effect of subliminal drive stimulation on the speech of stutterers. *J. Nerv. Ment. Dis.,* 155:14–21.

──────, Kwawer, J. S., Wolitzky, C., & Coron, M. (1973), An experimental study of aspects of the psychoanalytic theory of male homosexuality. *J. Abnorm. Psychol.,* 82:178–188.

──────, Lachmann, F. M., & Milich, R. (in press), *The Search for Oneself.* New York: International Universities Press.

──────, & Wolitzky, C. (1972), The effects of the subliminal stimulation of symbiotic fantasies of the defensiveness of "normal" subjects in telling TAT stories. Research Center for Mental Health, New York University, New York. (Unpublished.)

Spence, D. P. (1976), Clinical interpretation: Some comments on the nature of the evidence. *Psychoanal. & Contemp. Sci.,* 5:367–388. New York: International Universities Press.

Stein, M. H. (1979), Review of *The Restoration of the Self,* by Heinz Kohut. *J. Amer. Psychoanal. Assn.,* 23:665–680.

Stolorow, R. D., & Lachmann, F. M. (1980), *Psychoanalysis of Developmental Arrests.* New York: International Universities Press.

Stone, L. (1961), *The Psychoanalytic Situation.* New York: International Universities Press.

──────(1967), The psychoanalytic situation and transference: Postscript to an earlier communication. *J. Amer. Psychoanal. Assn.,* 15:3–58.

Varga, M. (1973), An experimental study of aspects of the psychoanalytic theory of elation. Unpublished doctoral dissertation, New York University.

Wallerstein, R. S. (1979), Discussant on panel on The Bipolar Self. American Psychoanalytic Association, New York City, December.

────── & Sampson, H. (1971), Issues in research in the psychoanalytic process. *Internat. J. Psycho-Anal.,* 52:11–50.

Wangh, M. (1974), Concluding remarks on technique and prognosis in the treatment of narcissism. *J. Amer. Psychoanal. Assn.,* 22:307–309.

Winnicott, D. W. (1965), *The Maturational Processes and the Facilitating Environment.* New York: International Universities Press.

Wolitzky, D. L., & Wachtel, P. L. (1973), Perception and personality. In: *Handbook of General Psychology,* ed. B. Wolman. Englewood Cliffs, N.J.: Prentice-Hall.

Zetzel, E. R. (1956), Current concepts of transference. *Internat. J. Psycho-Anal.,* 37:369–378.

CHAPTER 17

Therapeutic Influences in Dynamic Psychotherapy:
A Review and Synthesis

Morris Eagle and David L. Wolitzky

Our aim in this chapter is to extract from the preceding papers certain important themes and issues and to offer our comments on them. Our focus will be confined to the contributions in this volume, leaving aside the large extant literature on curative factors in psychotherapy.

Before discussing these themes, a cautionary note must be sounded regarding the very use of the term "curative factors." It would be more accurate, although perhaps awkward, to say "presumably curative factors" or "purportedly curative factors." For the fact is that we do not know, with any degree of rigor and assurance, what the curative factors in dynamic psychotherapy—or any kind of psychotherapy—are. In this volume, seasoned clinicians have brought their experiences, impressions, intuitions, and understanding to bear on this issue. What this volume provides, among other things, is: (1) a set of hypotheses regarding curative factors—to be used by, and measured against the experience of, other clinicians as well as to be tested more rigorously, and (2) a kind of informal test of reliability regarding curative factors. That is to say, although each contributor has considered a different aspect of dynamic psychotherapy, the emergence of a common set of overriding factors would give

NOTE: The authors would like to express their appreciation to Dr. Rita Simon-Eagle for her helpful comments and suggestions.

a degree of credibility to their importance and relevance to the process of psychotherapy. But again, the cautionary note must be introduced. As Kubie (1952) has pointed out, ordinarily psychotherapeutic sessions are rich sources for generating hypotheses rather than for testing them. The contributions to this volume likewise represent a rich source for our perusal.

Recapitulation of Contributions

Before commenting on the various themes and issues, it is necessary to summarize the views of each contributor. To a certain extent, the editor's Introduction has already provided such a summary, and we hope the reader will bear with the inevitable degree of repetition.

An orthodox and somewhat simplistic account of curative factors in psychoanalytic psychotherapy would be limited to two factors: (1) insight as a consequence of properly timed, effectively presented interpretations of resistance and conflict, and (2) the process of working through. While it would also be recognized that relationship factors (e.g., countertransference, positive and negative transference, therapeutic alliance) are important elements in the treatment process, their significance would be viewed as secondary in that they provide the context within which interpretation leading to insight can best be accomplished.

Hatcher provides a historical review of the concept of emotional insight as a mutative factor in treatment, emphasizing the therapeutic "split," or oscillation, between experiencing and reflecting, as well as the role of analytic self-observation and awareness in facilitating conflict resolution and ego mastery.

Hatcher reminds us that, as Freud developed the concept of resistance, he began to focus on the patient's role in bringing to awareness previously unconscious contents. In introducing the basic role of free association, the therapist no longer lifted repressed memories directly by exercising "his will" against the resistance. Along with this change came a shift from an emphasis on abreaction to the ego's gradual assimilation and mastery of unconscious contents. Freud also recognized that patients must *experience* their resistance and insight via the transference neurosis. As Hatcher puts it, following Strachey and Bibring, "emotional insight demands a balanced integration of emotional contact and intellectual comprehension into a full-bodied experience of the meaningfulness of an unconscious conflict." The patient has to realize that his feelings toward the analyst are "real, but not *really* real." This attitude requires an oscillation between experiencing and reflecting on one's experience. In Sterba's (1934) words, it requires a "dissociation of the ego" in response to interpretations.

Hatcher describes insight as a "complex process that depends on the integrated, sequential operation of several different ego functions" (e.g., controlled ego regression, detached self-observation). In what Hatcher calls "reflective self-observation," the content is seen as part of a context, i.e., as "an organized cognitive system of meaningfully related contents." The sophisticated elaboration of such contexts presumably enhances ego mastery and is therefore curative.

It is not at all clear from Hatcher's account how this process occurs. For the most part, he simply asserts the value of acquiring a meaningful, coherent, organized account of one's personality and behavior. At one point, however, he suggests that this increased self-understanding (i.e., the development of new contexts) must take a specific form; he quotes Hartman, (1939, p.63) who claimed that interpretations not only help uncover repressed material but "must also establish correct causal relations, that is, the causes, range of influence, and effectiveness of these experiences in relation to other elements." The idea that one can establish an accurate etiology of a neurosis by interpretation in adult analysis is, as we shall argue later, quite untenable.

While Hatcher does not consider the relative therapeutic efficacy of insight versus the therapeutic relationship, he does point out, citing Kris (1956) and Myerson (1965), that the motives for acquiring insight are complex and are often related to the state of the treatment relationship. For example, identification, compliance, desire for praise, the wish to merge symbiotically with the analyst, as well as conflicts concerning these motives can determine the degree to which insight or resistance characterizes the therapeutic process. Hatcher seems to be suggesting implicitly what Gill argues explicitly, viz., that in dynamic psychotherapy, the acquisition of insight cannot easily be separated or disentangled from the therapeutic relationship.

As a concluding comment about insight, we find it remarkable that so few articles or books have been specifically devoted to this topic, considering the traditional emphasis on this factor as a curative—if not *the* curative—factor in psychoanalysis and dynamic psychotherapy. The present discussion suggests that the therapeutic relationship, insights about this relationship, and insights about matters outside the relationship are three potential curative factors whose relative therapeutic value remains to be established.

We turn now to Kohut and Wolf, who, in describing their experiences with narcissistic personality disorders and narcissistic behavior disorders, stress the importance of permitting narcissistic transferences (i.e., mirroring and idealizing transferences) to develop. According to them, emphatic understanding on the part of the therapist facilitates the patient's access to archaic narcissistic needs and serves as a partial gratification of these needs. The patient becomes aware of, expresses, and accepts the old narcissistic needs, eventually transforming them into normal self-assertiveness and devotion to ideals. Elsewhere

Kohut (1977) has written of the therapeutic role of small doses of frustration land of "transmuting internalization" in helping build psychic structures that have not developed adequately. Kohut and Wolf draw a parallel between the mother-child relationship and the therapist-patient relationship (a parallel drawn by other contributors to this volume). In short, Kohut and Wolf believe that when mothering is adequate with respect to empathy and mirroring, the small and optimal doses of frustration (what Winnicott [1958] calls "gradual failure of adaptation") experienced by the infant permit the building up of the infant's own psychic structures.

What is noteworthy is the clear implication that, for narcissistic disorders, understanding and insight are secondary to the emphatic quality of the relationship. In other words, the therapeutic value of accurate interpretation derives from the fact that it expresses the therapist's emphatic understanding of the patient. As Gedo (1980) observed in a recent paper, Kohut's emphasis on empathy as a direct agent of healing, rather than as a tool of observation, represents a radical departure from the traditional value system in which the "absolute quest for knowledge" is primary. Some clinicians believe that empathy is the primary healing agent mainly for more disturbed patients, who make only limited use of insight; others believe that such use of empathy should be universal. (This controversy is touched on by other contributors.)

The mobilization of narcissistic transference discussed by Kohut and Wolf can be seen as a special case of the general issue of regressive phenomena in dynamic psychotherapy. (Of course, all transference phenomena are, in an important sense, regressive.) Tuttman's contribution addresses the role of regression in psychotherapy directly. Along with Kohut and Wolf, Tuttman believes that an important aspect of psychotherapy is the facilitation of infantile needs and other "fragmented regressive components" that the patient dreads reexperiencing. Tuttman, too, emphasizes the role of the therapist's acceptance and empathic understanding both in facilitating access to the infantile needs, and, via the therapeutic relationship, in partially meeting these needs. At Tuttman puts it, " . . . the skillful acceptance of regression to the traumatic developmental phases where something needed for growth was missing, and then facilitating understanding and growth from that point forward via an analytic relationship . . . are necessary steps in treatment." The affinity between this statement and the views of Winnicott (1958, 1965) and Guntrip (1968) will be apparent to the reader.

Like many of the authors in this volume, Tuttman argues that a neutral interpretive stance does not work with more disturbed patients; instead, he believes that "treatment can offer, ideally, a parallel of the mother-child 'facilitating environment.'" That the parallel is not complete is indicated by Tuttman's insistence that he does not advocate a "'milk-giving, hand-holding,' libidinally gratifying interaction" which, he believes, "often leads to more malignant pathology."

Another contributor for whom the curative aspects of the patient-therapist relationship are central is Volkan, who focuses primarily on more disturbed patients with defects in ego organization. Volkan's main proposition is that, for seriously disturbed patients, partial identification with the representation of the therapist is a primary curative factor. According to Volkan, this identification comes about through "introjective-projective relatedness." That is, the patient projects onto the therapist material from archaic self- and object representations. The therapist reacts in a positive, non-critical way, providing helpful interpretations of the patient's distortions. The patient then introjects the positive features of the therapist, a process which helps to "decontaminate," or rid, new representations of archaic ones and which strengthens "observing, integrating, and taming functions." Volkan reminds us that, as early as 1934, Strachey spoke of the patient's introjection of the analyst as an auxiliary superego, which helps to modify the patient's harsh, primitive superego. He also notes Rangell's (1979) point that, in the analysis of neurotic patients, there is "a constant series of microidentifications."

Levenson tells us that an interpretation is not a disembodied phenomenon without a context. Communication, he reminds us, has its pragmatics as well as its semantics. That is, therapists communicate and interact with patients not only through the content of their interpretations but also through their style, tone of voice, timing, etc. And they also communicate by remaining silent. Given the necessity and inevitability of interaction with the patient, a primary responsibility of the therapist is to act *authentically*. An authentic response, while it cannot preclude the possibility of error, at least increases the likelihood that the patient will be "engaged, experienced, and responded to." And it is this response, Levenson maintains, that is likely to be therapeutic and to foster growth.

Despite Levenson's somewhat different vantage point, his view resembles both Kohut and Wolf's stress on empathic understanding and Volkan's concern with differentiating archaic and new representations. Levenson's reminder that communication (including interpretations) has its pragmatics as well as its semantics provides still another perspective on the insight and interpretation–therapeutic relationship distinction. If what is communicated to a patient is a function both of the content, style, tone, and context of the interpretation, and of the nature of the ongoing interaction between patient and therapist, then it follows that interpretation cannot be sharply differentiated from the therapeutic relationship. Further, if the effect of an interpretation (or any other therapeutic intervention) is, in part, a function of *how* one makes it and who is offering it to whom, it also follows that the *personality* of the therapist and the match or fit between patient and therapist will be critical factors in therapeutic outcome. While one may learn a good deal about technique and dynamics, *who* one is and how one reacts to various people are likely to remain less subject to the effects of training and other forms of conscious control. But, as is implied in Levenson's chapter, these subtler and more "organic" features of the therapist are also communicated in the therapeutic interaction.

Silverman, Langs, and Gill articulate additional perspectives concerning the subtle personal influences, both general and specific, that are inevitable components of the therapist-patient interaction.

For Silverman, a frequent, though usually inadvertent, therapeutic agent is the activation of key unconscious fantasies. The activation is inadvertent in that it is unintended by the therapist; it is based on characteristics of the treatment situation, including aspects of the therapist's personality and behavior, of which he may be unaware. The two principal unconscious fantasies to which Silverman refers are symbiotic gratification and sanctioned Oedipal fantasies. Though insight is still assumed to be the principal agent of therapeutic change, according to Silverman these fantasies can facilitate the acquisition of insight if they are activated only occasionally and if they are analyzed at some point in the treatment. Silverman outlines certain conditions, however, in which these two fantasies can be allowed to operate silently—that is, without interpretation—and still enhance adaptation and therapeutic effectiveness. In such instances, sanctioned Oedipal fantasies and symbiotic gratification fantasies do not appear to have maladaptive consequences that require interpretation and thus can serve as "noninsight agents of change." In Silverman's view, these fantasies were implicit in earlier concepts, such as the "holding environment" (Winnicott, 1965) and "identification with the analyst" (Sterba, 1934).

Silverman's thesis requires clinical investigations of the influence of these fantasies on treatment outcome when they are: (a) occasional versus frequent, (b) mild versus intense, (c) used for defense versus adaptation, (d) allowed to operate silently versus when they are interpreted, and (e) interpreted at earlier versus later points in the treatment. Of course, the above points also apply to the curative factors emphasized by other contributers to this volume (e.g., Kohut and Wolf's prescription concerning the timing of interpretations of idealizing transferences).

In Gill's view, the therapist's role, his therapeutic intent, and his unique personality characteristics are of central importance to the treatment process. Gill argues that analysts may see certain of their behaviors as expressions of technical neutrality, when in reality these behaviors are the stimuli that trigger transference reactions. If the analyst is aware of these stimuli and if his intervention includes a reference to the cues in the analytic situation that may have prompted the transference reaction, he "will be respecting the patient's effort to be plausible and realistic rather than seeing him as manufacturing his transference attitudes out of whole cloth." Patients who are treated this way will "more readily consider their preexisting bias, that is, their transference."

Implicit in Gill's position is the feeling that analytic treatment often takes place in an atmosphere that the patient rightly regards as authoritarian, at least in the sense that the doctor is the repository and conveyor of truth. Thus, Gill makes it clear that he does not maintain an "absolute conception of reality" or see the patient as "distorting" that reality. We question this view, since every therapist, however tactful, presumably makes the final decision whether, and to what extent, the patient is displaying a "preexisting bias." Gill's states that different people (or the same person) can bring multiple perspectives to a situation. But, since Gill still emphasizes the value of insight, his "multiple perspective" approach seems to us to sidestep the issue of the significance of interpretive accuracy as a factor in treatment outcome.

In any case, Gill believes that the analyst should be more alert to transference allusions in material that is not manifestly about the therapist—what he calls "the here-and-now transference." If one interprets the here-and-now transference consistently, genetic material will tend to emerge spontaneously. Genetic transference interpretation, extratransference interpretation, and working through are also regarded as essential but are accorded secondary importance.

With respect to the relative weight to be given to insight versus relationship factors, Gill writes that "in the very interpretation of the transference, patients have a new experience. They are being treated differently than they expected." Transference interpretation is "not a matter of experience in contrast to insight but a jointing of the two together." In other words, both are required; they are inseparable. This view is persuasive and makes it exceedingly difficult, if not impossible, to determine objectively the relative importance of each variable as a curative factor in psychoanalytic treatment.

Langs also places great emphasis on the therapist's responsibility for the outcome of treatment. He believes that both psychoanalysis and psychoanalytic psychotherapy aim at "symptom alleviation through insight into unconscious processes and constructive introjective identifications." The latter derives from object relational and interactional processes and tends to be "broadly ego enhancing," while the former, if it consists of "affectively meaningful and validated cognitive insights," leads to "specific forms of nonsymptomatic adaptive resolutions of specific unconscious, conflicted fantasy-memory constellations."

Within this overall framework, Langs focuses on the inevitable countertransferences which, if improperly managed, can result in negative outcomes, stalemated treatment, and a lack of genuine insight. At best, unrecognized and unmanaged countertransference will lead to what Langs terms a "misalliance cure"—that is, "uninsightful symptom relief."

Through the use of case examples, Langs articulates the subtle interactional and unconscious processes involved in countertransferences and their impact on the patient. To cite one example, Langs describes how the patient can react to the therapist's countertransference by attempting to cure him, an effort that Langs views as a reliving of childhood attempts to "cure" maternal and other primary objects. In such cases, the therapeutic outcome depends on the analyst's awareness and management of the countertransference. Langs makes the strong claim that "There is little doubt that unrecognized countertransferences are the single most critical basis for therapeutic failure." At the same time, countertransference is "an essential component" of a good therapeutic outcome.

In advancing this position, Langs is clearly placing the responsibility for therapeutic failure mainly on the therapist, giving lesser emphasis to patient characteristics (e.g., motivation, psychological-mindedness) typically associated with positive outcome. It will be necessary, though difficult, to test the many implicit and explicit assumptions and hypotheses inherent in Langs's view. For example, Langs claims that: (1) every silence and intervention contains some element of countertransference, (2) nonvalidation of an interpretation (i.e., the absence of derivative, confirmatory material) is an indication of countertransference, and (3) countertransference influences "will override any other stated intentions or meanings of the therapist's interventions." To what extent and under what conditions these generalizations hold are vital issues in any theory of therapy.

Marmor also focuses on the personality of the therapist, but his concern is the curative potential of the therapist's interest, empathy, and warmth—qualities that Greenson and Wexler (1969) subsume under the notion of the nontransference or "real" relationship. Since interest, empathy, and warmth presumably cannot be simulated effectively, Marmor is referring here to the abilities and personality of the therapist as well as to the "fit" between therapist and patient. That is, particular patients may be more likely to call forth interest, empathy, and warmth from particular therapists.

Marmor also presents other factors that he believes produce change: the therapist's taking an active role in confronting defenses and resistances; the explicit and implicit approval and disapproval cues provided by the therapist; implicit suggestion and persuasion; catharsis and abreaction; and (along with Volkan) identification with the therapist. (This list is similar to those offered by Frank [1976] and Strupp [1976], among others.) As for the role of insight, Marmor maintains that, while it may be useful in facilitating change, it is not essential: if an accurate or "correct" interpretation is a key factor in change, how does one explain patients' favorable therapeutic responses "to analysts with disparate theoretical views"? This same question has led many to argue that what is useful about interpretations is that they provide, to borrow Fingarette's (1963) term, a coherent "meaning scheme"; the clear implication is that many different "meaning schemes" will be equally effective and useful.[1]

Stone's chapter also reminds us of the variety of factors that can be influential in producing change. Stone deals with an interesting therapeutic phenomenon that is rarely discussed in the psychotherapy literature—what he calls "turning points." He is referring to rather sudden and dramatic positive changes, for example, the sudden experience of new alternatives beyond the rigid either/or choices a patient has set for himself; the patient's sudden emergence from mutism to communication; the sudden amelioration of a crippling symptom. Stone notes that such turning points are unlikely to occur in the treatment of essentially chronic and/or characterological conditions; they tend to appear only in cases of more acute pathological states.

Stone discusses the factors that appear to make these turning points possible. Some of the more traditional ones are: the role of awareness and insight, including the cumulative effects of small insights which, at a particular point, can result in dramatic change; the experience and awareness of alternatives and choices (which, he points out, can be particularly important with suicidal

---

[1]This question is too complex to be dealt with fully and adequately here, but some points are worth noting. For one, so-called disparate theoretical views may only appear to be disparate. To a certain extent, different theorists may say very similar things in different ways. There are a limited number of themes in human development and in pathological disturbances, and different theorists may simply employ different theoretical language to refer to these themes. We must not take theoretical controversies at face value and assume that they always reflect substantive differences.

A related point is that different theoretical systems may focus on a particular aspect of a larger truth and/or take a particular perspective on it. Unless the different theoretical systems are logically contradictory, one should not assume that their equal efficacy means that any explanatory account is as good as any other. The belief that one can have multiple perspectives and/or emphases on a complex truth does not mean that any perspective will do; nor does it mean that different perspectives are equally valid or useful. With regard to this last point, we do not know whether a rigorous, systematic study would demonstrate that all theoretical perspectives are *equally* effective in therapy. It is possible that, while all might be somewhat useful, in given cases, one perspective would be more effective than others.

For example, on the basis of what is not known about multiple, complex phobias of which chronic agoraphobia is the core, it has become clear that a central dynamic issue in these cases is, to use Mahler's (1968) term, separation-individuation. Now, it seems to us that a perspective in which separation-individuation occupies a central role would be more effective than, let us say, a perspective that interprets agoraphobia primarily in terms of prostitution and street-walking impulses (Freud, 1933). If we are correct, the former perspective would be more effective because it is more accurate, more in accord with the case (for further discussion, see Eagle, 1979). The point is that one should not readily dismiss the importance of accurate interpretation—however complex and difficult it may be to formulate criteria for interpretive accuracy and however important other factors may be.

patients); unpredictable extratherapeutic factors, such as a fortuitous environmental change; and abreaction, particularly when a major trauma is involved. Stone also discusses the patient-therapist relationship in an interesting and enlightening way, and considers the influence of both therapist and patient variables on the nature of that relationship. Thus, along with other contributors to this volume, Stone believes that the patient-therapist relationship is a curative factor and, indeed, says explicitly that the kind of parental, desexualized love toward the patient of which Nacht (1962) speaks may play a critical therapeutic role with more disturbed patients. To this extent, Stone's comment is a variation on a theme sounded by Kohut and Wolf, Tuttman, Volkan, and Marmor.

But Stone has some interesting additional things to say about what makes the patient-therapist relationship therapeutic. Among other things, the therapist must enjoy working with the patient and must genuinely believe that the patient has sufficient assets to make a lasting recovery. While such an attitude is partly dependent on the patient's characteristics (e.g., characterological type) and the "chemistry" between patient and therapist, it also is a product of the therapist's experiences and personality structure. Thus, a therapist's own experiences may strengthen his or her ability to instill hope in a particular patient. (One is reminded here of Fromm-Reichmann's [1959] comment that one important consequence of the therapist's having experienced a successful analysis is that he or she is better able to sustain faith and hope in the therapeutic process, particularly when things are not going well.) Stone points out that therapists' insights into their own conflicts and countertransference reactions to patients may help them become more compassionate, accepting, and spontaneous in their therapeutic work.

Stone also speaks of therapy "as a tutorial program in which the patient is given individual lessons concerning hitherto problematic life situations." He notes that "obviously, the learning that occurs during psychotherapy, especially if it has centered on the transference, is of no utility unless the patient is able to apply it to analogous situations in his outside life." What Stone is referring to here is what Fried, in her contribution, discusses as working through.

Fried recognizes that the concept of working through has been variously defined, but the essential meaning she gives to it is the "self-innovative" learning of a new outlook toward oneself and the world. Along with Stone, Fried believes that an essential aspect of therapy, especially of the transference, is the exploration of new ways of thinking, feeling, and relating. It is here that transference interpretations can be most useful. But what is learned in therapy must be tried out outside of therapy in order for real change to occur. Fried makes the compelling point that therapy involves overcoming not only the resistance to insight and awareness but also the resistance to change in modes of behaving and experiencing. She argues that "the ego does not unfold spontaneously when conflicts are understood and removed." (Here is another contributor to this volume who is implicitly saying that insight is not enough.) In addition, fresh images of the self must be mobilized by the therapist's evocation of new responses through interpretation and the establishment of a new object relationship, as well as by the patient's success in trying out these new responses in the outside world. (The idea that new behavior on the part of the therapist—as well as on the part of group members in a group therapy situation—helps both to extinguish old responses and perceptions and to facilitate new ones is, in important respects, similar to Alexander and French's [1946] concept of the "corrective emotional experience.")

In his discussion of change factors in depression, Bemporad is also concerned with modes of living—with "fundamental systems of beliefs, modes of relating, and ways of experiencing the world." Bemporad's basic thesis is that the depressed patient is characterized by a premorbid pathological mode of living that predisposes him to depression. These modes include: a life pattern in which much of one's behavior is directed toward an attempt "to wrest praise from some dominant other who has transferentially replaced the parent," and the "dominant goal" pattern in which the individual "has precariously limited his avenues of esteem to one external source: that of fulfilling some great ambition." What is required in therapy with these patients, according to Bemporad, is first, the facilitation of awareness of these depression-predisposing modes of belief, of relating, and of experience; second, their alteration through the application of awareness and insights learned in therapy to everyday life. It is in the second phase that the need to change, the resistance to change, and working through occur. The third stage Bemporad refers to as "consolidations." He warns therapists not to assume a nurturing role or to permit depressed patients to idealize them. Bemporad believes such interactions will only perpetuate the patient's pathological mode. Instead, he urges that the patient's attempt "to distort the therapist into a needed transference figure" be subjected to "mutual analysis." Bemporad's view seems somewhat contrary both to Kohut and Wolf's interest in mobilizing narcissistic transference and to Tuttman's view of the therapeutic significance of regression. What may be involved here are different diagnostic categories (e.g., depression versus narcissistic disorders) as well as different degrees of pathology.

It would appear, however, that differences in conceptualization and preferred technique separate the contributors to this volume at least as much as do differences in the type and degree of pathology they encounter as therapists. For example, while Kohut and Kernberg presumably work with the same kind of patients, Kohut sees lack of self-cohesiveness as the central issue, with aggression as secondary, whereas Kernberg focuses on oral rage and envy.

They also differ in the technical implications of how the central problem is conceptualized.[2]

In Kernberg's view, the theory of psychoanalytic psychotherapy is not keeping pace with changes in theoretical views of personality and psychopathology. Specifically, patients with "severe character pathology and borderline personality organization" show "an intrapsychic structural organization that seems very different from the more usual transference developments in better-functioning patients." They show "contradictory ego states that reflect primitive internalized object relations, including primitive condensations of dissociated aggressive and sexual drives in the context of the relationship between part self- and part object representations that cannot be clearly located or differentiated in terms of ego, superego, and id structures." In arguing that the traditional psychoanalytic tripartite structural model and conceptualization of change do not fit these cases, Kernberg reviews the contributions of object relations theory that he believes are necessary to account for borderline pathology and develops the implications of his theoretical views for the conduct of psychoanalytic psychotherapy. Since his work, like Kohut's, has received considerable attention, we will limit our discussion to his view of the implications of object relations theory for a conception of curative factors in treatment.

Kernberg states that both psychoanalysis and psychoanalytic psychotherapy are appropriate treatments for mild disorders. By contrast, borderline patients respond poorly to both psychoanalysis and supportive psychotherapy. These and other findings from the Menninger Foundation Psychotherapy Research Project suggest that expressive, rather than supportive, psychotherapy is the treatment of choice for borderline patients. Stated succinctly, the central issues in borderline patients are envy and oral aggression, which lead to primitive splitting and ego weakness. The main therapeutic task is to help the patient become aware of and integrate split-off self- and object representations.

In cautioning against the traditional view that borderline patients should receive supportive therapy, Kernberg makes a crucial point. He argues against the idea that a very disturbed patient requires a warm therapist who can be internalized as a compensation for a poor infant-mother interaction, claiming that such a view results from a misreading of Winnicott (1958, 1965) and Loewald (1960, 1979). The key factor, according to Kernberg, is that the internalization of a benign dyadic interaction requires object constancy. Thus, with borderline patients, there is danger that an excess of support, warmth, and empathy will lead to "a primitive, pathological idealization of the 'good' therapist," and thereby prevent the patient's expression of aggression toward the therapist.

According to Kernberg, cases of severe psychopathology require changes in

---

[2]Of course, it is possible that Kernberg's patients are more disturbed than Kohut's.

the basic analytic paradigm of the systematic interpretation of transference by a neutral analyst. The following are some of his major technical prescriptions: (1) the immediate focus should be on the "here-and-now" primitive transferences that serve as resistances and genetic reconstruction should be postponed for later stages of the treatment; (2) analysis of the transference should not be systematic, but rather, should be codetermined by "the predominant conflict in immediate reality," the specific treatment goals, and "the immediately predominant transference paradigm"; (3) parameters can be introduced but should eventually be "reduced by interpretation"; and (4) interpretation and clarification should be used, but the therapist should remain neutral, using manipulation and suggestion only in instances of severe acting out.

In the context of the other contributions to this volume and the psychotherapy literature in general, Kernberg's chapter raises the question of the extent to which some of his theoretical and technical views are specific to borderline patients. For example, Gill seems to recommend an emphasis on the here-and-now transference in all cases, regardless of the nature of the psychopathology. With respect to the "systematic" interpretation of the transference, one wonders how systematic such interpretation really is, even in the case of the average neurotic. And the idea of introducing parameters when necessary and interpreting their significance later in treatment is common in analytic work with mild disorders as well. Finally, the problem of distinguishing structural versus "merely behavioral" change is a difficult one in any treatment, and we shall comment on it later in this chapter. In our view, these issues are unresolved and need to be considered in formulating a general theory of dynamic psychotherapy.

In the course of a clinically sensible, humane, lucid account of the treatment of schizophrenic patients, Lidz and Lidz succinctly state their view of what is curative as follows: " . . . the essential curative aspect of therapy lies in releasing these patients from the bondage of completing a parent's life, or of bridging the schism between their parents, to invest their energies in their own development." The Lidzes thus view excessive and conflicted symbiotic relatedness as the core intrapsychic problem in schizophrenia. A principal task for the therapist is to encourage the "patient's latent desire for individuation." Their discussion of the theapeutic process focuses on the development of trust, the confirmation of the patient's worth as a person, the avoidance of an omniscient role on the part of the therapist, and the maintenance of an optimal distance between the therapist and patient.

In presenting their clinical views and technical recommendations for the conduct of treatment with schizophrenics, the Lidzes appear to emphasize relationship factors rather than insight. To cite a specific example, "the therapist does not analyze the patient's mechanisms of defense so much as the distortions imposed by the parents' defenses of their own tenuous ego." As will be discussed in more detail later, the Lidzes are part of the general, though not complete, consensus that insight is less important than the therapeutic relationship in the treatment and cure of extremely disturbed patients.

Palombo focuses on the issue of the cognitive and experiential modes in which the patient presents his conflicts and fantasies. Basing his view on an information-processing model, Palombo argues that dreaming is essential to psychotherapeutic change. Central to his thesis is the proposition that "associative material that emerges during the analytic hour is worked through in the dreams of the following night and matched with related memories of past events that are already located in permanent storage." Failures in matching cause anxiety dreams, which, when recalled, are designated "index dreams." These are dreams in which the censorship does not allow for adequate matching. Material from the index dream appears in the dream of the following night as a day residue. When the "revised and expanded representation of the dream is rematched with the contents of the permanent memory," we have what Palombo calls a "correction dream." Apparently, in the correction dream there is an "active assimilation," integration, and working through of memories, fantasies, and conflicts in short-term storage so that they presumably become relatively quiescent elements in permanent memory. Or, as Palombo puts it, new understandings do not remain isolated in short-term memory. He claims that "the correction dream is one of the principal agents of therapeutic change."

Palombo illustrates his thesis with a series of dream reports from a patient whose case is described at greater length in his recent book (1978). Since it is difficult to pinpoint exactly when material has been assimilated, worked through, or integrated, it seems to us that considerable inference is required to label a given dream as a correction dream rather than an index dream. Palombo maintains that "the success of the correction dream seems to be a more reliable measure for the effectiveness of the therapeutic work than any criteria based entirely on what happens in the hour during which the index dream is reported." He concludes that "dreaming is not only grist for the therapeutic mill, it is the mill itself."

In elevating the dream to a preeminent position in the conduct of psychoanalysis and psychoanalytic psychotherapy, Palombo joins other writers who feel that dreams deserve a special status in treatment. He believes that Freud's (1911) comment that the dream should be treated like any other association has been incorrectly interpreted to mean that Freud was deemphasizing the role of dreams. Whether dreams—or any other *particular* form of mentation (e.g., waking fantasies, childhood memories—will differentially facilitate conflict resolution and adaptive change, and whether they should be accorded special therapeutic attention are open, empirical questions which are relevant to an explicit theory of therapy.

Having briefly described the nature of the various contributions to this volume, we turn to some of the general themes and issues that were raised.

Interpretation, Insight, and the Therapeutic Relationship

As would be expected in the context of psychodynamic psychotherapy, the three related therapeutic factors most frequently discussed in this volume are interpretation, insight, and the patient-therapist relationship. Although the three are interlocked, we believe it is possible, at least conceptually, to disentangle their relative roles. Of the three factors, the patient-therapist relationship is the most frequent overriding theme stressed by the various contributors to this volume.

Let us first consider the relationship between insight and the therapeutic relationship. As Slipp observes in his Introduction, the debate about insight versus the therapeutic relationship was already in full force in the Freud-Ferenczi controversy. In an important sense, that debate has continued among the heirs of Freud and Ferenczi, the former represented by traditional Freudian theorists, and the latter, through Klein and Balint, now represented by the so-called English object-relation theorists. For the former, insight remains the critical curative factor in psychoanalysis. It will be noted that Rangell's (1954) definition of psychoanalysis, cited by Slipp, places primary importance on insight and, indeed, makes no explicit reference to the therapeutic relationship (see also Gill, 1954). Similarly, in Bibring's (1954) formulations, insight through interpretation is the primary curative factor in psychoanalysis.

It is widely accepted that therapeutically useful insight requires the context of an ongoing relationship. Both Hatcher and Gill remind us of the importance of dealing with active feelings that have emotional immediacy. And it is also widely observed that offering a clarifying and insight-facilitating interpretation itself contributes to a therapeutic relationship. A number of contributors, however, explicitly or implicitly take the position that the patient-therapist relationship can have therapeutic effects quite apart from that of generating insight. Indeed, at least one contributor, Marmor, tells us that the relationship factor is primary and that insight is not necessary for therapeutic progress. And other contributors—Volkan, for example—while not taking the explicit position taken by Marmor, stress the role of factors, such as identification with the therapist, which would appear to be at least somewhat independent of insight. In effect, what is being said is that while insight may depend on an ongoing therapeutic relationship, the patient-therapist relationship can be therapeutic quite apart from insight.

It is worth noting a recent paper by Bush (1978), who argues that Freud himself placed greater emphasis on the role of the therapeutic relationship than on that of insight in effecting change and cure. He cites the following passage as evidence that Freud was not especially impressed with the therapeutic efficacy of insight:

If the patient is to fight his way through the normal conflict with the resistances which we have uncovered for him in the analysis, he is in need of a powerful stimulus which will influence the decision in the sense which we desire, leading to recovery. Otherwise it might happen that he would choose in favor of repeating the earlier outcome and would allow what had been brought up into consciousness to slip back again into repression. At this point what turns the scale in his struggle is not his intellectual insight—which is neither strong enough nor free enough for such an achievement— but simply and solely his relation to the doctor. Insofar as his transference bears a "plus" sign, it clothes the doctor with authority and is transformed into belief in his communications and explanations. In the absence of such a transference, or if it is a negative one, the patient would never even give a hearing to the doctor and his arguments [Freud, 1917, p. 445].[3]

We turn next to the role of interpretation and its relation to the therapeutic relationship. While the importance of interpretation is discussed by most, if not all, of the contributors, it does not occupy the central place it has been given in more traditional accounts. Furthermore, interpretation is often viewed as important, not primarily because of the insight and understanding it provides, but because it gives the patient a *feeling of being understood*. That is, the major importance of the insight derived from interpretation is viewed, not in terms of cognitive restructuring, but in terms of such relationship factors as feeling understood, the provision of empathy and mirroring, facilitating identification with the therapist, etc.

Interestingly enough, interpretation is still seen as a primary tool, but its therapeutic role is linked to relationship factors rather than to insight. It is in the act of making accurate and helpful interpretations that the therapist expresses his empathic understanding and helps the patient differentiate archaic representations from current ones. In short, providing an accurate and helpful interpretation is therapeutically important because in so doing the therapist functions as a good object.

A somewhat different aspect of the relation between interpretation and the therapeutic relationship is involved in the oft-debated question whether interpretations should be almost exclusively concerned with the transference situa-

---

[3]Bush cites this passage as evidence of Freud's skepticism regarding the role of insight as a sufficient basis for change as well as of his emphasis on the curative primacy of the therapeutic relationship. However, a close reading of this statement indicates that, rather than downgrading insight, Freud is stressing the role of the relationship in maintaining insights already achieved and in facilitating the process of working through in achieving a cure.

tion or should be concerned with a variety of extratransference concerns and experiences. In this volume, Gill's paper is a good example of the former position, while Bemporad's paper is a good example of the latter—insofar as he stresses the importance of offering interpretations of the patients' pathological life style, including their destructive belief systems, which are only indirectly related to transference reactions.

In this process of conceptual disentangling one can also look at the relationship between insight and interpretations. In traditional psychoanalytic theory, a most secure and unquestioned link is that between insight and interpretation. As noted above, however, that link is weakened in this volume. Feeling understood, rather than insight or understanding per se (or cognitive clarity and restructuring), is viewed by most of the contributors as the critical therapeutic aspect of interpretation. That is, while insight facilitation is seen as a legitimate function of interpretation, the provision of empathy by the "good object" is seen as its primary role. It is interesting to note that this attitude toward interpretation parallels, in important respects, general developments in the field of psychotherapy research.

For example, Bergin and Lambert (1978), after reviewing a good deal of the psychotherapy literature, conclue that the "power [of techniques] for change pales when compared with that of personal influence. Technique is crucial to the extent that it provides a believable rationale and congenial modus operandi for the change agent and the client." They add that "these considerations imply that psychotherapy is laden with nonspecific or placebo factors . . . but these influences, when specified, may prove to be the essence of what provides the therapeutic benefit" (pp. 179–180).[4] They make clear that, in their view, those "placebo factors" center on "an interpersonal relationship" with the therapist that "is characterized by trust, warmth, acceptance, and human wisdom" (p. 180)—a point of view quite similar to the one enunciated by Marmor in this volume.

Although Bergin and Lambert view the value of interpretation primarily in terms of its importance for the relationship, what appears to remain intact is the assumption that if insight is to be achieved the primary means of achieving

---

[4]A Grünbaum (1979) points out in an enlightening discussion of the concept of placebo, "nonspecific" and "placebo" cannot be equated. Placebo factors are no less specific than any other set of factors. Rather, it is only with respect to a particular theory specifying what is supposed to be effective (in relation to a particular outcome) that certain factors can be seen as placebos. For example, if one theorizes that interpretation and insight are the curative factors, and it turns out that the accepting *way* in which an interpretation is made is the curative factor, one would call the latter a placebo factor. But, (1) the placebo factor is no more and no less specific than interpretation and insight; and (2) it is a placebo factor only in relation to a particular theory. If one had theorized that authenticity of manner is a major curative agent, it would no longer constitute a placebo factor.

it (however important or unimportant that may be) is through interpretation. But this link is also attenuated by recent findings from a group of psychoanalytic researchers (Weiss et al., 1980) who present evidence that patients can develop insight *without* interpretation as long as they experience "conditions of safety" in the therapeutic situation. This finding suggests that the emergence of warded-off contents, which is necessary to and part of the process of insight, can occur simply as a function of the patient's feeling safe in the therapeutic relationship (following "enactments" with the therapist which constitute test passing). If one accepts the view of Weiss, Sampson, and their colleagues (Weiss 1971; Sampson *et al.,* 1972; Horowitz *et al.,* 1975; Sampson, 1976; Sampson *et al.,* 1977; Weiss *et al.,* 1980) that patients primarily want to master infantile traumas, conflicts, and anxieties (as opposed to the view that they primarily want to gratify infantile impulses and wishes), have unconscious plans to do so, and make unconscious decisions about whether to lift defenses and express warded-off contents, then it is not surprising that under appropriate "conditions of safety" insight occurs without interpretation.

One can certainly conclude from this work that insight and the patient-therapist relationship are not opposing factors. But one might also make the more sweeping claim that the therapeutic relationship is the primary factor, not only as a direct curative agent (as is claimed by some of the contributors to this volume) but as the critical determinant of insight. In other words, what is implied in this view is that the most profound, incisive, and well-timed interpretation will not lead to change if "conditions of safety" do not obtain and, in addition, that insight and change can occur as a direct consequence of the establishment of "conditions of safety."[5]

The concept of conditions of safety recalls Bush's (1978) suggestion that, at least in part, insight entails changes in one's perception of danger. For example, a patient may come to realize that criticizing the therapist will not destroy therapist or patient. If Bush is right, the patient's determination of whether a potential situation of danger had really changed would be influenced, not so much by the specific interpretation offered as by the general response of the therapist to criticism.

Degree of Pathology

Many of the contributors link their increased emphasis on the therapeutic relationship and their relative deemphasis of insight to the related facts that (1) they are dealing with more disturbed (rather than neurotic) patients and (2) they are describing dynamic or psychoanalytic psychotherapy rather than

---

[5]While this research demonstrates that interpretation is not a necessary precondition for insight, it does, of course, frequently generate insight.

so-called classical psychoanalysis. As cited by Slipp, Bibring (1954) acknowledged that in dynamic psychotherapy the therapeutic relationship assumes greater importance than it does in psychoanalysis proper. There is, moreover, some evidence that among the contributors to this volume, those who are not writing specifically about more disturbed patients (for example, Gill, Bemporad, and Langs) do place greater stress on the role of insight and less stress on other factors. With regard to the latter, we have already noted Bemporad's belief that, in working with neurotically depressed patients, idealization of the therapist—a transference development encouraged by Kohut and Wolf with narcissistic patients—is to be resisted.

But this general observation regarding the relation between the role of insight and the type of patient must be qualified. Marmor, for example, does not limit the lessened importance of insight to more disturbed patients. The context of his remarks regarding insight suggests that he means his comments to be general ones, applicable to all psychotherapy. Conversely, Kernberg, who deals with the more disturbed borderline and narcissistic categories, does not appear to minimize the role of insight.

The question thus is posed: what is the interaction between type and degree of pathology and the nature of curative factors? Are there specific therapeutic factors that are applicable to a particular type and degree of pathology, as well as general factors that are applicable across the board? Whether the changed conceptions of what is curative are applicable only to a limited range of more disturbed patients or to a wider patient population is one of the unresolved issues that emerges from this volume. (Ambiguity about this question as well as the larger question of the range of applicability of his self psychology can also be found in the work of Kohut.) It is possible that the more disturbed patients—those with narcissistic disorders, borderline conditions, or schizoid states—may represent today's modal patient and that the classically neurotic patient—if he or she ever did exist in pure form—may be a disappearing breed. One recalls Erikson's (1963) observation, which was made well before the recent preoccupation with narcissistic and borderline phenomena: "the patient of today suffers most under the problem of what he should believe in and who he should—or, indeed, might—be or become; while the patient of early psychoanalysis suffered most under inhibitions which prevented him from being what and who he thought he knew he was" (p. 279).

In other words, problems of values, self, and identity—which are so prominent in, for example, Kohut's (1971, 1977) descriptions of narcissistic personality disorders—may well be widespread phenomena. If that is so, the modifications in theory and technique that were presumably relevant only for a certain limited class of patients may well be applicable to a much wider range of patients. Indeed, as Gedo (1980) observes, many patients who are diagnosed by Kohut's followers as "narcissistic disorders" are indistinguishable from other patients in whom more traditional analysts found "significant Oedipal problems" but "no other sources of psychopathology" (p. 372). In short, whether so-called "narcissistic disorders" and certain classes of borderline conditions are distinguishable categories of psychopathology, qualitatively different from neurotic patients, or whether they mainly represent the predominant nature of today's neurosis, is an open question.[6] In any case, in the present context, the point to be stressed again is that the therapeutic factors—for example, the importance of the patient-therapist relationship—which some contributors suggest are mainly applicable to certain classes of pathology may be the critical elements in the general activity of all psychotherapy.

Warded-Off Contents and Therapeutic Attitude

While all of the contributors to this volume uphold the basic psychoanalytic emphasis on facilitating conscious access to warded-off contents (i.e., repressed and split-off material), they depart from traditional views in their conception of *what* is warded off and *how* one should facilitate access to this material. There is not a unanimous acceptance of the traditional assumption that warded-off contents are necessarily derivatives of sexual and aggressive drives. A number of contributors refer to various other contents. Thus, Kohut and Wolf discuss patients' lack of access to archaic narcissitic needs; Tuttman stresses their unmet dependency needs; Volkan emphasizes their archaic introjects; Bemporad focuses on patients' lack of awareness of their pathological program of living, including their pathological belief systems; Stone refers to lack of awareness of choices and alternatives; and so on.

With regard to the issue of what constitutes an appropriate and facilitating therapeutic attitude, a number of contributors claim that analytic neutrality (what Kubie [1975, p. 100] referred to as "analytic incognito") is not therapeutic and needs to be replaced by such attitudes as empathy, interest, and warmth. Further, the altered conception of the kinds of unconscious contents that are warded off is linked to this conception of a proper therapeutic stance. Thus, one finds some contributors talking about the legitimacy (and even necessity) of partial gratification of the patient's needs (including archaic and infantile needs). Such a position is incompatible with the traditional view of

---

[6]That is, the form of current pathology may be particularly "narcissistic" and "borderline" in nature. As far as we know, no one has adequately explained the recent veritable preoccupation with narcissistic and borderline disorders and the relatively sudden popularity of these diagnoses. We strongly suspect that an explanatory framework which goes beyond an appeal to early mother-infant interactions and includes broad social factors will be necessary to shed light on this phenomenon.

the warded-off contents; namely, that they consist solely of sexual and aggressive wishes. But when one holds that the warded-off material includes wishes centering on, let us say, the need for mirroring or idealization, the strictures against any therapeutic gratification do not seem as self-evident.

There is a good deal of ambiguity about the meaning of "neutrality" and a "neutral stance." Neutrality may mean an aloof and impersonal manner, with as close an approximation as possible to "blank screen" status—an approach that led Ferenczi (1919) to wonder whether the therapist was fulfilling the patient's neurotic expectations regarding the "bad" and rejecting other. Or "technical neutrality" may include such behaviors as not taking sides in the conflict; not being overinvolved, for one's own countertransference reasons, in one particular set of therapeutic goals; not being overinvolved in therapeutic outcome; not being seductive, manipulative, or sadistic; centering most of one's therapeutic gratification on the experience of professional competence. Interpreted in the latter way, neutrality need not be at all contrary to empathy, genuine interest, or warmth (see Kohut, and Wolf, this volume).

Weiss et al. (1975, 1977a 1977b) have done some interesting work relevant to the question of analytic neutrality as well as to the larger issues of insight and the patient-therapist relationship. They have presented empirical evidence that therapist neutrality is significantly associated with the emergence of unconscious, warded-off contents. When a patient tries to get the therapist to satisfy certain infantile wishes and the latter does not do so, the patient becomes more relaxed rather than more anxious. According to Weiss and Sampson, this response can be explained by the fact that most patients want to *master, rather than gratify,* unconscious infantile wishes; they hope to disconfirm the infantile beliefs and ideas that generated their conflicts and anxiety. However, in order to come forth with this distressing material, the patient must first determine whether "conditions of safety" prevail in the therapeutic situations—determinations that are made through tests unconsciously presented to the therapist.

In this context, one can see that it is not analytic neutrality per se that is important, but rather, the *degree to which it constitutes the conditions of safety developed in the therapeutic relationship.* It can be shown empirically that neutrality usually will constitute a condition of safety because, above all, patients need guarantees that the therapist will *not* be drawn into their infantile wishes. Rather than gratification of these wishes, they need assurances that the therapist will not be hurt and destroyed, will not be seduced or seductive, will not be "impinging" (Winnicott, 1958, 1965), etc.

Thus, to cite some of Weiss et al.'s examples: when a female patient learned that she was not actually hurting or destroying the therapist, she felt safer to express omnipotent wishes and fantasies; when a male patient felt assured that the therapist would not be seduced, he could then express his fear of homosexuality.[7]

Thus, a relationship is therapeutic to the degree that it constitutes a "condition of safety" for the patient. The condition of safety, in turn, will be a function of the individual dynamics and defenses of the patient, the "match" between patient and therapist, and the personality of the therapist, among other things.

Sharp distinctions between therapeutic neutrality and the "real" relationship are artificial (see Dewald, 1976). For one, the "real" characteristics of the therapist will always be apparent, even in someone completely emulating the "blank screen" role (see Gill, this volume); and two, the "real" characteristics and personality of the therapist are the vehicle for any therapeutic work that is carried out. Such work is not done by disembodied interpreters, supporters, or whatever, but by particular persons with particular characteristics and styles. We need to remind ourselves constantly that this is so. For the position therapists take on issues such as neutrality versus warmth, etc., may bear a complex and uncertain relation to *what therapists actually do in therapy and to the personal and interactional feelings and attitudes they convey.* It is likely that some therapists who espouse an extreme "blank screen" position may convey a great deal of warmth and genuineness, whereas other therapists who advocate such qualities in theory may be personally remote and aloof.

Being accepting of someone, being genuinely interested in someone, and feeling warmly toward someone are *organic,* personal—or more accurately, interpersonal—qualities that cannot be meaningfully generated by the knowledge that they are therapeutic. Every therapist enjoys working with certain patients more than others; every therapist is more genuinely interested in and feels more warmly toward some patients than others (see Stone, this volume). Here Levenson's point concerning authenticity is quite relevant. It is unlikely that merely presenting an attitude of acceptance, interest, and warmth will be experienced in the same way or have the same effects as the authentic behaviors and feelings. Even authentically expressed attitudes cannot be assumed to have the same meaning and the same effects for all patients.

While everyone would probably agree about the general applicability of certain ingredients in psychotherapy—for example, being nonjudgmental, accept-

---

[7]Slipp (1981) has investigated direct family interaction and has suggested that the patient's developmental fixation occured because the existing family dynamics corresponded to, and thus reinforced, the patient's unconscious fantasy; that is, aggression actually was considered as destructive in families of schizophrenics, whereas in families of hysterics and borderlines an Oedipal triumph seemed possible. Slipp believes that it is important for the therapist to resist the countertransference tendency to reinforce such conflicts. The therapist needs to contain the patient's projective identification and to respond differently than the patient's family did in order to permit the differentiation between omnipotent fantasies and reality.

ing, showing genuine interest—the meaning and impact of other ingredients would depend on the particular patient and therapist involved. For example, for certain patients at particular times in therapy, obvious warmth might be experienced as a seduction or as generally "impinging," thereby creating anxiety, mobilizing defenses, and decreasing the likelihood of access to warded-off material. This point is quite relevant to parallels drawn by some of the contributors between the therapeutic relationship and the parent-child relationship.

Parallel between Psychotherapy and the Mother-Child Relationship

It seems to us that the claim that therapy meets unmet archaic needs, and a general uncritical parallel between therapy and good parenting, involve the risk of overlooking the above (and other) considerations. That is, in most cases of psychopathology, it is not simply a question of meeting unmet needs on the order of a deficiency-compensation model—analogous to having a vitamin deficiency and taking vitamins to correct the deficiency. Rather, it is often more like having a deficiency and being conflicted about and/or allergic to the "substance" which could correct the deficiency. For example, someone deprived of love and nurturance is frequently precisely the person who experiences intense fear as well as need of intimacy and love. Hence, it is often the ability to resolve the conflict through clarification and mastery, rather than gratification, that is therapeutic.

The fact is, moreover, that an adult patient, however disturbed and regressed, is not a chronological infant. Hence, the parallel betwen the therapeutic relationship and the mother-child relationship cannot be complete. In discussing the role of regression in therapy, Tuttman tells us that offering empathic understanding and clarification are therapeutic, while milk-giving and hand-holding are inadvisable. But why are the latter inadvisable? Is it, as Tuttman suggests, because milk-giving and hand-holding are libidinally gratifying? Or is it because they are infantilizing, preclude mastery, and are, so to speak, age-inappropriate? Responding to someone with acceptance and understanding is age-appropriate for a adult, whereas milk-giving and hand-holding entail treating the patient regressively. Or, to put it somewhat differently, although an attitude of acceptance and understanding may facilitate the patient's access to regressive phenomena, it is not regression-inducing.

It must also be kept in mind that even when therapy involves gratifying the patient's more primitive and archaic needs, the gratification is generally *indirect, disguised, and symbolic*. Thus, Silverman writes about *unconscious and symbolic* gratification of symbiotic fantasies. And, as will be recalled by those familiar with Sechehaye's (1951) account of Reneé, her schizophrenic patient, therapeutic gratification of life-sustaining primitive needs such as eating initially had to be provided symbolically by Sechehaye. (Hence, the title of her book was *Symbolic Realization*. Such provision was necessary because Reneé's mortal terrors and conflicts concerned those very areas in which she had been deprived.

One sees this same phenomenon at work, in less extreme form, with other patients. For many patients, being emphatically understood may have the symbolic and nonthreatening meaning of a good maternal environment, while more direct provision of a maternal (and paternal) environment and more direct gratification of regressive wishes are likely to prove threatening and destructive. In clinical work, one can observe that such direct gratification is likely to evoke, among other things, fear of being seduced and overwhelmed, frightening and insatiable greediness, and rage at past disappointments and deprivations. Above all, one must remember that, as Loewald (1979) puts it, "the analysis of adults, no matter how much given to regression or how immature they are in significant areas of their functioning, is a venture in which the analysand not only is, in fact, chronologically a grownup, but which makes sense only if his or her adult potential, as manifested in certain significant areas of life, is in evidence" (pp. 163–164).

A more meaningful comparison between the parent-child relationship and the therapeutic one is, as Strupp (1976) points out, likely to center on the fact that the patient is in a dependent relationship, is subject to the influences that such a relationship entails, and is encouraged to substitute inner control and autonomy for such external influences—a process not unlike socialization.

Working Through

In describing each of the individual contributions, we have already spoken of the emphasis on working through as a therapeutic factor. Here we want to make the additional point that of the various meanings that can be given to the term working through, most of the contributors emphasize the process of trying out in one's outside life what one has learned in therapy, particularly about one's interactions with the therapist. As noted earlier, much of the discussion of working through is evocative of Alexander and French's (1946) concept of the "corrective emotional experience," as are other formulations in this volume. For example, Volkan's emphasis on the importance of helping the patient "decontaminate" archaic representations from new ones, in relation to the therapist, bears a resemblance to the concept of a "corrective emotional experience," notwithstanding differences in terminology and in broader conceptualization. There is one important difference, however; Volkan and the other contributors to this volume would be likely to reject Alexander and French's manipulative strategy of carefully targeting the particular "corrective emotional experiences," including the therapists' deliberate selection of certain roles to play. In other words, they would expect the so-called "corrective emotional experience" to evolve spontaneously in the course of the therapeutic relationship.

Pre-Oedipal versus Oedipal Factors and Self versus Drive Theory

Although we cannot discuss it at length here, we want to note that running through some of the contributions are the related issues of the Oedipal versus pre-Oedipal basis of pathology, and self psychology versus drive theory as the basis for conceptualizing personality development and psychopathology. These issues appear in a number of contributions concerned with patients whose pathology is characterized by disturbances in self-cohesion, defective ego organization, and early developmental difficulties. Furthermore, the pre-Oedipal versus Oedipal and self versus drive theory disputes appear to parallel the therapeutic relationship versus insight debate. That is, those conceptualizing pathology mainly in pre-Oedipal and self theory terms are more likely to focus on the importance of the therapeutic relationship, whereas those stressing Oedipal factors and drive theory are likely to emphasize the role of insight.

Research on Therapeutic Outcome

In the present context, where the main concern is curative factors in psychotherapy, the critical question is whether different theoretical conceptions—pre-Oedipal versus Oedipal, self versus drive theory, or any other—are associated with differential effectiveness (see Silverman and Wolitzky, this volume). There is some evidence (Gedo, 1980) that more favorable therapeutic outcomes may be associated with "focusing on certain pregenital issues" that may include the developmental antecedents determining the Oedipal fixation. Issues of this kind need to be investigated more systematically. While it is extremely difficult to tease out the weights of different specific factors in therapeutic outcome, the effects of certain broad variables—such as different theoretical conceptions and their respective areas of concentration in therapy—*can* be more systematically investigated.

Gedo's (1980) observation that the analysts at the New York Psychoanalytic Institute involved in the Firestein report (1978) found predominantly Oedipal difficulties, whereas the analysts of the Chicago case book (Goldberg, 1978) found mainly pre-Oedipal material and self difficulties, raises important questions. Were the New York and Chicago therapists *interpreting* and formulating the patient's productions differently or were there differences in the actual content of the material elicited from the patients? If the latter is the case, did the personality as well as the theoretical orientation of the therapist play a significant part in the kind of material elicited? For example, would a more aloof and authoritarian therapist be more likely to elicit Oedipal material? Here one must consider that the patients' very choice of therapist is likely to be influenced by their dynamic conflicts. These and other possibilities remind us once again of the importance of systematic therapeutic outcome studies in which the therapeutic effects of different variables are investigated.

Therapeutic Process

An important issue that needs to be pursued is *how* the various purported curative factors effect change. What specific psychological processes are involved? A careful microanalysis needs to be done in this area. Unfortunately, some of the concepts and functional relations posited by analysts and therapists are vague and need to be further sharpened and clarified. For example, what specifically is meant by "the building up of psychic structures"? And, as Gedo (1980) asks, how can the reliving of certain childhood experiences in the transference lead to the repair of developmental deficits? Are we, as Gedo suggests, really dealing with the acquisition of essential skills and the relative freeing of the learning process in the wake of such changes as increased trust and decreased grandiosity and anxiety? As a final example, how does one distinguish "structural" change from change that is "largely behavioral"? What is the measurable difference between "a partial increase in ego strength," the presumed outcome of psychoanalytic psychotherapy, and "a reduction in the rigidity of the ego's defensive structures," the presumed outcome of classical psychoanalysis (Kernberg, this volume)? These are all thorny issues that, so far, are neither clearly defined nor adequately resolved.

An Autonomous Theory of Psychotherapy

We believe that one of the general conclusions to be drawn from this volume is that we need to develop a quasi-autonomous theory of therapy which, in good measure, stands apart from theories of personality development, especially those concerning the etiology of pathology. That is, we need to establish an independent and strong empirical base of knowledge and understanding of the therapeutic factors that produce change and the processes by which they produce change.

In this volume, Silverman and Wolitzky outline some research strategies that could be used to resolve controversial issues and to generate a body of reliable clinical knowledge. How this body of knowledge and theory will then fit into theories of the etiology of pathology and of personality development will undoubtedly be a complex matter. What we cannot assume—as is often implicitly assumed—is that effective treatment mirrors etiology. For example, if empathic understanding is therapeutically effective, it does not necessarily follow that *lack* of empathic understanding was a significant etiological and historical factor in the patients' pathology. This possibly fallacious link between therapeutic effectiveness and etiology is particularly likely to be generated by the general analogizing between therapist-patient and mother-child interactions. Thus, if a particular therapeutic intervention or phenomenon (e.g., mobilizing a mirroring transference) is helpful, one conceptualizes it in terms analogous to "good" parenting that is therapeutic because it makes up for the etiologically significant "bad" parenting. Logically, this is equivalent to arguing that an underconcentration of aspirin in the blood is the etiologically significant factor in headaches.

Theories of etiology presented by clinicians are often built on adult patients' recollections of purported genetic *events,* such as mother's attitude and behavior toward the patient as a young child (even as an infant), with no corroboration other than the adult patients' free associations, dreams, and, on occasion, direct reports.[8]

As Gedo (1980) notes, in commenting on similar accounts, "the detection of a specific transference configuration was used, in a global way, to postulate the occurrence of an equally global, typical childhood emotional constellation" (p. 371). Furthermore, etiological theories regarding certain nosological categories (e.g., narcissistic personality disorders or borderline conditions) are developed on the basis of these data. It should not be necessary to point out that an adult patient's free associations, dreams, etc., however useful they may be as a guide to the patient's perceptions, feelings, and intrapsychic life, are likely to bear uncertain and complex relation to actual early events. If one wants to relate early events to later pathology, at the very least one has to have some firm, independent, reliable evidence regarding these early events. The most elementary notions of what constitutes evidence would make this point apparent, even self-evident.

If one wants to study the relationship between, let us say, patterns of mother-child interactions and later pathology, one needs to study mother-child interactions directly in longitudinal studies. This is not the same as studying an adult patient's perceptions, feelings, and memories of his early years, nor is it the same as inferring what the mothering must have been like on the basis of interpretations and renderings of the adult patient's productions. This is not to say that the therapeutic situation may not be heuristically valuable in generating hypotheses regarding the etiology and vicissitudes of patterns observed in adults.

---

[8]Such accounts often begin with the caution that the patient's *perceptions* and experiences (of mother's attitudes, behavior, etc.) are being presented, but they soon lapse into talk about the mother's *actual* behavior and attitudes. It should be noted that it is only the patient's *current* perceptions and memories (in the context of the therapeutic situation) that are available.

While the material generated in psychotherapy may not serve as solid evidence for a theory of etiology or a general theory of personality, it can and should provide basic data for an autonomous theory of psychotherapy—that is, a formulation of the necessary and sufficient conditions for therapeutic change. Quite apart from general theories of personality, it is important to identify those factors that lead to specific therapeutic outcomes. In the course of specifying these factors, we will need to attend to issues such as independent criteria for the validity and effectiveness of interpretations, placebo effects, and patient and therapist variables, separately and in interaction with one another. Our task for the future is to subject the many intriguing ideas and important clinical insights presented in this volume to controlled, systematic investigation.

REFERENCES

Alexander, F., & French, T. M. (1946). *Psychoanalytic Therapy*. New York: Ronald Press.

Bergin, A. E., & Lambert, M. J. (1978). The evaluation of therapeutic outcomes. In: *Handbook of Psychotherapy and Behavior Change,* ed. S. L. Garfield & A. E. Bergin. New York: Wiley, pp. 139–189.

Bibring, E. (1954). Psychoanalysis and the dynamic psychotherapies. *J. Amer. Psychoanal. Assn.,* 2:745–770.

Bush, M. (1978). Preliminary considerations for a psychoanalytic theory of insight: Historical perspective. *Internat. Rev. Psychoanal.,* 5:1–13.

Dewald, P. A. (1976). Transference regression and real experience. *Psychoanal. Quart.,* 45:213–230.

Eagle, M. (1979). Psychoanalytic formulations of phobias. In: *Integrating Ego Psychology and Object Relations Theory,* ed. D. S. Milman & D. Goldman. Dubuque, Iowa: Kendall-Hunt Publishing Co.

Erikson, E. (1963). *Childhood and Society*. New York: Norton.

Ferenczi, S. (1919). On the technique of psychoanalysis. In: *Further Contributions to the Theory and Technique of Psychoanalysis*. London: Hogarth, pp. 177–180.

Fingarett, H. (1963). *The Self in Transformation*. New York: Basic Books.

Firestein, S. (1978). *Termination in Psychoanalysis*. New York: International Universities Press.

Frank, J. (1976). Restoration of morale and behavior change. In: *What Makes Behavior Change Possible?* ed. A. Burton. New York: Brunner/Mazel, pp. 73–95.

Freud, S. (1933). New introductory lectures on psychoanalysis. *Standard Edition,* 22:156–157. London: Hogarth Press, 1964.

Fromm-Reichman, F. (1959). Personality of the psychotherapist and the doctor-patient relationship. In: *Psychoanalysis and Psychotherapy: Selected Papers of Frieda Fromm-Reichman,* ed. D. M. Bullard. Chicago: University of Chicago Press, pp. 100–104.

Gedo, J. (1980). Reflections on some current controversies in psychoanalysis. *J. Amer. Psychoanal. Assn.,* 28:363–383.

Gill, M. M. (1954). Psychoanalysis and exploratory psychotherapy. *J. Amer. Psychoanal. Assn.,* 2:771–797.

Goldberg, A. (1978). *The Psychology of the Self: A casebook*. New York: International Universities Press.

Greenson, R. R., & Wexler, M. (1969). The nontransference relationship in the psychoanalytic situation. *Internatl. J. Psychoanal.,* 50:27–39.

Grunbaum, A. (1979). Epistemological liabilities of the clinical appraisal of psychoanalytic theory. *Psychoanal. & Contemp. Thought,* 2:451–526.

Guntrip, H. (1968). *Schizoid Phenomena, Object Relations and the Self.* New York: International Universities Press.

Hartmann, H. (1939). *Ego Psychology and the Problem of Adaptation.* New York: International Universities Press (1959).

Horowitz, L. M., Sampson, H., Siegelman, E. Y., Wolfson, A. W., & Weiss, J. (1975). On the identification of warded-off mental contents. *J. Abnorm. Psychol.,* 84:545–558.

Kohut, H. (1971). *Analysis of the Self.* New York: International Universities Press.

――― (1977). *Restoration of the Self.* New York: International Universities Press.

Kris, E. (1956). On some vicissitudes of insight in psychoanalysis. *Internat. J. Psychoanal.,* 37:445–455.

Kubie, L. S. (1952). Problems and techniques of validation and progress. In: *Psychoanalysis as Science,* ed. E. Pumpian-Mindlin. Stanford, CA: Stanford University Press, pp. 46–124.

Loewald, H. (1960). On the therapeutic action of psychoanalysis. *Internat. J. Psychoanal.,* 41:16–33.

――― (1979). Reflections on the psychoanalytic process and its therapeutic potential. *The Psychoanalytic Study of the Child,* 34:155-167.

Mahler, M. (1968). *On Human Symbiosis and the Vicissitudes of Individuation, Vol. 1: Infantile Psychosis.* New York: International Universities Press.

Myerson, P. (1965). Modes of insight. *J. Amer. Psychoanal. Assn.,* 13:771–792.

Nacht, S. (1962). The curative factors in psychoanalysis. *Internat. J. Psychoanal.,* 43:194–234.

Palombo, S. (1978). *Dreaming and Memory: A New Information-Processing Model.* New York: Basic Books.

Rangell, L. (1954). Similarities and differences between psychoanalysis and dynamic psychotherapy. *J. Amer. Psychoanal. Assn.,* 2:734–744.

――― (1979). Countertransference issues in the theory of therapy. *J. Amer. Psychoanal. Assn.* (Supplement), 27:81–112.

Sampson, H. (1976). A critique of certain traditional concepts in the psychoanalytic theory of therapy. *Bull. Menninger Clin.,* 40:255–262.

――― Weiss, J., Mlodnosky, L., & Hause, E. (1972). Defense analysis and the emergence of warded-off mental contents. *Arch. Gen. Psychiat.,* 26:524–532.

―――& Weiss, J. (1977). Research on the psychoanalytic process: An overview. Bull. No. 2, March 1977. The Psychotherapy Research Group, Department of Psychiatry, Mt. Zion Hospital and Medical Center.

Searles, H. F. (1965). *Collected Papers on Schizophrenia and Related Subjects.* New York: International Universities Press.

Sechahaye, M. (1951). *Symbolic Realization.* New York: International Universities Press.

Silverman, L. H. (1978). The unconscious symbiotic fantasy as a ubiquitous therapeutic agent. *Internat. J. Psychoanal. Psychother.,* 7:562–585.

Slipp, S. (1973). The symbiotic survival pattern: A relational theory of schizophrenia. *Family Process,* 12:377–398.

――― (1981). The conflict of power and achievement in depression. In: *Object and Self: A Developmental Approach,* ed. S. Tuttman. New York: International Universities Press.

Sterba, J. (1934). The fate of the ego in analytic therapy. *Internat. J. Psychoanal.,* 15:117–126.

Strachey, J. (1934). The nature of the therapeutic action of psychoanalysis. *Internatl. J. Psychoanal.,* 15:127–159.

Strupp, H. (1976). The nature of the therapeutic influence and its basic ingredient. In: *What Makes Behavior Change Possible?* ed. A. Burton. New York: Brunner/Mazel, pp. 96–112.

Weiss, J. (1971). The emergence of new themes: A contribution to the psychoanalytic theory of therapy. *Internat. J. Psychoanal.*, 52:459–467.

—— Sampson, H., Caston, J., Silberschatz, G., & Gassner, S. (1977). Research on the psychoanalytic process. Bull No. 3, Dec. 1977. The Psychotherapy Research Group, Department of Psychiatry, Mt. Zion Hospital and Medical Center.

—— Sampson, H., Gassner, S., & Caston, J. (1980). Further research on the psychoanalytic process. Bull No. 4, June 1980. The Psychotherapy Research Group, Department of Psychiatry, Mt. Zion Hospital and Medical Center.

Winnicott, D. W. (1958). *Collected Papers: Through Pediatrics to Psychoanalysis.* New York: Basic Books.

Winnicott, D. W. (1965). *The Maturational Process and the Facilitating Environment.* New York: International Universities Press.

Author Index

379

Subject Index

Abreaction:
  analytic change and, 60–61, 63, 66
  defined, 4
  delay in transference interpretation and,
    115
  function of, 23
  turning point and, 268–269, 278
Acquaintance, knowledge by, 73–74
Acting in, 92, 98
Acting out, 11–12, 109
  by borderline patients, 32
  countertransferences and: countertrans-
    ferential acting out and, 99
    as effect of countertransference, 132
    and understanding roots of acting out,
      186
  extensive resistance and extensive, 108
  interpretation as, 95–96
    (See also Interpretation)
  as language, 91–92
  and maintenance of neutrality, 33
  by schizophrenics, 12n.
    sexual, 314
  in severe psychopathologies, 27, 30
  somatization and, 189
Action, dilemma between speech and,
  91–93, 100–102
Active (experiential) insight, 245–246
Actual analytic situation, interpretation in,
  107–119
  and connection of transference manifes-
    tations within actual situation,
    113–114
  and encouraging transference expansion
    within analytic situation, 110–
    112
  principle of encouraging transference
    expansion within analytic situation,
    107–110
  and relative role of transference resolu-
    tion within analytic situation, 116–
    119
  role of analytic situation in interpreting
    resistance to awareness of transfer-
    ence, 114–116, 124
Acute psychoses (see Psychoses)

Adaptation:
  neurotic, limitations characterizing,
    260–261
  pathogenic vs. adaptation-enhancing
    fantasies, 210
  (See also Unconscious fantasies,
    adaptation-enhancing effects of)
Adolescent disorder, schizophrenia as,
  302, 303, 313
Affect:
  analytic change resulting from cognitive
    awareness combined with release
    of, 60–61
  insight development and tolerance for
    unpleasant, 76
  (See also Emotional insight; Insight)
Affective holding function, 27n.
Aggression:
  family dynamics and, 370n.
  individuation and, 255, 256
  mobilizing, expressing, and processing,
    256–258
  self- (see Suicidal patients)
Agoraphobia, 267, 277, 357n.
Alter-ego-hungry personality, 55–56
American Academy of Psychoanalysis,
  Annual Meeting of (1978), 2
Amphetamine psychoses, 314
Analytic change (see Change)
Analytic introject, 156
Analytic self-observation, 86
Anger, therapeutic uses of, 184–185
Anna Freud/Hampstead Center Sym-
  posium on Insight (1978), 88
Anna O. case, 91, 180
Anorexia, 277, 314
Artistic creativity (see Creativity)
Associations:
  confirmatory, 324
  with dreams, 224–226, 231, 233, 235,
    236, 289
  Freud and nature of, 112
  of schizophrenics, 307, 308
  transference neurosis development and
    transference dominating, 111
  (See also Free association)

About the Editor

SAMUEL SLIPP, M. D., is Medical Director of the Postgraduate Center for Mental Health and Clinical Professor of Psychiatry at New York University School of Medicine. He completed his psychiatric residency at the University of California, Langley Porter Clinic and his psychoanalytic training at New York Medical College. Dr. Slipp is a fellow of the American Psychiatric Association, a fellow of the American Academy of Psychoanalysis, and a charter member of the American Family Therapy Association. He is on the editorial boards of *The International Journal of Psychoanalytic Psychotherapy* and *Family Process,* as well as being the editor of *Groups*. He has taught at the Stanford University School of Medicine, San Francisco State College, Mount Zion Hospital in San Francisco, the University of London Institute of Psychiatry, New York Medical College, and New York University School of Medicine. He has published numerous professional articles on psychoanalytic theory and treatment in schizophrenia, depression, and hysteria as well as on psychotherapy outcome research.